FRIENDLY FIRES

FIRES

*Recollections of a
Diplomatic Family*

VOLUME I

Friendly Fires, Volume I
Copyright © 2018 by Robert and Barbara Pringle

Published by Piscataqua Press
An imprint of RiverRun Bookstore, Inc.
32 Daniel Street
Portsmouth, NH 03801
www.riverrunbookstore.com
www.piscataquapress.com

ISBN: 978-1-950381-00-5

Printed in the United States of America

NOTE ABOUT THE COVER ART:

The cover of this volume depicts a scene from an Indonesian epic of Indian origin, stories from which are a main feature of Indonesia's renowned shadow puppet theater. Here the nobles of one of two warring families are holding council, aided by the droll but powerful Javanese-origin clowns, who serve, yet sometimes control, their masters. On the back cover, the tall figure facing right is Krishna Duta, the family's wily strategist and negotiator, of special interest to any diplomat. Anyone interested in Indonesian politics will want to know more about this ancient drama and its philosophical relationship with Indonesia's majority religion, Islam.

CONTENTS
Volume I

5. BEGINNING DIPLOMACY: *from Washington to Indonesia, 1967-1970*

6. INDONESIA (2), *1971-1974*

7. THE PHILIPPINES, *1974-1977*

Dedication

This book is dedicated to our extended families,
who helped us, especially our children,
at home in the United States
and visited us abroad from
Jakarta to Cape Town.

With a special shout-out to Jamie,
our ever patient long-distance
computer adviser.

Foreword

This is a joint memoir of life in and out of the US Foreign Service. It is intended for family and to a lesser extent for others interested in American diplomacy or in the countries where we served. Our primary objective is to write a narrative about who we were and how we lived, because we do not want to leave our children or their children knowing nothing about their forebears.

We regret that many people today, including us, are in this position. Bob, for example, knows virtually nothing about his maternal grandmother, or why she left Germany, and he has only one letter written by his maternal grandfather. Only the Pringle side of his family is well documented, thanks to the southern (Charleston, South Carolina) passion for such things. Both his parents were professional writers and historians, but family history was unfashionable in the New York and Washington of the early twentieth century where they lived and worked. Fortunately they did write many letters, in addition to what they wrote professionally.

Barbara has been better served and her family on both sides is well documented, not least thanks to her father Clarence, who was fascinated by his own ancestors, especially the Cade family, and traveled to England to find records of them.

In both our families, up to and through our years abroad, frequent letter writing was still the norm. This book was made possible by letters written to and from us, and then saved. We wonder how such family history will be possible in the age of the delete button, when electronic communications are seen as of the moment and further endangered by rapidly changing technology. In a few places, Bob's informal trip reports, written for the State Department, have also been used, as have some diary entries, although he kept a diary only sporadically.

These written sources have served as a valuable corrective to what we remember. We sometimes have up to three versions of what happened in any given situation: as Bob remembers it, as Barbara remembers it, and what we wrote at the time to family and friends. None of these versions is infallible, but by putting them together we hope that we have gotten closer to the truth. Because research and writing took over a decade, we have tried to avoid any use of "now" referring to a specific date, and "at this writing" means when the passage in question was written, not when the memoir was completed.

Bob's memory of his State Department career was recorded in an interview with Ambassador Ken Brown in March, 2015, as part of the oral history program conducted by the Association for Diplomatic Studies and Training. The interview occurred as he began to write this book and helped him considerably to organize his personal thinking about his Foreign Service Career.

The first three chapters cover some family history plus our individual lives before we met at Cornell in 1964. After that, the narrative is about both of us. Use of the first person can mean either of us, and which one we hope is clear from the context. The last chapter includes some of Bob's opinions on life in the Foreign Service and why its core values and practices are at risk, and Barbara's thoughts on teaching as a portable career.

It is a joint effort partly because we want to demonstrate the role of a modern spouse in a diplomatic career. This relates to the importance of living in a foreign country, with a family, as opposed to short visits without family, or communication by e-mail or Skype. At the beginning of our diplomatic career Barbara was officially a "wife," an appendage of Bob. Then she became a "trailing spouse," but the inequity inherent in this status has remained. At the same time the spouse's economic importance within the modern family has continued to grow, creating a dilemma, which now poses a growing threat to the Foreign Service as we have known it.

Bob's career ended officially in 2001, whereas Barbara briefly kept on teaching. We were not both fully retired until 2003. We have had plenty of time since then to enjoy family, pursue quasi-professional pursuits, from book writing to museum management, and to devote more attention to civic and charitable interests, as well as to travel both to countries we knew well, and others we had never visited. Aside from a few references, this post-retirement travel is not covered in this memoir.

The title, *Friendly Fires*, refers to a poem by Rudyard Kipling, who was a great favorite of Bob's mother. One stanza, slightly modified, reads:

> How can we answer which fire is best
> Of all the fires that burn?
> We who have been both host and guest
> At every fire in turn. [1]

It refers to hearth fires, not the kind that need to be extinguished by diplomats or soldiers. The stanza could have been written for Foreign Service families. We have frequently been welcomed in front of the warming fires to which Kipling was referring—by family at Christmastime in the US, by friends in England when we were students, by acquaintances in mountain get-away homes in Indonesia and the Philippines. But just as often, the welcoming fires in our Foreign Service experience have been cooking fires, over which the tea and the meal which is always offered to guests is prepared.

Many times we have been unexpected visitors—hiking into a longhouse in Sarawak or bouncing over a sand dune to reach a village in West Africa or fording a river in a tropical land like Papua New Guinea. And times without number we have hosted old friends or new acquaintances in our homes, whether in front of a hearth in our living room in Alexandria or Pretoria or with a meal prepared in a modern oven in any of our diplomatic residences abroad.

---

[1] Modified from *Rudyard Kipling*, "The Fires," in *Rudyard Kipling's Verse*, definitive edition, Doubleday, New York, 1940, p. 82. The original reads:
How can I answer which is best
Of all the fires that burn?
I have been too often host or guest
At every fire in turn.

1

Barbara: From Wartime Washington to Cornell, 1942-1964

In the wee, small hours of April 17, 1942, a family car sped, as fast as it dared with lights half-obscured to comply with wartime blackout regulations, from Buckingham Apartments in Arlington, Virginia, to Doctors' Hospital in the District of Columbia. There I was born, Barbara Ann Cade, first child (and first of four daughters) of Clarence and Charlotte Cade, and first grandchild of all four of my grandparents. Therefore, as an infant I was much doted upon and much discussed in family letters, which substituted for personal visits given the difficulties of travel during World War II. All my childhood and teen-age years, I was blessed to remain in this loving family atmosphere.

Antecedents

Cade, Riesch, Pettersen, Radlund—England, Germany, Norway, Sweden and Denmark—my antecedents were all northern European and all Midwestern—Chicago and the Wisconsin Dells. My father, Clarence Louis Cade, has traced our ancestry on his side many generations back through records and contemporary families in Lincolnshire, England, in his *magnum opus* "The Descendants of Joseph Cade and Sarah Musgrave, a Family Narrative." This exists in typescript form (1982) only; there are about a dozen blue paper bound copies of it scattered throughout the family.[1] In 1992, sensing an imbalance in our

---

[1] The original typescript, with numerous handwritten corrections and additions by CLC (i.e. the most recent and final version), as well as the original photos, is in our safe deposit box, awaiting the day I find time to scan it and get it, with emendations, into the computer.

records, I interviewed Mother, Charlotte Pettersen Cade, and produced a much shorter history of the past several generations of her family, "Pettersen-Radlund History," of which I have one copy, in a green, loose-leaf notebook, with my family records.

All my grandparents were first- or second-generation immigrants. The father of my grandmother Clara Cade, Great-grandfather Riesch, was the son of a "German" (Prussian) army soldier. He was born on December 14, 1866, and spent the first fourteen years of his life on a farm near Dannenberg, Germany. He emigrated, apparently with his whole family—at least, a pencil note on a scrap of brown paper tells the story of how he and three sisters, ages twelve, eight (Aunt Lizzie) and one-and-a-half, with his parents presumably along too, survived a dramatic boat trip from Hamburg to New York. The boat hit a sunken ship, and drifted helplessly for almost two months until the passengers, reduced to eating only rye flour soup, were rescued and taken to Glasgow. Their ship was repaired in Scotland and the family finally reached the US, where they settled in Bloomington, Illinois.

Clara's mother, whom I knew only as a small child when everyone called her "Munner," was born six months after her parents arrived in the same city, and seems to have spent the early part of her life there. At some time after their marriage, the young couple moved to Chicago, where "Gupe," as he was called by the time I knew him, apparently prospered, because they were able to buy a newly constructed white frame house in Oak Park, where my father was born years later. The Riesches had two children, my grandmother, Clara Dorothy, and my great-uncle Lou, whose proper name Louis became Daddy's middle name, Clarence Louis Cade.

On the paternal side, the story is more complete, and is told in detail in Daddy's *magnum opus*. Briefly, Great-grandfather William Harrison Cade, a twenty-one year old miller in west-central England near Manchester, married Cathrina McGrath in 1882. A year later, following relatives who had settled in Ohio and Illinois, they too emigrated to America. They had two children, Laura and her younger brother Joseph, my grandfather, born on Christmas Day in 1884. However, after Cathrina's early death, the children were sent, separately, to live with relatives, and Joe's early life, with two different families, was unhappy and did not result in a very high level of formal education. His father divorced a second (or maybe third) wife, Rhoda, whom Joe adored, and who had been, during his grade-school years, like a second mother to him, so much so that he was the only Cade who attended her funeral years later.

So Joseph Philip Cade went out into the world of work at an early age, first as an errand-running office boy, but by 1908 finding his life-long occupation—selling things. Two years later, he married Clara Dorothy Riesch; in 1914, he began his career-long association with Everson and Company, which sold lighting fixtures. He had the accounts for public buildings and Protestant churches at first, and became one of the company's most successful salesmen. When the Irish immigrant who had the Catholic Church account died suddenly, Joe took over that account too. His fortunes waxed and waned pretty much in sync with the country's economic and military fortunes, high during the Roaring Twenties, sinking during the Depression, recovering as things improved in the late Thirties and during World War II, when he served the government as an "expediter" of military materiel, and then gradually waning as his eyesight and hearing failed during the years after his return to Everson.

His two boys, my father Clarence Louis Cade, born in 1913, and his younger brother Arthur, called Art by his friends and Bud by his relatives, grew up in a loving but not wealthy or sophisticated family. At first they lived with Clara's parents in the white wooden house, but then the younger family moved out to a series of apartments in Oak Park. When the Riesches lost their house during the Depression, they moved in with the younger generation, so that in their later teens, Daddy and Art lived in a three-generation household. In those days, Gupe still worked; I don't know his occupation, but it was certainly not professional.

When Daddy received a full-tuition scholarship to the University of Chicago because he was among the top three graduates in his class at Oak Park High School, no one in the family realized that it did not include room and board too. Since the South Side of Chicago, where the university is located, was too far away from Oak Park on the west to allow daily travel to class, Daddy had to find a job quickly when he arrived as a student; with assistance from the Dean of Students he found a professor who needed a handyman, dog-walker, and all around assistant and boarded with him for the whole four years. After graduation, he helped significantly to cover the expense of Art's college education at Yale.

The final year at Chicago, Clarence met Charlotte Pettersen at a conference of student charitable organizations at the Baker Hotel in St. Charles, Illinois, a hotel for which his father had supplied some of the grander chandeliers. "I saw this stunning, low-voiced, blonde female on the podium and after the first session had the temerity to ask her to walk along the river and have an ice cream. Things have never been the same since."[2]

This stunning female was born in 1915 to upwardly mobile parents. Her father, Frank Otto Pettersen, had arrived in the United States as a small child. His father Nils, born into a poor family in the port city of Kristianstad, Norway, had begun a career at sea as a cabin boy at age twelve. While working his way up to ship's captain, he had honed his wood carving skills. Between trips, he had married the beautiful Aurora, much beloved by all who knew her, and started a family, which consisted of two boys (another had died as a child) when, in 1889, he decided to take a job in a toy factory in Chicago and bring them all to a new, more promising world. One of these boys was Frank Otto Pettersen, my grandfather, who was then three years old.

Nils' dreams came true. His carving skills made him a valued employee of the Mills Novelty Company during the winter, and in the summer, he captained the boss's yacht on Lake Michigan. He was able to buy land on the outskirts of the city and, with the help of his boys he built a large house for the family, which grew to include two more boys and a daughter, my famously dour great-aunt Nora.[3] In this family, Grandfather Pettersen, and probably all his brothers, graduated from eighth grade, which was very likely more education than his father had had—a benefit of their new homeland.

After Frank began paid employment at Sears Roebuck as

---

[2] Clarence L. Cade, "The Descendants of Joseph Cade and Sarah Musgrave, a Family Narrative," p. 36.

[3] After whom we named our first GPS device.

a stock boy, he kept right on taking correspondence courses, whether finally to achieve a higher diploma we do not know. But he moved steadily up in responsibility and salary at Sears Roebuck. He married late, at the ripe old age of twenty-eight, perhaps absorbed in his rise up the corporate ladder. In addition, his mother had died just before his twenty-first birthday and, being one of the older cohort of Pettersen children, he might have felt responsibility to his father to remain within the family home longer than usual.

However, Grandfather Pettersen certainly has to have been a very eligible bachelor. He owned a motorboat and shared picnics with groups of young people in forays along the Illinois River; some of these expeditions he recorded with the new box camera in which he owned a half share. In the summer of 1912, he chose to take his vacation at the Radlund family's Pine Glen resort at the Wisconsin Dells, one of several that Chicagoans reached by train for a week's respite near the Wisconsin River's weirdly-shaped rock formations and sandy beaches. No one else was expected that day and the Radlund brothers were busy with farm chores, so their sister Emma hitched up the small buggy and went off to the train station to meet the lone guest, who turned out to be that eligible bachelor.

Emma was the only one of my grandparents who completed high school. This is probably because she grew up in the city. Her father, John Radlund, a restless and imperious soul who had immigrated from Sweden to find a better life, had by the time she was born become a "loading boss" at the Chicago docks. In this job, he supervised the loading and stowing of cargo on ships, and he was paid well. He bought a house in Chicago, which accommodated his six living children, as well as his wife Katrina Meyer, an immigrant from Denmark, and his mother, who had come from Sweden. So Emma lived in a comfortably established family in a settled urban area, through, or almost through her high-school years.

The dating is unclear, and we do not know where Emma finished high school, but sometime shortly after 1900, her father got wanderlust again, and bought a "farm and resort" property near a small town called Kilbourne, later to become known as the Wisconsin Dells. He sold the Chicago house, and opened a resort at the Dells with the whole family as the labor force, except for a "lady-manager," who ran off with all the profits at the end of the first season. The family was left so destitute that John had to return to the city and work at the docks that fall and winter. Fortunately, my great-grandmother, also an immigrant who had sought a better life, had been reared as a milkmaid on an estate in Denmark where her father was a woodcutter. So she knew hardship and she knew the basics of farm operation too, and the family survived the winter. This they accomplished with the help of canned goods that had lost their labels in transit, which John scavenged at the docks, so the family often did not know what they would be eating until they opened the cans.

When the resort opened the next spring, following the theft, Emma was in charge of the finances, reservations, and other business aspects of its operation. Her siblings took care of the hospitality end, but Emma did bake all the pies. Later, my sisters, cousins and I enjoyed many more of her baked goods as desserts. I particularly remember her making pies with the blueberries we picked during a summer vacation on Prince Edward Island. The resort had a farm operation to supply most of the food served to guests, which Emma also managed. During this time she had a serious beau, who courted her by taking her out canoeing. He died of tuberculosis, and so she was older than usual for an eligible young woman when she met Grandfather at the train station. They married in 1914, perhaps because that was the year that Grandfather received a significant promotion and, presumably, a significant raise in salary. Mother was born the next year.

Charlotte Ann Pettersen [Cade] was born in Oak Park, Illinois, on June 18, 1915. Her first home was apparently an apartment that her parents were renting at 1040 South Clinton Avenue in Oak Park, after which they had a series of apartments in that new western suburb until at least 1922, which means that she started primary school somewhere in Oak Park. The date of the purchase of the Elmhurst house (451 S. Kenilworth Avenue) is unknown to me, as are details of Mother's early life, except that she was taken to the family resort at the Wisconsin Dells regularly for summer visits. She remembered that, as she grew up, she spent whole summers there, reading placidly for hours on the beach. Since she never used sunglasses, if they existed then, she wondered whether her macular degeneration late in life somehow resulted from all that reading in bright sunlight. Sometime during her toddler years, Aunt Alice was born, so the two sisters were close in age and grew up together.

Charlotte and Alice both graduated from York High School in Elmhurst, Illinois. Mother was valedictorian of her class, and, when I went to Cornell, she hoped that I would have her friend and competitor, the salutatorian, Prof. William Rea Keast, then a professor of English at the university, as my freshman English teacher. (It didn't work out that way, but I thoroughly enjoyed the classes taught by my professor, Arthur Mizener, a noted scholar of F. Scott Fitzgerald.)

Being able to send his girls to college was a mark of success for Grandfather Pettersen, so Mother, having skipped a year somewhere during grade school, went off to college at Northwestern University at age seventeen in 1932. She must have boarded there, at least during the week, during her freshman year, because it was a change when Grandfather had financial difficulties during the early years of the Depression and she returned to live at home and commute daily by car, with Aunt Alice, for the next one or two years. As a senior, she was president of her beloved Delta Delta Delta sorority, and by then Grandfather could again afford to pay for her to live on campus, this time at the sorority house. She graduated Phi Beta Kappa with a degree in English, a solid command of Latin, and some kind of teaching credentials. For the next one or two years, she taught English in Sibley, Illinois, somewhere southwest of Chicago.

Being the eldest daughter and preceding the restless and questioning generation of the mid- and later 1960s, I was heavily influenced by the pattern of my parents' lives. I took it for granted that schoolwork was to be done on time and well; also, in general, I assumed that teachers and other adults in my life knew best and did not question their direction. Until I made the surprising decision to marry a man who was about to set off for London and Borneo for the first two years of our married lives, I followed their direction in many ways. I learned Latin early, starting with a tutorial at home for the first year. Then I chose French as my modern language, with the happy result of being able to have that wonderful summer on a Girl Scout exchange in France after high-school graduation.

When it came to picking a college, I agreed with Mother who decided that Radcliffe would clearly not be suitable, because it had no lovely, expansive campus like Northwestern's (an opinion reversed by Kathy's time). So my choice was between Cornell and Swarthmore, big or little, and I chose big. Mother had a good sense of letting all of us make independent decisions—but within a sensible framework laid out for us. I also rushed three times and eventually pledged a sorority, Pi Beta Phi, where several of my Cincinnati friends were sisters, because Mother had always considered her membership in a sorority as such an important part of her college experience. For me, it never was, and though I have remained friends with several of my sorority sisters, I think I could have spent the time devoted to Pi Phi much more constructively.

Finally, as a senior at Cornell, thinking that I really should leave with some professional credentials, I earned a New York state teaching certificate by taking twelve hours of teaching courses as I wrote my honors' thesis, a decision I have never regretted since it enabled me to find interesting and remunerative (slightly) employment as I followed Bob on his Foreign Service assignments abroad and at home.

Mother, unlike her own mother but just like me, met her husband during her college years. However, she and Daddy had a properly extended courtship of a few years, during which she taught English and Latin and directed high-school plays, among other duties, at that high school in Sibley. They married in June, 1938, while Daddy was selling pots and pans for Mr. Burnett, the father of a university friend of Mother's, in Michigan, but shortly thereafter moved to Washington, DC, when he took a job as a personnel officer with the newly created Social Security Administration.

Washington

Upon marrying, Mother had to resign her teaching position. In the Midwest of that era, her family and friends would have interpreted her continued employment as an indication that Daddy could not provide adequately for her and their prospective family. In addition, many places of employment, emphatically including schools, did not retain young married women because, as a result of the Depression, they considered it fairer to employ men or single women who had no other source of support. Mother, I am sure, enjoyed the freedom to explore Washington, DC, when she and Daddy first arrived, and she did volunteer work for the Red Cross until, and perhaps after, I arrived in April, 1942.

The story has it that Mother, expecting me and therefore taking it easy, as was the practice then, was darning socks (!) and listening to the Texaco weekly broadcast of opera live from the Met when the attack on Pearl Harbor was announced to the American public. Washington went on wartime status, which included the blackout that caused Daddy to drive her to the hospital on pitch-black streets with his automobile lights half-covered when labor pains began in the middle of the night in April.

Even though Daddy was at first exempt from the draft because of poor vision and his status as the father of an infant, as the war dragged on he enlisted in 1944 as an officer in the Navy, with the specific job of helping to run the civilian personnel effort at the Washington Navy Yard. The Navy had discovered that its hugely expanded core of civilian workers were not good at taking orders in military fashion, and needed the services of experienced personnel officers immediately. Therefore, he never underwent basic training or risked being sent to sea. His service, rather, was to help keep sailors well supplied with the munitions and stores they needed. And sometimes he had to stay, as duty officer, all night. On such occasions, when he did not come home for supper or bedtime, I envisioned him standing on a roof somewhere looking for enemy planes—surely not the case.

With the entry of the United States into the war and my birth four months later, Mother had her hands full, to understate the case. Her work included coping with the extra demands of rationing, making do in the kitchen, mending clothes so they would last longer, and being responsible for a newborn baby. All this comes to life in an eloquent handwritten daily schedule on a page which apparently was torn out of her account book:

5:45 up	2:00-2:30 feed
6-6:30 feed baby	2:30-4:00 nap
6:30-7:00 dress, make bed	4-5:30 leisure
7:30-8:30 breakfast	5:30-6 [prepare] supper
8:30-9:00 wash dishes	6-6:30 feed
9-10 bath	6:30-8:00 supper & dishes
10-10:30 feed wash	8-10 leisure
10:30-12:30 household	10-10:30 feed
12:30-1:30 lunch & dishes	10:45 bed
1:30-2:00 store	

There followed a list of weekly chores: "Monday—our washing; Tuesday—ironing; Wednesday—mending; Thursday—ironing; Friday—cleaning."

This was the period when infants were nursed at fixed intervals, not on demand. I seem to have adjusted just fine to that regime. The arrival of Jane eighteen months after my birth must have added to this complicated schedule and reduced the time devoted to leisure. As to ironing twice a week, all Mother's dresses as well as Daddy's uniforms, the latter having to be always just so, must have accounted for the hours spent on that chore.

With all this going on, Mother undoubtedly did not waste energy worrying about her lack of a career path. She was doing what she had been brought up to do, and voracious reader that she was, she certainly was not letting her mind deteriorate. Intellectual pursuits, as well as entertainment, were "leisure."

During that time, we lived in the Buckingham Apartments in Arlington. Years later, shortly after Mother's death, when I sent Daddy an article about "Arlington Today," he wrote back: "The Arlington [article] was nostalgic in depth. I wish Mother could have seen it. She always had a deep affection for Buckingham because the owner . . . let her have a 2 bedroom apt. (notwithstanding a long waiting list) because she was pregnant with Jane." Getting that larger apartment was a coup for Mother, because housing was at a great premium in wartime Washington. This garden apartment complex, one of the earliest in the DC metro area, still exists, and is now home to many recently arrived immigrants.

*Lt. Clarence Cade and Charlotte Cade out for a rare date without baby
Jane and toddler Barbara, shortly before the end of World War II.*

Montreal

After the end of the war, Daddy took a job at ICAO (the
International Civil Aviation Organization, an agency of the
newly created United Nations) in Montreal. The family moved
into a brand-new "semi-detached" (i.e. two together, just
like 216 Wolfe Street) house, which was the first one he and
Mother owned, in the just being developed suburb of Mount
Enterprise. Mother continued the same kind of young mother's
life, with a slight "foreign" twist. Coming from immigrant
backgrounds, she and Daddy had wanderlust, and might
have enjoyed going even further afield, but further afield was
mainly either war-torn or still very primitive. Besides, as many
letters show, the proud grandparents in Chicago considered

Washington, DC, and then Montreal entirely far enough away from the Midwest to take their darling grandchildren.

Kathy and Susie were born in Montreal in December, 1947, and January, 1950, during the banner years of the postwar "baby boom," so even though Jane and I started kindergarten one after the other shortly after we moved, Mother still had a life of diapers and bottles for most of our stay in Canada. Susie's birth occasioned a couple of amusing stories. She was born at the large public hospital in the city, apparently on a busy night, and Mother wound up in the charity ward, for lack of empty beds in the private rooms. Therefore, Susie was brought to Mother to nurse almost immediately after her birth. Mother, experienced by then, informed the staff that babies do not want to be fed right after birth, and asked them to take her back to the nursery so she could sleep. They told her that all charity patients had to nurse their babies because they might not be able to afford formula. Mother, who had every intention of nursing Susie, ultimately won that round.

Given that there were three others of us still at home, a family friend, Mr. Parks, had come over when Daddy took Mother to the hospital and stayed until the new father returned home. He did not remain for the birth; Dads were definitely NOT expected to be in the delivery room at that time. But after Mother called and announced the news that a fourth daughter had arrived, Daddy called his father-in-law with the happy news and distinctly heard him say to Grandmother, "It's another damn girl." Of course, everyone has always loved that other damn girl, and Daddy never seemed to mind his single sex family—he just helped us all earn our Girl Scout handywoman badges, taught us to fish, took us camping with Mother, played tennis with us—and waited until he had sons-in-law and grandsons to discuss sports seriously. We did, however, learn the basics of both baseball and football from watching games with him on that little black-and-white TV.

For Jane and me, the six years in Montreal were glorious ones. I had a posse of friends on our block, four little girls of the same age: Christianne Damien who went to the French Catholic School; Maxine Valiquette in the house attached to ours, who attended the English Catholic school; Joanne Walker and I, along with Jane and her best friend, Bea Redpath, who attended the public school, at that time an English-language institution. The latter housed classes from Grades 1 to 11 (the final one in Quebec then) in the same building, so Jane and I went to kindergarten in the changing room at the town skating rink. Coming home for lunch, we walked back and forth twice a day. These trips, all bundled up in our blue-wool-with-red-piping Red River coats, hoods, and red knitted scarves and leggings, were non-stop fun, even if the school was about a half-mile away. Letting the buckles on our boots freeze was another bit of fun; before classes could start, we had to stand in front of the radiators and unfreeze them so that we could take off our boots, which we wore over our leggings and shoes.

After school, to save Mother washing, we changed out of our uniform blue pleated tunics, white blouses, and long cotton stockings to "play clothes" and were sent outside to play. In winter that meant putting on our snowsuits and boots and going to the skating rink, the final year with Kathy in tow on a sled, with two-runner baby skates strapped onto her boots. One year, Daddy even flooded the back yard for our own personal rink. Or we could ski down the slope in Christianne Damien's backyard, or make igloos in the piles of snow which the municipal snow blower threw up on our lawns. In any case, Mother was not about to have us using up our after-school energy inside the house. By the time we did reappear, we were content to play with our dolls, coloring books, blocks and other toys in our upstairs playroom/bedroom.

There were no libraries near us, so we read the same dozen or so books over and over; *Heidi* and *Anne of Green Gables* were my favorites. Jane and I also wrote books together, the main characters of which were Ingly and Spanny, obviously a reference to two far-away lands to which we had been introduced in our geography classes. The story that survives tells a tall tale about their travels around the globe in a magic mattress/boat. It was also fun, just before supper, to listen to children's radio programs, one of which, as I recall, was a continuation of Anne of Green Gables' adventures, another a Canadian serial about Maggie Muggins. There had been a disastrous theater fire in Montreal shortly before we arrived, so children under some age that we hadn't reached were not allowed in movie theaters while we lived there. Every once in a while, we went to a cowboy film or one out of the Disney studios at the Town Hall; maybe that's the reason I never got into following film in a big way.

The only world event I remember was the visit to Canada of then Princess Elizabeth and Prince Philip. Brownies and Girl Guides helped to form the honor guard along her parade route, and I was disgusted when I had to look after Jane, who on that occasion stood with my company of Brownies rather than her own. That happened because she had just had her appendix out, and her Brownie leader refused to take responsibility for her. Had a crisis occurred, I'm not sure that I (or my leader) would have been better at coping. But we did see, and wave to, the royal couple after waiting more than an hour while Prince Philip inspected the interesting telescopes at the Mount Royal Observatory.

Vacations in those days were all about seeing family. Sometimes we took the long train trip to Chicago to visit the grandparents, and sometimes, usually in summer because

Barbara's paternal grandparents, Joe and Clara Cade, vacationing at Lake Champlain with her and her sisters: from eldest to youngest— Barbara, Jane, Kathy, Susie.

they drove, they came to share a vacation with us. The first I remember was the cottage on Prince Edward Island where we picked blueberries and Grandmother Pettersen baked them into awesome pies—if we could refrain from eating too many while we picked them. This vacation, which must have occurred when I was about five or six, was also the one where Mother and Daddy first tried to teach me how to swim, by throwing me to each other from sandbar to sandbar. I thought I was going to drown, and I couldn't imagine ever mastering this dangerous skill.

Later, we spent two long summer vacations at more peaceful, from my point of view, Lake Champlain. The first was in a little cottage at Chazy Landing; the most memorable event there was finding a dead mink in the water pump when we, the first renters of the season, arrived. We detected his presence by the smell, for apparently freezing nights had just ceased. That stay was otherwise so much fun that the next summer Mother and Daddy rented a larger cottage for a month or two and not only did both sets of grandparents spend time with us, but we also had a steady stream of weekend visitors from Montreal. By that time, I had mastered the art of staying afloat.[4]

As for us visiting Chicago, it was a stamina test for Mother to get us all there on the train. With four little girls under ten, she always took a roomette, with two bunks and a pull-down bed, also a private toilet. For a couple of years, Jane refused to have anything to do with the latter, for it opened directly on the tracks and could be used only when the train was in motion—very scary! The trip via the northern US (probably the Canadian National Railroad connection with the New York Central) was direct, but more than 24-hours long. The shorter route, via the Canadian Pacific, required a change of trains in Detroit. You can imagine Mother trailing four of us, with luggage (probably in the care of a porter, but still . . .), through customs and immigration to the new train. And she no longer had the roomette for the trip from Detroit to Chicago.

On one such trip, at Christmas, Daddy took time off and came with us. That was the year of a major snowstorm in

---

[4] There are some scenes from these vacations on the "family" CDs, made from various home movies. These now exist, courtesy of Jamie, as "family movies_JamieRip" on our computers.

Chicago on the day we were leaving for home, and we were delayed in traffic. As Grandfather hurried to try to make the train, another car sideswiped his Cadillac. "Keep on driving, Daddy," said Grandmother. "We need to get Charlotte and the children to the train." It was still very difficult to get long-distance train reservations. So we kept on, and upon arrival at the station, Mother leaped out with baby Susan and said, "I am making this train with the baby, even if the rest of you don't." We did, and when we arrived, the train was still sitting on the track, without an engine. We older girls fooled around in the parlor car, the final one with a rounded end, with comfortable seats that spun back and forth and lots of space to run around. En route, it would be a smoky bar full of stuffy grown-ups, but in it we happily passed the next three hours until the train left.

In 1951, Mother and Daddy decided it was time to return to the US and rear us girls in our own country. Ironically, one of their main concerns was that we be well prepared to attend college here, but when I got to Cornell, I discovered that about ten percent of my fellow students were, indeed, Canadian. As it was, Daddy found an administrative job at the newly opening Taft Sanitary Engineering Center, the first air and water pollution center in the United States, and we moved to Cincinnati.

Cincinnati

I don't remember any particular trauma connected with the move, and therefore didn't think too much about moving Jamie and Anne with us as we followed Bob on his Foreign Service assignments. The only hiccup as far as I was concerned was that Mother insisted I not practice with my ice skating class for the final ice show at the end of winter in case we had already moved by then. We hadn't, and I was dejected, not because of non-participation, but because I didn't get a red velvet skating dress, trimmed in white fake fur, which seemed to me then the height of elegance. My Barbara Ann Scott doll had one.[5] When we left Canada, I was ten, and Mother suggested

---

[5] Barbara Ann Scott was a famous Canadian figure skater, who won a gold medal in the 1948 Olympics. You can actually Google "Barbara Ann Scott doll" and see her in her skating costume.

I was old enough to give her to our cleaning lady's daughter, whose family couldn't afford such an expensive toy. I did, but I remember being sad at the parting; perhaps ten was a bit soon to give up a favorite doll.

Daddy had to start his new job in Cincinnati on January 1, 1952, but he and Mother had decided to sell the Montreal house without a realtor to realize a greater profit in order to help offset the cost of a new house in the more expensive Cincinnati market. At some point they had made a trip together to Ohio and decided to settle in one of the two most highly regarded school districts in the area, Mariemont, east of the city, and later letters indicate that finding an affordable dwelling there was not easy. Mother therefore remained with all four of us in Canada until late spring, and Daddy's frequent letters show concern that coping with the stresses of a Montreal winter and four little ones, plus the financial uncertainty during the period they were responsible for two mortgages, was too much for her.

He was especially concerned when a stomach complaint, which turned out to be a diseased gall bladder, laid her low for a couple of weeks. Grandfather Pettersen helped to lessen the financial strain with an interim loan. Mother toughed it out and finally a buyer appeared. Daddy spent his spare time taking care of the formalities of purchasing the new house, which were prolonged as the previous owners moved out bit by bit, and then sprucing things up inside while he slept on a cot and gradually bought a few pieces of new furniture. Finally in May we all arrived in our new home.

Three out of four of us kids had a smooth transition. I found fourth grade to be full of friends, taught by a male teacher, a novelty, and altogether welcoming. The teacher, Mr. Davies, did not immediately earn my respect because he thought Canada had nine provinces, and I *knew* it had ten. My parents explained that he didn't yet know that Newfoundland had just been made a province, but at that point I was not impressed with him, as teachers were supposed to know everything.

Kathy didn't settle in quite as well as the rest of us. At age four, she was still too young for kindergarten, so she made friends with the daughter of the village doctor, who lived down the street, and four days after our arrival badly broke several bones in her leg by trying to stop one of those two-child gliders on their swing set. She was stuck in a heavy ankle to thigh plaster cast for at least two months, and then had to wear clunky tie shoes for several years. Her immobilization was, however, responsible for the purchase of our first television, which offered such wonders as Howdy Doody and, later, the Mickey Mouse Club.

Of course, Daddy got sports, but he never would have indulged quite so early after the expensive house purchase and move just for that. Later when I was in high school, I remember enjoying *The Hit Parade*, a presentation of the ten top popular songs, each accompanied by a skit or dancing, on Saturday nights after coming home from football and basketball games. Mother, of course, loved the dramas. So that little black-and-white screen gave the whole family a lot of pleasure, all three channels of it.

Kathy's broken leg was also responsible for our first family pet. A neighbor brought over a box turtle for her to observe, and that was the beginning of years of turtles as pets. After Kathy recovered, a sort of sandbox was constructed in the back yard for the turtle, and we fed him (or her) worms and vegetables. At first, we let each turtle go in the woods for the winter, but later, when we found tiny turtles in spring, we put them in the box and they hibernated just below it and came back to see us the next year.

One of the great advantages of the house at 6508 Park Lane was "the woods," a ravine formed by a small creek flowing towards the (Little?) Miami River. It was part of the untouchable watershed of that river, and so a permanent bit of nature in which to search for all sorts of living creatures, blooming plants, interesting trees, pretty stones, fossils, etc., etc. I earned several Girl Scout "proficiency badges" by making observations in the woods. We were instructed to stay away from an old boathouse, which the adults thought might harbor unsavory characters, but otherwise were allowed to explore the woods alone or with our friends. Later, after I was gone, a path through the woods provided a welcome short cut to the new municipal swimming pool.

Mariemont is a planned community, built between the two World Wars by a philanthropist, Marie Emory, with the expressed objective of mixing classes in one harmonious suburb. So in the 1950s there was inexpensive rental housing for working people, especially war widows, as well as individual dwellings, some of them quite roomy for the day, in the village. It had only one church, ecumenical, read mainline Protestant, the Mariemont Community Church. As far as I can remember, in high school I had no fellow students who were Jewish (which accounts for the fact that, upon arriving at Cornell, I was astonished to discover that Judaism involves much more than just worshipping God differently from Christians). The few Catholic residents of Mariemont simply worshipped in Madisonville, the next town over. Segregation was not legally imposed in the Cincinnati area, but the only two black ("Negro" as we then said) students in the Mariemont schools were the children of the high school janitor, who were much younger than I. For reasons that it never seemed to me important to ask about, black residents of southwestern Ohio lived in various parts of the city of Cincinnati or in the rural countryside, not in the suburbs.

Life for children in Mariemont was easy, because schools and friends were all within walking distance. It was legally a village and its population was small, so everyone who wanted could participate in every exciting activity that occurred. Thus it was that, only in seventh grade, I rode around in someone's Dad's convertible celebrating the victory of the high school varsity basketball team when it became Ohio State Triple A (smallest schools) champion. From junior high on, my girl friends and I went to all football and basketball games, and in seventh and eighth grades, we had a rotating supper club, potluck style, before each home game. I remember that our mothers became very annoyed if we tried to burn various food items, like carrot sticks, in the candles. Every year, all Girl Scouts and Brownies marched in the Memorial Day parade, as did the mayor, the school band, the American Legion, and I don't remember what other worthy organizations.

Girl Scouts and camping played a significant part in my life. Scouting was a major avenue to the outdoors, not only because of summer camp, but also because our troop, in late grade school and junior high, when Mother was the leader, went on several overnights a year. Most, if not all, of those took place at established camps of the Cincinnati Girl Scout Council, so the tents or cabins were already there to sleep in.

On one winter overnight, famous in our family, Mother sat up all night feeding coal into the furnace and grading semester exam papers for a seventh-grade geography class which she had taken over as a substitute for a teacher who walked off the job. Experienced as an English teacher (read grammar and essays to correct), she wrote a fill-in-the-blanks exam for geography, and then had to consider every student answer which was not the one she expected, to discover if it, too, was possible. The venue was an old, cold farmhouse, which had been a stop on the Underground Railway prior to the Civil War. At least it had acquired a furnace since then.

The best effect of Mother's being the Girl Scout leader was that she came to the conclusion that our family could camp for vacations in suitable comfort in a huge, canvas, walled tent that took four of us to set up. While Susie and Kathy stayed with the Grandparents Pettersen in Grand Rapids, Jane and I and our parents explored the Lower and Upper Peninsulas of Michigan and the Canadian north shore of the Great Lakes, as well as parts of Minnesota and Wisconsin, during high school summer vacations. The final expedition while I was at home involved a trailer and, I think, included all four daughters. It is worth recording that Mother's camping came with two conditions: a bakery stop for chocolate or sweet rolls for breakfast almost every day and funds for one, or in extremis two, nights in a motel if we arrived somewhere in the pouring rain (i.e. no setting up camp in the rain).

While Mariemont High School was considered one of the top three in Greater Cincinnati (the others being Walnut Hills in the city and Wyoming in the western suburbs), it was not particularly strenuous academically. I had plenty of time to participate in interscholastic sports, where I did not shine but helped provide the requisite number of players for various teams. I can remember doing math homework on the sidelines of girls' basketball games (for which I was a guard, not a forward, because I was hopeless when it came to getting the ball into the basket). I worked on the *Chieftain*, the yearbook, and was editor my senior year. My class produced a fine book, because there was plenty of talent for the endeavor,

*A stroll down the street where the Cade family lived after returning to the
US: Park Lane in Mariemont, Ohio. Barbara, the teen-ager, walks with her
maternal Grandmother, Emma Radlund Pettersen, and her mother, Charlotte.*

among others, my friend Nancy Reynolds as art editor and
two boys, Joe Schumaker and John Allee, both of whom went
on to become professional photographers with their own
studios, as photo editors.

The two most noteworthy achievements of those years
were to be elected Governor of Ohio Girls' State, a mock state
government run by the American Legion Auxiliary not only
in Ohio but in most other states too, and to be chosen one of
twelve Girl Scouts to represent the United States in an exchange
program with the French *Guides de France* and *Eclaireuses* (the
former Catholic, the latter Protestant). Of the two, there is no
question that the latter left a much more lasting legacy for
my future life. Not only did it consolidate my command of the
French language, which I had been attempting to learn since
third grade in Quebec province, but also my hostess in Lyon,
Michele Besson Antoine, is still a close friend, though distant
in miles. My other hosts, the Paulets, the family of a perfume-
factory owner—I shall never forget the scent of lavender that

pervaded their home in Montpellier—chose me because they had four daughters just like my family. I enjoyed my time with them, including a camping trip in the Pyrenees and another through western Germany, Switzerland, and eastern France. However, not one of them proved to be a good correspondent, and we lost touch after a few years.

My time with the Bessons was full of life lessons. *Papa* was a top trouble-shooter for *Electricité de France*, a senior level blue-collar job. Yet in 1960, fifteen years after the end of World War II, the family still lived in a one-spigot, cold water flat, with a toilet that you poured water down to flush, and no bath or shower. (That was somewhere else in the apartment building.) There was one bedroom, and Michele and her brother slept on one side of the living room in beds partitioned off with curtains. During my visit, Robert, the brother, was fighting in the Algerian War as a conscript, and I remember that every morning the first thing that happened was that a paper was bought and the list of casualties checked. Happily, right at the end of my stay, he surprised the family by returning home, and he went on to become a butcher in Lyon.

But *Maman* was a peasant girl, and we soon went about forty miles southeast to the family farmhouse in the village of La Chapelle de La Tour du Pin, where I had my first exposure to living on a farm—not your mechanized American version, but a set-up straight out of the European Middle Ages. The Besson family, then headed by Michele's maternal grandfather, owned several different plots of land with different sorts of fields—one an orchard, one with wheat, one for fallow and grazing, and so on. Vegetables grew in the farmyard, along with a goat, several hens, several mature walnut trees, and various other types of food production. I was enchanted, but also amazed. Imagine going to the farm down the road and bringing back the milk for breakfast the next morning. Or trampling pears to make pear wine. Or learning how to make goat cheese, either soft or hard. Or to make an apple pie in a wood-fired oven. There was no end to the fascination, but I must also say that I have never since had culture shock as great as I did upon my return to the United States, where new interstate highways and shopping centers were being developed all over the country, after that experience in postwar France.

Mother and Daddy met the student ship in New York harbor with a trunk full of the clothes, manual typewriter, and AM radio that I would need to start my freshman year at Cornell University, to which we proceeded directly. I, on the other hand, had a round of Camembert for Daddy which, after nine days in one of my bags near a steam pipe on the ship, might possibly never have been tasted by him, though he was gracious about accepting it. This undoubtedly forbidden import had bypassed agricultural inspection on the docks, all twelve of us Girl Scouts, dressed up in our formal uniforms, not meriting a second glance from them. So north we drove to Cornell, to rest a couple of days with Mother's college chum, Louise Shallenberger, who lived in Elmira, just south of Ithaca. I had a terrible cold, and I can remember sitting on a bed directing Mother what to put in the trunk for Cornell and what in the duffel bag going home to Cincinnati.

Cornell

As I reread my correspondence during my four years at Cornell, September, 1960, to June, 1964, I am astounded at the amount of growing up I did there. The maturing occurred where it is supposed to at a first-rate university—on the intellectual side—but also on the life in the big wide world side. It is true that I had not been overly cloistered during my pre-college years. I had traveled alone fairly widely before I left home for upstate New York—to Chicago for Easter with the Grandparents Cade (with Jane, but I was the responsible older sister), to Colorado and Illinois and finally Europe with the Girl Scouts, and to various conferences and workshops within Ohio. But all these were planned by others, financed ahead of time by parents, and well chaperoned by adults. Plus they were all of fairly short duration.

At Cornell I walked into a situation in which I was responsible for planning my own days, all 24-hours of them, getting to classes that occurred helter-skelter throughout the week all over campus, deciding how many enticing extracurricular activities I could engage in and how many concerts, plays, and serious speeches I could spare time for. For Daddy, who had had to work all the time he was at the

University of Chicago and then contributed heavily to Uncle
Art's education at Yale, it was a mark of honor to be able to
provide his girls, all four of us, with a college education. So
I never worked during the school year, though I did hold a
summer job when no other plans intervened, which was only
two out of the four summers.

The biggest changes came as I pulled away from my
interesting and pleasant, though rather sheltered previous
life. It comes naturally to most children to absorb a great deal
of their parents' life philosophy, whether explicitly taught or
implicitly learned by observation. Having matured during
the Depression, Mother and Daddy managed our household
very frugally while I was a young girl, but I had never felt
constrained by the economies in our upbringing, even if I was
vaguely aware of some of them, like limits on new clothes
purchases. By Susie's high-school years, there were more
restaurant meals and other extras, but as I started college
they still had all of us to educate, and they were also keenly
aware of the need for a cushion in case of another national
financial calamity.

At college I had a small allowance, over and above the
approximately $2000 per year that it cost to study at Cornell
and to live in a dorm there in the early 1960s. Slowly I became
aware that many of my fellow students were operating on a
larger budget than mine, and that I would have to pick and
choose among expenditures above room and board. I was
horrified with a nearly $50 bill for books my first semester,
and Mother gently pointed out that next semester I should
purchase used textbooks. I either carpooled or took the bus
and train back and forth from Cincinnati to Ithaca, and the only
plane trip was home for my final spring vacation senior year.

In my efforts to compromise between doing what I would
have liked versus spending my money wisely, the biggest
challenge was to walk the quarter-mile plus from my classes
back to the women's dorm dining rooms for lunch each day.
Meals there were included in my room-and-board fee, but if
I remained on the Arts Quad, where most of my classrooms
and the libraries were located, I had to pay for lunch again. In
midwinter or busy exam periods, that posed a real quandary.
Besides, it was more fun to eat at the student union or a

graduate dorm cafeteria than at the cloistered women's dorms.

In loco parentis was the phrase that described the university's view of its responsibility toward women students in the early 1960s. Hence the all-meals-in-the-dorm rule. Women also had a nightly curfew, 10:30 on weekdays, later, but not much, on Fridays and Saturdays, and exceptionally until as late as about 2 a.m. on special party weekends. In no cases except for visiting parents or grandparents were overnights away from the dorm allowed in the Ithaca area. In my freshman year, a Girl Scout friend and I were making a presentation in Albany; we flew up and needed to stay overnight in a hotel. For that, the Cornell Dean of Students' office required a letter from the Albany Girl Scout Council assuring that it would see to our well being and proper behavior. Speaking of proper behavior, coeds, as women were called, wore skirts to class, period—unless it was snowing, and then we could wear slacks. I had quite a supply of tights to go with those skirts most of the academic year.

Once, I managed to break the no-women-living-off-campus rule, but it didn't end well from the university's point of view. When I was a freshman dorm counselor my junior year, a refugee from Estonia had a room on my corridor; she had fled with her parents ahead of the Soviet conquest of the Baltic states. They had settled in upstate New York, where her father passed away. A few months into her freshman year, her mother died too. They left her well provided for in financial terms, but they also left an apartment full of treasured family furniture and other possessions, in Albany I think. She was facing rent for the apartment, plus room-and-board payments to Cornell for her final three years of college. After what her family had been through, she was mature beyond her years, and also a good student. I persuaded the Women Students' Dean to allow her to get an apartment in Ithaca and to make that her permanent home, with all her family possessions, during school terms as well as vacations.

This was the year when Cornell was tentatively moving toward more freedom for women, and senior women were going to be able to live in university apartments. Her apartment would be off-campus and a good friend of hers, also from my corridor, would live in the apartment with her. After my graduation, I heard via the grapevine that unfortunately the friend had entertained a male friend in the apartment and had become pregnant by him—exactly the danger that the university was citing to keep women in dorms and even to try to regulate what went on in graduate student apartments off campus. We know the end of that story, but I wish I knew what finally happened in the lives of both young ladies involved in my story.

Another new challenge was to manage my own health care. Even my bout of stomach flu, or whatever it was, on the Girl Scout trip to France was thoroughly taken care of, albeit with treatments unfamiliar at home, by my French family in Montpellier. But when I walked across campus with a date to a polo match sometime during freshman fall semester, I apparently dressed fashionably rather than warmly. My toes were very cold when I went to bed and, frighteningly, the next morning, one was still numb. My freshman corridor adviser sent me to the clinic, where the nurse pronounced that the skin nerves were frozen and that they would gradually warm up, over the next week. My reaction in the next letter home was to write "Next time I have to walk to a polo game, I'll wear tights and snow boots *and* those wool socks I got in the Alps."

The other big issue that I had resolved by the time I left Cornell was the whole question of exclusionary social groups, which on the university scene meant sororities and fraternities. For Mother, her membership in Delta Delta Delta had been a highlight of her college experience; she was president of the Northwestern University chapter as a senior. So I rushed the first time I could, during intersession in January of freshman year, then again in the fall of sophomore year, and finally during intersession sophomore year, when my friends from Cincinnati offered me membership in Pi Beta Phi. Of course, they were having a fine time living in the chapter house as sophomores (juniors traditionally didn't), but I could not spend my second sophomore semester there. So my experience may have been atypical, but I found very little meaningful in the various activities of the sorority, and I hated rush. During my junior year I observed, "I really question the selective principle, but especially the superficial bases on which we discuss these girls. As a VP [dorm counselor], I have come to realize that in girls I wouldn't have come to know on first impression there are positive likeable qualities." On the plus side, I made some new friends in the sorority and established deeper ties with the Cincinnati friends who had invited me to join. Still, by senior year, I avoided as many sorority meetings as I could, and I did not live in the house. My only real contribution was to be chosen for Phi Beta Kappa, so our chapter could brag on that news in the alumnae magazine. And I did knit the only garment I ever knitted, a burgundy pullover sweater, with collar, during rush my junior year. I still have it, along with my lasting friendship with Lois Wyman Dow, as my best memories of Pi Beta Phi.

I arrived at Cornell from a thoroughly Republican family and community. However, I have nearly always voted Democrat in national elections, and I think that both parents, by the end of their lives, had moved much closer to many of the values that the Democratic Party of the 1980s and 90s stood for. In 2008, Daddy was even going to cast his vote for Barack Obama for President, but he did not have the chance. Regardless of party choice, I understood from Mother and Daddy that interest in politics and voting was every citizen's obligation.

From leadership positions at MHS, plus the Girls' State experience, I was predisposed to get involved in student government at Cornell. In a much more heterogeneous electorate than prim and proper Ohio Girls' State, I didn't win either of the elections in which I ran for Cornell Student Government, but more important, a year-and-a-half's involvement in the National Student Association (NSA), including attendance at their national convention between my sophomore and junior years, convinced me that I was not cut out to sit through endless debates either. In the latter case, it didn't seem to me that any meaningful action would follow from those debates, and, in fact, when action did come on civil rights and the Vietnam conflict, though many students were involved, the leadership did not come from the NSA. One good episode in my NSA involvement on the Cornell campus, though, was organizing a day-long seminar on nuclear weaponry, specifically the danger of radioactive fallout, for which Hans Bethe, the Nobel laureate who was teaching at Cornell, agreed to be the principal resource person. I will never forget that seminar, and the willingness of such an eminent person to spend a whole day sharing his knowledge with lowly students.

Influenced by my high school experience, I also tried out for the yearbook, the Cornellian. I made the staff, but like student government this proved to be a dud as far as suggesting an interesting ongoing life occupation. One year of being a copy editor at the yearbook persuaded me that simply putting together other people's work was a dead end, though all my life I have enjoyed creating family photo albums, and most recently photo books online. And I have done plenty of copy editing for the author in the family.

In academic areas, all kinds of new ideas, way beyond just new facts, were flooding into my consciousness. As a freshman in an honors section of the required English course, I wrote home in regard to a long essay on Ernest Hemingway that "it is difficult to write for a person [Arthur Mizener, a noted F. Scott Fitzgerald scholar] who knows so much that you can't bluff or ignore inconvenient facts." I can remember walking back from a botany lab, a long trek from the agriculture campus across Triphammer Gorge to my dorm on a dark, cold afternoon that first semester, and wondering how I was ever going to manage four years of intense study, noisy dorms, my own laundry, and constant exams all alone. That is about the last time I can recall feeling unable to cope until I left four years later. Academic success did not come without lots of work, but most courses were not difficult. Beginning Russian was boring, as learning vocabulary always is, and I did not became really fluent in my year and a half of studying the language. However, I have never been sorry about the insight into a completely different world, which that language study, plus several later courses in Russian history, gave me. (Later, I wished that Bob would get an assignment to the USSR so that I could really master the Russian language, but that was not to be.)

I learned the importance of choosing courses on the basis of the professor, not just the write-up in the course catalogue. An excellent, though at times very puzzling, French literature course taught by an abstract-thinking professor, showed me the limits of my talent in this direction. Just who exactly is "*Je*" in Proust's *Les Fleurs du Mal*? I still don't understand that question, and received a very low grade on that hour exam, but I aced the final when the main question was "Which book that we studied did you like best, and why?" I had brought Montaigne's essays, which I had enjoyed and pondered a lot. Apparently, in the same professor's estimation, I did a good job of explaining why. Some of my classmates, who chose the only book they had read, had a harder time with their answers.

My history major gave me lots of practice in evaluating information from various sources, both written and oral, and my honors thesis, which required interviews, taught me how to deal with the latter. Dr. Edward Fox, an expert in modern French history, was my major adviser, and he steered me in that direction for my thesis. I managed to get a fellowship for summer research in France, courtesy of the Woodrow Wilson Center at Princeton. The Algerian War was then winding down, and I chose as my topic the fate of the *Pieds Noirs* ("Black Feet," a reference to the fertile soil in which European settlers had planted vineyards and other agricultural fields on the Mediterranean plain of Algeria) as the Algerian uprising gradually made remaining in Algeria untenable. The *Pieds Noirs* were mostly second- or third-generation farmers from parts of the European Mediterranean littoral like Portugal, Spain, and Italy; many families were not originally French.

Based upon interviews with scholars and administrators in Paris, all of whom were very generous to a young, inexperienced scholar, and a brief stay in Algiers, I concluded that the *Pieds Noirs*, who were already beginning to flee to the southern coast of France, around cities like Marseilles and Montpellier, would have a terrible time fitting back into metropolitan society. I was totally wrong; as I found out when we began to transit Paris on our way to various Foreign Service posts, they had almost immediately begun to move north and were indistinguishable in French society a decade later.

By my senior year, life was very different from that of a freshman. I was living in one of those experimental townhouses with my sophomore and junior-year roommates, Helen Menges (now Knoll) and Charlotte Fremon (now Danielson). I no longer had a trunkful of possessions, for as Mother observed in a letter to Grandmother Pettersen at the time of my graduation: "I'm a great one to talk, but I am urging her to get rid of everything she doesn't need, but I'm afraid that she has inherited the Grandfather-Mother traits, although she is more efficient about storing it and claims that all of it is essential." ("SPOT ON!" comments Bob.)

My final semester at Cornell was also different academically from the previous seven. I was commuting to Ithaca High School several days a week in my apartment-mate Charlotte's antique convertible, a big hit in the school parking lot, in order to do practice teaching there. The university had an agreement with the New York State education authorities that if Cornell certified an honors student as fully trained in his/her subject, by adding six hours of education theory classes plus practice teaching, New York State could grant a permanent teaching certificate. And so I was preparing to earn my living while I was writing my honors thesis and, at that point, expecting to go on to graduate school. As things turned out, given my peripatetic life later on, it was one of the most important decisions I ever made.

The biggest change in my life also occurred that semester. It started this way, as described in one of my increasingly infrequent (and now misplaced) letters home: "Tonight we are going to a party given by our friend with an Indonesian roommate."

2

Bob: New York City to Deerfield, 1936-1951

I was born early on the morning of November 12, 1936, at Doctors Hospital in Manhattan. My father lost a five-dollar bet that my birth would be on Armistice Day. I was the third of three children, preceded by Geoffrey, born with severe brain damage in 1926[1] and Margot, born in 1932.

Both my parents were writers. My father grew up in New York City with his older brother, James Maxwell, better known as "Uncle Max." Their father, my grandfather, also James Maxwell, had moved north from Charleston, South Carolina, in about 1900, supposedly because he wanted to escape the South with its racist politics. (My father may have been spinning this a bit.) He was the son of yet another James Maxwell Pringle, "Papa's Pa," the Episcopal minister who, in order to avoid acknowledging the Pringle family baldness, had a succession of wigs each a little longer than the next. Once a month he would go to the barbershop, get a "haircut," and pop out wearing wig number one in the series. He's the same one who had a brand new church in Columbia, SC, which was burned by General Sherman during his famous or infamous "March to the Sea." It is now a park and Papa's Pa is buried in St. Phillips' graveyard in Charleston. (My father would later discover, as would I, that some of his Charleston cousins, who had long memories about kinship, were wonderful people.)

Grandfather James Maxwell Pringle became a retail druggist in New York, which is almost all I know about him

---

[1] Dr. Laurence S. Kubie letter to Harry Rosenfield, November 5, 1958, and other material in Bob's folder on Geoffrey.

beyond his Charleston ancestry. There he met Anna Dorothea Juergens, who had run away from her family in Lübeck, Germany, via England. She was only nineteen years old. Her split with her family was apparently bitter and she never wanted to return to Germany or to speak German, according to my father. Both she and James died before I was born. A German I met somewhere once told me that there was a large

Bob's paternal grandparents,
Anna Dorothea Juergens and James Maxwell Pringle.

Jewish Juergens family in Lübeck, and it would be fun to go there and try to find out more.

In general I know very little about my paternal grandparents: we have only one photograph of him and three of her. My father always spoke very affectionately of them, and he even spoke a little German, but neither he nor my mother, although both professional historians, was interested in family history. It was unfashionable in the sophisticated New York of the 1930s, and we all thought it quaint of the Charleston cousins to make such a fuss over second cousins umpteen times removed.

Both my father and Uncle Max grew up in New York City and attended De Witt Clinton High School, the hotshot public academic high school of its day. Both went on to Cornell

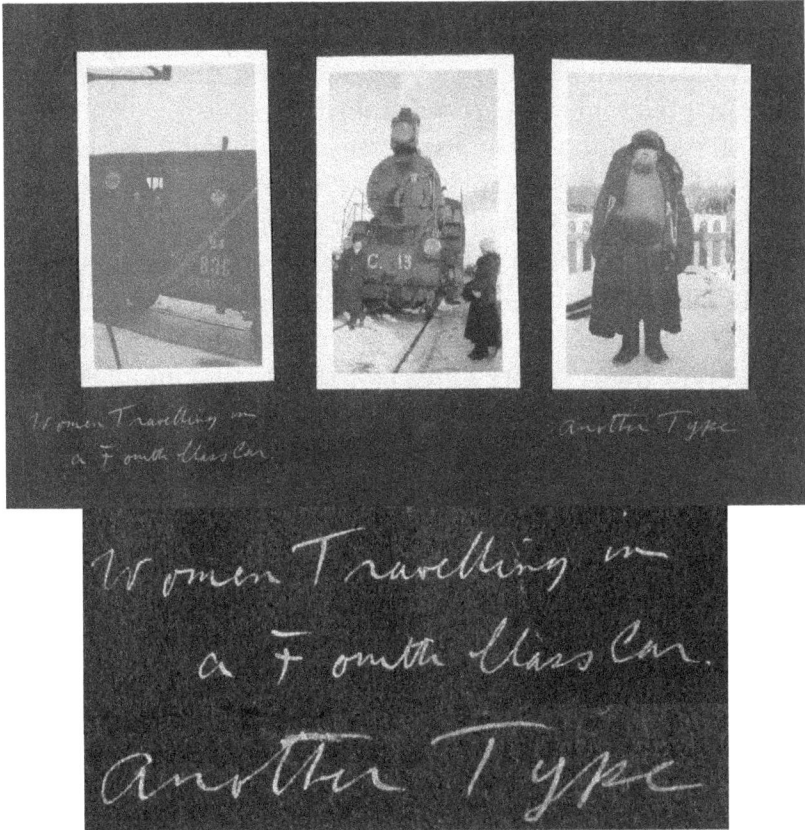

Uncle Max took evocative photos of his wild ride through Revolutionary Russia in 1917, courtesy of what is now Citibank. The captions (enlarged above) read: (left) Women travelling in a Fourth Class Car and (right) Another Type.

University, were enrolled in ROTC, and served briefly in World War I, although too late to go to France or be involved in any fighting. Although the College of Arts and Sciences at Cornell was (and is) not a state school, the Pringle brothers don't seem to have had any trouble paying for it. They may have had New York State Regents' scholarships. My father (and maybe Max also) made some money selling aluminum pots and pans at Chautauquas[2] during the summer and from

---

[2] Chautauquas, organized loosely into a "Chautautqua movement," were educational summer camps highly popular during the late nineteenth and early twentieth centuries, often featuring well-known speakers such as William Jennings Bryan.

door to door in upstate New York. My father belonged to a
fraternity, played tennis (although not competitively) and,
much more important, was very active on the *Cornell Daily
Sun*. That led him to a career in journalism.

Uncle Max (known by us as "Unkie") initially worked for
First City Bank of New York, today Citibank. In 1917 the bank
sent him as part of a small team of Americans to open a branch
in Russia, on the eve of the Bolshevik revolution, no less. After
trying the impossible in both St. Petersburg and Moscow, he
and his colleagues had to be evacuated over the Trans-Siberian
railway, and then via Korea and Japan to China, taking marvelous
Dr. Zhivago-esque photos along the way. He ended up working
for the future Citibank in Shanghai and other locations for
several years. After that Unkie became a mortgage banker and
retired with Anne to California. [3] After his death, she gave his
Russia photos to my mother and we eventually passed them on
to the Library of Congress, which was delighted to have them.

After Cornell and the army, my father worked for a series of
well-known New York newspapers including the *Sun*, Joseph
Pulitzer's *World* and the *Globe*—I'm not sure in which order—all
of them defunct by World War II. In 1926 he married my mother,
who graduated from Smith in about 1918 and had come to the
big city for work and excitement. The marriage lasted nineteen
years. My father gradually switched to free-lance magazine work
for the *New Yorker* and others. His first book, *Alfred E. Smith, a
Critical Biography,* was published in 1927. (It was not in fact
very critical; my father adored Smith.) This was followed almost
immediately by *Big Frogs*, a collection of essays about prominent
Americans, published originally in the *New Yorker*, the *Outlook* (a
trendy intellectual magazine of which he was also an editor for
two years), *Harper's*, and *World's Work*. Of the *Big Frogs* essays,
the most interesting from today's perspective was "His Master's
Voice" about Ivy Lee, who was a flack for the Rockefeller family
and a pioneer of modern, high-powered PR.[4] From this time on,
except for his government work in World War II, it was his free-

---

[3] For the rest of his Russia photos see http://www.loc.gov/pictures/
search/?q=pringle%20james%20maxwell&sg=true.

[4] Henry F. Pringle, *Big Frogs*, New York, 1928. A Japanese translation of *Big
Frogs* was published in 1929 and my father received a wonderful gilt-silk
embroidery-bound presentation copy, which we still have.

lance magazine work that supported the family.

His life of Theodore Roosevelt was published in 1931 and won the Pulitzer Prize for biography, solidly establishing his professional reputation.[5] The TR book remains in print and is still (in my unbiased opinion) one of the best. Unlike more recent biographies, such as Edmund Morris's, it saw and poked fun at the slightly preposterous, jingoistic side of TR (no one in the know *ever* referred to him as "Teddy") without at all neglecting his greatness. The hagiographers charged that HFP treated TR as "*opera bouffe.*" Well, on one level he **was** *opera bouffe*. My father later revised and updated the book, eliminating most of his youthful cynicism and making it less interesting. If you read it, you should definitely read the first edition, not the one that is currently still in print.

This was followed by two volumes on William Howard Taft, done with the full cooperation of the Taft family, although, suspicious of my father's New Deal sentiments, they didn't much like the results. Taft was admirable, but not very exciting, and neither is the book; I've never been able to read it through.[6] Perhaps not surprisingly, it remains the definitive biography of Taft. HFP always wanted to do another book on the fascinating, intensely hostile relationship between TR and Woodrow Wilson, but World War II and the need to support a family got in the way.

My father was Professor of Journalism at Columbia from 1932 to 1943. This was never more than a part-time job in which he played editor, assigned tasks to student reporters, and critiqued their work. He greatly enjoyed it and many of his students went on to be famous, including reporter Marguerite Higgins and pollster Sam Lubell. Later, thanks to old family friends Delia and Ferdinand Kuhn, a Pringle Fellowship in Journalism was established at Columbia in his honor. It still exists (except that it is now a memorial lecture and an award).

---

[5] Henry F. Pringle, *Theodore Roosevelt, a Biography,* New York, Harcourt Brace and Company, 1931.

[6] Henry F. Pringle, *The Life and Times of William Howard Taft, a Biography*, New York, Farrar & Rinehart, 1939, 2 vols. Doris Kearns Goodwin used it a lot in writing her book *The Bully Pulpit: Theodore Roosevelt, William Howard Taft and the Golden Age of Journalism*, New York, Simon & Schuster, 2013, perhaps partly because there were so few other books on Taft.

Life in Manhattan

Looking back at the way the Pringle family lived in pre-World War II New York City is like dimly perceiving a different planet. Writers didn't generally make much money, then as now, but in the Great Depression if you were employed at all you could live startlingly well by modern standards. The photographs of my father taken at this time are quintessential successful young author, holding a pipe. By the mid-1930s we had a duplex (two-floor) apartment at 8 East 96th Street, just off Fifth Avenue, across the street from Central Park.[7] We have a photo of yours truly on a Shetland pony in the park, age about four, gleefully labeled by my mother "the non-horseman at the start of his career!" My earliest memory is dropping toys out of the 13th or 14th storey window—I can't remember whether I was caught doing this or not. Tom Dewey, then the New York City police commissioner and already getting into national politics, lived in the building across the street.

We had at least two full-time servants, including Yama, a Japanese cook (who stayed in the US and lived until after World War II), and an English nanny, Mabel Stratton, affectionately called "Mamie" in our family, who was devoted to my mother and remained with us, except for a trip home right after the war, until she went to work for the Auchincloss-Bouvier family (Jacqueline Kennedy's parents) in the early Fifties. She was always more like a member of the family than a servant, and she went to Wyoming to help my sister, *gratis*, with her first child in the 1960s. My parents went to Bar Harbor, Maine, in the summer, and later

Mable Stratton (Mamie), my sister Margot and newborn me in Mamie's lap, probably in Sheridan, Wyoming.

---

[7] Earlier addresses included 2 Grace Court, Brooklyn Heights, and 60 Gramercy Park.

Margot and Bobby shown dressed up, perhaps for Easter, probably at the Episcopal Church of the Heavenly Rest, which we attended, thanks to Mamie, not far from our apartment at 8 East 96th Street.

to Sheridan, Wyoming (Eaton's Ranch, etc.). In the mid-1930s they went on a cruise through the Panama Canal on the *SS California*— "The Good Ship Lollypop." Photos show them having dinner with the captain, wearing paper hats, and of course playing shuffleboard. They moved in the literary set and knew authors like James Thurber, E.B. White, and the famous editor of the *New Yorker*, Harold Ross.

My father's magazine work took him all over the country, including Hollywood, source of many stories[8] and a friendship with Joan Crawford, which he talked about a lot, somewhat to Kate's annoyance, in later years. He was a member of the Century Club, perhaps the thing he was most proud of except graduating from De Witt Clinton High School. I'm not sure if we had a car or not, but of course you didn't really need (or want) one in New York City, then as now. We had the best medical care, even though health insurance didn't (as far as I know) yet exist. The Taft book is dedicated to my mother's prestigious gynecologist-obstetrician, Dr. I.C. (Isadore) Rubin, "who has supervised the publication of two far more important editions." (The TR book is dedicated simply "To

---

[8] There was, for example, his story about the time he borrowed an acquaintance's Rolls Royce in Hollywood. When it broke down he called the Beverley Hills Rolls agency and asked for help. The man who answered his call asked to speak to the driver. My father explained that he was the driver. "We do not approve of owner operation," the man said, and hung up.

H.H.S.")

Politically, my father was a fervent liberal and internationalist. As World War II approached, he was a strong advocate of US intervention and an opponent of the America First movement. He talked about this on radio shows, and got hate mail from the pro-Nazi German-American Bund. He was not even close to being a communist, but no doubt had some acquaintances who were, because left-wing politics in this country were polarized on this score. He and others like him looked back on the "phony war" in the summer of 1940 and the subsequent German invasion of France as a completely agonizing experience.

My mother's political opinions were similar but less fervent and also less predictable. Neither parent was religious, nor were any of their parents, as far as I can figure out, although HHS did become a serious Episcopalian later in life, when she joined Christ Church in Alexandria. The story is that it was Mamie who dragged me off to the Episcopal Church of the Heavenly Rest in Manhattan to be baptized, without my father knowing about it, not that he would have objected very much. As my mother grew older she dropped her interest in psychotherapy and became an increasingly ardent Christian, believing that all good works in modern life "stem from the sixteen words that changed the world, 'As you do it unto the least of these, you do it unto me.'"[9]

Mother's New England Roots

My mother was a complex personality, to put it mildly. She was born December 9, 1899, and always resented that she didn't quite wait until the twentieth century. Her father, Charles Huntington Smith, grew up in rural western Massachusetts. He was of deep-rooted New England stock, with Smith and Huntington ancestors going back to the earliest days of the Massachusetts Bay Colony. His only surviving letter to her, which he typed, is a fascinating

[9] Helena Huntington Smith letter to Dear Children, January 27, 1957. This letter is among Bob's files on HHS; others are in a special collection of her papers at the library in Sheridan, WY; at my sister Margot's house; and some, relating to the Teddy Blue book, at the Historical Society of either Wyoming or Montana.

Helena Huntington Smith, my mother, sitting at the feet of her mother, Anna Marion Smith, and Charles Huntington Smith, at home in Amherst, Massachusetts, when he was teaching at Deerfield Academy. Note the meticulously arranged books, the painting of a French cathedral and some narcissi in bloom. The locomotive prints would have been upstairs.

description of subsistence farming in New England, written apparently in response to questions from her, and was probably (although he doesn't say so) based on life at his father's farm, or that of some other close relation:

I'm sorry I have been so slow. You have some rather altitudinous ideas of farming and widows and the like in New England seventy-five years ago; the Leonard Smith farm in particular. It was way up the hill to begin with, three miles from the P.O.

and the nearest store. The farm maintained about five cows, a horse, three or four pigs, probably twenty or thirty hens, a few apple trees, a pear tree or two, some currant bushes and a dog. (It has all gone back to the jungle years ago. I'll take you up there some time.)

The cows supplied the milk and butter, occasionally a little cottage cheese. (Dutch cheese it was commonly called.) In the fall, the ample cellar would contain enough potatoes to last until new potatoes were ready—the last of July. There would be a more or less generous store of beets, carrots, turnips, winter squashes, maybe onions, barrels of apples, all in sufficient quantity to last til spring, a barrel or two of cider, some of which later turned into vinegar, a barrel of salt pork (with the hams smoked and hanging in the attic). These last two together constituted the entire meat supply on most farms, with an occasional chicken on Sundays.

Bacon was never cured nor served separately; salt pork (fat mostly), was the standard. The grease which fried out made the gravy for the potatoes.

Sometimes a two-foot trench would be dug in the garden, straw placed in the bottom, and cabbage placed in it, heads down. Then boards were put over the trench and the whole covered with earth and straw or leaves, deep enough to make it frost proof. In the winter when cabbage was to be on the menu, the snow would be shoveled off, the trench opened sufficiently to allow the removal of what was needed, and then all made snug until next time.

In the barn would be plenty of hay and (sometimes) oats for the winter, with an abundance of corn fodder (that is, what is left after the ears have been broken off). There would be a corn bin, or crib, containing enough corn (on the ear) for the winter. When the supply of corn meal was getting low, six or eight bushels of the ears would be run through the corn sheller, which removed the kernels from the cob, and a bag or two of the grain would be taken to the grist mill where it was ground into meal. This was used for making johnny cake, vulgarly known as corn bread, which was often the only bread, but some farmers would have a patch of rye, or less commonly wheat, which they took to the grist mill, same as the corn.

In the Leonard Smith family (and this was not unusual under

like circumstances), a lot of the work was done by the mother and grandmother.

As to "going to market," which seems to trouble you—there was no such thing. On the weekly visit to the post office, a basket of eggs would be taken along to exchange for salt, or sugar or molasses, some calico, pins and needles, thread, unbleached cotton cloth, or what not. There might also be a few pounds of butter, a few potatoes in the spring when the less thrifty found themselves eating short, a ham or two, or even half a hog at butchering time. Now or then there might be young pigs or a shoat or two. (A shoat is a quarter grown pig.) In fall there might be a peck or two of beets, or a few turnips, or half a dozen squashes, or a calf or a yearling. (And remember that is not y-e-a-r ling, but yerling.)

As to haying, ploughing, getting in the winter's supply of wood, and the like, the neighbors would agree on a day or two to get together and go up "to do the Widder Henry's haying," or whatever it might be. People had neighbors in those days. God bless them.

Not much real money changed hands when I was a boy. Many a family would not see as much cash in a year as you spend on beauty parlors and other "fixins" in a month.[10]

My mother went on and on about what a tyrannical character her father was, and I was warned to be on my best behavior around him. I now recall that despite his fierce snow-white mustachios he was always kind as could be to me. When she wasn't emoting about her own mental problems, blamable on him, mother recognized his strong points. She said that there were three things he loved: gardening (he was a prize peony grower), railroads, and of course the classics. We have pictures

[10] Charles Smith letter to My Darling Daughter, from 28 Dana St., Amherst, MA, August 15, 1941. The ending of the letter describes how he had been once been overcharged by the conductor of a local train that took him into South Deerfield to visit a friend, making him hand over his "pocket piece" (lucky coin). The next day his mother marched down to the station, met the same train, and, with an audience looking on, made the offending conductor give it back. That is almost all we know about the boyhood of CHS. While the "Leonard Smith" referred to in the letter may have been his father (and my great-grandfather), I am not sure—a commentary on how little I know about my family except for the Charleston Pringles.

proving that he took his young wife train watching on their honeymoon in 1895, and I remember him recounting with pride that he knew Charlie Hogan, the engineer who drove the New York Central's *Empire State Express* to a world speed record, 112 miles an hour, in 1899. The big steam locomotive prints I have always kept on my office wall were his.

The Smiths adored and doted on their only child. They originally named her Helena Whitney (later replaced by Huntington) Smith, and early photographs are so labeled. They took many photographs of her—a strikingly beautiful child radiating placid innocence—which just goes to show that childhood photos can be misleading. The pictures are also a great example of the fine work done by small town portrait studios in those days. It was her mother who pushed her into writing. In 1910, she got a poem Helena wrote (with a little help from mother?) into the *St. Nicholas Magazine*, the leading children's periodical of its day. The author, then ten years old, was paid one dollar (we have the payment letter):

A Midsummer Query

Pretty Little Firefly, sparkling through the night,
What do you do, the whole day through
Before you take your flight?
Do you spend your time in hollow trees
Where little squirrels dwell,
Or sleep away the summer day
In yonder leafy dell? [first verse only]

Grandmother Smith was herself a talented writer of light verse and author of *Mother Goose and What Came Next*, published in 1908, in both the US and Britain, and although she was certainly a sweet retiring soul she was also extremely bright. I have no idea how much education she had. She had a series of thoroughly spoiled Japanese spaniels with names like MoMo and ChoCho, who also show up in the old photographs. My favorite poem of hers, which may also have been published in *St. Nicholas*, cut to the quick about Theodore Roosevelt:

The President

Who keeps the nations well in sight,
To see if they are doing right,
And separates them when they fight?-
The President.

Who keeps his eye upon the meat,
To see that it is fit to eat,
And makes the butcher wipe his feet?-
The President.

Who scorns the nature fakir bold
Whose tales mislead both young and old,
And will not have such twaddle told?-
The President.

Who hunts the moose and caribou
The fox, the bear, the kangaroo
And hunts the haughty magnate too?-
The President.

Who catches them by tens and twelves
And in their secret action delves
And makes them all behave themselves?-
The President.

Who grapples with the much discussed
And very, very wicked Trust,
Resolved to lay it in the dust?-
The President.

In short, who is with zeal imbued
To see that we are duly shoo'ed
Along the path of rectitude?-
The President.[11]

---

[11] Although we cannot find a reference to the exact issues of the *St. Nicholas Magazine*, copies of both poems are in the looseleaf albums of family memorabilia compiled by Bob.

Even with tongue palpably in cheek, it makes you yearn for the likes of TR, doesn't it? I wonder whether Anna Marion Smith was as browbeaten by her husband as my mother liked to maintain. We have only one surviving letter from her, presumably written in 1939, congratulating her talented daughter on the publication of *We Pointed Them North*, but expressing revulsion at the content:

Have you any idea what the attitude of the present-day West is likely to be toward a book of this kind? Personally I should think they would hate being reminded of the revolting coarseness and brutality of their pioneer origins. For I don't know where or when, in all human history, one can find humanity on a lower plane or with fewer redeeming qualities. However, that's what they were, and there is no way of escaping the facts.[12]

Although her parents sometimes had to struggle to understand their only child, they did their level best to support her. They made sure that she got a good education and were in general very proud of her writing career. Grandfather Smith was a graduate of Amherst (class of 1885) and his daughter went to Smith College—whose choice it was I don't know— and graduated in the class of 1921. Helena always professed to have loathed Smith and had her name deleted from her fiftieth reunion mailing list because she thought she looked a lot younger than she really was and didn't want the fact of her age/college class to compromise her professional life.

Back to Charles: he worked briefly for the Chicago and Northwestern Railroad, and then settled down to the itinerant life of a schoolteacher in New England and nearby western New York state. He taught first in Peekskill, NY; later in Mohegan, NY (where he taught at a private academy); and finally at Deerfield Academy in western Massachusetts, where he taught Latin and Greek from 1923 to 1942. The Deerfield students called him "Beaver" Smith, although not to his face, because of his mustache. In about 1940 the Smiths moved from Deerfield to Amherst, where they bought a house at 28 Dana Street, which

---

[12] Mrs. Charles Huntington Smith letter to My Dearest [daughter], April 7 [no further date], neatly typed. She obviously typed well, as did her husband.

they called "Dunmovin"—really! Grandfather commuted to his teaching job for the rest of his career, no doubt terrorizing legions of other motorists in the process.

Deerfield's headmaster, the famous Frank Boyden, loved my grandfather because he was a great teacher, remembered as such by students bright and tenacious enough to master his Latin and Greek, and also because he was a folkloric New England character of the kind that Mr. Boyden collected the way some people collect antique cars. There was, for example, Deacon Greenough, the village bachelor who paid his cleaning lady 25 cents a week. At age eighty he discovered that she was saving money, so he married her. One of Mr. Boyden's stories about Grandfather Smith, which he was still telling at evening meetings when I was a student, described his explosive backward exits from his garage, which could be heard all over town. Then in his eighties, he had only just learned to drive.

No complaints: it was only because of Mr. Boyden's affection for CHS that, with trepidation, he gave me a three-year scholarship in 1951. My high school education at Deerfield rescued me from my immediate family and later got me into Harvard (see below). Grandfather Smith lived until his early nineties; Anna had died only a year or two earlier. He passed away in 1952 when I was a student at Deerfield; the memorial service was held in the red brick village church which we were required to attend every Sunday. One of Grandfather Smith's students has summed him up:

> Mr. Smith was a man so venerable that he looked like a 19th century schoolmaster; recalling him now, I think of photographs of Darwin as an old man. He had silky white hair, a bushy white mustache and a white goatee, and he wore the black suit and high collar that befitted his age and dignity. But his eyes were young, and so was his passion for the classical world.
>
> He had turned his classroom into a small outpost of ancient Rome. Huge framed photographs of the Roman Forum and the Colosseum hung on the walls, and he had sent away for plaster statues of various Roman gods.

Hermes on tiptoe, beckoning the other gods, was on his desk, and the Winged Victory stood nearby, still sending her message about beauty and line down through the ages. Mr. Smith knew that the icons that inhabit the classrooms of our youth can exert a lifelong spell, and in my case he was right. When I got to Italy during World War II, I used my first five-day pass to hitchhike to Rome. It took me two days to get there and two to get back, over the Apennines in winter, but the day in between was one of the most memorable of my life. I knew my way around the Forum because I had stared all one year at that photograph.

Although I always liked Latin, I didn't love it until I got to Mr. Smith's class, finally getting beyond Caesar's dreary wars and Cicero's prim orations to Virgil's *Aeneid* and Horace's odes, finally discovering that the wonderful language also had a wonderful literature. It was from Mr. Smith that I first glimpsed what was meant by 'humanist' and 'liberal education' and in a lifetime of travels no city has called me back as often as Rome.[13]

We know little about my parents' early married life. One can imagine Helena, trying hard to shed her cramped New England background, being swept off her feet by Henry, the glamorous, up-and-coming, big city reporter. There is no question that HFP helped her a great deal to get on her feet as a writer; indeed he kept on helping her sporadically after they were divorced. She did a number of short pieces for the *New Yorker* that were far from her eventual interests; for example, a profile of the Polish pianist Paderewski,[14] and another about the reform-minded warden of Sing Sing Prison.[15]

[13] William Zinsser, *Writing about Your Life,* New York, 2004, pp. 20-21.
[14] [Ignaz Paderewski's] "Double Life," *The New Yorker*, November 29, 1930.
[15] "Counsel for the Defense," a profile of Lewis E. Lawes, a famous reform warden of Sing Sing Prison, sometime in 1926, as indicated by a handwritten note on a clipping. *The New Yorker* did not indicate issue or date on each page at that time.

In 1933 she wrote a novel, *Damned if They Do*,[16] about problems of childbirth, which was more than slightly autobiographical in tone and no doubt owed much to the difficult deliveries of Geoffrey and maybe Margot. The book lacks the punch, conviction and style of her best non-fiction, but it was successful enough to be reprinted in a British edition. Its feminist emphasis was well before its time, and is apparently now recognized as such. But Helena was not a feminist as the term is understood today, maybe because she enjoyed men too much. Nor for that matter was she an ideological liberal, as my farther tended to be, although she certainly supported liberal causes on a case-by-case basis.

One thing is clear: in 1930s New York City there was nothing all that remarkable about a two career family, or a woman writing under her maiden name, and HHS rarely suggested feeling discriminated against except for some resentment at finding it easier to sell articles to female-oriented publications such as *Woman's Home Companion* than to mainstream magazines. At one point she also played with a byline, Huntington Smith, that didn't identify her as female, but she used it only a few times. Having a husband who sympathized with her professional ambitions and the wherewithal to have full time help made what she did look easy compared to what some of her descendants are experiencing today!

HHS Discovers the West

By the Thirties, Helena was developing a major professional interest in the "The West," meaning American cowboy country, the area between the Missouri River and the Continental Divide; it was there that she wrote two books which will be around for a long time, one of which is a classic. The West also broke up her marriage. It all began with a summer in and near Glacier National Park when she was (according to her account) twenty-one years old, thanks to "Aunt Hattie," who was perhaps not an aunt but a cousin named King. Trapped in an unhappy, childless marriage with a boorish but wealthy husband, Hattie showered gifts and attention on pretty,

---

[16] Published in New York by William Morrow in 1933.

precocious Helena. We have a photo of the glamorous "Aunt" dressed in an incredible Edwardian dress that must have cost the equivalent of thousands today.[17]

The Glacier trip blew mother off her feet: not so much the famous high mountain scenery, but a guided trip to a white-owned cattle ranch on the rolling grassland of the adjoining Blackfoot Indian Reservation. She was entranced by the big-sky scenery, by the cowboys, and by the free-and-easy attitude toward sex, all so different from what she had known in New England:

Before the summer was well under way I was punch drunk, as one wonder followed another. Horses! ... I had had a horse frustration since I was nine years old! The West in 1928[18] was horses. [After trail rides in the Park] I went to bed nights aching in every bone and transfigured with bliss ....

The top hand [at the ranch they visited] was a great blonde hulk of a man named Ira—pronounced "Arey"—and he was a strange mix of brutishness and delicacy. [She must have been reading D.H. Lawrence.] We went on long rides almost every day ....

I lost my cultural virginity with a bang, and here is the way it happened. We were all seated around the long supper table one evening when there was a thunder of hooves followed by a commotion outside and here came Ira, back from a few days in town—jingle, jingle, clump, clump, all six feet of him—red face, fiery shirt, batwing chaps flapping, kids screaming "Arey! Arey!" and a chorus of ecstatic dogs. He sat down and proceeded to regale the table with an account of his adventures in the big city of Browning, the capital of the [Blackfoot Indian] Reservation. I was dreaming along, not paying much attention, when a

---

[17] "Aunt Hattie" is easily confused with Helena's real Aunt Harriet, who was her father's sister. Harriet married a wealthy man (we have pictures of them on vacation in New Zealand apparently around 1910), lived in Pasadena, and shared mother's interest in psychiatry; they corresponded for years. The question of who took Helena to Glacier in 1928 remains uncertain. My recollection is that mother always told us it was Aunt Hattie. However, according to a slim file of Helena's notes to her psychoanalyst, Dr. Granatir, the source of the long quotation below, it was an "adoptive aunt" named Leila from Chicago who summered in Glacier every year. "Leila" may have been Hattie; her name does not recur elsewhere that I've been able to find.

[18] If this is the correct date, she was quite typically fudging on her age when (elsewhere) she refers to being 21 years old; she would have been 29.

sentence jolted me awake:

*"And I hadn't hardly gotten to sleep when the girl said 'It's time to get up.'" "The girl said," **The girl said,"** . . . If a Fourth of July cannon cracker had exploded in my brain, the detonation could not have been louder—Ira had been shacked up with a dame in a whore house, and here he was telling the world about it with perfect matter of factness, including his employer's wife and a young woman visitor who was not yet dry behind the ears. There was quiet amazement around the table—nothing more.*

Later after I went to bed I started trying to sort it all out. You could say anything, any time: a dead weight of generations rolled off my shoulders. I wanted to whoop and holler. This was freedom, liberation, glory, hallelujah! . . . The more I thought the more I saw. Ira's casual, unseemly remark meant much more than casual freedom: it meant that women were not sequestered in a mental nunnery but were free to share in the world of men, 'crossing the line' at will—(and I am not talking of a color line).[19]

I'm not sure exactly when mother's professional (as opposed to emotional) involvement with The West began, but by the time I was born she was well into cowboy country research and the family had taken to summering at dude ranches in Sheridan, Wyoming, where my sister Margot lives today.

By 1939 she was gathering material for a novel about cattle country (to have been entitled *The Centaurs*) when, fortunately for all concerned, she ran across a Montana pioneer named E.C. Abbott, but known far and wide as Teddy Blue. The resulting as-told-to classic, *We Pointed Them North: Recollections of a Cowpuncher,* is one of only two first-hand, authentic accounts of the range cattle industry,[20] which has since become such a central part of the American national

---

[19] The quotation is from autobiographical scraps, the oldest of which dates to May, 1939, in our files mentioned above in Footnote 9; HHS later reworked this material and was hoping to publish it, tentatively entitled "A Personal Memoir," and, as of 1978—when she was already at the Woodbine Nursing Home in Alexandria—she was writing to the University of Oklahoma Press about it.

[20] E.C. Abbott and Helena Huntington Smith, *We Pointed Them North, Recollections of a Cowpuncher*, New York, Farrar & Rinehart, 1939. The other is Andy Adams, *Log of a Cowboy*, New York, 1903.

mythology. In a sense the book came pouring out of Teddy Blue himself and, as HHS said in the introduction, her job was to capture his language and "not mess it up by being literary," which sounds easy but took real talent, if not genius. The book is a delightfully honest look at a heavily fictionalized chapter in American history and is still great fun to read. Teddy Blue died within a short time of its publication, as if he had been waiting for someone to appear and help him get it done.

A few years later, Helena did another as-told-to memoir with Nannie Alderson, wife of the founder of Eaton's Ranch in Sheridan, the place that pioneered so-called dude (guest) ranching. *A Bride Goes West* told a less sweeping story of pioneer life than the Teddy Blue book, but its emphasis on the role of women has insured that it too will be in print for a long time.[21] I should have mentioned that Larry McMurtry drew on *We Pointed them North* for the *Lonesome Dove* trilogy, as he has frequently and generously acknowledged.

As time went by my father increasingly resented mother's romantic involvement with the West even as he continued to help her with her writing, and it eventually drove a wedge between them. Until World War II took him to Washington, his work was in his beloved New York and he resented her long absences Out West. He didn't mind horseback riding now and then, with jodhpurs, not blue jeans, and preferably in a riding ring or Central Park. But he was basically neither outdoorsy nor macho, and he sensed, no doubt correctly, that my mother's fascination with cowboys had a more than platonic side to it.

Washington in the McCarthy Era

After the war began we moved to Washington. Before that Mother, Mamie, Margot and I unsuccessfully attempted to stay in Wyoming for the winter of 1941- 42 at our summer place on the Yentzer Ranch, not far from Eaton's.[22] When the

---

[21] Nannie T. Alderson and Helena Huntington Smith, *A Bride Goes West,* New York, Farrar & Rinehart,1942.

[22] The house we were renting from the Yentzers was later moved about ten miles to 1149 Pioneer Avenue in Sheridan, where my sister Margot bought and still lives in it, as of 2017.

weather went below zero, we moved into town and boarded with a villainous lady named "Catty" Carter. Margot and her friend next door aroused Catty's wrath by passing secret messages back and forth between second floor windows on a pulley system made from string and butter cartons. Isn't it funny what you remember from age five?

My father was already in Washington at a new job as Director of the Writers' Division (aka Publication Division) of the Office of War Information (OWI). This was a momentous experience for HFP, and the friendships he made at OWI lasted for the rest of his life. He didn't like Washington, which was racially segregated and a cultural desert compared to New York or even Philadelphia. But that was irrelevant: he loved his job, believed devoutly in the war effort, and thought FDR was a great man, as did all of us. Passing formative years under a president who was almost an object of worship ill-equipped me for later life!

At OWI my father hired Arthur Schlesinger, Jr., who describes him as "a slight, short, balding, businesslike man with a twinkle in his eye."[23] HFP and OWI are liberally mentioned in Schlesinger's autobiography, *A Life in the Twentieth Century*:

> The Writer's Division was an unusually cohesive group with uncommonly high esprit de corps. Henry Pringle was a father figure for the younger people. He was wise, wry, considerate, protective, with the uncommon gift of phrasing criticism in the most courtly and acceptable way, "a marvelous, even-handed, very intelligent man," Archie MacLeish mused forty years later. We were drawn together by our devotion to Pringle, by the job, as we understood it, of writing honestly about the war and by the fact that we were true believers in FDR's New Deal and his Four Freedoms. We shared MacLeish's conceptions of OWI as an educational agency

---

[23] Arthur Schlesinger, Jr., *A Life in the Twentieth Century*, New York, 2000, p. 265.

providing, as he wrote to the president, 'a full
knowledge of what we were fighting for.'[24]

Schlesinger also records that "the occasional Pringle parties
seemed to be straight out of the Twenties, with drunken
hilarity, noisy argument and pervasive mutual affection."[25]
Maybe, but if so things quieted down considerably after my
father married Kate.

OWI was in one sense an ancestor of USIA, but it was aimed
entirely at a domestic audience. Literati of the caliber of poet
MacLeish and novelist John Dos Passos wrote pamphlets
exhorting Americans to support the war effort and explaining
what we were fighting for. As Schlesinger emphasizes, they
believed that truth was on our side and fiercely resisted
efforts to deviate from it for the sake of propagandistic
impact. That kind of thing was what the Nazis did. My father
left OWI—to be more accurate, he was fired—in 1943 after
leading resistance to a plan to introduce "Madison Avenue"
methods, known more recently as "spin." Arthur Schlesinger
says: "Both Pringle's Writers' Division and Hank Brennan's
Graphics Division were now to be placed under ad men. The
Writers' Division, as we saw it, was to become a glorified
advertising agency with a cage full of copy writers to leap
around as the 'idea' men directed."[26]

As the reference to the Graphics Division suggests, OWI also
made those great "Loose Lips Sink Ships" war effort posters.
My father brought many of them home and we had quite a
collection in the attic for years until someone—probably my
mother—pitched them out, her usual panicked response to
dealing with the material exigencies of moving.

The war also had a big impact on HHS. On April 16, 1942,
she wrote a "Dear Henry" letter from Tucson, where she must
have been working on a magazine article:

---

[24] Ibid, p. 287.

[25] Ibid, p. 280. In the same passage Schlesinger notes that my parents did
not share the "pervasive mutual affection" because their marriage was
breaking up, and he refers to HHS as "attractive, intelligent, competitive
and sometimes devastatingly frank."

[26] Ibid, p. 291.

My first sight of America at war . . . . The army, big construction, trailer camps, and workmen and honky-tonks; and a million dollars' worth of guns arriving by freight trains . . . . And then there are convoys full of black[27] troops coming back from the Pacific Coast, where they have been on guard duty since early January.

It was America at war. War may be terrible and regrettable, and is, but by heaven its effect on America is wonderful. I'd never have believed the whole picture of this country could change so much in a short time. No more phony glitter—and all of a sudden *my* kind of men are everywhere—in uniform or out of it—soldiers or workmen—in pictures and in the flesh. This has become the picture of America so swiftly—like someone waving a wand—that when I saw Homo Americanus of a year ago—stoop-shouldered, puffy-faced, in baggy slacks—wandering among the keen-faced young men at the airports, he looked as dated as a Gibson Girl . . . .

The letter was published in the *Saturday Evening Post* as "Letter of the Week," according to a note on the typescript we have. One can only imagine how my father felt about it!

In Washington the family rented a row house at 1640 Argonne Place, uphill from the zoo in what is now called Adams-Morgan. We could hear the lions roaring on hot, unair-conditioned summer nights. It was the kind of house that would be selling for close to $1 million in today's Washington. We considered it dull and plebeian, but in the World War II housing market, beggars weren't choosers. There were three bedrooms and a glassed-in back porch on the second floor, but only one bathroom. (My mother and father complained a lot about that.) My parents were in the front, master bedroom; Mamie was in the larger of the two others, and I was in the third.

Margot got the third floor, attic bedroom where she could indulge the teenage need for privacy, display her numerous

---

[27] "Black" was unusual usage at this time, vis-à-vis "Negro."

collections (from sea glass to toy horses), expel me to downstairs when I hung around too much, and tape pictures of Gregory Peck and Lawrence Olivier on the ceiling over her bed. I adored and admired Margot—we were always allies in the family war games—and I never yearned for an older brother instead of an older sister. I spent a lot of time in Mamie's room listening to the radio while she knitted. Her favorite program, on Sunday night, was Edgar Bergen and Charlie McCarthy.

The neighborhood was of course totally white, with some Jews but no Latinos or other minorities. We had big apartment blocks on all sides and I got to know the shortcuts through all of their basements as well as the adjoining alleys, which doubled as somewhat unsanitary playgrounds.

Our second-story balcony closely adjoined the identical houses on either side, which led to an amusing episode. Our first dog was an extremely intelligent mutt named Nonnie, for Anonymous, because we couldn't decide on a name. He was housebroken, but liked to be let out on the upstairs porch now and then, for all we knew with no ulterior motive. He realized it was part of our house, hence off limits for toilet functions. We had seen him jumping over the railing to explore the neighbors' porch, but thought nothing of it. All went well for several months until the neighbor happened to glance out at his own porch and discovered several months' accumulation of dog poop, which we had to go over and clean up. Nonnie was a free spirit and eventually ran away.

Well before their separation my parents were fighting a lot, although not violently. Margot and I were never the subject of abuse; rather, they competed, sometimes bitterly, for our affection. Margot remembers all this as traumatic and damaging. I don't remember it like that, but I was four years younger, which no doubt made a big difference. This pattern continued after the divorce, which took place in Sheridan in early 1944, not long before HHS left for Europe (see below). There was almost always a row over where we would spend Christmas, often because "Daddy and Kate" wanted to plan things in advance, which my mother couldn't or wouldn't do.

A Second Mother

By 1943 my parents had separated and my father was living with Katharine Douglas, "Kate" to all of us, who was also employed at OWI. For a time they rented a small house near the intersection of 30th and Dumbarton Streets in Georgetown. I was mightily impressed because next door lived an Admiral Davis, who had commanded the USS Enterprise at the time when, at the low point of the Pacific war, it was the only US aircraft carrier in service. He had married a WAVE named Tuckie, known to all and sundry as "The Navy." Just down 30th Street was a famous Georgetown hostess who had spectacular Christmas parties. After their marriage in 1944, my father and Kate bought a larger home at 3319 N Street, a three-story Victorian town house, also in Georgetown. Under the divorce settlement my father paid my mother $300 a month in alimony plus $100 in child support for each of us. We were supposed to stay with him for one month yearly, a provision which got blurred a lot by events.

Kate, who became our second mother, came from an old California family. Her father, William Wallace Douglas (known as Will), was born in Xenia, Ohio, in 1863. His father, James Ball Douglas, a silversmith and talented musician, played in an army band during the Civil War. Afterwards, James moved the family first to Topeka and later to California, where he farmed alfalfa near San Bernardino. The second move interrupted Will's engineering studies at the University of Topeka, but he later flourished on the West Coast. In 1887, he became executive assistant to the Governor of California, then held a job writing banking regulations, and then founded a bank of his own in Sacramento. Finally, he moved to Berkeley, where he worked for the rest of his life for the Bank of Italy, which became the Bank of America, eventually as chief of personnel.[28]

Kate's mother, Helen Elizabeth Cooper, was born in Virginia City, Nevada, where her father, Thomas, was a mining engineer at the great silver mine on the Comstock Lode, the first major discovery of silver in the US. I think the Coopers were originally Canadian. Being a mining engineer was a

---

[28] Personal information from Kate.

"Daddy and Kate" in the living room at 3319 N
Street in Georgetown, Washington DC, with Archy,
their bad-tempered cocker spaniel.

peripatetic profession in those days of constant gold rushes. Kate told me when we were serving in Pretoria that Thomas had visited South Africa during the Boer War to check up on a gold ore-stamping mill he owned there. I remember hearing that at one point Helen taught in a frontier school near Virginia City. Will and Helen were married in 1909—I have no idea how or where they met—and eventually lived in (and built?) the fine, pseudo-half timbered house at 163 Alvarado Drive in Berkeley, which we looked up when David and Anne were living in the area. The one extant picture of Kate's mother in her youth shows a lovely young woman with a self-confident air.

Will loved the outdoors and was an early member of the Save the Redwoods League, the pioneering organization of California conservation. The family did a lot of camping out in the Sierra Nevadas and elsewhere, as well as taking full advantage of the Bay area's cultural and educational opportunities.

Helen was the prime mover behind Kate's relentlessly thorough education. Once she had graduated from Berkeley, Kate was packed off on a kind of grand tour of higher education in France, Spain and Germany, learning to speak both French and Spanish fluently. After that, in the late 1930s, she went east to work for Time Inc. in New York. She once told me that, like many early Time Inc. employees, she was offered partial payment in shares of stock, but turned down the offer. Big mistake! From New York, she gravitated naturally to wartime Washington and the Office of War Information, where she met my father. There ensued what Schlesinger calls "a well concealed office romance."[29]

Kate's mother Helen was a passionate liberal and loved visiting us in Washington, where it was Daddy and Kate's job to provide her with a constant diet of small dinners attended by bright, liberal people. Then she could go back to California with her intellectual batteries recharged. She had white hair, worn in what appeared to be 1920s flapper style, with keen wit, a gravelly voice and perpetual cigarette in a cigarette holder. I always found her great fun to be around. From Kate and her mother I learned early on that northern California was a totally civilized place, quite unlike the southern half of the state, with its Republicans and Hollywood glitz, surviving only on water stolen from the north. A devoted friend, a Mrs. Ellis, gave Kate's parents the little Chinese jade (etc.) carved ships that we now have.[30]

HHS Becomes a War Correspondent

In 1944-45 Helena went to Europe for over six months as a war correspondent for *Woman's Home Companion*. She had already been writing on war-related topics for that magazine and *Colliers*,

---

[29] Schlesinger, *A Life in the Twentieth Century*, p. 280.

[30] Helen died in 1965. I wrote that she was a "a great old lady, a magnificent rich blend of California frontier and Berkeley intelligentsia and we will miss her." About this time, Kate was marrying Mark Massel. Bob to Dear Mother, from Kuching, December 28, 1965.

but of course was eager to get closer to the front. She went first to
London, and then to Germany, which the Allies had just invaded.
We have wonderful army photographs of her in her official war
correspondent's uniform (I wish she had kept THAT!), peering
myopically into the breech of a howitzer, sorting through her
musette bag, and partying with her colonel boyfriends.

She had a very active social life, which netted a pile of liberated
German artifacts for us children (especially me): genuine SS
and Wehrmacht officers' hats, the former complete with ultra-
sinister silver skull-and-crossbones insignia; bayonets, both
dress and ordinary, and a huge Nazi banner with a silver fringe

Mother in her official war correspondent
uniform peers into the breech of a big army
artillery piece, somewhere in Europe in 1944.

which had hung inside the courthouse in Aachen, where she
spent some time. It was hard to figure out what to do with this
stuff since displaying it was clearly not on. All of it except a very
dull, non-dress bayonet got lost or jettisoned in later moves,
along with the OWI "Loose Lips" posters.

The Army tried to keep lady correspondents out of harm's
way, well behind the front lines, and of course the *Companion*

wanted pieces with a female angle, which in those days didn't include combat stuff. But Helena happened to be nearby in early 1945 when the German Army punched through the Allied lines in the Ardennes in a last desperate offensive, the Battle of the Bulge, and she got close to the fighting. The results were published in *American Heritage*, although not until 1957, under the awful title "A Few Men in Soldier Suits"[31] (not her idea). It's about the handfuls of non-combat troops, cooks and clerks, who suddenly had to drop their frying pans and typewriters and go out with primitive rocket launchers ("bazookas") and try to stop German Tiger Tanks. It is by far her best piece on the war.

Once back in the US she kept on writing about the war effort, including one piece for the *Companion* entitled "You Can't Keep Them Down," about early women test pilots. The *Companion* didn't allow authors to have two bylined articles in one issue—I can't establish what the other one was—so she signed it "Margot Roberts," for my sister and me.[32] Mother continued to be very productive until the mid-Fifties. One of her most interesting articles, "Mrs. Tilly's Crusade," published in *Colliers* late in 1950,[33] was about a white Georgia aristocrat in her sixties fighting for racial justice in the South, a decade before the heyday of the civil rights movement.

During Helena's absence in Europe, she sublet the house on Argonne Place, and Margot and I descended on N Street, accompanied by Mamie, who regarded herself as the guardian of mother's interests (mainly us) in her absence and sent her weekly letters on engraved stationery headed "Mabel Stratton, 3319 N Street, Washington 7, DC." The first of two surviving letters is about the great drop-kicked football episode on my eighth birthday, November 12, 1944:

Dear Mrs. Pringle:

Well, the last of Bobby's guests has just departed and on the whole it has been a great success although we did get off to a disastrous

---

[31] *American Heritage*, August, 1957.

[32] The Margot Roberts article was published in June,1944, and we have a print copy of it along with other HHS articles. A recent book on the subject quotes it: "According to Roberts . . . "

[33] *Colliers*, December 30, 1950.

start this morning. Mr. and Mrs. Pringle returned home from New York at 9 p.m. last night. I had the breakfast table nicely set with as much as possible and the gifts put around his plate with your gift of a football on his plate. He was overjoyed when he saw it because he has talked so much about having a good one. It is a beauty, price $5.95. Breakfast was almost ready and Bobby started to open his gifts, naturally the football was opened first. Mrs. Pringle and I were called to the front door to settle an argument with the newsboy when suddenly there was a great crash coming from the direction of the dining room—Bobby had kicked the football plonk in the middle of the table!

Orange juice and milk went all over the place, splashes on the chairs, wall, Margot's dress, hair, etc., to say nothing of the mess on the table. Daddy was furious, I felt like crying, Mrs. Pringle spoke not a word, Margot began to clean up. The colored paper on his other gifts began to run and all presents had to be quickly unwrapped. Poor dear Bobby, he always seems to do the wrong thing. It was the act of an impulsive child to be sure but what a mess! Daddy took the ball away from him for an unspecified time and our day looked like being ruined.[34]

You can sense that Mamie really quite enjoyed this episode. However once the birthday party began in the afternoon things returned more or less to normal. The funny thing is that I never liked football nor was I any good at it—but I had discovered that I could kick a ball fairly well!

Life at 3319 N Street was troubled in other respects. Daddy and Kate knew that Mamie was on Helena's side and they increasingly concluded that she was also a bad influence on us, since we had obviously outgrown any real need for a nanny. On January 12, 1945, as HHS was apparently about to return from Europe, Mamie wrote her that there had already been one "unpleasant scene" and asked my mother to give her strict instructions to move us back to 1640 Argonne Place on the first of February, "otherwise I am quite sure he will not let us out of the house 'til you are actually back.'" As for me,

He is coming along nicely and is more interested and at ease

---

[34] Mabel A. Stratton (Mamie) letter to Mrs. Pringle, November 12, 1944.

with other boys. Kate is rather touchy and likes to be praised a lot and poor Bobby made a dreadful faux pas one night in their hearing about a highly sherry flavored desert she had made— not knowing she'd made it. But my goodness you don't expect a child of eight to be perfect all the time . . . . Do you wonder I turned on Mr. Pringle one morning and told him to stop picking on the boy. He does his chores and he's cheerful and willing . . . . He does far more than Margot did at the same age . . . .

The person who was really suffering from this comic opera situation was no doubt Kate, who must already have been wondering why my father couldn't pay a little less attention to his ex-wife and their progeny, not to mention their nanny, and a little more attention to building a new life with her. A less long-suffering person would have walked out on him.

Mamie ended her letter to HHS with a flurry of rationing news:

Did I tell you that I sent Mrs. Smith [my grandmother] your no. 33 sugar coupon and a few days later it was cancelled? I was feeling worried about it when back came a letter from Mrs. Smith saying she had cashed it in immediately and how very thankful she was and grateful too. I was so relieved because otherwise it would have been wasted. They spring these things on us overnight. All meat is back on the rationing list again and butter is 24 cents a lb. I've already started to buy in a few things as I see them—things that are difficult always at the Safeway.[35]

Once we were back at 1640 Argonne Place, life resumed as before. My best friend, Jackie Moran, lived at The Ontario, a once (and now again) palatial apartment house, long since condo-ized, with huge rooms and very tall ceilings. His sister Patty was also Margot's friend, but the hub of her social life had shifted to Meadowbrook and Pegasus stables, in the further reaches of Rock Creek Park near the District line, where she and her equally horsy friends got to exercise people's horses and flirted with the stable boys.

After the war ended Mamie went back to England to visit her family and stayed for about a year. It seemed like an

---

[35] Mabel A. Stratton (Mamie) letter to Mrs. Pringle, June 12, 1945.

eternity, and we had to put up with a series of unsuccessful substitutes, the worst of whom was a vast Swedish woman named Haywie (phonetic). We also had a series of black cooks, since although both mother and Mamie could cook, Mamie rather well (I loved her very British shepherd's pie), neither of them felt it was their calling to do so.

Mamie stayed with us out of sheer loyalty; she must have been getting paid a fraction of the going rate for English nannies, especially over on Embassy Row, where a number of her friends worked, including the incomparable Nanny Bowden, whose aphorisms included, in regard to children's messy eating, "It will be messier where it's going." Nanny Bowden worked only with high-priced newborns. Much later she, Mamie and another nanny from their bridge group retired to a small house in downtown Newport, Rhode Island. We corresponded with Mamie until her death years later.

After my father left OWI in 1943, he was awarded a Guggenheim Fellowship to work on a history of World War II, which never got off the ground. This was to require high-level government cooperation, hence the framed "OK on Henry Pringle" memo from FDR, which he always kept on his study wall, and which I still have. In connection with this, he was a consultant for the US Army Air Force and the Secretary of War. He also went to Europe, although he never published anything about this experience.

At the end of the war he resumed his free-lance work, increasingly for the *Saturday Evening Post* but also on occasion for *Nation's Business*, *Holiday* and other magazines. He and Kate worked as team in interviewing and writing. He pounded away in his second-floor study at 3319 N Street, often working after dinner, churning out eight or ten articles a year, our bread and butter. Unlike HHS he did not touch-type, but he did use eight fingers and was fast and accurate.

It was hard work, even though he and Kate were reimbursed for travel expenses, at least by the *Saturday Evening Post*. The editor often sent articles back for major revisions, sometimes two or three times, and very occasionally did not accept them at all. My parents were of course paid by the article. My father's study was lined with books, including lots of war books such as Samuel Eliot Morison's fourteen volumes on US

Naval Operations in World War II, all of which I read, as well as much more on TR, Taft, Wilson and their eras—his main area of interest—which I found less fascinating.

Plumbing Morison, I discovered there had been a *USS Pringle*, a destroyer launched at the Charleston Navy Yard in 1941. Late in the war it went to Okinawa and was sunk by a *kamikaze* bomber with heavy loss of life. The *Pringle* was named after a remote Charleston relative, Rear Admiral Joel Roberts Poinsett Pringle, a senior officer of the battleship fleet during World War I. (For those of you still of child-bearing age, remember "Poinsett" if you are looking for a Pringle family name. In the event of a girl it could be changed to "Poinsette" or even "Poinsetta.")[36]

A Year in Switzerland

I attended Sidwell Friends School for second through fourth grades, from 1943 to 1946. It was not the excellent school that it later became, and had shed all traces of Quakerism. About all I remember about it is hating football, which all boys were required to play.

Then one year there was the famous Fathers-Sons Football Dinner. Fathers were pressured to attend and mine, hardly your great sports fan, did his duty. Slingin' Sammy Baugh, the Redskins' star quarterback, had been invited to attend and speak, which he did at length. Then there were 16mm movies of Redskins games, lots of them. The gym where this was happening was hot and crowded, and my little friends and I were in the front on the floor, where we proceeded to get in a scuffle and kick over and break the screen with a great crash.

That ended the movies, so we all got to go home. I was clearly one of the culprits responsible for ruining this great father-son bonding experience, and I was very surprised not to be scolded by my father; instead, as we drove home, he seemed rather pleased. It took me a while to figure out why.

Summers I attended Camp Chewonki near Wiscasset in Maine, now an environmental foundation. It had its high points, including a lovely lake and a nature counselor who taught us

[36] Not to be confused with Joel Roberts Poinsett (No "Pringle"), who was the first US minister (then the equivalent of ambassador) to Mexico and probably related somehow to the admiral.

to eat ants (the red ones were sweetish, the black ones were sour). We made lots of spore prints from mushrooms. Some evil child discovered you could catch garter snakes and then decapitate them in one of the traps that were kept in the nature room, why I have no idea. I didn't do anything useful like learning to sail.

I left Friends in 1946 and went to Georgetown Day School, which we learned about from one of father's liberal OWI friends. It was supposed to be "progressive" in the terminology of the day, which meant that it was very informal and that it was the first school of any kind in the Washington area to be racially integrated. (It is now a thriving, top-line independent school.) I liked it from the start. The school was then located in a rambling, early nineteenth-century farmhouse off Nebraska Avenue, where the NBC headquarters now stands. The farmhouse had been a speakeasy during prohibition, and the woods which covered most of the huge property were full of exotic debris, including unending troves of old champagne bottles.

GDS in those days ended at seventh grade, sort of. We sat on the desks and called the teachers by their first names. You progressed at your own speed. There was emphasis on dance and art, but it wasn't ideological. The headmistress, well known in Washington liberal circles—she was a friend of Eleanor Roosevelt—was Agnes Inglis O'Neil, always addressed as "Ag." For "sports" we wandered in the woods unearthing old bottles, playing scratch softball, and building dams and catching salamanders and crayfish in the creek that separated the GDS property from McLean Gardens on Wisconsin Avenue. Ag was cheerful and down to earth. She seemed to breathe through her ever-present cigarette.

In the summer of 1947 I attended Redbrick Camp, which she and her farmer husband owned in the Catskills. Redbrick was like GDS only more so. The antique farmhouse had a chink in the bricks where bees flew in and out, leaving streaks of wax and bee manure on the wall. In the basement there was a wooden tub filled with water where eggs were kept. This worked quite well: if an egg got rotten, it filled with gas and floated to the top of the tub and could be removed.

There was riding and hiking, or campers could (without adult supervision) wander across the hills to a rural general store. There we bought corncob pipes so we could smoke pigweed, a common local plant resembling desiccated brown goldenrod. There was a "Backwards Day," beginning with dinner and ending with breakfast. Partway through the summer we older kids took off by car, camping out around the northeast, including Quebec and Maine. It was immensely entertaining from start to finish. Ken, one of the two counselors who led us, had been a Marine on Guadalcanal. He told us he was the only man in his company not to contract malaria, then got it when he was home on leave visiting relatives in Mississippi.

In the fall of 1947 mother returned to Europe, for the North American Newspaper Alliance (NANA). We have a folder of articles she wrote, mainly on the progress of communism. She recognized that even in the east, most Europeans were going communist only under duress. She loved Italy and Poland.

This time I went with her, while Margot again remained with Daddy and Kate at 3319 N Street. There was no time for me to begin school at GDS; instead I took a few French lessons and spent some time at a most peculiar institution, the Gaunt School, located in a handsome Victorian building on Connecticut Avenue just above where the Washington Hilton is now. The man who ran it had some sort of connection with Chiang Kai-shek, and aside from the "school," the rest of the building was a boarding facility for Chinese military officers doing lord knows what.

I remember flying to Europe on a TWA DC-4 with Mother, the stops at Gander (Newfoundland) and Shannon (Ireland), and the endless and quite good meals. It took days, or so it seemed. I was then deposited at Le Rosey, a boarding school in Switzerland, while mother set off for Eastern Europe. Mother chose the school not out of any affection for Switzerland but because the rest of Europe was still largely without basic amenities such as hot water. It was located in and around a small chateau at Rolle, on Lake Geneva. In the winter the entire school moved to Gstaad in the Bernese Alps. It has since become one of the most expensive schools in the world, but in 1947 it was still quite affordable.[37]

---

[37] By 1960, it was being called "The Prince of Private Schools"—as in the article with that title in the September,1960, edition of *Holiday* magazine.

Total immersion in a foreign school at age eleven after the beginning of the school year was not fun. Le Rosey was bilingual in French and English, in that order. On my first day in French class I was blasted out of my seat by the teacher, Mme Stickel, for responding to her with "Oui" instead of "Oui, Madame." Eventually I did learn some French, which was quite useful later on.

When I got sick I went to an infirmary featuring liberal application of scalding, evil-smelling poultices made from burlap and filled with what smelled like spoiled oatmeal. If that didn't work, you had to lie on your stomach while little glass jars to suck out the inflammation were prepared. They were first coated with some sort of oil, which was then lit with a match, and then applied to your back. The fire inside the jar went out, creating a vacuum which stuck the jars to your back. The vacuum was sufficiently strong to be painful. This continued until you were covered with them, armadillo-style; they clinked together when you moved.

But after a week or two of such painful mysteries things got a lot better fast. Mme Stickel became quite friendly after I mastered "Oui, Madame" and the rest of school was as nice as could be. Before I knew it we were boarding a train to Montreux, where the Rhone exits the High Alps into Lake Geneva. We got a glimpse of Lord Byron's picture-postcard Chateau de Chillon, then took the mountain-climbing Bernese Oberland Railway to Gstaad, where the entire school was ensconced in three big chalets above the resort town.

I never did learn to ski worth a damn. There was lovely deep snow on the ground when we arrived—and none whatever fell after that. What little was left on the world-class ski runs around Gstaad quickly turned to mud and ice. I had no money for good skis, so the school issued me an ancient pair with no metal edges—deadly on ice. Anyway, after a month or so even the good skiers were reduced to going on long mountain walks for exercise.

Our guide was often an evil-tempered German language teacher who terrorized us about accidentally (or otherwise) kicking rocks off the precipitous trails. Although he was Swiss, the British and American boys called him Himmler and Hitler behind his back. We knew that Switzerland had not been on our side during the war. The fascination and mild suspicion this generated was heightened by the fact that the Swiss military was still totally equipped with World War II German equipment. We could actually see the infamous Messerschmitt 109 fighters landing at a military airstrip down the valley, and we discovered that our male teachers had German-style helmets as part of their Swiss citizen army equipment, always kept wherever they lived.

In the spring we went to back Rolle. I was getting good grades, and I loved certain classes, including one on drawing (which I always wished I'd been able to continue), and another on Swiss geography. We had to learn the productions of all twenty-six cantons, the linguistic breakdown (French, German, Italian or Romansch) and the percentage of Catholics and Protestants in each. The student body was a crazy mixture, including quite a bit of royalty—the future king of Belgium, Baudoin; the young future Duke of Argyle (named Campbell of course); lots of Indian princelings, and the future (now reigning) Aga Khan, Karim, and his brother, Amin.[38] Karim was stolid and haughty, but Amin was a charmer. They both had special food flown in from Pakistan—including fresh mangos, not shared with the rest of us. They were, of course, Muslims, but I certainly didn't know that. The school food was quite good. The best thing about it was the Sunday night "*Souper Suisse*," consisting of hot chocolate, Swiss cheese, small boiled potatoes and delicious brown bread. We went on a field trip to Annecy, in French Savoie across the lake. It still looked very threadbare compared to Switzerland.

Every week we got paid our allowance, in my case one Swiss franc, worth 25 US cents, which I could spend in the town of Rolle on whatever I wanted, including little chocolate bottles with real liqueur inside, quite a change from Hershey bars. There was a winery right in the middle of town where you could see huge, red-stained wooden casks, as big as houses, being cleaned and repaired. The main railroad line from Geneva and points north to Rome ran between the school playing fields and the lake. Trains whizzed past with exotic labels like "Simplon-Orient Express" on the *wagons lit*. On a clear day you could see Mont Blanc across the lake. Inspired by my drawing class, I

---

[38] Previous "Roséens" had included the future Shah of Iran, Prince Rainier of Monaco, and Prince Alexander of Yugoslavia. *Holiday*, September, 1960, p. 53.

drew a sketch of how it looked in one of my letters to Mother.

The school got more relaxed as the weather warmed. There were cherry trees around the chateau and every night, instead of dessert, we went outside and ate cherries—and threw them at each other. Then, before I knew it, it was over. I didn't want to leave. But I had a soft landing, spending the summer of 1948 with cousin Mary Pringle Fenhagen and her children at the Rhode Island shore.

Margot had switched to the Madeira School from public school, entering as a day student junior in 1947. Contrary to what some people now think, DC public education was lousy even before racial integration in 1954. There were no schools for the talented, like De Witt Clinton in New York. To get into Wilson, the only really good high school, you had to live in its neighborhood, which neither of my parents did. Margot did not want to leave public school, but she was bribed to do so by the prospect of being able to ride at Madeira, plus the fact that one of her stable boy friends at Meadowbrook had gotten a job at the Madeira stable.

My father and Kate were the prime movers behind this change and worked hard to make it a success, equipping Margot with everything from clothes to dancing lessons. "I'm sure Margot told you about the very elegant party Anstiss has invited her to," my father wrote HHS. "Kate and she will shop for a suitable evening dress tomorrow." Margot had known Anstiss McCormick in New York when they both attended Brearly, and took a dim view of her, much preferring her manurey stable crowd.

While the switch to Madeira went very well in the end (Margot graduated in 1949 and went on to Cornell), my father never stopped fretting about the expense. He wrote to HHS on August 9, 1948, just after her return from Europe with me:

As you requested on the telephone last night, I send you herewith the itemized cost of Margot's schooling and clothes [$1006.72 for tuition and fees, $327.25 for clothing and other expenses] . . . . I think any fair person would agree that the $1,333 is a relatively small part of what we did, to our very great joy and satisfaction, for Margot while you were away. Katharine spent many hours working with her at her French, Latin and English

. . . . She repaid us over and over again, both in companionship and in the really distinguished work that she did.

Katharine and I have discussed this again and again, several times with Margot [who was then sixteen]. We are unwilling to meet any of the expenses of Madeira unless the child lives with us, under an arrangement comparable to last year. Of course she would be with you week-ends depending on the degree to which you are in town, her desire to go to the stable and her homework.

Under such circumstances we will meet the Madeira bills for next year. To be accurate, Katharine will pay them as, with the cost of Geoffrey,[39] insurance, taxes and increasing prices, I could not meet them were it not for her very small income.

And we will also give serious consideration to postponing our adoption of a French orphan girl until next spring.

Yours,
Henry

Needless to say HHS was not about to agree to such an arrangement, and things continued much as before.

Adolescent Malaise

On my return from Switzerland I spent another year at Georgetown Day School, but the school stopped at seventh grade. In the fall of 1949, I enrolled at Landon, in Bethesda, remaining there for two years until I went to Deerfield. I had a great geography teacher the first year at Landon, Mr. Diefenderfer. All his pupils maintained current events scrapbooks, and my subject was China. It was the year the Communists were conquering the country, so I had plenty to cut and paste even though I didn't understand half of it.

But the next year was not good. Landon's founder and head, Landon Banfield, was a pompous idiot, interested only in sports. The faculty seemed demoralized. My ninth-grade English teacher, Mr. Eden, lost control of his classes and I was

---

[39] At this point Geoffrey was still in a private institution. Only later was he transferred to St. Elizabeth's in Washington, which, being a federal government institution, was free.

apparently one of the culprits. I was frequently assigned to "Saturday Study Hall," which meant going out to Bethesda on Saturday mornings, not to study, but to work in the resident faculty's gardens and even clean their dogs. My father was furious. He said he could find plenty of chores for me to do at home. He was even more upset when Eden called and asked his advice about getting out of teaching and becoming a professional writer.

I could have gotten into serious trouble. At Camp Chewonki, I had learned to shoot, courtesy of the NRA's extensive recreational program. Later I wanted my parents to buy me a rifle and one of them did so. It was a .22 caliber bolt-action Marlin. I used to take it from N Street downtown to a rifle range on Capitol Hill on the Cabin John–Union Station streetcar, which passed right in front of the White House. No problem, in those days.

But now I discovered it was great fun to go hunting squirrels with a friend around his suburban home. Once we shot one and, mortally wounded, it fell down a neighbor's chimney. In the ninth grade, I boarded for a time at Landon while mother was away working, and became pals with a thoroughly unwholesome character who, among other things, introduced me to the fascination of shoplifting. I don't recall that I ever stole anything myself, but I certainly watched him do it.

Then one afternoon I looked on in horror as the Woodward and Lothrop police picked him up and ushered him away weeping. They paid no attention to me, but I was therapeutically terrified by the experience. My parents never learned anything about this or the squirrel hunting idiocy.

I took the Cabin John streetcar to Chain Bridge to go fishing when the herring, shad and white perch were running up the Potomac to spawn in the spring. Herring do not feed in fresh water but you can "snag" them almost by the bushel by throwing an unbaited treble hook into the swift current and reeling it in with a series of jerks. Daddy and Kate were not wild about this activity of mine, because it made a huge mess in the kitchen and the "buck" herrings were incredibly bony and almost inedible. The "roes" (females) had eggs, not unlike shad roe and very good to eat, but not good enough to compensate for the mess. I finally ended up giving most of the fish to other fishermen, mostly blacks who salted them down in barrels, a method which supposedly dissolves all the bones. Today in March and April you will find large groups of Vietnamese and other immigrants exploiting this fishery below Chain Bridge.

Since the Potomac gorge is very rocky I lost a lot of tackle, and when I saw an advertisement in *Field and Stream* saying that you could order a mold and make your sinkers from scrap lead, I ordered one. You heated the lead in a saucepan (hopefully not one of Kate's favorites) on the kitchen stove and then poured molten lead into the mold, not without occasional dribbles here and there, compounding the mess made by the fish. Why my parents allowed me to do this is one of the minor mysteries of my upbringing.

Apart from bouts of incipient delinquency, my life as I approached high-school age was going well in many ways. I was now old enough to enjoy my father and Kate's frequent dinner parties and to join in the conversation. Guests included Father's OWI friends, like Jack Fleming (father of Phil), foreign policy editor for *US News and World Report*, Ferdinand (Ferdie) and Delia Kuhn (their son Philip became a professor of Chinese History at Harvard), and others from that crowd. There were Arthur Schlesinger, Jr., and Abe Fortas, not to mention his formidable, cigar-smoking wife Carol, a highly successful tax attorney. She had a silver Rolls Royce and later, when I started smoking cigars, used to give me one of her very expensive Havanas whenever they came to dinner.

We were sometimes joined by Kate's mother, Helen Douglas, on her annual visit to imbibe all the latest news in Washington. There were old friends from New York like Philip Hamburger, senior writer for the *New Yorker* (he lived until 2005), who during the war had driven us to fits of laughter when, with a comb in his lip, he would do screaming imitations of Hitler. There were a few Foreign Service Officers like Kay Bracken, an extremely talented linguist who had served all over the Middle East although she had no formal education beyond high school, and today would surely have been an ambassador by the end of her career.

There were the Stroups, Russell and Louise. Russell was our minister at the Georgetown Presbyterian Church, while Louise Baker had been a colleague of Kate's at OWI. Russell was an eloquent preacher with strong liberal convictions, which caused my father as well as Kate to become regular churchgoers. Later, he baptized both Annie and Jamie, who reciprocated during Annie's pre-baptismal visit by accidentally destroying an antique Italian statue at their retirement home in McLean; while the adults were talking they had been sent out to play in the garden and had decided to climb on it.

After my father and Kate wrote an article about Howard University, and another about the shortage of Negro doctors, they became fascinated with the problems faced by black Americans. They became good friends with several Howard faculty members, including the Warner Lawsons (he was Dean of the School of Music and Director of Howard's renowned choir), and the John Hope Franklins, also frequent guests at 3319 N Street.

The parties at 3319 N Street were particularly exciting during the McCarthy era, when liberal Washington felt the country was facing a major threat. I remember one of my father's old Hollywood friends, Anne Revere, who was in town testifying at a McCarthy hearing investigating communists in Hollywood. She told him where to go, and pumped all of us full of adrenalin. But her blacklisting by McCarthy resulted in her not being able to get another job in Hollywood for two decades.

It is hard for people to understand now, I think, how frightening McCarthy was, mainly because, like most skilled demagogues, he played unerringly to a prevailing paranoia, and thereby seemed more powerful than he really was. McCarthy's demagogic appeal was rooted in cumulative shock and disbelief over the loss of America's atomic monopoly, the fall of China, and then the Korean War. With unsettling speed these events rudely shattered our illusions that the sacrifices of World War II had secured our future. People could not believe that all this could have happened had we not been betrayed from within, so McCarthy's search for scapegoats seemed logical to many scared Americans. Should we ever have another global economic crisis coupled with a serious external threat, you could reasonably expect something similar to happen again.[40]

Interesting as it was in many ways, Washington in the Forties and early Fifties remained culturally deprived, causing natives of New York and Philly to snort with derision. The town still didn't have a decent symphony orchestra. There was the National Gallery (thank God) and a few smaller galleries such as the Corcoran and Philips, but not much else. The Smithsonian was a monument to cobwebs and increasingly irrelevant government science. When my parents did an article about it for the *Saturday Evening Post* the title was "Uncle Sam's Attic." Washington lagged far behind Cincinnati in cultural achievement, as Daddy and Kate noted when they did an article on that city, perhaps in their Cities of America series for the *Saturday Evening Post* in the mid-Fifties.[41] Washington still showed its rural southern upbringing. Blacks aside, there was as yet little resident diversity, except for some Jews (no German, Italian, Polish, Greek, Asian or Hispanic communities).

The city's worst feature of course was segregation, abhorrent to liberal northerners like us, and even to our liberal Pringle cousins in Charleston, SC. If you had Negro friends, you couldn't meet them for a meal at the Woodward and Lothrop lunch counter. At a time when good restaurants were still few and far between (and equally segregated), department store lunch counters were important. Because of segregation, Washington was without any theater for a decade, more or less. The New York-based actors' union refused to play at the National, the only major theater, "National" in name only because the audience was still segregated even when the actors were not. Road shows of major New York plays did not come to DC. Washington had only the Gaiety Burlesque on Ninth Street.

Few whites ventured into black Washington, with its chain of segregated movie theaters along U Street: the Lincoln, the Booker T, and several others. Although segregation ended in 1953-54, in large part due to the efforts of Dwight Eisenhower, the heavy hand of witless Congressional rule and the absence

---

[40] This paragraph was written before the election of Donald Trump in 2016.

[41] A search did not turn it up among the articles they did for the *Saturday Evening Post's* Cities of America series, so it may have been for another magazine.

of democracy at the local level remained a big problem in the District of Columbia. Perhaps most important, Washington had little in the way of truly local financial resources to draw on for philanthropic or cultural purposes. Of course, we did have the Washington Senators, always in seventh place, trailed only by the St. Louis Browns.

I can't say I was greatly disturbed by Washington's cultural and athletic failings as a young teenager, despite hearing the adults grousing about it. I enjoyed going to Washington Senators baseball games at Griffith Stadium, which loomed like a giant gasworks at the end of U Street, and I didn't mind that much that they were always in seventh place. Lee Miller, a friend of mother's from the *Washington Daily News* (long since defunct) and the biographer of Ernie Pyle, used to take me to games, along with his nice lady friend, Rosemary. He taught me how to keep score on his custom-printed scorecards.

The stadium was awesome. It had a towering right field wall, over which few home runs were ever hit. Then it went off in a series of angles to a very deep center field, often the scene of inside-the-park homers. It seated only about 27,000 as I recall, but that was plenty to contain the long-suffering Senators fans. I listened to baseball on the radio as well. For away games, the local radio station was too cheap to send a reporter out-of-town. Instead a guy sat watching a teletype ticker, and he would cover the game as if he were there: "It's a long fly ball into deep left field, McGrubnick is racing back . . . etc." But you could tell what was going on because there was no crowd noise; instead there was only the teletype machine audibly chattering away in the background.

The city's rural southern character had an upside; just across the river in Virginia you could get into gorgeous countryside with real farms in twenty minutes. With Margot at Madeira, as well as my fishing expeditions in the spring, I enjoyed occasional trips into DC's neighbor state.

Our lifestyle was otherwise simple by modern standards. Washington had about half a dozen restaurants worth mentioning. We rarely went to any of them. One exception was the Oriental, a Chinese place on the corner of Wisconsin and R Streets, where we ate when living with Daddy and Kate perhaps three or four times a year on the maid's night out. There were plenty of books around both houses, but only a handful of records. At Argonne Place we had the "Warsaw Concerto" and "Oklahoma!"—that was it. Daddy and Kate had a few more records. Nobody was into singing or performing. Someone is supposed to have offered me piano lessons at some point; I don't remember it and it certainly wasn't pushed very hard.

Both my parents worried about money constantly, but neither had health insurance—it was unheard of. You paid the doctor the same way you paid the milkman. At Argonne Place, to augment my allowance, I had a paper route, but it was the tabloid *Washington News.* I had to walk miles, carrying the papers in a cloth bag, to make a few bucks a month. I was extremely envious of the *Washington Evening Star* delivery boys who served a much higher density of subscribers and made a lot more money, plus they were issued shiny wooden wagons with iron wheels. In those days the *Star*, not the *Post*, was far and away the most prosperous newspaper in DC.

Margot and I did find the more regimented atmosphere of N Street difficult at times. It was partly that Kate, an innate perfectionist and a punctilious planner, never got used to having kids around. For example, although her meals were always exquisite, the portions were, well, frugal. But when Margot and I, waking up at night and feeling hungry, snuck downstairs and ate some leftover or other from the icebox, we would inevitably find out that we had thoughtlessly devoured something being saved specifically for Bertha's lunch next Thursday. (Bertha was our black maid from Clifton Forge, WV, extremely correct, punctilious and hard working herself, as well as very pretty—we always wondered why she never got married.)

Much later we discovered that we had both independently devised the same solution. Instead of consuming one leftover, the trick was to nibble a little from several, plus maybe a shaving of cake or a cracker or two (only from an already open box) and a swig of milk. Everything had to be in imperceptible moderation. It usually worked and perhaps it was good life training.

Then there was Archie, the cocker spaniel. Our various dogs at 1640 Argonne Place were all mutts: Nonnie, Andy, and one other I can't remember. But my father and Kate always wanted to do things properly, and that meant a pedigree, papers, etc. Archie, named for OWI colleague Archibald MacLeish, was the result of inbreeding normal for pedigreed dogs of popular breeds, handsome but neurotic, and he bit people often enough to give my father and Kate something else to worry about. So they bought a female named Penny, after the then-popular comic strip character Penny Pringle, about a Bobby Sox teenager, in the vain hope that she would calm Archie down. Penny was as painfully shy as Archie was aggressive.

It is not totally clear why my father and Kate never had children of their own. My father suggested at various times that they couldn't afford the financial burden given what they were doing for Margot and me, especially alimony and child support payments. Geoffrey was also a significant expense before they got him admitted to St. Elizabeth's in the late 1950s. I'm not so sure that was the real reason. For one thing my father's health was not what it should have been for a man in his fifties. He smoked heavily (Philip Morrises), he got no exercise worth mentioning, and he had a growing drinking problem (usually bourbon Old Fashioneds, at least on formal occasions), which became increasingly noticeable.

Above all, he was a pathological worrier, and he never stopped fretting about my mother. This must have been extremely distressing to Kate, and the worrying no doubt played into his physical problems. I should note that fitness, like medical insurance, was an almost unheard of concept among the intelligentsia of those days, and the medical profession was still denying—or really didn't yet understand—that heavy smoking was lethal.

By 1950 I was going nowhere fast. Landon was not working for me, but there didn't seem to be any attractive alternatives in the Washington area. My mother thought of Deerfield, but we couldn't afford it. Nothing daunted, she talked to the headmaster, Frank Boyden, who prided himself on his ability to salvage problem boys. Boyden listened, and with obvious misgivings agreed to accept me in the fall of 1951, the beginning of my sophomore year. It was understood that Deerfield would pick up whatever expenses the family couldn't cover, meaning most of them, all this because of Boyden's loyalty to my grandfather. Boarding school was exactly what I needed, and in retrospect it is clear that Deerfield was my salvation.

3

Bob: Deerfield, Harvard, Army, and Marriage, 1951-1964

Deerfield Academy

I felt at home at Deerfield from the beginning. Mr. Boyden's seamless benevolent despotism made it a curiously relaxed place. There was no disciplinary system, no demerits or other sanctions, and certainly no student government. Everyone knew that any serious problem would get the headmaster's personal attention. He claimed that he had never expelled anyone from the school, or hardly ever. What he did in the event of a serious problem was to call the parents and tell them they should find another school. And of course it worked, for over sixty years. He decided everything—admissions, scholarships, who got into Harvard or wherever.

He was in his fiftieth year as head when I arrived. The school, founded in 1799 as a typical New England village academy, had been on the verge of extinction when it offered him, fresh out of Amherst, the headmastership. In the end he reigned longer than Victoria. He had lots of quirks and a streak of narrow mindedness. The school had been co-ed and he quickly ended that, being on the whole uncomfortable with girls. His politics were unconventionally Republican, useful for fund-raising in New York City, at which he excelled.

He loved buildings and sports. He both coached and played on the three important teams—football, basketball and baseball—until about World War I. The story is that someone once picked him up and carried him for a touchdown. He was indeed quite short, even dumpy by the 1950s, with an owlish face and hair parted in the center. He didn't at first glance look like an authority figure, even when he was driving his famous horse and buggy around the school. At the evening meetings we all had to sit on the floor so he could see over us. You could tell a Deerfield boy by his flat rear end (which, unfortunately, didn't last into middle age). He favored rumpled blue serge suits.

Boyden's pronouncements usually began with "Now boys ..." and were sprinkled with aphorisms, endlessly repeated, of which the most notorious was "Finish Up Strong." He could also be very amusing (e.g. his stories about New England characters like Deacon Greenough and my grandfather, Charles Smith). Of course he was a New England character himself. Attendance was compulsory at all meals, classes, afternoon sports, Sunday morning church (in the town church), Sunday evening hymn sing, daily evening meetings, and there was a final check at bedtime. The only really free time was Sunday afternoon. Yet I did not find it oppressive and I don't think most students did, although there was a fair amount of grumbling.

One of his legendary habits was having his "office" in a large space where the main school building corridors came together and everyone had to walk by him going to and from classes. He had the ability, à la Winston Churchill, to take catnaps, sometimes interrupting a meeting with a visitor to go into another room to take a phone call (i.e. sleep for ten minutes) and then return and continue the meeting.

Beyond the legends, Frank Boyden was sheer genius, not immediately obvious. I wrote home about his ability to sense the mood of the school, to tell exactly who or what was causing trouble. He was adept at recognizing merit in faculty, even teachers who differed from him in almost every way, and then getting them to stay at Deerfield, although they might not like a lot of things about the school or about rural New England. He showed this trait in making virtues and funny stories out of my grandfather's eccentricities. He showed it with Dick Hatch, a talented English teacher and a good friend of my parents, who tried to escape by writing a dirty novel under a pen name.[1] Even that didn't get him fired, but he finally escaped anyway and ended up teaching English at MIT for many years. Boyden showed it with his own wife, Helen, a very different personality, amusingly irreverent about him, and a fine chemistry teacher in her own right.

This essential tolerance and skill with people permeated the school and made it a pleasant and rewarding place to be for those of us who were not athletic and did not fit Boyden's conventional ideals of young manhood. Although we were constantly supposed to be doing this or that, it was often possible to carve out a niche and do something else. So, for example, it was OK in the spring for me to escape from tennis (now I wish I hadn't) and go fishing with Mr. Poland, my biology teacher. Once I caught a big walleye in the Deerfield River and the kitchen prepared it for my table at dinner (all lunches and dinners were sit-down with a faculty member present), and for a moment I glowed in the unaccustomed admiration of my peers. I don't mean to suggest I didn't have friends; I did, but we were something of an intellectual and social fringe group.

Deerfield was good academically, but not great. Mr. Boyden never claimed that it was; he always granted that Andover and Exeter were better academically. After beginning as the town school, Deerfield had, after all, been primarily a fifth-year finishing school for local farm boys being prepped to get into Amherst. The science courses were excellent. The rest was variable. I had one really good math teacher, A. Phillips Bill; I only wish he had pushed me harder. I did well enough in the subjects I was good at, including English, French and history. Therefore, I took biology and chemistry, but was allowed to skip physics, a mistake. I got in the habit of loafing through on B's and a few A minuses, which was to continue at Harvard.

I began photography, having inherited Grandfather Smith's Kodak 35 camera, and spent a fair amount of time in the darkroom of the new Activities Building. I liked taking pictures of the lovely old houses along the village's main street. I enjoyed debating and I acted in a couple of school plays. I learned from my friends to appreciate classical music. I also

---

[1] Also author of *The Curious Lobster* and *The Curious Lobster's Island*, under his own name. My copies were given to Zoe and Penelope for Christmas in 2005.

enjoyed the Sunday evening hymn sings and the Deerfield tradition of all students singing in the school chorus. Volume was what counted; there were no parts. We sang songs like "Jerusalem" and of course the lovely Deerfield Evensong, with lyrics by Richard Hatch and music by music teacher Bob Oatley, who survived for decades in spite of a rather visible drinking problem—another example of Boyden's tenacity at holding faculty. I did well enough at all this to have Mr. Boyden include me on his annual list of recommendations for Harvard. I left Deerfield in a warm glow of having loved the place.

My best friend was Arthur Johnson, the son of Captain Irving Johnson, commander of the *Yankee*, a square-rigged brigantine on which he and his family explored the remote Pacific and wrote numerous articles for the *National Geographic*. Arthur was something of a loner and although he was wiry and fit as could be from years of crewing a tall ship, he was definitely one of our slightly-at-odds-with-the-rest-of-them crowd. In my senior year I got to visit the *Yankee* in Gloucester, her homeport, where she was preparing to leave on another voyage. I was hoisted up one of the masts to chip paint. I remember suddenly, to my surprise, feeling a terrible pang because I would not be going with the ship. The *Yankee* survived financially only because Captain Johnson charged crew members a fee, so it was not on for the captain's son's best friend to be taken along for free. He operated successfully for years, but finally sold the *Yankee* in favor of a less strenuous vessel suitable for cruising the canal system in Europe. The new owner lost the *Yankee* within a year or so in an Atlantic storm.

My friend Arthur Johnson died quite young of cancer. Recently I got to know his son, Cliff, by this time a senior State Department lawyer, who was eager to know more about his father, and brought his two young sons to dinner to hear more about their grandfather.

Moving South, to Alexandria

My parents continued to squabble over when and where we would live with whom, and over how father's child support payments would be handled. He did not trust HHS to dispense the child support money for us, and was constantly trying to send it directly to the school in question, through us. This continued until his death in 1958. My mother felt it was none of his business to do more than give the money to her. Whenever she found out we were cooperating with him, we were subjected to charges of backstabbing and betrayal. These outbursts never lasted long, but they were most unpleasant.

While I was at Deerfield, the major event was my mother's move to Old Town, Alexandria. She was persuaded to do so by Barbara Mustin, an emaciated, alcoholic, chain-smoking Southern belle friend-of-a-friend straight out of Tennessee Williams, but also bright and funny. Her perpetually fed-up husband, Henry, had an evening news program on WMAL, the radio station of the *Evening Star*. His office was in the *Washington Star* building at 12th and Pennsylvania Avenue, right over the loading docks where fleets of trucks picked up papers as they came off the *Star*'s big rotary presses. He was an avid fisherman and often took me smallmouth bass fishing in the Potomac, below Great Falls on the Virginia side.

I did not like the idea of moving to Alexandria, which seemed like the other side of the moon. It still smacked of antique Southern. The Greyhound bus station at King and Washington streets still had the old black and white facilities, even though the busses were no longer segregated. Alexandria's congressman, Howard Smith, a leader of the civil-rights-blocking Southern Democrats and powerful chairman of the House Rules Committee for decades, still had his office on South Fairfax Street, near where we lived.

Getting to Alexandria from Washington was a pain. It involved a change of busses and usually a very long wait at the Old Post Office on Pennsylvania Avenue, the building much later acquired by Donald Trump. Mother moved anyway. For a time she lived on the second floor of Joydons, an antique store on South Washington Street owned by Don Davis, the best of her World War II bomber pilot beaux, now happily married to a British war bride, Joy. Then for a while she had an apartment at 119 Prince Street. Then in 1952 Barbara Mustin persuaded her to buy 103 Prince Street, which she did for about $9,000 with some of her small inheritance from her father, plus some help with the mortgage from my Uncle Max, James Maxwell Pringle, who was by then a moderately successful mortgage banker. No one had the foggiest notion that the tiny house might be a good investment, as it turned out to be.

The house had been built around 1800 by John Harper, who owned the big brick warehouse next door, which later became the Christmas Attic. To save money he simply built 103 against the warehouse, with no separate wall of its own. It had no yard and no basement, but it did have three fireplaces, very tall ceilings, and a gorgeous Adams period mantelpiece in the master bedroom. I lived in the attic, "Robert's Roost," where Jamie later had his bedroom.

Although migrants from Washington had been renovating old houses since the 1930s, Old Town was still relatively undeveloped. There were no restaurants in the lower King Street waterfront area except for the Seaport Inn, at the corner of King and South Union. The old warehouses were still warehouses, or vacant empty shells like the one across the street from 103 Prince Street, since converted to a dwelling. The Torpedo Factory, now an art center, where some of the tragically defective torpedoes of World War II had been made, was still being used to store records from Nazi Germany. Coal trains en route to a power plant went through the tunnel on Wilkes Street and turned north down the middle of Union Street, past our front door. Once they passed the Torpedo Factory, the right of way was fenced. The engineer would then speed up, and the loaded coal cars would rumble past at forty mph within fifty feet of our house, making it shake, rattle, and roll.

It was terrifying, sickening. I am telling you and telling everybody that no house can go through an earthquake like this once or more every 24 hours . . . . I am not a hysterical woman. I have got common sense. And I tell you that when a house shakes as badly as this it is proof that something is wrong and very, very wrong; and that if repairs are not made it will be too late.[2]

The house was nearly the death of mother. She got caught up in a mess of maintenance problems. They began when the city

[2] HHS letter to Andrew Merle [presumably of the Southern Railroad], December 12, 1956.

dug a sewage line on Union Street and the settling that resulted was aggravated by the train vibrations. Cracks appeared in the old walls. She was certain that the house was going to collapse. She wrote screaming letters to contractors as well as to the Southern Railroad urging them to take action.

When an inspector told her the foundations needed more support, she went to Uncle Max once again, persuading him to pull strings so she could get a new loan to finance the insertion of some steel beams in the crawl space. It seems to have worked, because when we acquired the house a few years later, we had no more structural problems. 103 Prince Street has not fallen down yet, although the plaster ceiling in the dining room did collapse at one point, terrifying Pax, our small dog (we were not home). But since then it has been beautifully restored and remodeled. True, the coal trains no longer thunder down Union Street; there are hordes of tourists and diners-out instead.

Beginning in high school, I had a succession of summer jobs. In 1950 my mother, Margot and I made our first post-World War II trip to Wyoming, this time in Grandfather Smith's gas-guzzling Oldsmobile (Hydromatic Fluid Drive) sedan, which we had inherited. My first job was helping to care for Brown Swiss show cattle owned by Bea and Carlo Beuf, part of the transplanted, polo-playing petty aristocracy which had settled around Big Horn, nestled under the front range of the Big Horn Mountains near Sheridan.

Bea's mother was a Gallatin, descended from Albert Gallatin, an early and influential Secretary of the Treasury. Others in this Big Horn crowd were the offspring of British "remittance men," as they were called—the second sons of nobility who were sent abroad to amuse themselves on the American frontier, living on "remittances" from home. One such family was that of future Wyoming Senator Malcolm Wallop, which included the Earl of Portsmouth, quite high in the line of succession to the British throne. You can see why Queen Elizabeth felt at home in Sheridan when she visited relatives of her stable manager living there. Mamie used to refer to the whole collection as the "Gallops and Wallops."

In any case the Beufs were delightful people. The work wasn't hard, consisting of a little stable cleaning and escorting the big but gentle animals to state fairs in Billings, Montana, and Douglas, a small town where the Wyoming State Fair is still held. Bea's husband Carlo was an Italian count, poet and literary critic; he had a little log cabin of his own, down by a small mountain stream, where he wrote his poetry. The Beufs had two children, Cesco and Sandro, who was about my age, so there was no lack of company.

The house was built of logs with big picture windows facing the mountains, decorated with wonderful Crow Indian beadwork and other artifacts collected by Bea's mother, who was a great friend of the Crow tribe.[3] We went fishing in ponds formed by damming the small stream; they were full of huge rainbow, brown and brook trout. We ate some and released others in the icy, spring-fed swimming pool where they lived quite happily since it wasn't chlorinated. There were dogs all over the place. Every evening, we all ate dinner, prepared and served by an expert staff, together. I learned to drive that summer while attending polo games, on the margins of the big field. My father, who knew the Beufs from visits before he divorced my mother, loved them; they were his kind of cowboys, and I must say I did too.

My next summer next job was quite different, haying at the NX Bar (from its brand, <u>NX</u>). This ranch was owned by another Big Horn brahmin acquaintance of mother's, Alan Fordyce, but the resemblance ended there. Fordyce did not live on the property; instead he had a foreman, Jack Reisch, who took an instant dislike to me. There was no gorgeous view, no wine with dinner (although we did all eat together with Reisch's family), and certainly no swimming pool. Indeed there was no running water in the bunkhouse for the first half of the summer, and I went a month without really bathing. It was a big place, 45,000 acres, near Decker, north of Sheridan just across the Montana border. It was mostly very dry, but included some bottomland, which produced hay to feed cattle during the winter. My job was to help pick up and stack the baled hay.

As a laborsaving device, we used a horse and wagon. That

---

[3] The entire Edith and Goelet Gallatin Collection of Indian artifacts, named for Bea's parents, was later acquired by the Brinton Memorial Museum and is on display at a new annex built for it there, not far from the former Gallatin Ranch where I worked.

way the guy who drove the horse could stand on the wagon and help load bales, which could not be done with a tractor. This meant that the operation could be accomplished more easily with only two people. Once or twice I had to harness the horse, which was a fearful challenge. The big work horse was gentle enough, but getting the harness untangled and on him was hard for someone with little manual dexterity and no sense of spatial relations. I worked with a Cheyenne Indian named Phil Harris, who was married to a white woman and lived down the road in a little place of his own. The NX Bar has now been turned into a game ranch, where you can shoot wild animals for a fee. Much of the Decker area has been terribly scarred by mammoth open-pit coal mines; the whole area is part of the much publicized Powder River Basin.

Another summer I worked at the 4D, more like the Beufs' in terms of congeniality, but a real cattle ranch; it was located on Tongue River near the Northern Cheyenne Reservation where Margot was about to start teaching. The owners of the 4D, Albert and Annie May Brown, were originally from Mississippi. Albert had died, but Annie May, a handsome grey-hired lady, was very much alive and a Southern character to end them all. One of her trademark dinner table exclamations was "Ah just LOVES tuhnup greens." Big cottonwood trees sheltered the main house on one side, with a row of bunkhouse units and the kitchen-dining room building, where everyone usually ate, on the other side.

Albert's son, "Buster" Brown, was the boss, and most un-cowboy-like. He always wore a small hat, not a big one, and was continuously chuckling about something or other, but he knew the cattle business. Many of the local ranchers ran their cattle on the nearby Northern Cheyenne reservation, on land leased from the Indians. Down the dirt road a few miles to the north was Birney: a small school, a scattering of houses, and the requisite bar, which was the Saturday night gathering place. Not far away was the Bones Brothers dude ranch, owned by relatives of Nanny Alderson (subject of my mother's book, *A Bride Goes West*).

I arrived at the 4D via the "mail stage" from Sheridan, actually a station wagon operated by a legendary character named Diener. He didn't charge passengers anything, but they had to help deliver mail and freight (things like tractor tires) to the ranches scattered along the forty-mile route. The day I arrived, he had a return passenger from the 4D, the roughly three-hundred-pound Mexican cook who was being fired for drinking and ill temper. Diener looked on with trepidation as she was loaded into his vehicle. For the rest of the summer Buster did all the cooking himself, but he had no clue what he was doing. There was always a side of beef hanging in the cold locker, and he would just hack off the nearest hunk for dinner, regardless of anatomical provenance. It was a standing joke.

When there was no haying, I was relegated to the vast vegetable garden behind the main house, source of Annie May's tuhnup greens. It was irrigated, but never weeded except by me. I hated this job because it was utterly boring, and there was no one to talk with. It seems strange that I got to like gardening later in life. The 4D and Birney would make a book, if someone hasn't written one already, but that is Margot's subject. She was to live in the neighborhood for many years and would write a different book, *Working Cowboy*,[4] about one of her many friends from the area, plus another, *Horseback Schoolmarm*,[5] about her job teaching in a one-room school not far away.

The Harvard Crimson (and Harvard)

I got to Harvard in the fall of 1954 and was assigned to live in Weld Hall; then as now all freshmen lived in the Harvard Yard. Weld was a huge Victorian pile with offices on the lower floors and freshman rooms on the top, all arranged around a huge circular atrium and in need of maintenance. The first thing of any note that I did was to sleep through a couple of my initial hour exams, prompting a letter from the Dean of Freshmen to my alarmed father. I resented the letter and could not understand what all the fuss was about—Mr. Boyden had never done anything like that!—but I didn't repeat the mistake.

My freshman roommate was a Chinese student, Tsing Yuan, whose father, a scholar in the classical Chinese sense, had been

---

[4] Margot Liberty and Barry Head, *Working Cowboy, Recollections of Ray Holmes*, University of Oklahoma Press, 2002.
[5] Margot Liberty, *Horseback Schoolmarm, Montana, 1953-1954*, University of Oklahoma Press, 2016.

the head of the National Library in pre-revolutionary Beijing. The family went into exile when the Communists took over and his father wandered from one job to another at the great libraries of the world. No wonder that with this background Tsing was relentlessly serious and could not understand my indifference to study. This became a real irritant when I started competing for the *Crimson* and often wandered back to the room late at night, waking him up. From his perspective, I must have been a royal pain in the ass. I remember listening with disbelief when he told me that China was a great country with plenty of resources, and that it was not at all difficult to read and write Chinese—he had been doing it all his life. I lost track of him for decades and was very surprised to encounter him at my Harvard 50th Reunion.

I had a small scholarship (about $200 a year, 10% of 1954 annual tuition plus room and board), but I was expected to work as well, so I got a job as a "student porter" cleaning bathrooms in the residential houses where all students lived after their freshman year. I remember being amazed at the contrasting conditions of the rooms I cleaned, from primly neat to total pigsty. We "porters" were not exactly popular, because we had just, by university fiat, replaced a traditional corps of local maids ("biddies") adored by generations of hung-over students for their maternal ministrations. In any case, the tedium of gazing into a few too many toilet bowls brought me enough money to live on.

The *Harvard Crimson* soon became almost the be-all and end-all of my college experience. I tried out as a photographer, just to be different from the rest of my family. The first high point of my "comp" (for competition) was a photo of the Harvard Union's gate at night, after a storm left wet snow plastered all over it. The second high point was my assignment to illustrate a proverb, "Fools march in where angels fear to tread." I got some of my friends from Weld Hall to get dressed up as *Guys-and-Dolls*-type card sharks and posed them in the splendid room in University Hall where senior faculty meetings are held. To accomplish this, we just snuck in when no one was looking. I was reassured on a recent visit, when daughter Anne took us to see the same room, that half a century later it was still left unlocked and accessible to random visitors.

Then there was the "sex picture" assignment. By this time I was dating a Radcliffe freshman, Jo Ann Abraham, and I posed her on a sofa, looking pretty but totally clothed. This evoked hoots of laughter from my mentors because it was not exactly "sex," even by the standards of the 1950s. My more sophisticated colleagues found some Simmons girls, not as pretty but willing to expose a little more flesh. Still, for better or worse, I was elected to the *Crimson*.

For me as for many others it was an addictive experience. Putting out a daily paper was very time-consuming, requiring all of us to work at least a full day every week. But the *Crimson* was also a social black hole. Many of its "editors" (everyone was and still is an "editor;" the real editors are "executives") came to Harvard primarily to be on the *Crimson*, not to study in a formal sense, with newspaper careers in mind. Such people hung out there endlessly. In those days, we owned a flatbed press built in about 1885 and two linotype machines.

The linotype was your original nineteenth-century Rube Goldberg fantasy. By means of a keyboard, it arranged little brass molds of letters, dropping them with an inimitable combination of clink and clatter into a line which, when filled with lead, produced a slug of type. All this was serious and potentially dangerous machinery: if you did the wrong thing on the linotype keyboard you produced a "squirt" of molten lead, and the ancient press was potentially lethal.

So we had two professional printers, Art Hopkins, a *Crimson* legend, and a young apprentice (who turned out to be a passionate railroad fan). The basement and rear of the building at 14 Plympton Street was rented to the Crimson Printing Company, a commercial printer which technically employed Art and his assistant, and, more important, produced a cacophony of printing noises and smells all day long which provided a soul-lifting professional atmosphere. Today of course everything is digital and I have no doubt that the building is a lot duller. Upstairs on the third floor there was the "sanctum" with a small kitchen and sofas suitable for sleeping if necessary. I spent the better part of one summer living there.

The "comment books" were another time drain. Each day's editorials were posted in one, where all editors could write comments. The second, so-called "news" comment book, was supposedly for reaction to news articles, but mainly for general gossip and debate. We all used our initials, so I was RMP, inevitably articulated as "Rump." There were lots of little tribal customs such as RIITPOTME, pronounced "ripotme," meaning "Red ink is the property of the Managing Editor," who ran the news page. Anyone except this worthy who erred and used red ink in a comment book evoked a barrage of scribbled RIITPOTMEs. The first managing editor I knew was Jack Rosenthal, later (along with many other "crimeds") a senior executive of the *New York Times*. We were all very conscious of our distinguished alumni, beginning with FDR.

There was a lot of pranking and semi-professional horseplay, requiring much time-consuming effort and travel. Putting out parody editions of rival university dailies was one favorite stunt. We did this in Princeton with a fake issue of the *Daily Princetonian* reporting that their star football player had been incarcerated for mugging a local youth on the eve of the Harvard-Princeton game. It is unlikely that anyone was fooled.

Of course, nothing pleased us more than irritating the Harvard administration, which we did frequently. One weapon was the so-called "Confidential [sic] Guide" to undergraduate courses, which printed often unflattering and insulting reviews of professorial and teaching assistant performance, sometimes based on very scanty evidence. Another annual ritual, equally annoying to University Hall, was smoking out and revealing the recipients of honorary degrees, supposed to be secret until awarded. And there was a lot of other sheer foolishness, such as stealing the bronze Ibis from the tower of our rival, the *Harvard Lampoon*. Our specialist in this prank was the very talented cartoonist and human fly, perpetual student David Royce. He always labeled himself as "class of '53, '55½, '56," but I don't think he ever actually graduated. Once stolen, the Ibis would be taken all over town and posed for pictures in various locations, allegedly with the "Poonies" in hot pursuit. I suppose, to be charitable, we were like puppies playing, sharpening our teeth for later use.

The *Crimson* would have been fine for a year or two, but I ended up spending far too much time there and neglecting anything approaching serious study. With all the time I spent reading comment books I could easily have become fluent in Chinese, or least made a start in that direction. Since I had passed the Harvard language requirement on admission, I didn't have to study languages at all, so I didn't. I came within an inch of flunking my natural science general education requirement, a pitiful, watered-down geology course for amateurs, because I found it boring and cut most of the labs. It all makes me shudder just to think about it. I did have some wonderful courses, like Humanities 3, taught in small sections by classics scholar William Alfred; his evocation of Aeschylus made me begin to appreciate Grandfather Smith.

Occasionally there was a teacher who would not tolerate this kind of nonsense. The most notable in my experience was Frederick Merk, a wizened, elderly man still teaching well beyond the usual retirement age—he had been a student, then colleague of Frederick Jackson Turner, author of the frontier thesis in American history. Merk's course on the History of the Westward Movement (aka "Wagon Wheels") was loaded with quizzes and map tests asking such questions as "Where was the center of hog production in 1840?"[6]

You knew what he was up to when you saw him peering

---

[6] Below is a typical Merk hour exam, dated November 1, 1956, in its entirety, courtesy of classmate Bryce Nelson:

> I. (40%) Take (a) or (b):
>> (a) Draw up a list of the discoverers of the Mississippi River and indicate the claim of two of them (two expeditions) to the title.
>> (b) Write an account of the Iroquois attack on the Illinois in 1680, and your opinion as to its origins and its bearing on LaSalle's enterprise.
> II. (40%) Take (a) or (b)
>> (a) "By the Ice of Helvost Sluys [I still have no idea what this means] in 1803 the destiny of the Mississippi was changed." Explain. Do you have any reservations as to the correctness of this assertion?
>> (b) Compare the activities of speculators in the public lands of Massachusetts in c. 1760 with those in Kentucky in c. 1773.
> III. (15%) Locate *five* on the map:
>> French Creek; Treaty Line of Lochaber; Saluda Gap; Ottawa River; Boone's Wilderness Trail; Transylvania; Wautauga Settlements.

around the lecture hall: if you cut his classes more than once you would get a little hand-written note inquiring after your health. Harvard professors weren't supposed to do that kind of thing. The course ended with a superb survey of US public lands policy, which grew out of our frontier experience and is still highly relevant to our daily concerns. It is the only Harvard course from which I kept my notes.

Merk's skills were not always focused on the Wild West. I was lucky enough to hear him give the two big survey courses on American History, filling in due to a faculty gap. His technique was to offer three versions of every major issue: one based on the textbook, one on other assigned readings, and a third contained in his lecture on the subject. Often no hint was given as to which version was correct—that was up to the student to decide and defend when exam time came. For many undergraduates who were accustomed to history courses as declarations of revealed truth, rather than never-ending debate, this was a priceless exercise, if confusing at first.

In the process of looking for easy courses, so-called "guts," I strayed into some other interesting courses, such as Samuel Huntington's on the role of the military in US society, taken mostly by ROTC students but fascinating nonetheless. (Huntington was not yet famous.) Many of the more popular courses had nicknames: Abnormal Psychology ("Nuts and Sluts"); History of the Caribbean ("Bananas"); History of Maritime Trade ("Boats") and my favorite, Fine Arts 1 ("Darkness at Noon," because it was on Monday, Wednesday and Friday at 12 o'clock and slides were always shown). The nicknames were used in conversation, as in "May I borrow your Nuts and Sluts notes?"

There was one nicknamed course, or pair of courses, that matched Merk's for teaching skill and scholarly content. They were collectively known as "Rice Paddies," more formally a year-long history of East Asian Civilization,[7] taught by two experts, John K. Fairbanks on China and Edwin O. Reischauer on Japan, who took turns lecturing and delighted in accusing each other of mistakes. This was intended to stir attention from

---

[7] I forget the exact wording of the course names; they were part of Harvard's General Education program.

students who might be hung-over or napping, and it did. First offered in 1939, "Rice Paddies" eventually led to two superb, jointly authored volumes: *East Asia: the Great Tradition*, and *East Asia: the Modern Transformation*, the first of which was published in 1958, the year I graduated, and both of which remain good reads and invaluable reference works.

The *Crimson* did enable me to quit cleaning toilets and make money as a photographer for the *Harvard Alumni Bulletin* instead. For a while I also did odd photo jobs for the university news office, run by a gentleman named Bill Pinkerton. This came to an end suddenly when, in the absence of his regular photographer, Pinkerton asked me to take a picture of the university deans at one of their meetings. After the formal picture I was told to take another with everyone hamming it up to amuse one of their colleagues who was absent due to illness.

The assembled deans decided to pretend to be begging for money—maybe Harvard's endowment investment was not yet as successful as it has since become. One dean grabbed a silver platter and held it out, collection-style, while McGeorge Bundy of Arts and Sciences proffered a blank check and a pen, and so on. Pinkerton swore me to secrecy, but allowed me to use the *Crimson's* speed graphic and take the film back to our darkroom for processing.

There I discovered that the joke had produced a rare image of President Nathan Pusey, normally the most wooden-faced person on earth, flashing a warm smile. The *Crimson's* stock "mug shot" of Pusey was awful, and I decided that no one would notice or care if I made two new ones from my masterpiece, one facing each way so Pusey would always be looking towards the article he accompanied, and of course cropping the image down to his head only, so only I would know what it really was, or so I thought. Then I made two engravings and stuck them on a *Crimson* shelf for future use.

But when we finally ran the photo months later for the first and only time, Bill Pinkerton was not fooled for an instant. There was an immediate explosion in the Harvard news office. The fact that the picture printed was the reversed version convinced Pinkerton that I was deliberately deceiving him. He called me in a rage and said I had betrayed his trust, I would NEVER work for the news office again, anyone could see from the cropped picture that something funny was going on (part of an outstretched hand was visible behind Pusey's ear) and I was to bring the engravings and all other prints of any description to him immediately to be destroyed (he already had the negative). It was embarrassing because he knew my father, which was the only reason he had given me odd jobs in the first place. However, after all this, I could not resist keeping one large, uncropped print, and the picture was, many years later, published in an anthology of the *Crimson*.[8] Am I glad I lied and betrayed Pinkerton's trust? Yes. (Do not show this to Zoe, Penelope or Alexander until they are grown up.)

Summer jobs continued to be varied and usually interesting. One year I spent a summer working in a department store in Washington, on the theory that it would earn more money than a ranch job. I ended up as the stock boy in the "remnants" part of the yard goods department. It was definitely the dullest thing I've ever done, with the possible exception of declassifying documents for the State Department after retiring. One summer Arthur Johnson, my friend from Deerfield, lived with me at 3319 N Street. My father and Kate were away, presumably in Union Village, Vermont, where they had started to rent a summer place. My Dad liked Vermont; there were old friends summering nearby, and it was within easy driving distance of the Dartmouth Library if he needed to do some research.

Arthur and I managed to stay out of trouble except for one very hot, late summer weekend when we rented a canoe and paddled it up the C&O Canal. When we got to the District line we decided to put the canoe in the Potomac River, which parallels the Canal, and come back with the current, not realizing this would take us over the dangerous rapids at Little Falls. Fortunately Arthur was very good with boats of any kind and I was at least a good swimmer, and we did nothing worse than capsize. A lot of people have drowned in this way, and now there are signs all over the place warning people not to approach these dangerous rapids.

One Harvard summer I worked for the *Quincy Patriot Ledger*, a great little newspaper covering Boston's South Shore

---

[8] *The Harvard Crimson Anthology*, ed. Greg Lawless, 1980, pp. 192-93.

area. I made a connection that would prove useful later, when I supported myself while coming home from army service by writing for them. Also, armed with new cameras and photographic expertise, I spent time taking pictures of steam locomotives, then rapidly vanishing from American railroads. In the summer of 1957 I wrote the Union Pacific and got permission to ride their 4000 class engines over the continental divide between Cheyenne and Laramie. These were the biggest steam locomotives ever built, almost half a football field long, the same kind as in the picture I got from Grandfather Smith, and they were on the verge of being cut up for scrap, being operated only during the fall harvest freight rush.

The westbound trip was disappointing because we were coupled behind a gas turbine locomotive on the front of the train. But the return trip from Laramie across the Wyoming uplands in the middle of the night was perfection. I even got a chance to play fireman. There was no shoveling involved; these engines were far too big to be hand-fired. You adjusted steam jets that blew the coal, lifted by the mechanical stoker from the tender, onward into the cavernous firebox. Like all steam locomotives, the 4000's were rough-riding and filthy, but they produced magnificent sounds, not least from their deep-pitched whistles. After that ride I felt I could die happy. (Photographs are in a separate, unpublished photo album.)[9]

The mid- to later 1950s were in general a time of declining productivity for my parents. Both were, I believe, tiring of the grind of freelance magazine work. My father was convinced that its day was over, and repeatedly urged me not to go into journalism. Instead he thought it would be wonderful if I became a physician, which, partly as a result, I never seriously considered. We discovered this perverse aspect of child psychology years later when we urged Annie, then at Madeira, to at least *think about* the University of Virginia as a college possibility, since she didn't have any clear preference, and as Virginia residents it would have saved us a lot of money. So of course she never applied to U VA. We were overseas at the time and not exactly micromanaging her college applications.

_____
[9] One of the Union Pacific's 4000 class locomotives is being restored in Cheyenne as of 2016, but it will take several years.

Yes, it turned out well in the end.

Both my parents were drawn to longer-term projects. In mother's case, this involved a long struggle to write a book about rodeo and rodeo cowboys. At one point it was going to be preceded by an article for the *Saturday Evening Post*. Discouraged by the editors' reaction to an early draft she asked my father for advice, and he responded with a long letter. It is pretty clear that at one level, and in spite of everything, he was still in love with her:

Your letter and the manuscript came late yesterday afternoon . . . . I wired you immediately . . . . Naturally I was very much distressed by the gloom of your letter. Still, I didn't take it too seriously, either. I've known you to be at the end of your rope in the past; yet you always find a new length of rope to grasp . . . . It is of course just not so when you say that you can't write. You have done it for years . . . . I enclose a bunch of notes for what they are worth . . . . Bob's letter [to her, from one of the Post's editors] is discouraging. But Bob always is . . . . We [he and Kate] did three drafts of our latest, the Community Trust job, before they finally bought it . . . . You are worrying too much about writing like Colliers or the W.H.C. [Woman's Home Companion]. Frankly I don't get your apprehension . . . . Forget all that and write like yourself. And that is damned good . . . . Write like Helena Smith. Katharine and I have always thought, with envy, that your piece about the blind soldiers[10] was one of the best magazine articles ever written. And it was. [11]

But the rodeo article was never published, nor was the book, despite an enormous investment of time and effort.

Mother was further distracted by her psychiatric ailments, real or imagined, all of course allegedly due to her tyrannous father. She spent a lot of time and money on psychiatric counseling, including the better part of one summer at a well-known therapy center in Stockbridge, Massachusetts. Not long afterwards, she turned to religion, which was certainly a lot cheaper and at least as effective.

---

[10] "Five Days of Darkness," *Woman's Home Companion*, December 17, 1945.

[11] HFP letter to HHS, from Union Village, Vermont, September 8, 1953.

In the late Fifties, she began working on another major, and ultimately very successful project, the story of the Johnson County War. This was to be a full-fledged history of a conflict between small frontier cattle owners and wealthy absentee ranchers in Wyoming, rather than an as-told-to biography. The research and writing of it would occupy her both in the West and in Alexandria for more than five years, until publication of *The War in Powder River* in 1966. (The rest of the story is told in Chapter 8.)

My father and Kate continued to work hard, but my father's declining health must have affected his productivity. In the mid-Fifties, they were hired by the Rockefeller Foundation to do a history of the General Education Board. It was a Rockefeller philanthropy established in 1902 to support education, primarily in the South, where at that time public education still barely existed. The Board would later be criticized for supporting segregation; this was no doubt true and to some extent unavoidable. My father died of lung cancer on April 8, 1958, before the book could be published. The Rockefeller Foundation turned it over to a former president of theirs to complete, instead of allowing Kate to finish it, much to her understandable annoyance. She felt that the Foundation's in-house author significantly diminished the book's impartiality and frankness.[12]

My father's death came less than two months before my graduation from Harvard. The last two years had been less than wholly satisfactory. I dated my classmate Jo Ann Abraham until some time in my junior year, when we broke up. This distressed my father and Kate, who had met her parents in Paris (he was a senior executive of UNESCO) and liked them instantly. It was also awkward for one of my best friends, Tom Shankland, since his fiancée, Becky Hogue, was Jo Ann's best friend; they were both Quakers and had attended the George School together before Radcliffe. It was not pleasant for me for a while, but all ended well and Jo Ann married another classmate, David Reiss, soon after graduation. They live in

---

[12] Raymond B. Fosdick, *Adventure in Giving: the Story of the General Education Board, a Foundation Established by John D. Rockefeller*, based on an unfinished manuscript prepared by the late Henry F. Pringle and Katharine Pringle, Harper and Row, 1962.

Washington, have grown-up children, and Jo Ann, like her husband, is now a psychiatrist. After that I had an erratic social life, mostly dating Radcliffe student and fellow *Crimson* photographer, Bobby Blitman.

In 1953, after graduating with a degree in anthropology from Cornell, Margot moved to Montana and found a job teaching in a rural, one-room school. She recorded her experiences there in a diary, which, as mentioned earlier in this chapter, was published years later with the title *Horseback Schoolmarm*. It quickly sold well, one-room schoolhouses having become a thing of the folkloric past. That winter she started dating a cowboy, Forrest Jerome Liberty, "Timber" for short. In 1955 they were married in Miles City, Montana.

The idea was that they would acquire cattle and run them on leased government or Indian land. The cattle would multiply (it works just like compound interest) and eventually they would be able to buy their own place and become cow country gentry. Margot would have time to pursue her anthropological interests with the Northern Cheyenne while Timber ran the cattle business. It didn't work, partly because even then land prices demanded far more capital than such a plan could generate, and the marriage foundered in large part on this problem. There were two children: Paula, born in 1959, and Henry, born two years later.

In 1954 Margot had achieved her goal of teaching on an Indian reservation; she got a job at the Birney Village Primary School on the Northern Cheyenne Reservation. "Indian Birney" was located not far from the other Birney, "White Birney," described earlier, but there was little resemblance between the two. Indian Birney was a scattering of primitive log cabins with red shale roofs, as devoid of sanitation (etc.) as any African village. The kids came to school speaking only Cheyenne, but they also knew enough American Indian sign language to be able to talk silently behind the teacher's back, which was not good for discipline. (These children are now among the tribal elders, the last to speak Cheyenne fluently, if at all.)

I visited Margot and took various pictures later used in her book, *Cheyenne Memories*, published by Yale University Press in 1967. And I met her co-author, Northern Cheyenne tribal historian John Stands in Timber.[13] John always doused himself with Absorbine Jr., giving him a spicy trademark smell. He was also a charming, soft-spoken man with an encyclopedic knowledge of his people and a very level head, as well as a great sense of humor about their present prospects, which at that point looked grim. In fact, the Northern Cheyenne tribe has done much better than any of us would have expected at the time.

Having learned something of the fascinating history of the Cheyenne people, I decided to do my undergraduate history thesis about them, focusing not on their heroic struggles against white conquest but on the less-known story of what happened to them after they fled from Oklahoma (with the US Army in hot pursuit) and got what they wanted—a reservation on the northern plains, in Montana. In the spring of my senior year I went to Washington and found a great deal of relevant material in the National Archives. I got a *summa cum laude* minus on the thesis, which despite my lackluster course work, was enough to enable me to graduate from Harvard *magna cum laude*. For the first time, I experienced the zing that results from original historical research, the fun of finding the pieces and seeing what emerges when you put them all together. Professor Frank Freidel, the senior reader, a well known biographer of FDR, commented: "I have read a good deal about Indians, but have seen nothing which illustrates as well as this the way in which our changing Indian policies affected a single tribe. The implications of the thesis are a good deal broader than the title would suggest."[14] Boy, did that make me feel good! This experience and what I learned of anthropology from Margot gave me a lasting interest in ethnic diversity that eventually led me into Southeast Asian studies, with a focus on tribal minorities, at Cornell, and also

---

[13] John died in 1967. More than three decades later, original source material on the old cultures had become so scarce that Oklahoma University Press published in full the texts of all Margot's interviews with him. The book was dedicated to me and had one of my photos on the jacket: John Stands in Timber and Margot Liberty, *A Cheyenne Voice: the Complete John Stands in Timber Interviews*, Oklahoma University Press, 2013.

[14] Reader's comment [unattributed, but I found out who it was] on Robert M. Pringle, "The Northern Cheyenne Indians in the Reservation Period," thesis submitted in partial requirement for the degree of Bachelor of Arts with honors in History (Harvard College, Cambridge, MA, March 20, 1958).

influenced my Foreign Service career.

Once graduated, I was at loose ends. I had absolutely no idea what I wanted to do with myself. I did not want to commit to graduate school just to escape military service. The Peace Corps did not yet exist. So I decided to join the Army, if only to get my military obligation out of the way. In 1958 we were at peace, between the Korean and Vietnam Wars, so there was little danger of getting blown to bits. There were two options: six months active duty, plus eight years of reserve obligation, or two years' active duty plus a shorter reserve obligation. I chose the latter, hoping I could parlay it into an overseas assignment. Mother was egging me on, inspired by an Army friend, Colonel Shinn, who kept telling her what a wonderful experience it would be. To avoid waiting for my draft board to act, I decided to enlist for a two-year term (a purely bureaucratic distinction, or so I assumed, from being a two-year draftee).

Meanwhile I had a summer to kill before the Army would deign to induct me, so Bobby Blitman got me a job being the photography counselor at Camp Sebago Wohelo in South Casco, Maine. It was run by Halsie and Dotty Gulick, scions of the founders of the Campfire Girls, and was among the very first girls' camps in the country. It was there, in the Gulicks' living room, that I learned about keeping stout scrapbooks for each child, in which one would put everything from birth certificate onwards. The Gulicks did this for their children, and we later did it for Jamie and Annie, even using the same kind of indestructible scrapbooks until they stopped making them.

The US Army and Korea

The Army, which occupied my next two years, was pretty much of a lark. It began at Fort Holabird in Baltimore, thence via train (antique Pullman cars being stockpiled by the military) to Fort Jackson in Columbia, SC, once home of the Reverend James Maxwell Pringle, "Papa's Pa." Feeling very superior, but careful to conceal my Harvard background, I brought along a two-volume paperback edition of *War and Peace* to read during basic training. The latter consisted mainly of learning to fire the M-1 rifle, plus a good deal of PT and going on hikes through the sandy pine barrens of the huge reservation. I got to throw one hand grenade, discovered I was physically incapable of squatting with my feet flat on the ground (not good because this was one of the required rifle firing positions), and also that I have very bad directional hearing.

From the very beginning, it was a lot like "Beetle Bailey." The Army was very diverse; the train coming down from Baltimore had been full of Hungarian freedom fighter refugees. My basic training company was one-third Puerto Rican draftees, none of whom could speak English, or if they could they weren't letting on. Furthermore, they were all without exception labeled as "Santiago" on their fatigues. "Santiago" is apparently a nearly universal honorific final name in Puerto Rico, but not a real surname at all, which the Army had been unable to figure out. So these guys played dumb whenever asked to do something unpleasant, to the vast amusement of the rest of us.

The food compared favorably for the most part with other institutional food I had experienced, except for the infamous SOS, "shit on a shingle," creamed chipped beef on toast. KP, or "kitchen police," which we took turns doing, was however no joke—an awful all-day grind of scrubbing huge pots and pans. The outstanding thing about my basic training was that we were the last company at Fort Jackson to live in tents, albeit erected over concrete slabs, rather than permanent barracks. It was winter and the tents were heated with coal stoves, the flues of which constantly got jammed with soot in the middle of the night. The Army was terrified that we tent-dwellers would all catch pneumonia, and treated us with kid gloves as a result. I wrote to mother about peacetime life in the citizen Army:

We have both a professional opera singer and a professional rock'n roll guitarist in the next tent, but the latter had his guitar taken away for playing after lights out, and the former sings only for appreciative audiences, so things are fairly quiet. But at least every other night one of the stovepipes on our two GI stoves gets plugged up and everyone is routed out by noxious exhalations and shreds of soot. Everyone prances around in their GI drawers, pounding on the offending stovepipe with pokers and waving flashlights in the smog. The best remedy devised so far consists of climbing up to the peak of the tent and dropping coal down the chimney. I haven't volunteered for this yet.[15]

---

[15] Bob letter to Dear Mother, November 30, 1958.

I got one interesting break when Margaretta, Mrs. St. Julien Ravenel Childs, one of my wonderful Charleston cousins, came up to Columbia to help with an effort to desegregate the city parks. Somehow, she got the Army to release me for a day and suddenly I was off the base and in a room with all these earnest people, black and white, talking about desegregation in the Deep South in 1958. This was still well before the heyday of the civil rights movement. Margaretta and her two sisters, Mary and Eleanor, were also into historic preservation and Pringle family history, but Margaretta was the most expert on the latter and also the most politically active. There was a joke about her elderly black maid finally dying of exhaustion because Margaretta made her sign so many petitions.

Basic Training lasted only two months. At the end we were herded into an auditorium to be assigned an "MOS," or "military occupational specialty." Anyone with a skill of interest to the Army would be assigned accordingly; the rest went on to advanced infantry school, aka "the real thing." I figured if I told them I was a history major I would end up as a clerk-typist and die of boredom, so when queried I said I was a reporter-photographer. The guy interviewing me looked at his list of MOS's and said, "We don't have an MOS for that; you can be either a journalist or a photographer, but not both." So I chose "photographer."

I was forthwith assigned as a photographer, without further training, to White Sands Missile Range, north of El Paso, Texas. Although there was a big color photo lab there, with lots of fancy equipment, the interesting photography (i.e., pictures of missile firings) was all done by highly paid civilian government employees. All we military got to do was assignments like photographing promotion ceremonies and the grisly remains of the often lethal traffic accidents on the highway crossing the base.

I still had more than twenty months left in the Army so I asked if I could go to Korea, which was only a one-year tour. Many draftees with the same term of active duty as I had were being sent there against their will. But I was told I could not, because unlike them I was technically a "reservist." I was discovering that when it comes to mindless bureaucracy, the military wins the prize hands down.

When I complained about this annoyance to mother, she

promised to pull a few strings in Washington. Her friend Col. Shinn had already arranged for a pleasant two-week interlude at the US Army Information School at Fort Slocum, NY, located on a small island off New Rochelle (and needless to say long since closed, razed and replaced with mega mansions). There I learned how to do troop information courses under combat conditions, with blankets for bulletin boards, flashlights, and so on, as if such a thing would ever happen. Now mother went to another friend who was the head staff person for the senior US senator from Montana (who was aging, so this guy ran his office) and he wrote a letter to the Army about me.

The next thing I knew I was being escorted around the base by an irate officer, being processed for onward assignment to Korea. "You realize you have ruined your military career by using political influence," he told me. He was right; I was never promoted again, so I left the Army as a Private First Class, not a Specialist Fourth Class. Shortly thereafter I departed for Korea on a big grey troopship from Fort Lewis, Washington. It took three weeks, beginning with a gorgeous cruise through the San Juan de Fuca Strait, then degenerating into tedium. The ship was well organized to keep a couple of thousand GIs occupied (make work is where the peacetime military excels), mostly doing hard and unpleasant tasks connected with food, paint, the removal of old paint or cleaning of toilets. However, I linked up with a few other college graduates, and we wangled an assignment to run the ship's tiny library. Better yet, we discovered we could lock the door at night and sleep there among the paperbacks, as opposed to being jammed into the hold with everyone else. We finally disembarked at Inchon, Korea, on October 2, 1959, but not until after a taste-whetting stop in Japan at Yokohama.

I was assigned to the information office of the United Nations Command /US Forces Korea /Eighth US Army (the military particularly loves overlapping bureaucracies), which occupied the old Japanese base at Yongsan, on the edge of Seoul. As this implies we were still under a UN command, headed by the same American general who commanded US troops, even though the fighting in the Korean War had been over for five years; indeed I believe the UN Command fiction is still in place today since there has never been a peace treaty. There was still a battalion of Turkish troops on the DMZ, and right across the courtyard from my barracks was a multinational UN honor guard: Turks, Thais, Brits and Americans.

The work was rarely exciting, and sometimes sad. I remember in particular writing standardized press releases whenever a US Army truck ran over a Korean, usually a child, in some village on the busy supply route between Seoul and the DMZ. I did get to do occasional photo essays for the military newspaper, *Stars and Stripes*. I also did some interesting freelancing, including an article for the *Harvard Alumni Bulletin* on a fellow Harvard grad, Ensign Eugene Pell, also assigned to Seoul. I arranged to photograph him on a patrol through the friendly half of the six-mile-wide DMZ between North and South Korea, which was already going back to wilderness and has now become one of the world's more extraordinary wildlife preserves.[16] Once I went to the wild and beautiful east coast to take pictures of a North Korean MIG-17 that had just defected to the South.

My information office job allowed me to go regularly to Panmunjom, the site in the DMZ where the Military Armistice Commission met, Chinese and North Koreans on one side, Americans and some other friendly power on the other, with the DMZ line running down the center of the table, all under the purely nominal supervision of "neutral nations." "Our" neutrals were the Swedes and Swiss, "theirs" were the Czechs and some other communist country. For us the point of visiting was to get a photo of your buddy with a scowling North Korean or (better yet) genuine Red Chinese soldier in the background. Most of this farce was still in place when Barbara and I visited Panmunjom forty years later.

We got two R&R ("rest and recuperation"—ha!) trips to Japan during our one-year tour, via military air, a relic of the war days. There we could stay at absurdly cheap Japanese luxury hotels commandeered by the US occupation. One could (although I personally never did) pay for a week of bar-hopping in Tokyo with a few blocks of Korean seaweed, thousands of tiny sheets pressed together, prized in Japan for

---

[16] "Ensign in Korea," Photographs by Robert M. Pringle, *Harvard Alumni Bulletin*, April 2, 1960, pp. 515-519.

making sushi, but at the time unobtainable there due to the trade ban between the two countries.

Korea itself was very interesting. I wrote home:

Much has been done since the near-total destruction of the war—Seoul changed hands four times—but the city is still a fright. It boasts slums the likes of which I've never seen before or even heard of, whole hillsides covered with "houses" made out of tar paper, old packing crates, and flattened out oil drums.[17]

Once my friend Herb White made a sign labeled "Pangloss Memorial Bridge" and hung it on an overpass above one of the more ghastly slums. We thought we were terribly clever since no one but us would get the reference to Dr. Pangloss, who in Voltaire's *Candide* constantly opined, "Everything is for the best in this the best of all possible worlds."

The Koreans had still not reestablished relations with Japan, the hated ex-colonial power. We had a huge economic aid program, but it was crippled by corruption. Except for a few refugees, all the smart, educated Koreans were in the once industrialized north; the southerners were all country bumpkins, or so everyone said. All things considered it seemed indisputable that South Korea would never amount to anything. By the time this was written, South Korea had the world's tenth largest economy. I think of this now whenever I hear someone describing a country or a continent as hopeless.

My unit, the Eighth Army headquarters company, was an unmanageable mass of about 700 Americans, mostly draftees, many of them college graduates. We lived in an old brick Japanese barracks intermingled with KATUSAs, or "Korean Augmentees to the US Army." They got paid Korean Army wages, $1.20 a month, and considering the amount of invective they overheard from their American roommates about all things Korean—all the men were thieves, all the women whores, etc.—it's a miracle they didn't all hate us. The same KATUSA system was used to provide most of the riflemen in the nominally American combat units along the DMZ.

The fact that the Army of 1960 was a peacetime, non-

---

[17] Bob letter to Dear Family, November 24, 1959.

professional force resulted in a weird social mélange. College-graduate enlisted men could have officers and USAID officials as friends. One of my colleagues, Norm Sweet, had been a Pentagon civilian official in charge of military aid to Korea until he got drafted. (The Defense Department did not give deferments to its employees.) So he ended up as a messenger at the Yongsan HQ, serving the same colonels and generals with whom he had been working as equals only a few months earlier.

One thing the Army taught me was that there is no consistent correlation between brains, education and status. I knew some brilliant enlisted men, some of them career military, who aspired to nothing more than a relaxed existence and a pension after twenty years' service. On the other hand, one of the stupidest people I encountered was a West Point colonel who was handsome, military-looking, and no doubt came from an established middle-class background.

We Americans all had civilian Korean houseboys to clean our barracks, shine our boots, make our beds, and polish our belt buckles. We paid them with cigarettes we bought at the huge Yongsan PX; they would sell the cigarettes on the local market for many times what they cost us. One could also make a lot of money giving English lessons to Koreans, as I did. The prevalent eagerness for education should have told us something about the future of Korea.

But for most of us, Korea's main attraction was a big enlisted men's club full of beer drinking GIs and their girl friends or "moose," GI slang derived from a Japanese (not Korean) word for "young woman," *musimaya* if I remember correctly. The officers of course had their own more elegant club, and sometimes their own Korean girl friends, plus a golf course. In other words, the whole HQ UN/Eighth Army/ USFK setup was a classic military garrison, not to be confused with the two front-line units further north which still faced a potentially dangerous enemy. Many of us in Yongsan were physically out of shape—I put on a lot of weight—and could not have shot our way out of a wet paper bag.

Some "moose" married their GI boyfriends with the intention of remaining in Korea after their husbands left, with PX privileges of course, supporting their extended families by reselling cigarettes and other goodies on the black market.

This offended the American wives of officers, some of whom were on accompanied tours, because these Koreans of dubious social status created congestion in the PX, energetically shoving their way to the front of any line. The American wives made such a fuss that they persuaded the stupid West Pointer I mentioned earlier to deny the Korean wives PX privileges. Of course he couldn't legally do so, and his ban lasted only about 24 hours, because in addition to the retired prostitutes there were also many proper Korean wives married to American civilians who worked at the base.

However all this got dull fast, and my friends and I started looking for more interesting things to do. We discovered that Korean food was delicious, and that we would not get lethally ill from eating it downtown (as the Army wanted us to believe). We discovered the Royal Asiatic Society, British in origin, which put on cultural programs at the old royal palaces in Seoul, and ran tours to nearby historic sites. Through our KATUSA friends, one of them an aspiring pianist, we met a number of university students. One of my English students was a diminutive Korean high school girl, Chai Kum Ja, who became our constant companion. We also got to know members of the large US Embassy staff. We discovered that USAID had a lot of 4-H pamphlets and manuals, but no way to deliver them.

Of this came a brilliant idea: since we had some genuine farmers among our Army colleagues, and since our Korean student friends could act as guides and interpreters, why not start a 4-H club in one of the mud brick and thatch farm villages which were then common around Seoul? The next step was to persuade the underemployed J-5 (civil affairs unit), headed by a motherly WAC officer, to authorize an all-terrain, three-quarter ton truck for 4-H use. This led to many happy weekend afternoons on the banks of the Han River, in areas long since completely covered with high-rise apartment blocks. Today in order to see a farm village in Korea you must drive fifty miles to a museum of traditional rural life, as Barbara and I discovered when we visited Seoul in 2001.

My first year abroad went by quickly. During this time I had become a good friend of Herb White, a Georgetown University

The now-vanished village of Suk Sill, where we had our our our 4-H Club, showing the villagers, some of the Korean university students who translated for us, and one of several GIs from farming backgrounds who also worked with us. Herb White, with whom I later traveled back to the US, is the soldier in the second from bottom row on the left.

graduate and fellow Washingtonian.[18] He discovered that if a soldier got separated from active duty in Korea, the Army would still honor its commitment to get him home if he presented his separation orders at the nearest US base within one year. It seemed like an open invitation to see a little more of the world, so we did exactly that. After leaving the Army in

---

[18] It took me years to realize that Herb, despite his marriage, was homosexual, at least half of him was, although it was obvious enough that he was not interested in girls. He was a master of charm-tinged overstatement, much of which turned out to be true. His marriage, which he talked about a lot, was to me explanation enough at the time. Later Barbara and I got to know his wife, Clare Racine, from a wealthy Canadian family, but I did not fully understand his whole complex story until she explained it to me after his death in 2007. (She had been mostly but never totally separated from him for years.) He had in the meantime become a prominent patron of the Washington, DC, arts community, held wonderful parties at his house in Adams Morgan, which Barbara and I enjoyed thoroughly, and for a while owned, among other real estate, a popular restaurant, "Herb's," at 2121 P Street, well known *inter alia* as a gay hangout. His obituary said of him, "Straight people knew him as straight, gay people knew him as gay." Kriston Capps, "Herb's World, a Guide to Herb White's Footprint on D.C. Arts Scene," *Washington Citypaper,* June 28, 2007 at http://www.washingtoncitypaper.com/arts/article/13005566/herbs-world.

mid-November of 1960, I spent a few weeks waiting for Herb to get separated. I lived in a house belonging to the family of our Korean pianist friend, "Greg" Kim. Originally northerners, they had relocated to the southern city of Pusan. The house was for the use of Greg and his siblings while they were attending university in Seoul.

Fall is kimchi-making time, and when I arrived Kim's very energetic mother was on hand to make a supply for the winter: cabbage, *daikon* (big radishes), red pepper and garlic, in equal amounts it seemed, layered into big ceramic jars buried in the yard and allowed to ferment. The house had a cement *ondol* floor with flues running under it. Coal briquets are burned at one end of the house and generate hot gasses that heat the oil-paper coated clay floor. It's a big improvement over the Japanese system of *tatami* mat floors with tiny coal-burning braziers, but then the Korean climate is colder. An *ondol* floor works fine unless it hasn't been maintained and there are cracks in the floor, in which case you can die from carbon monoxide poisoning, which several GIs did every year while visiting their Korean girlfriends, despite stern warnings from the Army about the wages of sin.

Productive Travel Home

I have covered the trip home elsewhere in detail,[19] so I will touch only on the high points here. Herb complicated matters by getting a temporary job with Lockheed on Okinawa, preparing C-130s for delivery to Indonesia,[20] so I used the intervening time to travel widely in Japan with another friend, and Herb and I rendezvoused in Hong Kong. From there we proceeded

[19] See the large scrapbook about the trip containing photos, my *Quincy Patriot Ledger* articles, and my letters home. It owes its existence to the government shutdown of 1996 that gave me some spare time. I printed the photos in it in a makeshift darkroom at 103 Prince Street in the early 1960s. The negatives for these photos have gone missing; my archival capacity improved only after I married Barbara in 1964.

[20] The C-130 transaction was controversial, since many observers were convinced that Sukarno was a crypto-communist; these planes would later be used to support his campaign to "crush" Malaysia, which we would witness from Sarawak (see next chapter). I have no idea what Herb did in Okinawa, but it was probably some kind of clerical work.

by French (*Messageries Maritimes*) steamer to Saigon, then to Cambodia and Angkor, Thailand, Malaya and Singapore. After that, a whole month in Ceylon, as it then was. From Ceylon we bought rail tickets to Calcutta (nine dollars a ticket). We went to New Delhi, Nepal and Pakistan by air, rail and hitchhiking.

We wanted to go through the Khyber Pass and Afghanistan, but the pass was closed so we took the weekly train across Baluchistan, the part of Pakistan just south of the Afghan border, from Quetta to Zahedan, which is the Iranian border post. From Zahedan we hitchhiked on trucks to Shiraz, where Margot's best friend from Madeira, Louise Laylin, was living with her Iranian husband, Narcy Firouz. Then we continued across Iran and Turkey, arriving in Istanbul in early October, 1961. I got home about a month later from Mildenhall Air Force Base in England.

To finance the trip I borrowed some money from Herb; to this day I am not sure if I ever paid him back in full—he died in 2007. I earned more by writing articles for the *Quincy Patriot Ledger*. They paid me $15 an article plus $5 per photo. The articles were published as big spreads opposite the editorial page. I sent them the copy, negatives and captions by airmail, and they would send me a check via American Express to our next destination. Once I got going on the free-lance work, the income was enough to pay my travel expenses.

My favorite article, naturally, is the one about the train ride from Madras to Calcutta on the *Howrah Mail*. I also wrote articles for the Roman Catholic Maryknoll Missionary magazine, including one which got me into the South Vietnamese countryside just as the American phase of the war was about to begin. It already looked like a very dicey proposition.

What were the high points of the trip? Certainly exploring back-country Japan, especially the "fourth island" of Shikoku. The Norwegian freighter ride to Hong Kong as the only passenger, with the Chinese crew setting off New Year's firecrackers in the steel passageways, was a trip in every sense. The mad dash from Saigon to Phnom Penh via taxi, through potentially hostile territory, was certainly the scariest episode. Visiting Nepal in the first year of its opening to tourism was probably the most photogenic stop. The train ride in the water car across the cindery wasteland of

Baluchistan to Iran was also memorable and photogenic.

Last but hardly least was our stay with Louise and Narcy in Shiraz: I will never forget seeing Qashqai tribes in full migration along the road, shooting wild pigs at night from a careening Land Rover, and making rubbings of the bas reliefs at Persepolis, which is near Shiraz, with cotton cloth and oil paint purchased in the Shiraz bazaar. The Shah was still in power, but Louise and Narcy nevertheless had problems with the Iranian Army, which felt that their experimental farming got in the way of its tank maneuvers. Louise would survive Narcy and become a good friend of my Foreign Service colleague Ann Swift, who was among the embassy officers taken hostage in Teheran in 1979.[21]

Although we did not go to Indonesia, most important insofar as my future was concerned was my introduction to Southeast Asia. I liked the region's wonderful diversity, with its blend of great and little traditions: Indian, Chinese, European and tribal. I was already inclining toward a Foreign Service career, but I wanted to get some sort of higher degree first. Southeast Asia struck me as a good part of the world to specialize in. As soon as I got home I began to investigate graduate school and ended up settling on Cornell, which had by far the strongest Southeast Asia program anywhere. But I had a year to kill before the fall 1962 semester began, and I needed a job, as mother kept reminding me.

A Reporter in Washington

Thanks to George Watson, a *Crimson* friend, I ended up at the Pat Monroe News Bureau located in the National Press Building in downtown Washington. This was a peculiar

---

[21] Louise remained in Iran for decades, even after the death of her husband and the fall of the Shah, and she became well known internationally for her discovery of "Caspian Ponies," an ancient miniature breed of *horses,* not ponies (as she knew perfectly well). She told this story in her autobiography (Louise Firouz with Brenda Dalton, *Riding Through Revolution*, with an introductory note by HRH Prince Phillip, Shippensburg, PA, 2013). I wrote a letter home from Shiraz describing the way Louise and her family were living in 1961; it is currently in an envelope of correspondence filed in the scrapbook mentioned in the previous note.

operation run by a wealthy ex-reporter who liked the glamour of the Washington press world; he cannot possibly have made enough money from his Bureau to do more than pay his office rent. We provided Washington coverage for a strange collection of publications: the *Lincoln* (Nebraska) *Journal*, the unrelated *Albuquerque* (NM) *Journal*, *Chicago's American*, *Editor and Publisher* magazine, and *Western Farm Life*. The dailies were either too lazy or too poor to have their own Washington correspondents, but they didn't want to rely totally on the wire services to cover Washington-origin news of local interest. The *Lincoln Journal* was by far the strongest of the lot, run by the Seacrest family, part of a high-minded Nebraska establishment. *Chicago's American* was pathetic compared to the *Chicago Daily News*, but now and then they had errands for us to run. The *Albuquerque Journal* was almost equally awful, but it was interested in some Washington topics, such as Indian policy and the progress of water projects to be located in New Mexico through the Congress.

We spent a lot of time covering the congressional delegations from Nebraska and New Mexico. But Chicago wasn't worth the trouble. Of the thirty Chicago-area House members, nearly all were Democrats firmly controlled by the old Daley machine and, as in any authoritarian polity, they were too scared to speak to the press independently.

I had several memorable experiences during that year. One involved writing a three-part, first-person autobiography of New Mexico's senior Senator, Dennis Chavez, for the Albuquerque paper, with material provided by his office. The result was complete crap about how "I got up every morning at dawn to work in the bean fields . . . " and so on. As the offspring of talented biographers, I felt only slightly ashamed of myself for doing this. Then there was the joy of writing a monthly market column for *Western Farm Life*, a chore which rotated among Pat's three city-boy reporters. We accomplished this by rewriting the relevant Department of Agriculture press releases dumped on our doorstep, jazzing them up to sound inside-dopesterish: "According to inside sources, pork belly prices will probably peak by late August . . . ," etc. I had nightmares about mobs of mad Colorado farmers descending on Washington to lynch us for mis-forecasting white pinto bean futures.

My brush with LBJ's famous temper was also unforgettable. I had been working late at the Senate Press Gallery when the then-Vice President got on board my elevator and, assuming I was the elevator boy, asked to go to another floor. His confusion was understandable since most of the Capitol staff in those days, including the "police," were students working their way through college, hired by their senator or congressman. I tried to oblige him, feeling it was the courteous thing to do, but I got the floor wrong, at which point he blew up and gave me a tongue lashing. When I explained that I was only a reporter and didn't really understand what was where, he instantly became civil. This occurred at a time when everyone in Washington was gossiping about how, after having been the hugely powerful Senate majority leader, Johnson was pining away in his nothing job as Vice President under Kennedy.

The best episode involved JFK himself. I often went to his press conferences, held in the State Department auditorium, but never dreamed of trying to ask a question. However, on this occasion I had gotten a call from the *Albuquerque Journal*. They told me that New Mexico's Indians were upset because the just-announced Peace Corps would work only in foreign countries, and not with equally poor American Indians. I was to ask the President to explain this injustice. It was late August and all the regular White House reporters were in Nantucket or some other vacation spot. Kennedy recognized me and I asked the question. Nodding gravely, he said he didn't know; someone would get back to me. Goodness what a fuss ensued! By the time I got back to my office, Sargent Shriver was on the phone asking me to come see him so he could explain that creation of a domestic program similar to Peace Corps was already being considered. It was a front-page story in Albuquerque. I liked the fact that Kennedy had taken the question seriously and calmly admitted his own ignorance.

Despite such fun and games, I did not have second thoughts about not going into journalism. I didn't like the pack mentality, with everyone running after the same "big" stories, designated by consensus. And I believed what my father had said about the increasing insecurity of the profession. But my brief journalistic experience was to come in handy later.

Cornell

I began to think about the Foreign Service partly because of repeatedly meeting FSO's who impressed me as the kind of people who would be interesting to work with. My experiences in Korea and on the way home had reinforced that impression. But I had never forgotten the McCarthy era and its witch hunts. Why not, I thought, get a relevant higher degree first? That way if I felt had to quit because I disagreed with government policy, or was purged or fired, I could fall back on teaching (or so I rather too easily assumed), especially if I had a PhD and managed to get my dissertation published.

My search for where to apply settled easily on Cornell—more specifically, to seek a PhD there in Southeast Asian history. I liked what I had seen of Southeast Asia on my trip through part of it in 1961. I knew that Cornell had the best Southeast Asia Program in the country, with Yale the only close competition, and I had always admired that university based on both my father's and Margot's experiences there. I was attracted to anthropology but didn't want to major in it, because the discipline was already rent by disputes between those who felt it should be "scientific," relying on quantifiable data, versus those who wanted a more historical or impressionistic approach.

So I chose history, with minors in anthropology and political science. Although I didn't know it, the senior political science professor at Cornell and Director of its Southeast Asia Program, George Kahin, was a strong proponent of historical methodology. This mattered because political science (or "government" as Kahin preferred) was also on the verge of a struggle over historical vs. numerical methodology, and, as Margot's experience would later show, bad things could happen to graduate students who got caught on the wrong side of such debates.

I already had a thesis topic in mind. Influenced by my undergraduate work on Margot's Northern Cheyenne Indians, and aware that Southeast Asia was full of "hill tribes" and other minorities, I thought it would be interesting to apply the same approach as I had with the Cheyennes in Montana. This would mean studying a particular "hill tribe" and its relationship with the dominant society in some important country. I wanted to write something that could be published as a book with some popular appeal, not just an academic treatise.

An extraordinary trio of scholars dominated the Cornell Southeast Asia Program: George Kahin, already mentioned, a leading expert on Indonesia; Frank Golay, economist and specialist on the Philippines; and George Echols, linguist and moving force behind the Cornell library's unexcelled holdings of Southeast Asian material. The Program did not award degrees in "South East Asian Studies." Instead, everyone had to major in a discipline, history in my case.

The Program itself was resolutely cross-disciplinary, and all Cornell students and faculty members with an interest in the region, from archeologists to plant pathologists, were encouraged to participate in it. Faculty and library combined to attract leading scholars of Southeast Asia from all over the world. Cornell trained many Indonesians and other residents of the region who went on to illustrious careers at home. Foreign Service Officers came to Ithaca for year-long area training, a program now unwisely dropped.

One of the visiting faculty members during my time was D. G. E. Hall, a prominent Burma specialist (former Rector of the University of Rangoon) and author of the standard text on modern Southeast Asian history. A towering, white-haired figure with a booming bass voice, he could lecture on any aspect of Burmese history in thirty-minute, one-hour or two-hour versions. One of the new hires, also British and a former student of Hall, was O. (for Oliver) W. Wolters, who became my advisor and was without doubt the Most Unforgettable Character of my Cornell experience. He arrived at Cornell unfamiliar with (and slightly terrified of) American academic culture, wherein graduate students took courses, instead of doing straight research, and had to be told the specific pages of books to read, instead of, as in the UK, being handed a forty-page bibliography and expected to fend for themselves. But he was a tolerant man of enormous intellectual reach and perpetual, infectious excitement.

After graduating from Oxford, Wolters had started his career in the Malayan Civil Service as a specialist on the ethnic Chinese, first studying the language in China. He was captured when Singapore fell to the Japanese in February, 1942, and spent time on the Thailand-Burma "Death Railway," of *Bridge on the River Kwai* fame. After the war he served as a District Officer in Malaya. Then, during the Malayan Emergency, he was an advisor on psychological warfare to British General Gerald Templer, helping to quell this ethnic Chinese communist insurgency. After retirement he wrote a PhD thesis on the history of Srivijaya, an early trading port on the Straits of Malacca, based largely on Chinese pharmacoepia and records of trade with Sumatra,[22] before coming to Cornell in 1962, at the same time that I did.

Wolters taught early Southeast Asian history, meaning up to about 1500. There were often big gaps in the factual record, hence ample room for creative interpretation, not to say imagination. He always lectured from a loose-leaf notebook, replacing old material with his latest news from the deep past. He was balding, with thin red hair, and wore baggy suits and a shapeless fedora hat. Euteen, his Malayan Chinese wife, speaks English with a British accent even more proper than his was. (He died in 2000, but we still correspond with her.) After my rave reviews, Barbara audited his course. Wolters adored her because she took in all the material and asked intelligent questions. Later we occasionally sailed with him on his boat on Lake Cayuga, an experience almost as exciting as his lectures, due to his somewhat erratic boat handling.

As a thesis advisor he was ideal. My topic was far from his own academic specialization, but it was heavily concerned with grass-roots colonialism, and he had most assuredly been there, done that. Moreover, while many of my colleagues could not imagine why I was intending to forsake academia and work for the government, already under a cloud because of the Vietnam War, Wolters thought my choice was both natural and praiseworthy, and cheered me on. (I still find myself hoping that I lived up to his expectations.)

I had no problem paying for my graduate work. Fear of international communism had stoked a boom in foreign area studies. Under the National Defense Education Act (NDEA), the government paid all tuition plus room and board if a student took at least one foreign language course. My

---

[22] Published as *Early Indonesian Commerce: a Study of the Origins of Srivijaya*, Ithaca: Cornell University Press, 1967.

choice was Indonesian, which works in both Indonesia and
Malaysia, as well as in Brunei, Malay being the same language
as Indonesian, with minor variations, as with "English" and
"American." I wanted to learn more about Indonesia, which I
had never visited, and Cornell was the place to do it—Kahin's
Modern Indonesian Project was in many ways the heart of
the Southeast Asia Program. NDEA covered summer study
as well, and in 1963 I took a summer course at Yale taught
by Tapi Omas (Simatupang) Ichromi, daughter of a famous
Indonesian general.

In addition to Kahin and Echols, resident Indonesia
specialists included graduate students already back from
fieldwork: Ben Anderson, Dan Lev and others. There was a
constant stream of academic visitors and alumni, like Jamie
Mackie and Ruth McVey, and a rich of supply of Indonesian
graduate students including Taufik Abdullah, Soemarsaid
Moertono, Soepomo (who married an American woman
when his wife died at Cornell), Mary and Filino Harahap, and
Toenggoel Siagian (more about him later); also Singaporeans
"Daisy" Chan Heng Chee, much later to be Singapore's
ambassador to the US, and historian Edwin Lee, whose family

*A Cornell Southeast Asia Program party. From left to right: Australian
visiting scholar Jamie Mackie, Rhondda Osborne, Bob (the photographer), D.G.E.
Hall, author of a standard text on Southeast Asian History, two unidentified
graduate student guests and, at far right, our close friend Milton Osborne.*

would entertain us warmly and often in Singapore. Milton Osborne, an Australian specialist on Cambodia, was our closest friend among the graduate student contingent. We have enjoyed our friendships with many of these people ever since, and it was of course invaluable knowing the Indonesians when we arrived in Jakarta with the Foreign Service in 1970.

I discovered that the requisite course work for my PhD was a pleasure. Cornell required senior faculty to teach undergraduate courses, so students in some of my classes were a mix of graduates and undergraduates. Classes were small, never over one hundred, and the content was always good, often superb. What a contrast with Harvard! And of course Barbara, as an undergraduate, had had the same experience in spades, as she makes clear in her own discussion of Cornell. My best-ever big course, in terms of teaching virtuosity, was one on Communist Chinese government, taught by John Lewis. The climax was a series of lectures on what it meant to become a communist in contemporary China, the China of the Cultural Revolution, a process akin to high intensity religious conversion. It made you feel as if you were experiencing this catharsis yourself.

One semester I volunteered to be a teaching assistant for Professor Kahin in his course on US Foreign Policy in Asia. Before he started, Kahin sat me down and told me gravely that I should not be worried when I discovered that I was consistently giving higher grades to women than to men. It was not a reflection on my libido. It was simply that the women, being mainly Arts majors, tended to be more academically inclined than their male counterparts, a greater proportion of whom came from the state schools that make up the majority of Cornell's unusual public-private composition.

At first I lived on a farm about a forty-five minute drive north of Ithaca on Lake Cayuga. This was cheap but not very handy, so I began sharing an apartment with Toenggoel Siagian in College Town, just off campus.

We Meet in Ithaca

Exactly how Barbara and I met is a little unclear. The first time we both remember was at a dinner party hosted by me and Toenggoel. Like most Indonesian male students, Toenggoel had never cooked a meal at home, but now, if he wanted to eat Indonesian food, he had to prepare it himself. He rapidly developed culinary skills and turned out to be a social asset with culturally adventurous Cornell coeds. As Toenggoel puts it, with typical Batak directness, "My job was to provide the food, Bob's was to provide the girls." Barbara, Charlotte Fremon, and their third apartment mate, Helen Menges, were early invitees, and things proceeded from there.

Our first conventional date was at an unremarkable restaurant on a steep street between the campus and downtown Ithaca. It was the end of winter and there was ice everywhere. Barbara slipped and fell, knocking me off balance so that I fell on top of her, a prophetically pleasant experience, at least for me. (From Barbara: Of course I was wearing fashionable high-heeled snow boots.) Various lunches together at Sage Hall (Barbara being less reluctant to pay for lunch on campus by then), tennis games (not anywhere near championship level), and expeditions into the countryside in Charlotte's car followed.

At about this time, I was invited to join Telluride House, a residential academic fraternity founded and endowed by a wealthy Colorado mining magnate.[23] It has a choice mid-campus location on "Libe Slope," the hill below the two main Cornell libraries. As a graduate guest, I got free room and board and a stimulating— sometimes too stimulating—intellectual environment.

Each year Telluride's members recruited new undergraduate members who were offered free room, board *and* tuition. It was assumed that anyone chosen by Telluride would automatically be accepted by Cornell. A few graduate students like me were invited to join and there were one or two senior guests. During my time, the most prominent of them was Francis Perkins, FDR's famous Secretary of Labor. She spent several years there, a delightful lady and a relief from the rather precious intensity of the student membership.

Everything about Telluride was self-consciously intellectual. Residents ate dinner together and since my knowledge of classical philosophy and political theory was minimal I often

---

[23] The name "Telluride" comes from the kind of ore mined at the Colorado town of the same name, now better known as a ski resort, where the founder invented an electrical process that made his fortune (there is a monument to him on the edge of town) and this was the source of his charitable activities.

had no idea what conversations were about. Although I did not realize it, I was witnessing part of the birth process of the neo-conservative movement. Paul Wolfowitz, son of a Cornell math professor, was Telluride's student president the year I was there. For a time, I shared a room with Abe Schulsky. Years later, during the presidency of Bush II, Paul, then Deputy Secretary of Defense, became a major advocate and architect of the Iraq war. It was in this role that Paul recruited Abe to set up a separate DOD intelligence unit, because he didn't like what the CIA was telling him about Iraq.

Barbara sometimes came to dinner at Telluride. She already knew Cornell undergraduate Clare Selgin, Paul's girlfriend and future wife. Clare was just back from an AFS summer program, during which she had studied dance in Indonesia, and she told us that if she had stayed there any longer, she might never have come home. Under President Reagan, when Paul was offered any ambassadorship he wanted, she persuaded him to choose Indonesia. At one point Bob applied for the post of Political

A typical scene at Telluride: visiting scholar Alan Bloom, author of The Closing of the American Mind *(right of center) greets C. Van Woodward (sitting), noted scholar of the American South, for a casual lunch, discussion (and . . . ? Frisbee) while students hover around.*

Counselor under him, but did not get the assignment, probably just as well, because our basic political philosophies were too far apart.

That notwithstanding, no one ever accused Paul of stupidity, and he was an excellent ambassador to Indonesia.[24] He is well remembered by the Indonesians because he was keenly interested in them and their country, as was Clare. This was partly because he felt that Indonesia, with 200 million mostly moderate Muslims, could be a counterweight against radical Islam, an idea that, at this writing, is still around.[25]

Telluride's superstar in Bob's time was philosopher Alan Bloom of the University of Chicago, author of *The Closing of the American Mind*. His lead line was that the last political theorist worth studying was Machiavelli, with the possible exception of Claude Levi-Strauss (although Levi-Strauss was an anthropologist). The Telluride students hung on his every word—it was like watching a prophet with his disciples. It got quite painful at dinnertime. Bloom later played a prominent role attempting to face down violent student protests against the Vietnam War, which to his disgust nearly paralyzed the university.

Barbara's graduation was a big deal for both sides of the family. Of course, Clay and Char were proud of their first daughter's college success; as valedictorian of the class, she led the senior class procession. Equally significant, they, and Jane and Susie who were with them, met Bob for the first time, both at the ceremony and later at a memorable party at the farm house which Milton and Rhondda Osborne were renting.

---

[24] Paul Wolfowitz's tour as Ambassador to Indonesia was from April 1986 to May 1989.

[25] I think it is safe to say that Paul's view of the world was heavily weighted by his concern for the long-term safety of Israel, a concern shared by many members of Telluride. That, of course, meant achieving an atmosphere less hostile to Israel in the Middle East generally, and especially among Muslims. He was intrigued by Indonesia because, while it has a larger Muslim population than any other country in the world, larger than all the Arab countries combined, its variegated Islam has historically been mostly moderate. Why, then, does Indonesian Islam not have more influence in the Middle East? Could the US not influence the Indonesians in that direction? I suspect that he discovered, as ambassador, that the answer to the last question is "only on their schedule."

*Cornell graduate with her proud parents and two of her sisters, the
younger one clearly bored by this event, still eight years in her future.*

Part of its memorable-ness was that I got thoroughly soused.
Nevertheless, I was invited to join the family for dinner at the
Taughannok Farm Inn, a required stop every time the parents
visited Cornell because Barbara's mother, Charlotte, loved a
good restaurant and she already knew about this one.

A couple of weeks later, on July 4, I proposed to Barbara.
When she called home with the big news (no e-mail or Twitter
then), Charlotte's reaction was that, when the family saw us
waving good-by to them, all ready for one of our slap-dash
tennis games, they had suspected something was up. We think,
inside, they were delighted, both by Barbara's choice of their
first son-in-law and by the fact that we would soon be off on
a big adventure, for they themselves had always wished to
see more of the world than they had so far been able to visit.
However, sometime during preparations for the wedding,
Charlotte remarked to her eldest daughter, only half jokingly,
that if she had enough money to visit Borneo—where by this
time we knew we were going—she would visit Rome and
Greece instead.

I had decided to do my thesis on the history of the Iban
people of Sarawak, today part of Malaysia, on the island of

Borneo, a subject which fit well with my broader interest in Southeast Asian minorities. I would focus on the relationship between the "tribal" Ibans and the quasi-independent "White Rajahs" who had been their "colonial" (sort of) rulers. I had already received a grant from the London-Cornell Project, co-sponsored by Cornell and London Universities to cooperate on social science research in Southeast Asia and China. My grant would include a term of preparation in London followed by a year of fieldwork in Sarawak.

I now went to anthropologist Bill Skinner, the Cornell chair of London-Cornell, and told him I was getting married and that Barbara was planning to accompany me to Borneo, hoping that my grant would be increased to include her travel also. "Well," Skinner replied, "We will have to increase your stipend. We have a continency [sic] fund for situations like this." It was the height of the Cold War and the funding for foreign area research was still easy.

We spent the rest of the summer of 1964 in Ithaca. I found a room in College Town. It was all terribly proper and we did not live together; instead Barbara roomed with Lois Weyman (Dow), a friend from Cincinnati, who was also staying in Ithaca for personal reasons. Bob's landlady, a formidable character reared in a sod house on the Kansas frontier, liked us, partly because Barbara knew what she was doing when she was mending bed sheets (which Charlotte had done when there were still six beds in use at 6508 Park Lane). However, she made it clear that Barbara would not be spending the night on her property. She did acquiesce to Barbara's visiting as late as midnight once she learned that we were engaged.

We were married in Cincinnati on September 26, 1964, at the Mariemont Community Church. The occasion was a big family affair, and we were lucky to have all four of Barbara's grandparents in attendance, as well as Aunt Alice and Uncle Richard Sidell and some of the Sidell cousins. But the only school friend of either of us who could be there was Nancy Reynolds, one of Barbara's closest high-school pals. It was, after all, September, and most of our high-school and college friends were busy at their jobs; airline travel was also relatively more expensive and flights less frequent than they are today, so weekend trips for weddings were harder to arrange.

All four of Barbara's grandparents helped to celebrate our wedding at Mariemont Community Church; from left to right, Frank and Emma Pettersen, the happy couple, and Clara and Joseph Cade.

Bob's mother and sister Margot came, but his best man, Herb White, did not, owing to a communications glitch. Barbara's Uncle Rich filled the gap at the last minute in admirable style. The Maid of Honor and the bridesmaids were Barbara's sisters Jane, Kathy, and Susie. Ron Theobald, soon to be Jane's fiancé, but then a fairly new boyfriend, was drafted to increase the number of ushers. The reception, a modest affair with wedding cake and champagne, took place at the Kenwood Country Club. Since we were abroad for Jane and Ron's wedding and Susie's to Bennett, we don't know whether subsequent Cade weddings became more lavish as prospective college funding became less an issue. However, we were certainly happy with the big family gathering, with lots of Mother and Daddy's Mariemont friends, that sent us off, married and feted, on our way to our overseas adventure. And perhaps someone had a small birthday cake at home for Clay, whose fifty-first birthday got lost in the wedding excitement.

Honeymoon on the SS France.

We set out for New York and London via Washington, spending our first night at the Golden Lamb in Lebanon, in a bed allegedly used by Charles Dickens. (The room is now for display only, and off limits to overnight guests.) Char and Clay stood us to a rented Ford Mustang, chosen by Clay with the advice of the bridesmaids, which we navigated through West Virginia to Washington. We spent one evening with Bob's missing best man Herb and his wife, Clare, at the fancy hotel he managed near Winchester, VA.

Kate hosted a reception for us at her house at 2911 O Street in Georgetown. She had not come to the wedding because she felt it might it cause problems with Helena. She invited many of Bob's father's and her old friends. It was a great party, although Barbara had a bad moment when, in the middle of a conversation with Arthur Schlesinger, Jr., she bit into a cherry tomato which exploded all over her stunning green velvet dress and his suit. Oh for a photo of that! (The dress is, however, visible in a photo taken on board the *France*.)

Thence, nothing daunted, it was on to New York and a four-day crossing on the SS *France* to Southampton. Bob's Uncle Max (James Maxwell Pringle) and Aunt Anne came to see us off with a bottle of champagne to enjoy on the crossing. While we were still in port, a French brother and sister came by to ascertain if the cabin would be suitable for the honeymoon trip of the sister, who was about to get married. Not knowing that we spoke French, the brother announced that it would not, because it didn't have a double bed. He was wrong.

The *France* was 1,035 feet of ocean liner, steam-powered of course, only two years old at the time. It was supposed to and did summon memories of the fabled *Normandie*. Being French, it included a kennel and walking area for dogs. There were a few glitches. Our table for ten included one couple who never ceased complaining about the food; the *France* was a two-class ship and someone had told them that tourist class was as good as second class on Cunard liners, which they judged it not to be. When we asked for a separate table for one evening so we could enjoy our bottle of champagne from Uncle Max, the staff first located us immediately next to our regular table, but when we asked to be relocated, they did find a more distant table for two. Still, there was an awkward moment at first.

Bob wrote a thank-you note to Clay and Charlotte from the ship:

In spite of striking longshoreman, we sailed at 3 a.m. on Thursday. Barbara and I were on deck to see the darkened Manhattan skyline slip away, and later the brilliantly lighted Statue of Liberty. Even in the wee small hours, leaving NY by ship is still quite a show. Since then we have been leading a thoroughly lazy and delicious existence. Breakfast is served around 9:30 and we don't even think of making that. For another hour there are croissants and coffee for "les retardaires" and sometimes we just barely manage to attend. The other meals are all huge and lovely . . . . [26]

It is sad indeed that real travel by ship is no more.

---

[26] Bob letter to Dear Char and Clay, October 6, 1964.

4

London, Sarawak and Cornell, 1964-1967[1]

We stayed in London for six months. All London-Cornell researchers spent a term at the university from which they did not come, before embarking on field research. This enabled everyone to take advantage of the two universities' complementary assets. For example, Cornell was especially strong on Indonesia and Thailand, while London was better, not surprisingly, on Burma and Malaysia. In addition to course work, Bob combed the material on Sarawak at the Colonial Office and interviewed retired Sarawak Civil Servants, which involved trips to pleasant corners of the country, mostly in places like Kent, in the relatively warm south.

Preparing for Borneo

Barbara studied medieval history, anticipating her eventual return to that subject when we came home. Both of us took courses in Malay at the School of Oriental and African Studies (SOAS), part of the London University complex, under a pair of slightly absurd retired colonial officials, Barrett and (Haji) Bottoms. Bob studied British-style anthropology at the London School of Economics, similarly part of the London complex, where one of its professors, Stephen H. Morris, who had done

[1] Much of this chapter appeared as "Between Two Worlds: Research in Sarawak, 1965-66," *Borneo Research Bulletin*, Vol. 46, 2015, pp. 303-343. There is more detail and many more photographs on our trip to the Kelabit highlands in "Bario Diary, June 3-27, 1966" in *Borneo Research Bulletin*,Vol. 41, 2010, pp. 211-249.

*At home in front of the friendly, though miniscule, gas fire
in our North Finchley apartment. We also had a paraffin
(aka kerosene) heater which we carried from room to
room with us when we were in our tiny abode.*

research in Sarawak, was immensely friendly and helpful.

We found an apartment at 14 Chislehurst Avenue, North Finchley, which had good underground connections to the London University area. Our landlady was a nasty bit of work, the beak-nosed widow of a British army officer (it was easy to see why he had pre-deceased her). Central heating was as yet rare in the UK, so we bought a kerosene ("paraffin") space heater. You had your choice of "pink" or "blue" kerosene brands, exactly the same except for the color. We learned the mysteries of multi-stop British high-street shopping in the era before supermarkets, the frustrations of British banking (you could cash a check only at the branch where you had an account), and the joys of finding change to work a public telephone. One variety took four huge old pennies—some still in circulation dated to the reign of Victoria; others worked with one thick, octagonal "thruppenney (three penny) bit." The latter were hard to come by, but four pennies or more in your pocket risked wearing a hole in it. Bob especially liked the charming, antique inefficiencies of British rail (many beautiful mainline steam locomotives were still in service).

We took a long weekend trip to Scotland, marveling at the beauty of the countryside even in overcast late fall weather. In Edinburgh we visited all the requisite sights including the National Portrait Museum. Bob wrote half in jest to Cousin Margaretta, saying he hadn't found any Pringles there. He got back a letter saying he hadn't looked in the right rooms, and telling us where they were, but to date we haven't returned to view the paintings.

We saw lots of plays. One of the first was the musical *Camelot,* which cost us a total of 17 shillings,[2] including transport and a light dinner. We enjoyed the long, mild English autumn, but by December we were using our heater full-time and still seeing our breaths in whatever part of the flat it wasn't. There was of course no Thanksgiving holiday, but the traditional English Christmas festivities were lengthy and fascinating—including, for us, *Toad of Toad Hall*, and a magnificent *Messiah* with large chorus and orchestra, performed at the Victoria and Albert Hall. Later we heard Martin Luther King preach at St. Paul's Cathedral on his way to Oslo to accept his Nobel Prize, and in late January we joined the crowds lining London streets for the funeral of Winston Churchill.

We shopped, acquiring our fancy china, eight full settings of Royal Doulton for $360, a late wedding present from relatives and Mariemont friends who having been told of our travel plans were also informed that a check for purchases abroad might be the most appreciated gift. Barbara acquired a stylish tweed coat on sale at Harrods. In general we had no trouble living on our London-Cornell stipend of $300 a month, supplemented by checks from Barbara's parents for special purposes.

We had a busy time with new English friends and old ones who were also doing graduate work in England. At 18 Rutland Gate, in the ultra classy, deepest West End, we passed one unforgettable evening with Lady Anne Bryant, who was the niece of Vyner Brooke, the last White Rajah, and was married

---

[2] Adjusted for inflation, about $15 in 2010 US dollars.

to noted historian Sir Arthur Bryant. [3] Anthony W.D. Brooke, Vyner's son, also attended. He had been heir to the Brooke throne when Sarawak was transferred to the Crown in 1946, amid some bitterness and turmoil stirred up by those who wanted the Brookes to remain. We didn't raise that probably still-sensitive subject, but instead listened to Anthony's idealistic views on the need for world government, all the while being plied with gin and "French" (meaning vermouth) = Martinis.

On Christmas Day we were entertained by Michael Ayling, a friend we knew from Telluride House, and his family, somewhere north of London. Michael's father was a wealthy car dealer, and the Aylings took us out to a multi-course dinner at a fancy restaurant at noon and then served us a huge high tea, which we enjoyed to the hilt in the afternoon. Next, after a very short walk, came a bibulous "supper." The Aylings had heard that all Americans suffered from the cold in England, but they had central heating, and they turned it up full blast for our benefit. We, of course, had dressed warmly in anticipation of a house heated by a few fireplaces. Thus stupefied by temperature and food, we were treated to a terrifyingly fast drive back to London chauffeured by Michael in his fancy new car. Upon arrival, we discovered that the water pipes in the unheated attic of our upstairs flat had frozen, leaving us with no water and the possibility that the pipes might burst. We opened the trap door to the attic, collapsed into bed, and hoped that whatever heat might still be in the flat would rise and prevent a flood. It did.

In late January Mrs. Mollison, our harridan landlady, finally went too far, yelling upstairs at Barbara for having an overnight guest (her Cornell roommate, Helen Knoll!), although this was not against the terms of the lease, as she claimed. Bob was speaking on American foreign policy, as part of a USIS public diplomacy effort, at a girls' school outside London and was away overnight when Mrs. Mollison blew up. Barbara called a

<hr>

[3] This connection was made thanks to Otto Doering and his wife Barbara; Otto was doing a master's thesis at LSE on Brooke administration and had ferreted out many Brooke and Sarawak connections by the time we arrived in London. He later went to Kuala Lumpur to work for the Ford Foundation, and Barbara stayed with the Doerings there in 1970 when Annie was born.

friend, Nigel Phillips, who came over in his car, helped to load all our worldly possessions—a trunk full of clothes and bed linens, some books, the paraffin heater, and a few dishes and kitchen supplies—and off she went to his house, replete with his wife Hazel and two small children who had to be watched lest they get too near the coal grates in the fireplaces. There we spent a few days before we found a new flat in Golders' Green, the Bohemian quarter of London, at 40 Rotherwick Road,[4] where we stayed until we left for Sarawak.

Our new landlady was very different and altogether delightful: Gertrude Rachel Levy, an authority on the history of epic poetry, whose book *The Gate of Horn* we have upstairs, but have yet to finish reading. The flat, located in an English basement that looked out on the garden, was a tiny "bed-sitter," meaning a living room with a folding bed plus a water closet (toilet), period. There was one cold-water tap in the living room, and the "kitchen" was a stone counter with an electric burner sitting on it. To keep food cold, you put it on the windowsill of said water closet, which worked fine during our January to March stay there. We did have friends over, but needed extra chairs and china if we had more than two guests. Sponge baths could be managed by heating water and using a washcloth, but for our weekly (or so) baths we made prior arrangements with Dr. Levy and used the tub in her bathroom.

As spring came to London, which it did rather nicely in 1965, Bob was getting his thesis outline into his head, and we were ready to head for Sarawak. Bob had a friend, Adam Clymer, in Moscow working for the *Baltimore Sun,* and we decided that it would be fun to visit him there, claiming to be cousins and thereby avoiding the outrageous and normally inescapable Intourist fees demanded of anyone visiting the Soviet Union. Bob duly filed an application at the Soviet Embassy saying that we would be staying with Cousin Adam. But a month or so before we were supposed to leave, we heard on our rented radio that an American reporter had been expelled for scuffling with a cop in Red Square while covering some sort

---

[4] If you Googled "40 Rotherwick Road" when this was written (about 2015), you could see the front of the house; our bed-sitter was on a lower level at the rear.

of demonstration. It sounded like Adam,[5] and it was. So we booked through Italy and Greece instead. Months later, after we were already in Sarawak, we got a letter from the Soviet Embassy in London saying, without further explanation, that our visa request had been denied.

The trip out, on Swissair, was great. Charlotte had equipped us with advice on what to see in Rome, especially in the Forum, for which she had filled a whole air letter (those old blue folding ones) with step-by-step descriptions of what the ruins we were seeing had once been. We had a great time buying picnic lunches to enjoy on the Appian Way. We got cheap seats at the Rome Opera for a Verdi opera (but can't remember which one it was). A side trip to Siena, our only venture out of Rome, was a high point. Surely among the most dazzling of Italian hill towns, its beautiful central plaza still bustled with local residents going about their daily activities.

Similarly in Greece, hordes of visitors and tourist busses were still in the future. We remember climbing the dirt path to the Acropolis by the light of the full moon to enjoy the panoramic view in the calm of the evening. Exploring the classical ruins on the hill and in the ancient Agora below, as well as various temples and other sites scattered throughout the present city, was like wandering in a local park, with little traffic and few crowds to dodge. A day trip by bus to Delphi, of oracle fame, gave us a taste of the countryside.

After brief stops in Bangkok and Kuala Lumpur, we had a pleasant two days in Singapore enjoying the hospitality of Edwin Lee and his father and taking an iconic photo of Life in the Tropics—Barbara sitting beneath a coconut tree on Changi Beach drinking the water of a coconut. This perfect South Pacific island scene is ironic, given that we were in the region's most advanced metropolis *and* on the site of its future airport. Then, on April 17, 1965, Barbara's twenty-third birthday, we took the weekly Malaysian Airways Comet (jet) flight to Kuching.

---

[5] Adam later worked for the *New York Times* for many years, and was accorded national attention when President Bush, chatting with Dick Cheney in 2000, called him a "major league asshole" over an open mike.

Life in Kuching

Our landing in Borneo was a bit rough. The Sarawak Museum was our official host under a new arrangement with Cornell whereby the Museum, which is to say its famously irascible Curator, Tom Harrisson, also the Government Ethnologist, would host Cornell researchers. Not unrelated, Tom himself, about to lose his job because Sarawak was transitioning to independence as part of Malaysia, was thinking of a job at Cornell. But the Museum had misread our cable and met a lesser morning flight.

The arrival of the once-a-week Comet, however, was a Happening, and half of Kuching was always on hand to meet it and have a drink at the airport restaurant. When no Museum representative showed up, a couple of friendly New Zealanders employed by Caterpillar gave us a place to stay and the use of their car—they were about to leave town for a few days—until we made contact with Tom and settled in.

It was an exciting time to be in Sarawak, roughly the size of Pennsylvania with a population of 820,000 (today it is over two million). When independence loomed for both Malaya and Singapore, the British didn't know what to do with their two big Borneo colonies, Sabah and Sarawak. They were also afraid of what might happen to Singapore, an overwhelmingly Chinese city-state being set adrift in a sea of less than wholly stable Muslim Malay neighbors. Malaya didn't want Singapore because its Chinese majority would reduce Malaya's Malays to a minority—unthinkable.

Hence the idea of "Malaysia." Throw the two Borneo colonies, now British Crown Colonies, in the pot with Singapore and Malaya and voila! a *non*-Chinese majority of "natives," although just barely. There were two problems. Most of the "non-Chinese" of Sabah and Sarawak were not Malays (i.e., not Muslim); they were animist and/or Christian tribal people. But no one consulted them. And no one knew what to do with the ancient, British-protected Sultanate of Brunei, the historic overlord of northern Borneo AND possessor of oil.

The oil had been found, most inconveniently, almost under the palace of the Sultan after he had been reduced to penury by his quasi-British neighbors, Sabah (founded as a British-protected Chartered Company) and especially Sarawak (before World War II ruled by a private family, the Brooke "White Rajahs"). The two of them had progressively annexed almost all his territory, leaving a residue of ill feeling. He did not want to share his oil money with some upstart "Malaysia," or his prestige with the Sultans of Malaya; his pedigree was longer than any of theirs.

So the British architects of Malaysia concluded that Brunei and its oil could remain under British protection for the time being—a battalion or two of Gurkhas would do it—and hopefully there would be no more ructions like the 1962 Brunei Rebellion in which a handful of radical Malays with Indonesian connections had almost unseated the Sultan.

At the time of our arrival, Malaysia had been legally in existence since 1963. But its birth had been complicated by strenuous opposition from Indonesia, where Sukarno needed foreign policy crises to maintain nationalist ardor. So he had launched a campaign of armed "Confrontation," consisting of sporadic attacks against the new Federation of Malaysia, mainly into its Borneo territories. Thanks to Indonesia's military weakness this conflict was in general a sporadic, low-cost war, but people did get killed, and much of the fighting that took place occurred along the Indonesia-Sarawak frontier, portions of which were quite close to Kuching. On top of this, the ethnic Chinese of Sarawak, especially their youth, had been attracted to communism by the Maoist rebellion in Malaya—the so-called "Malayan Emergency." For a time, as we would see up close, unhappy Sarawak Chinese in rural areas were resettled in fenced areas modeled on the New Villages established during that conflict.

The actual transfer of power from British Sarawak to Malaysia was just getting underway as we arrived. Senior British civil servants like Tom Harrisson still manned most key posts. Many of them were disturbed by the forced delivery of Sarawak to its wealthier neighbor, and they feared for the future of the non-Muslim native peoples like the Ibans, who they thought would be forced into a Muslim Malay mold once they lost the protection of a sympathetic and generally progressive colonial regime. Into this complex situation marched a colorful array of British and Commonwealth military: special forces (more correctly, "Special Air Services" in British idiom), helicopter and fighter plane units, intelligence specialists and renowned army regiments like the Gurkhas with all the trappings of Empire.

After our arrival, things moved quickly. Bob met Tom Harrisson and Benedict Sandin, an Anglican mission-educated Iban whom Tom was grooming to succeed him as Curator of the Sarawak Museum. Sandin was the unofficial tribal historian of his people and had published many small books and articles on Iban history and folklore. However, Tom felt he needed a more substantial publication to achieve sufficient prestige to be an effective curator. It was Bob's job to help him do it. In return, Sandin would help Bob sort out the relationship between the Brookes and the Ibans. Bob would also get access to the Sarawak State Archives, hitherto closed to foreign historians. Bob's relationship with Sandin turned out to be a model of collaboration between local and foreign scholars, who all too often did not contribute much in return for the information they collected. What Bob would do was similar to what his sister Margot had done with John Stands

Benedict Sandin, historian of his Iban people, poses in front of the Sarawak Museum with a model war boat of the kind once used by Iban headhunters and their allies from the southern Philippines for coastal raiding.

Barbara explaining the parliamentary system of government to student teachers at Batu Lintang Teacher Training College.

in Timber, the Northern Cheyenne tribal historian.

Tom had promised to help Barbara to find a job at the Batu Lintang Teacher Training College, and he did. The advent of Malaysia had inspired the British to get serious about education for Sarawak's rural people, hitherto largely neglected. This meant training students with only primary education to go into upriver areas, often accessible only by boat, to teach and open new schools. Batu Lintang Teacher Training College, Sarawak's first tertiary education institution, was located on the site of a World War II Japanese internment camp and used many of its buildings. Tom's help was needed because the British educational establishment, still in power, regarded Barbara's New York State certification, earned at Cornell University rather than a teacher training institution, as dubious or worse.

We stayed temporarily in Museum guest quarters, a tiny wooden house on Satok Road, on stilts with a row of orchids trained on a big trellis in front. Barbara wrote to her family:

This place has one thing in common with [state park cabins in the US]—ants. I could curse them; they get in everything. They spoiled a pound of sugar, invaded some cookies which I salvaged by re-baking, got our dinner which I left in a pan on the stove one night when we went to look at a house, and devoured two bananas another night. Now I hang bananas from the ceiling and put everything in the icebox. The other drawback is a baby monkey, a family pet next door, who wails for his mother for about an hour just before dawn every morning. Even Bob can't sleep through him.[6]

---

[6] Barbara letter to Dear Family, n.d., but probably late April, 1965.

We didn't realize that the monkey was a full-grown gibbon, not a baby, and that gibbons are famous for calling loudly just before dawn. It is supposed be the one of the more romantic sounds of the tropical forest. We finally adopted the tactic of throwing him (her?) several overripe bananas each morning, which gained us an extra hour or so of rest.

Within a few weeks we located a house to rent for the balance of our stay. The owner, a Chinese customs officer, had been posted to Miri, near Brunei. It was a small concrete house on concrete stilts, with the kitchen, dining room, and carport underneath, and a bedroom and living room upstairs. It had a squat toilet and no hot water; the latter made it hard to wash dishes, especially after cooking Australian lamb, the cheapest meat available in Kuching. There was a small balcony where every evening we split a can of Tiger beer (the top Malaysian brand) and listened to the news being broadcast from the capital: "*warta berita dari ibu kota negara, Kuala Lumpur*," words that still resonate with us. We watched the sunset and an occasional RAF Delta Dagger fighter lazily returning to its base from a patrol over the Indonesian border, its rockets clearly visible under its wings, reassuringly unexpended.

Just beyond our house began an ethnic Chinese settlement, where every wattle-and-daub house was hidden by vegetation—a horticultural maze of gardens, fish ponds, banana and coconut trees, and dwellings. From where we sat on our balcony it looked like an imaginary tropical rain forest. It was reputedly full of communist sympathizers, and we once saw an army patrol going into it. Rumor had it they were looking for a clandestine printing press.

The local Hash House Harriers, a TGIF-style institution which combines hounds-and-hare running with copious drink, was especially popular among Commonwealth expats; once while we were relaxing on our porch in the early evening, "the Hash" ran past our yard and through the community, which probably did little to win hearts and minds there. The primary school in this "rural" Chinese maze-cum-village had one of the best scholastic records in Kuching. The address of our house, quite the most poetic we have ever had, was 123 Iris Garden, 2½ Mile Rock Road, Kuching, Sarawak, Malaysia.

Iris Garden—Orchid Garden would have been more

accurate—was quite convenient to Batu Lintang, a little less so for the Sarawak Museum where Bob worked, but excellent exercise on a bicycle, and we immediately bought two of them for commuting. We enjoyed the ongoing controversy in the Kuching press about whether or not cyclists should be allowed to pedal "two abreast," regarded as a basic human right by the peddling cohort and a nuisance by the far less numerous motorists, who lost the argument.

Bob's work with Benedict Sandin consisted of helping him compile a history of the Iban people before colonial (Brooke) rule, drawing on his vast collection of oral genealogies (so-and-so, the son or so-and-so, etc.). Bob tried to use them for dating by estimating the number of years between generations. This was tricky, partly because women married much younger than men. Also, although the genealogies go thirty or more generations into the past, at about fifteen generations before present all are grafted onto a standard corpus of mythology. Before this demarcation all of them are largely the same.

With Bob's help, Benedict did indeed produce a book, *The Sea Dayaks of Borneo before White Rajah Rule*,[7] and Tom Harrisson, to his great credit, made sure that Bob's cooperation with Sandin was substantial. He then sweet-talked Macmillan (UK) into publishing both Sandin's and Bob's books and, later, his own on the Sarawak Malays. He told Macmillan that the Americans were madly buying any books even remotely relevant to the Cold War and that they could only make lots of money from publishing these books, which surely did not turn out to be true!

We led a varied and interesting social life. We got to know Barbara's fellow teachers at Batu Lintang, Colombo Plan and other aid workers, US Peace Corps volunteers and staff, the British and Commonwealth military, quite a few of the departing British civil servants, and all kinds of visiting scholars. One of our favorite Brits was Tim Marten, the Deputy High Commissioner, the Queen's representative in Sarawak, who took Bob on some fascinating tours of military posts and development projects. Marten, Winchester and Oxford educated, created a mild stir by marrying Anne Tan, a lovely

[7] London, Macmillan, 1969.

Chinese lady. He explained that some of the older Sarawakians still expected him to be all plumes and pith helmet, and not to fraternize, especially with the Chinese.

We overlapped with two US Consuls, Bill Brown and Bob Duemling; the latter became a life-long friend. He was a terrific amateur architect and made the Consulate residence into a showpiece; when we had him to dinner at Iris Garden, he was shocked by our squat toilet and suggested that I was maltreating Barbara by housing her in such a place.[8] The Kuching consulate was established only because of Confrontation, allegedly as cover for a CIA post, and there were only three consuls before it was closed, depriving Bob of achieving his greatest Foreign Service ambition.

Kuching, reflecting the best side of post-World War II British colonialism, was easy to live in. Its rain-washed tropical climate was pleasant, and it was spacious and sparkling clean. Thanks to a new waterworks, you could drink the water, and malaria had been eradicated all over Sarawak. (It has since made a partial comeback especially in the interior.) The town was virtually untouched by World War II, unlike Jesselton, its counterpart capital in Sabah, and its colonial charm was yet to be disrupted by development. On one side of the Sarawak River was the English Gothic Astana (palace) of the Brooke Rajahs, later used by British and Malaysian governors, as well as Kuching's whitewashed old fort, by this time purely symbolic. There was still no downtown bridge; you had to pay three cents (US) for a hand-paddled water taxi to get across.

Downtown Kuching was on the other side of the river. Facing the Astana was "Main Bazaar," a row of Chinese shophouses dotted with small but pretty Chinese temples affiliated with the different language groups. Behind that were more shops and most of the Brooke-era government offices. Everyone liked to eat out at the "night market," where you could order food from surrounding food stalls. Iban vendors often peddled wooden hornbill carvings and other handicrafts there.

Not far away was the parade ground, or *padang*, the best hotel, the Sarawak Museum, the residences of senior civil

---

[8] Robert Duemling, who later married Louisa Copeland Dupont, a Philadelphia Biddle by descent, was Ambassador to Suriname, and, after that, Director of the Building Museum.

servants, and the Anglican Cathedral. The Malays had their own quarter of stilted houses and canals, near the big mosque. In front of the mosque was a pushcart that sold curry-seasoning paste. You asked for enough paste for X pounds of Y meat (lamb, chicken or fish). The first time Bob bought some, he got it wrong and mistakenly ordered X pounds of *paste*, resulting in the world's hottest curry. After trying to dilute the heat by recooking the meat with lots of potatoes and new coconut milk, Barbara finally had to admit defeat and throw it away.

In front of the Museum was a park with an ornate bandstand where the police band played every Sunday. People of all backgrounds dressed up and came to listen and eat *kacang es,* a concoction of shredded ice, sweetened condensed milk, bright green gelatin, and red beans. We liked it too, and since Kuching had a clean water supply, indulged in a glassful whenever we could.

On weekends we could bike down to the excellent municipal swimming pool, or go to the races, which featured ponies from North Borneo adept at galloping through tropical downpours. We remember losing two dollars Malay (sixty cents US), the minimum bet. Friends on leave sometimes loaned us their cars, which enabled us to visit Land Dayak longhouses south of Kuching. One of them, Kampong Giam, had a small waterfall excellent for swimming. It was there that we once unexpectedly spent the night and participated in a harvest festival, during which Bob, dressed in a borrowed white shirt, handed out prizes for the children's field day.

The Land Dayaks or *Bedayuh* are different ethnically from the more numerous and warlike Sea Dayaks, the old term for Ibans, and in the Brooke era they had more often been victims than headhunters. However, they kept the heads they had taken in a separate head house, which we got to see. Long into the night, the eating, drinking, and dancing continued.

North of Kuching, toward the sea, Bako National Park was a good weekend destination. It didn't have much except a murky beach, this being a coast of mud and *nipah* palm swamp, where the rivers bring down too much sediment from the rainy interior for coral to survive. On one outing Barbara collided with a large jellyfish, resulting in a very painful sting. Fortunately there were British troops nearby equipped with

Energetic graduate students, we not only rode our bikes everywhere in Kuching, but once biked out to hike up the nearest "mountain," the top of which we reached just in time to enjoy a quick view of the surrounding jungle before clouds closed in for the rest of the day.

gin and some kind of pain-killing salve.

Late in our stay, we chaperoned a joint Girl Guide-Boy Scout camping trip from Batu Lintang to Santubong, not far away. All we remember is the hassle of persuading the students to hire two boats to go downriver, rather than dangerously (by our standards) overloading one. The boys had planned to sit on the roof, but few of the students could actually swim.

Bako was where Tom Harrisson and his wife Barbara had a project, one of the first of its kind, to teach jungle survival skills to orphaned orangutans with the help of a bad-tempered wild adult. For years Bob has relished and told a story about how Tom took a very senior colonial official and his pompous wife to see the project. The visit ended disastrously when the mentoring orangutan, named Arthur, assaulted the party and went prancing back into the forest with the top of the official wife's bathing suit wrapped around his head, munching on her camera. This supposedly led to the relocation of the project to Sabah. Unfortunately Bob's diary, read recently for the first time in decades, has a less colorful version, which merely states that Arthur was a bit neurotic and enjoyed "mildly mauling" sightseers.[9] This demonstrates how too many cocktail parties can make a hash of oral history.

At first Bob worked mainly with Benedict Sandin on his own project. Then he began going through Brooke-era records with the help of archivist Loh Chee Yin. He would frequently ask Sandin for his views, and often got another version of events, which usually agreed on basic facts but often, to his delight, provided a very different interpretation of them. Benedict was from the relatively well-educated Saribas district, and many people assumed that his knowledge was restricted to his home region, but this was not the case. Indeed the Ibans had more history in common, and much more sense of shared cultural heritage generally, than most people realized.

Later Bob would accompany Benedict on long interviewing sessions in remote areas, where Benedict would sit on the longhouse verandah with the *tuai rumah* (headman) as the two of them counted back on their respective genealogies. They would keep track of the generations with bits of straw placed on the floor mat, as they sought a common ancestor—bespectacled Sandin with his short hair and white shirt, every inch the missionary product, and the lean, wiry headman with tattooed throat and/or long hair, the picture of a retired headhunter. Sandin also interpreted, because although Bob had some knowledge of Iban, which is close to standard Malay/Indonesian, he could not deal with rapid-fire exchanges or specialized vocabulary.

When in Kuching, Bob would bicycle downtown for lunch, select a small restaurant on the ground floor of a Chinese shop, of which there were dozens, and order a bowl of yellow noodle soup with slices of pork on top. The Chinese, inveterate snackers, are always eating. Kuching is famous for *laksa*, a coconut and shrimp curry soup favored as a mid-morning snack, as was "*pao*," large round dimsum, as yet unheard of in the US, stuffed with meat or bean paste. Coffee was brewed in what looked like a long, very dirty sock hung around a metal rim through which

---

[9] Bob Diary entry for December 2, 1965. It refers to a "fat expat" being the victim of Arthur's misbehavior, not a senior official, and no mention of a bathing suit. It is true that the project was relocated to Sabah.

the shopkeeper, with much fancy arm motion, poured boiling water; the result was served with sweetened condensed milk. Yum!

All Chinese coffee shops were operated by Hailam Chinese, people who speak the Hailam language, originally from Hainan off the south coast of China. Most of about half a dozen Chinese language (not dialect) groups in Sarawak had similar occupational-linguistic linkages, as in if you spoke French, you must be a pastry chef. Another example: all Henghuas were either bicycle shop owners or fishermen. Shop owners lived over their shops and never really closed. The colonial government had valiantly tried to make them close on major holidays—based on the most un-Chinese assumption that too much work is unhealthy—but the shop door was almost always left open a crack, in case you really wanted to buy something. One of Bob's favorite Chinese enterprises was the Borneo Studio, at 57 Carpenter Street, which sold photo supplies and developed film. The proprietor did the best black-and-white processing he has ever experienced anywhere. Even his smallest prints were superb, and some of his work will adorn the photo volume that goes with this book.

Barbara at Batu Lintang

Barbara enjoyed our shared adventures as much as Bob did, but most of the time he was sequestered in the Sarawak Museum archives. She needed a job of her own, one that would contribute to her own professional future, and that was found, as mentioned above, with Tom Harrisson's assistance. However, the Sarawak education bureaucracy, still almost entirely British, took a full year to recognize her American teaching credentials. The result was that she was originally paid much less than other (UK or Commonwealth) expatriates working at Batu Lintang. This stupidity had a happy ending: when it was finally corrected, Barbara received a welcome bonus of about US$1,000 to spend on our trip home. That glitch aside, Batu Lintang was a wonderful experience. In Barbara's words:

Sarawak was my first encounter with a non-Western society, and Batu Lintang was loaded with special challenges. The first major lesson I learned (I was already supposed to know it, but sometimes experience is a better teacher than books) was that whatever you are trying to teach, you have to start at the level your students have already reached. No curriculum can change that basic truth—though you might have to admit that you didn't get the whole curriculum taught, in the very real sense that your students don't know all of it yet.[10]

A class I will never forget illustrates that point perfectly: When I decided to make a timeline in Sarawak history class one day and found out that my students did not know how to measure with rulers, I wound up teaching them how to use a ruler and to read inches and feet. They had to skip learning Western concepts of time, like centuries. This was a class of young men with four years of schooling, from the Iban longhouses farthest upriver. Their parents, or some of them, were expert oral historians who knew how to date events by linking them to generations, not by written timelines.

Those at the college ranged from students like them, many older than I, who would go on to staff, or even create, schools that reached only to Primary Four (the fourth year of primary school). Their own best students would go somewhere slightly less remote to finish Primary Six. The vast majority of our students at Batu Lintang were themselves Primary Six graduates who were preparing to teach in outstation towns and less remote longhouses. Leaving the mainly urban Chinese language schools aside, only the very best students in the primary grades in Sarawak would finish their educations with four years of secondary school, and be high-school graduates after ten years.

Batu Lintang had one class of high-school graduates, ten Chinese from various towns, one Iban, and one Malay. They were the elite and were aiming, if successful in their first years at an elementary school, to go on to further training and become secondary school teachers themselves. The secondary schools in 1965 were the province of expatriate teachers, a few Malays from Malaysia, and only the occasional Sarawak citizen. Many of our Peace Corps friends were

---

[10] Barbara letter to Dear Family, n.d.

involved in something called the Primary English Medium Teaching Scheme, designed to train local teachers to teach all subjects in primary grades in English.

Fast forward: when we returned for a visit in 1972, we were astonished to find not a single foreigner still teaching at the primary or secondary level in Sarawak. All the teachers were Malaysian, some from Sarawak, many from the peninsula—and all classes in primary school were taught in Malay. English was taught as a second or third language, and only began to be used as a language of instruction in other subjects in secondary school. In 1965, we would never have believed that such a rapid transformation could be possible.

Even my elite class had a long way to go when they arrived at Batu Lintang. One day in Sarawak History, we were studying Iban culture, and the Ibans had been the feared headhunters of former days. One of the urban Chinese students asked his Iban classmate if he would still take a head today if given the chance. The immediate reply was "Yes," clearly implying "of course," to the consternation of his classmates. In fact, inter-ethnic relations among Sarawak residents had been generally calm since independence, but my students certainly gained a new idea to think about that day.

My Chinese students were subjects as well as consumers of my Sarawak history teaching. I asked them to record what Chinese linguistic group in Sarawak they belonged to, where their forbears had first settled, and what their fathers did professionally. They turned out to come from four of the commonest language groups, Hakka (or Kheh) being the most numerous, with 12 students, then Foochow (10), Hokkien (5) and Teochew (4). All were learning Mandarin and English, but the old distinctions were only beginning to fade. The surveys helped the students, and me, to understand the Chinese role—and their own places—in Sarawak history.

A digression by Bob: The great book on the subject of Sarawak's ethnic Chinese was and still is Ju K'ang T'ien's *The Chinese of Sarawak, A Study of Social Structure*, published by the London School of Economics anthropology department in 1950. T'ien had been part of a team assembled for the British Colonial Office by a famous anthropologist, Edmund Leach, to survey the various ethnic groups of Sarawak, in order to help Britain to manage its newly acquired Crown Colony. Stephen Morris, Bob's mentor at LSE, was also on the team. Each member studied a certain ethnic group: Morris did the Melanau, William Geddes did the Bidayuh, then known as Land Dayaks; J.D. Freeman did the Iban, T'ien did the Chinese, and Tom Harrisson did the Malays, although not until much later.

But as T'ien finished his work in Sarawak in 1949, he faced a big problem. His home, China, had just become Red China. Some of Sarawak's Chinese had become ardently Maoist. T'ien had been studying them—for the Imperialists! According to Morris, he was quite apolitical, but he wanted desperately to go home to his wife and family. He went to Morris for advice. Morris said, "Don't worry, here's what you do. Next time [the most radical Chinese organization] has a rally, you go there and make a speech blasting the British and praising Mao and everything he stands for. It will be in the papers the next day, and the governor will expel you from Sarawak."

And so it happened, and everything apparently went well for a time. T'ien went home to China and returned to his professional career there. Only several years later did Morris hear from him. His message was short: Thank you, I am fine. That was not the end of the story, however; he was incarcerated and tortured during the Cultural Revolution, which broke out in 1966, and his talented pianist wife committed suicide. However, later he was able to resume his career as a respected specialist on non-Han minorities. In 2002 he paid a return visit to Sarawak at the invitation of the Chinese community that he had studied decades previously, and as of 2016 he was still alive and working in China.[11]

End of Bob's digression. The Batu Lintang faculty was expected to participate in all aspects of college activity, and so one of Barbara's contributions was to be leader of the senior Girl Guide company. This led to marching in various parades, the famous boat trip to Santubong mentioned above, and undoubtedly numerous long-forgotten service projects.

---

[11] I learned the first part of the T'ien story from my LSE mentor, Stephen Morris; the second, covering what happened to him after his return to China, is based on information from Clifford Sather, especially his "Notes from the Editor" on page 1, Vol. 33 (2002) of the *Borneo Research Journal*, which he edits.

Batu Lintang also got me involved in Sarawak history. Not that I didn't have a dose of that at home. But Bob's study concentrated on the period from 1831 to 1941, and I was teaching on the site and in the buildings of what had been the World War II Japanese internment camp for European women and children in the Dutch East Indies. I don't know whether I had read Agnes Keith's *Land Below the Wind* and *Three Came Home* before I arrived, but if I hadn't, someone lent them to me early in our stay. Of course, preparation for the Sarawak history course lessons led me to find out more.

The proof-by-archeology lesson came when the college decided to dig a demonstration fishpond, so that students could replicate this protein-enhancing activity in any school at which they would teach. One Saturday morning, all faculty and students gathered at the chosen site, a field on one side of the campus, and dug out the dirt in a huge rectangle. It must have been clay soil, because it was deemed ready to hold water, and it was duly filled. The mistake was to stock it with fish the same day. On Monday, when someone went over to inspect the pond, the water had vanished and it was full of dead fish. Investigation revealed that an old drainage pipe had been nicked, and that is how the water had seeped away. That pipe could have come from only one source, the old Japanese internment camp drainage system.

Batu Lintang also got me involved in Sarawak art. No one who visits the state can fail to be attracted by the curvilinear designs in black, red, yellow, white and green that characterize the painting and carving of the upriver people. The art teacher, a long-time expatriate resident named Susie Heinze, encouraged the use of local motifs and subjects while she introduced students and Kuching artists to new techniques.

One of Susie's most successful young artists was the batik painter Ramsey Ong, from a famous Kuching Chinese family. Together they were experimenting with this technique using Ritz dyes, which require boiling to bring out maximum color and to set it. But batik is a wax-resist technique, and strong German cold-water dyes were not yet available in Sarawak. So the two attractive paintings which I bought from him, muted in color to begin with, faded from the sun as they hung in our living room in Kuching. Stenciled designs painted on fabrics were more successful. I modeled and for years afterwards enjoyed wearing a blue shift decorated with a spray of stenciled white flower blossoms.

There was no shortage of art to collect. We acquired several carvings, including two hornbills and a canoe carrying hunters, from upriver people who came into the night market to sell their work. In the Sarawak Museum shop we found several Iban *ikat* blankets, called *pua*, that we liked and could afford, which meant that they were not of highest quality, as measured by the clarity of the design; fine *ikat* work is not supposed to be fuzzy, as many cheap textiles from Eastern Indonesia are today. Somewhere, right at the end of our stay, we acquired a smaller piece of much more delicate and exact weaving that had been a woman's skirt.

Although we were not collecting beads at that point, we could not help but notice the Kenyah, Kayan, and Kelabit beadwork, and we brought home a lovely small basket decorated with seed beads, as well as a man's throat decoration of seed beads wound in a cylinder. I also acquired two interesting strings of women's beads, both made primarily of large, deep red carnelian beads, one with turquoise beads interspersed. As I recall, some of our beadwork was purchased in longhouses, but the young woman we met at Nanga Antawau on the Balleh was the only weaver we ever encountered (and photographed) upriver, and she was weaving for ritual use at home, not for sale.

Travels in the Interior

In June 1965 we got our first look at Iban country. The proximate cause was Barbara's trip to oversee nineteen of her students doing practice teaching at Betong in the Second Division, about 125 miles west of Kuching by mostly dirt road. She was assigned to a vacant government house, a small blue bungalow on stilts. It was the dry season and very hot as well as dry; every house had a rain barrel to catch runoff from the roof, a system which we were later amazed to find is rarely used in other tropical, underdeveloped countries. One virtue of the house was that, having been unoccupied for a while, it had a barrel full of water. So Barbara and the three women practice teachers could wash and bathe in comfort. The male students, on the other hand,

Elsewhere upriver Bob accompanied Sandin while he compared oral history accounts with Iban headmen and genealogy experts like Penghulu Ngali, on Sandi's left at Tappang Pungga longhouse, Nanga Delok.

had to hike the better part of a mile to a stream, where they bathed, washed their clothes, and then, hopefully upstream, filled cans with drinking and dishwashing water. We must have boiled our drinking water in Betong.

Life in Iban country was a real adventure for some of Barbara's students, especially those (mainly Chinese) from urban areas. "Mrs. Pringle, Mrs. Pringle!" one of them told her on our first day in Betong, "Some of my students live in longhouses!" [12]

I accompanied Barbara and her students on the trip out, occupying myself by visiting local longhouses and chasing down old court records at the administrative headquarters. In Betong, as in most outstations, the architecture of Brook rule was still apparent: a government fort, named after a female Brooke relative (in Betong it was "Fort Lili") where the Resident or District Officer had his office; a cluster of Chinese shophouses, in town either along the river or around the *padang* (town square); a Malay (i.e., Muslim) *kampong* (village) or two downriver, and Iban longhouses upriver, scattered along streams coming down from the interior.

This geography was fascinating because it expressed the

---

[12] Bob and Barbara letter to Milton Osborne, July 9, 1965.

Rajahs' ideas of what was safe, proper and administratively convenient. There were no Chinese in rural areas before the Brookes arrived, and Muslims and pagans were not separated from each other. But the Brookes were wary of Muslim influence over the pagans because Muslim nobles had preceded them as rulers, and so they decreed the upriver/downriver separation. They made it illegal for Chinese to "live amongst Dayaks" (i.e., in longhouses), because they thought the Chinese might cheat the Ibans, who might react by taking Chinese heads.

I interviewed old men who had served on the Rajahs' expeditions against rebels, which sometimes included thousands of warriors. Ibans subject to being "called out" for such service were not paid, but they were allowed to take the heads of the enemy, and because of their military function they paid lower taxes than other people. This practice, unique to Sarawak, enabled the Brooke state to survive in its earliest days, and it continued well into the twentieth century. Near Betong, I interviewed one old man who had killed and beheaded a famous rebel in 1918 and was still mad because the District Officer later made him return the head to the rebel's family so that peace could be made with the insurgents.[13]

I did not stay with Barbara the whole time she was in Betong. Instead I returned to Kuching periodically, sometimes by bus, sometimes by hitching rides with aid workers or the British military. I felt pangs about this arrangement and wrote her at least one letter, in addition to making several visits:

Dear better half:

Somehow this business of a month [apart] didn't seem nearly so long until it happened. Well I suppose we will both survive.

I am worried about you and I confess that I feel slightly guilty about leaving you in Betong, especially with all the alarming headlines. Thank heaven for the Peace Corps anyway.[14]

---

[13] Bob Diary entry for August 17, 1965.

[14] Bob letter to Barbara, July 10, 1965. There were two male Peace Corps volunteers in Betong. Rather than "protectors," they were friends, with whom she regularly dined each evening at one of the shop houses in the Bazaar, for thirty US cents a meal.

A few days later Barbara wrote reassuringly to Clay and Char:

Bob definitely got the worst of this deal by having to go back to Kuching and read [Sarawak] Gazettes. I've spent the weekend absorbing Dayak [Iban] life firsthand. I went with a charming girl student of mine [McKenna Samuel] to visit her uncle's longhouse over Sunday night (Monday was a holiday – Prophet Mohammed's Birthday). The house was interesting because it has followed all the Agriculture Department's instructions about chickens in coops, pigs in pens, cats and dogs properly cared for. Therefore there are no pigs groveling below the house or mangy dogs or chickens fouling the ruai [common veranda]. Without Bob (i.e., a woman only) I didn't cause much of a stir, and got a chance to see daily life in full swing. In the morning all the young adults leave to tap rubber—the trees grow helter-skelter on the hillsides. The women come home and wash and cook; the men prepare the latex into sheets—smells horrible. The main pastime is talking; the radio is mainly a young people's entertainment.[15]

At a neighboring longhouse, she also attended an all-night funeral mingling Christian and pagan ceremonial, part Anglican church service, part recital of long traditional chants. The coffin of the dead was displayed on the veranda and the funeral featured much drinking of rice wine and spirits—the dreaded "arrack"—plus speeches about the dead man, and a midnight snack. Then she went to sleep, provided, as a visitor, with a mattress, but through it she could hear the women at the coffin wailing until six a.m., when it was taken to the missionary church for a burial service. "I came home, fortified myself with a cup of coffee and went off to watch four poor lessons and one good one by my practice teachers," she wrote.[16]

Later we were to see a four-day long *gawai antu* (feast of the ancestors) at Melayu, a neighboring longhouse. This was a major celebration, one of the most important in Iban tradition. They were held only every decade or two, the same kind of ritual as Barbara had seen but on a much grander scale, attracting hundreds of visitors, including many foreigners, a

---

[15] Barbara letter to family, July 13, 1965.
[16] Ibid.

sizable proportion of whom drank too much, as was expected. Barbara joined the young women processing around the veranda wearing Iban dress (with tops covered, perhaps due to missionary influence).

Travel between Kuching and Betong was interesting because for a considerable distance the road paralleled the Klingkang Hills, which marked the frontier with Indonesia, and at least twice we had to stop because a British rubber-tired tank just in front of us was firing shells toward the border. Once we caught a ride in a similar vehicle when escorting some of Barbara's student teachers home from a track meet. "Eyes did pop somewhat when this iron-coated

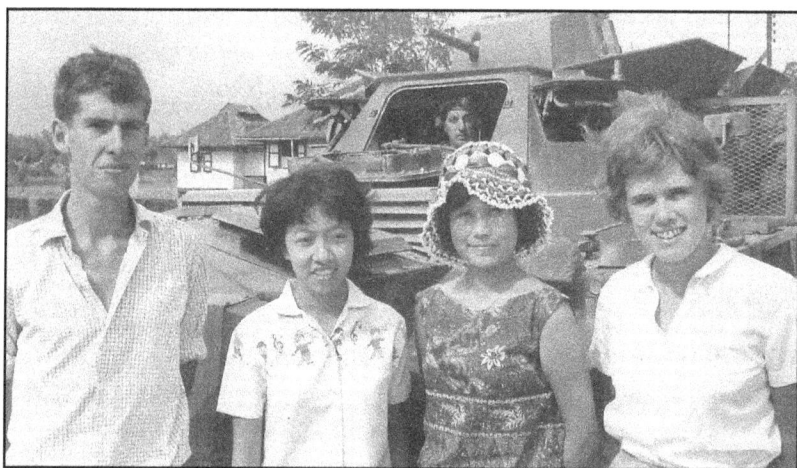

Taking student teachers on field trips had certain unique features in 1965 Sarawak: here Barbara, a British VSO volunteer, and two of her students have just returned to Betong from an athletic field day to which the transportation was provided by British troops stationed in Sarawak to help its former colony fight a border war against Indonesia.

monster disgorged us not far from Fort Lili, in front of our little blue house," I wrote.[17] We were covered with dust, head to toe.

Things got even more interesting after an Iban policeman who happened to be the half-brother of the new Chief Minister

---

[17] Bob Diary entry for August 17, 1965.

of Sarawak was killed in late June during an attack on a police post, eighteen miles from Kuching, in an area populated mainly by Chinese pepper farmers. As a result they were all moved summarily into guarded compounds where they had to remain at night. It was never quite clear to what extent the pro-communist Chinese were in league with the anti-imperialist Indonesians, but it was assumed they might be. On one trip we picked up a Chinese language leaflet dropped by the military warning all Chinese (only) where they had to be after dark. (I pasted it in my diary.)

I wrote on July 6, after returning to Kuching:

For the next fifteen miles we drove through Sarawak's new Emergency, still wet behind the ears. Numerous checkpoints and we were almost flattened by a tank careening around one corner at 40 mph plus—you'd never dream a tank could corner so well! I had heard the Chief Minister's broadcast early this morning . . . telling those [the Chinese] inconvenienced that it was their own fault for nourishing subversion. . . . The bazaar [at Samarahan] was jammed with Chinese. Military everywhere. Just beyond the bridge, shiny new barbed wire fencing going up—watch towers at the corners—lights strung along the fence . . . . Only they aren't New [Villages] at all. What they are doing . . . is moving the Chinese rural population into bazaar areas where they will sleep in houses and schools! There will be five such areas between 25 and 15 Mile [indicating distance from Kuching].[18]

I doubted that New Villages would work as well as they had in Malaya because the ethnic mix in Sarawak was very different, and all of this was going on within sight of a hostile Indonesian frontier. Maybe so, but as things turned out the villages ceased to be needed because Sukarno passed from power in 1966, Malaysia worked pretty well when it came to making money, *inter alia* from stripping away Sarawak's forests, and radical Chinese youth grew, and sobered, up, for multiple reasons.

Back in Kuching my relationship with Tom Harrisson was

---

[18] Bob Diary entry for July 6, 1965, recording several days' events.

never dull. I wrote to Milton Osborne:

Harrisson allows as how he's been offered a job, or rather what I gather would be a Claire Holtish[19] sort of sinecure, at Cornell; this has made my position here a good deal easier. I see very little of him, which is just as well, since the difficulties of working with him have not been exaggerated. He is even better than my female relatives at doing 99 things at once, frantically, in order never to have to really face up to any of them. Surviving involves ignoring endless bluster and insult, but I'm working at it.

I recently showed him a paper I'd written on the early Brooke state—the same one I sent to Dr. Wolters before leaving London—and he criticized it on the grounds that I'd pictured James Brooke as economically motivated, which I certainly had not, in terms of American power politics, whereas in fact his motives derived from something mystical in the ethic of the English gentry. He also said the paper was snide, facile, etc., etc. Then he turned up at the Museum this afternoon, peering seriously over his semi-spectacles, assuming that I would be in a terrible temper because of his comments. I never met anyone with such a capacity for reading his own personality into other people.[20]

I wrote in my diary, "I am becoming everyone's consultant about how to get along with TH [although] the fact of my survival owes little to me personally—don't we know it!"[21] In fact my survival had everything to do with Harrisson's pending Cornell employment, which I couldn't talk about. In the event, Tom's relationship with Cornell was brief, although his wife Barbara had a longer stay there.

Life at 923 Iris Garden settled down into a pleasant regime. We acquired a cat and a dog creatively named Kitty and Puppy. As we recall, Kitty came from a longhouse near Betong; like most local cats she had a kink in her tail, according to legend so that Malay princesses could hang their rings on it when they bathed. We christened her "Pepper" for the color of her

---

[19] A reference to Claire Holt, author of *Art in Indonesia*, who had a well-deserved position at Cornell for many years.
[20] Bob letter to Milton and Rhondda Osborne, July 9, 1965.
[21] Bob Diary entry for September 4, 1965.

feet but could never get over calling her Kitty. Puppy staggered in our gate one day and collapsed in a pile of skin, bones and mange. We nursed him back to health with a generous diet of frozen kangaroo meat, very cheap, from Ting and Ting, the local supermarket, plus the ministrations of the local vet, who was astonished that anyone would take an interest in, and buy medicine for, a mere mongrel dog.

After a period of mutual hostility the two of them learned to play with each other, with Kitty usually initiating the romp, adding to the animal cacophony of the neighborhood. Next door to us was a wealthy Chinese family from Shanghai, their house protected by floodlights, a stout barbed-wire fence and big guard dogs. That was OK, but the local curs on their nocturnal prowls enjoyed calling these well-fed hounds names through the fence. When we complained about the resulting uproar and loss of sleep, Mr. Shanghai said, "Outside dogs come and make noisy, what can I do?" On the other side was another Chinese, Mr. Ha, several of whose ornamental goldfish Kitty, to our surprise, had the gumption to slip through his fence and eat.

Visitors continued: the Doerings from Kuala Lumpur (where, because of them, Annie would be born five years later); Barbara's college classmate, Elaine Emling; George Elliston, polymath geographer met in London who was doing research on a fishing village in Malaya; and Ferdinand and Delia Kuhn, authors and close ex-OWI friends of the Henry Pringles. The Kuhns admired our little house, which seemed quite comfortable for Borneo, and reported with great amusement to all and sundry when they got home that we had told them we were historians, not anthropologists, and didn't need to live in primitive circumstances. When Barbara got sick (not seriously as it turned out), the Scottish ambulance unit quartered in some nearby Chinese shophouses took her to Kuching's clean, pleasant hospital, where, as a Sarawak Government employee thanks to her job at Batu Lintang, she paid thirty cents (US) a day and was soon well.

We kept on traveling, a lot. In August we went up Sarawak's

biggest river, the Rejang, as far as Nanga Antawau[22] on the Balleh tributary. It marked the limit of migration imposed by the Brookes to keep the warlike Ibans under control, and the limit was still maintained at the time of our visit. Further upstream there was nothing but forest (alas, not for much longer). At Nanga Antawau we met young Iban women still weaving *pua*, the famous tie-dyed blankets; making one was the female counterpart of taking a human head. However, this skill was rapidly vanishing in the longhouses we visited.

Coming downriver, at Kapit we met Leonard Linggi Jugah, who was the son of the most prominent Iban leader, Temenggong Jugah, on vacation from his studies at Hull University in England.[23] We continued down the Rejang to Sibu, and then set off to Kuching by ocean-going launch, down one flaccid stream and back up another, through endless boring miles of *nipah* palm swampland, because there was not yet any road along the coast. We spent a night at Kabong, a big Malay fishing settlement of grey houses on stilts over grey mud. The trip took eighteen hours of boat travel; with the road that now exists it probably takes thirty minutes or less. Finally we reached Betong and the familiar route back to Kuching.

At about this time we learned that Singapore had not seceded from Malaysia, as originally reported, but rather had been kicked out by the Muslim Malay leadership of Malaya. This was a source of great concern to the pagan and Christian people of Sarawak, who now feared more than ever the consequences of integration into a Malay-dominated Malaysia.

In October Bob traveled alone to Lubok Antu on the Indonesian border, to see if it would be safe to return later with Benedict to interview Iban informants in the rugged

---

[22] Nanga means "mouth of a stream," i.e. the place where a tributary flows into a larger river.

[23] Leonard Linggi Jugah became a respected leader of the Ibans and is known today as the founder of the Tun Jugah Foundation, devoted to the preservation of Iban culture. His wife, whom we never met, created a large workshop in the splendid Foundation Museum to revive dyeing and weaving skills and was instrumental in collecting high quality *puas*, many of which are now on display in the museum.

headwaters of nearby streams. Lubok Antu itself is at a flat place on the frontier, a route between Sarawak and the great Kapuas River on the Indonesian side. It is a region that had figured heavily in Iban history. Now British military were in the old Brooke-era fort. The man in charge was a non-commissioned officer, Sergeant W. "Butch" Woodward, and his main job was gathering intelligence from Ibans, who were still crossing the border freely despite Confrontation. There had been fighting nearby and every evening the British fired a couple of "harassing fire" howitzer rounds into Indonesian territory, mainly for psychological effect.

Butch would ask his informants to give him news of the Indonesian units on the other side. Once, when a new artillery piece was reported, he gave one of them a camera so they could take a picture of it, which they did. On presenting him with the resulting film, the Ibans asked for extra prints, which they had promised to take back to the Indonesian gun crew. These Butch duly provided. It was definitely a laid-back kind of war. Butch didn't hesitate to share this kind of thing with me. He was concerned about mutilation of British/Commonwealth dead and asked me to write a description of Iban burial customs, which I did and sent back. I suppose that I am listed somewhere in old British intelligence files as a "source."

In December we went back to the Rejang, this time going all the way up the main river, passing Kapit and portaging around the famous Pelagus Rapids, as far as Belaga. To get there we needed a pass from the Resident of the Third Division at Sibu, then one of the very last expatriates to hold such a post.

Our pass form read:

Permission is hereby given to visit areas above Kapit,
[then, typed in]:
1) They should report to the DO and Police Kapit & lodge copies of their programme with them.
2) They should not proceed above Belaga. [This was probably because there had been, months previously, Indonesian raids in the extreme upriver areas, and we ignored it.]
3) Valid from 8th to 20th December, 1965
Signed, A.R. Meikle,
Resident, Third Division

I wrote beneath Meikle's signature "Last of the Mohicans!"[24]

From Kapit onwards we got a ride with a friendly British officer transporting some Punan Lusong to serve in the Border Scouts along the Indonesian frontier. We left Iban territory and passed longhouses of "Upriver Melanau," still-pagan peoples related to the better-known coastal Melanaus who had converted to Islam. Above Belaga, settlement was entirely "*orang ulu*," (literally "upriver people") meaning, mainly, Kenyahs and Kayans. They had highly stratified class systems—hereditary chiefs, a middle class, slaves—the other end of a societal spectrum from the classless, "democratic" (or anarchic) Ibans. From the *orang ulu* people came the famous art motifs widely associated with Borneo that Barbara had already encountered at Batu Lintang, displayed in painting and beadwork, not to mention music and dance.

Going upriver we saw a really big crocodile, at last, sunning on a sandbar. In the Archives' old *Sarawak Gazettes* there were constant accounts of people being "taken" by crocodiles, often snatched from their riverside bathing places, but by 1966 big ones were a rarity thanks to the skin trade.

At Belaga we stayed in the scruffy bazaar (twenty-one shops in two sections) with Russ Wilson, a gruff Australian Colombo Plan group headmaster, who was not pleased to see us, although he warmed up a bit after a day or two. Our biggest adventure was an overnight trip further up the Balui (as the uppermost segment of the Rejang is called) to Long Linau.

From Bob's diary:

We are just back from . . . a Kayan longhouse at Long Linau . . . . This thanks to the Tuai Rumah, one Taman Bulan, previously encountered at the [Sarawak] Museum, to which he was then flogging various Punan objets . . . . We left [Belaga] about 11 a.m., waiting two hours because the river, according to Taman Bulan, was too high. This we believed, later. Wong Bakun is the big rapids above Belaga, and it has to be negotiated to be believed. I have never seen nor dreamed of such a furious river. Thrills and chills were added to by the ailments of our 40 hp motor—it actually conked out at the head of one lesser

---

[24] I pasted the pass in my diary.

but still scary rapids—they did get it started again in time. The problem here is sheer volume of water—had it been any higher our motor could not have pushed [our boat] through the fast parts and a couple of times as it was we were hanging! . . . [sic] Tremendous leaping swirling current between sheer rock walls. The scenery is often gorgeous—almost alpine hills dropping to the water's edge— one lovely stretch before the rapids covered with bright green hill paddy [rice] fields. The final approach to Long Linau is through a last dramatic gorge-rapids at the head of which the longhouse is located, together with a new dispensary and primary school . . . .[25]

At Long Linau we enjoyed typical longhouse entertainment, and Bob observed that Kayans were lovely to look at, especially the women. "Beadwork adds to the American Indian impression—the most spectacular is on the baby carriers which are apparently unobtainable at anything under a mile-high price."[26] (We finally bought a Kayan beaded baby carrier when we returned to Sarawak in 2007.) Boat, fuel, and crew cost under US$20 for the round trip from Belaga to Long Linau, which Bob felt was exorbitant. Today the entire river above Belaga has been flooded by a much and justifiably protested dam, named Bakun for the rapids we negotiated, that will—or may, some day—provide power to mainland Malaysia. Transmission lines have not yet been built.

On our return we got a ride in a Medical Department boat with a "traveling dresser" and, as assistant, Peace Corps volunteer Bruce Cheliowski. We stopped at twenty-nine longhouses, mainly Upriver Melanau, but also four Iban and some Kayan, to give DPT shots (Diptheria, Tetanus, Whooping Cough), the basic immunization of childhood. Bob wrote:

People were by and large very cooperative about the shots, despite struggles and tears and shouts of "Enggai!"—"I don't want!" Frequently mothers couldn't bear to see their offspring jabbed, and the dirty job was delegated to Granny.[27]

Of these stops, we found Punan Ba the most interesting;

---

[25] Bob Diary entry for December 13, 1965.
[26] Ibid.
[27] Bob Diary entry for December 19, 1965.

it was an upriver Melanau longhouse with 33 "doors" (= families) and 303 people. It had huge *belian* (ironwood) house posts and a number of beautifully carved burial posts (*keliring*), similar to the one in front of the Sarawak Museum, on top of which the preserved remains of chiefs were given secondary burial. Each elaborately carved post was erected over a sacrificed human, or so we were told, and capped by a huge flat rock—until age and rot took its toll. (Punan Ba burned down in 2008, according to a YouTube entry.)

Much further downstream, we turned left off the main Rejang at Kanowit, into the rugged hinterland, to visit a charismatic Scot, J.K. [John Kennedy] Wilson, who was running a famous counter-current development program in an Appalachia-like region. We were physically much closer to "civilization," but in reality much further away, because these streams, often full of rocks and beautifully overhung by trees, were much harder to navigate than the main river, and the area had been fraught with Iban unrest for decades.[28]

Wilson had worked for the Sarawak government, but he was philosophically opposed to big-spending, top-down programs, so he quit and set up his own private operation. He thought the Ibans should stay put, stick to their culture, and learn things that would benefit them within it. The few who had to get educated were best off in cold-water boarding schools in Scotland, where he sent a number of them. He bypassed Iban authority, such as it was, effectively becoming a sort-of chief himself. Missionaries? Not if he could help it. While there, we saw a group of Ibans setting off to join the Border Scouts. The departure ceremonies included killing a pig on the longhouse veranda and reading the lobes of its liver for omens. The Iban participants were the lean, muscled, tattooed variety. And the veranda was decorated with *pua*, some of which may have received heads when they were first woven.

We celebrated Christmas at Wilson's place, purchasing

---

[28] This period in Sarawak's history did not seem to fit in my dissertation and subsequent book, but I did cover it in a separate article, Robert Pringle, "Asun's 'Rebellion': The Growing Pains of a Tribal Society in Brooke Sarawak, 1929-40," *Sarawak Museum Journal*, Vol. XVI, Nos. 32-33 (New Series), 1968.

some Cinzano at the otherwise Spartan longhouse co-op store as our contribution to the festivities. Barbara was as usual a big hit with the Ibans, who were familiar enough with European males, but had seen relatively few European women, especially not young ones. "Are there others like you back in Kuching?" one old lady asked her. By this time we were used to providing evening longhouse entertainment, whether joining in the dancing (our inability to do the twist very well put us leagues behind most Peace Corps volunteers) or telling tall tales.

Skyscrapers had been much described by previous visitors, but polar bears were a favorite tall-tale subject—there *could not be* bears of that color! Although longhouse dwellers knew all about brownish bears, white ones did not exist in their world, and that made it all the more fun to hear about them. On another occasion a woman lost her temper at Bob for showing the assemblage how contact lenses worked. She thought it was some sort of outrageous hoax, especially because he would not let her try his on. On a sadder note, a woman once asked why we had no children, and Barbara explained about birth control pills. That led to a conference followed by a second question: if we had a pill *not* to have children, did we have one that would enable would-be mothers to *have* them? At the time of our visit, malnutrition, especially protein deficiency, often plagued upriver people and hindered conception in a society which, like most traditional societies, placed great value on children.

Further downriver in a different world around Sibu, we had our first look at the Foochow Chinese. These Methodist Chinese and their American pastor, "Tuan Hoover of Borneo," had been subject to persecution in China following the Boxer Rebellion. Hoover persuaded the second Brooke Rajah to invite them to Sarawak and give them land around Sibu to grow rice. They soon discovered that they could make more money by growing rubber, and that no amount of government regulation could prevent them from getting more land from the Ibans. Before long these ferociously effective, cognac-swilling capitalists were also dominating the nascent Sarawak timber industry. It would rapidly get bigger and they richer along with it, and once the Borneo supply of logs was largely exhausted, Sarawak Foochow companies would be—and still are at this writing—stripping tropical timber as far away as New Guinea and Suriname.

All that was in the future, but Bob got a glimpse of it when he interviewed Ling Bieng Siew, boss of the as-yet embryonic timber business in the Rejang. He was a caricature of the gimlet-eyed Chinese tycoon with "a very air-conditioned office and a very sexy secretary in a green dress."[29] He gave Bob a long lecture about the challenges and travails of entrepreneurship and a lot of baloney about how the timber further upriver (as yet unexploited) probably wasn't worth anything.

Back in Kuching we celebrated Ramadan in late January by crossing the river, along with everyone else in town, to call on the Governor, Datu Abang Haji Openg bin Sapie'e, and ask his forgiveness, according to the standard Ramadan formula, for any offenses, physical or spiritual, that we might have committed against him during the past year.

In April we visited Mukah, a small coastal town inhabited by Muslim Melanau people who lived by producing starch from the pith of sago palms. It was eaten in Sarawak and used for making laundry starch and tapioca abroad, and was once a major Sarawak export. These Muslims had still-pagan ethnic relatives living in the deep interior, some of whom we had visited a few weeks earlier. The Mukah people lived in single houses (not longhouses) over canals stained a rich brown by peat. Some of the burial posts from their pagan past were still standing. One of them gave me a tiny, old Vietnamese ceramic jar in which he had kept a pungent liniment, which we still have, and it still smells of liniment.

In 2008 Bob sent copies of the pictures he had taken in 1966 to his family, via Ann Appleton, an anthropologist working in Mukah. By this time the man who gave us the little blue-grey jar was the village patriarch. The old photos enthralled them, and in return, they sent us new photos of the whole family posing with them.

By the time of the Mukah visit, it was clear that Bob would be ready to wrap up his research and leave Sarawak by early summer, but he was not, under the terms of the London-Cornell program, supposed to be in London until the beginning of the fall term in September, so that he could give some seminars

---

[29] Bob Diary entry for December 6, 1965.

reporting his research results. What to do? The ever-generous London-Cornell Director, Professor Skinner, said not to worry, they would pay our way to travel around mainland Southeast Asia for two months, thereby using up the intervening time. It would, he thought, be good for Bob's future career, whether he went into academia or not! And so it was.

Kelabit Country

However, we still had not yet visited Sarawak's other great river, the Baram. There were not very many Ibans there, but we didn't want to miss the famous Kelabit people, or the "heart of Borneo" plateau into which then-Major Tom Harrisson had parachuted at the end of World War II as part of an operation to unleash the head-hunting dogs of war against the hapless Japanese. So we packed our baggage for direct shipment to the US, found a home for Kitty (Puppy had died of a type of distemper which attacked young dogs before they could be vaccinated with the regular vaccine), and enjoyed a round of farewell parties. Most of them took place at Chinese restaurants, causing Bob to comment that parting was such sweet-and-sour sorrow. The most memorable moment at these events occurred at a dinner given by Dr. Danny Kok and his former Peace Corps volunteer wife, Liz. There was a lull in conversation as we ate soup from a steamboat at the end of a long meal, and Barbara, endeavoring to transfer a fish ball with her chopsticks from the pot in the middle of the table to her bowl, dropped it into her beer glass. The loud hiss startled everyone, and led to much merriment about non-Chinese ineptitude with chopsticks, etc.

Bob had revived his relationship with the *Quincy Patriot Ledger*, and would write several illustrated articles for them about our travel home. The first, however, was about the Peace Corps in Sarawak.[30] It seemed to me, based largely on the views of the outgoing Peace Corps Director in Kuching, that Washington had abruptly decided to send too many volunteers to certain countries that were welcoming. One was

---

[30] Robert M. Pringle, "Peace Corps Seen Overstaffed in Sarawak," *Quincy* [MA] *Patriot Ledger*, July 30, 1966, p. 2.

Malaysia. In Sarawak, it was getting to the point where they were forming little colonies in outstations and socializing with each other rather than getting to know the local people. Moreover, during our stay, as volunteers were being posted further and further upriver, some were unhappy about accepting posts in longhouses, rather than in towns.

Tom Harrisson gave a copy of the article to the *Straits Times*[31] reporter who covered Sarawak, and the result was an article in that major newspaper based on it, which was then picked up by the Singapore bureau of *Pravda*, where it duly appeared. Needless to say I was alarmed, fearing that it might end my prospects of joining the Foreign Service. However, the State Department security people apparently never noticed it. A few years later, I discovered that the sudden influx of Peace Corps volunteers in Sarawak had been the result of a famous episode in Nigeria, where a new volunteer had written a postcard to her family telling them how awful the country was. The Nigerians read it and terminated the program, leaving a large contingent of Nigeria-bound volunteers-in-training who had to be sent somewhere else.

On June 1, we left Kuching by Air Malaysia DC-3 for Miri, the town where Brunei's oil was refined. Then, from its airport at nearby Lutong, we caught the weekly "Twin Pin" (Twin Pioneer short landing and takeoff aircraft) for Bario, the principal Kelabit settlement. The airline weighed us and our knapsack and suitcase, as it did all passengers and their bags and bundles. One quite fat Chinese trader who traveled back and forth regularly was so heavy that he was not allowed any baggage.

The Bario people knew we were coming, because Tom Harrisson had told them. So did the British military, which included a unit of the famous Gurkha mercenaries from Nepal.

[31] Geoffrey Geldard, "Peace Corps in Sarawak Under Fire: 'Just Colonies of US College Kids'," *The Straits Times*, November 11, 1966. Harrisson sent me a copy inscribed, "Bob, We hung this one on dear old Geoffrey." Of course, wicked Tom came close to hanging it on me too, as he probably realized. The new Peace Corps country director, Michael McCone, who had replaced the one whose criticisms had given me many of the ideas for the *Patriot Ledger* article, wrote a letter to the *Straits Times* which it apparently published—I have only what appears to be a proof copy—accusing me of gross inaccuracy.

Our plan, which we more or less followed, was to remain in Bario for a few days, then hike down to the main tributary of the Baram, where we would hire a boat back to the district headquarters, Marudi, before ending our stay in Sarawak. Before leaving Bario, Barbara acquired a pair of Gurkha boots for the hike; they kept out the leeches much better than Bob's tennis shoes did, and she used them for years.

Our Baram adventure turned out to be one of the highest points of our stay in Sarawak. It lasted from June 2, when we arrived in Bario, to June 27, when we left Marudi. Bob had his two Leicas, one for color and one for black-and-white, and the resulting photos tell the story of our Baram trip better than anything he can write.

We knew that everyone was accustomed to foreigners associated with the Sarawak Museum showing up and asking for help with mysterious projects. Michael Fogden, an ornithologist and today a well-known wildlife photographer, had been in the same area not long before we were, so at first the Kelabits assumed we must also be looking for birds. No, we explained, we wanted to talk to people about history. Well, that was OK too. Unfortunately we didn't get interested in birds until we were in Burkina Faso many years later, and we didn't even have a pair of binoculars with us.

The Kelabits were different from any group we had seen previously, with their irrigated rice fields (rare in Sarawak) and their stout, well-constructed longhouses. They seemed to be doing an exemplary job of pursuing modernity on their own terms. They had converted to evangelical Christianity, but had not necessarily given up drinking, long hair, or extended ear lobes for wearing earplugs or suspended earrings.

They had a great relationship with the British military, one that now seems almost impossibly harmonious in the light of later experience in other "low intensity" conflicts. It built on a heritage of good relations with the Brookes and the British who succeeded them, and the economic benefits— free helicopter rides, used fuel drums (excellent for all kinds of construction), and jobs building barracks as well as serving in the paramilitary Border Scouts. It also helped, we thought, that the British military were so light on the ground. The Brits didn't have the kind of heavy logistics and support

Dapat Arang and his wife greeting us at Pa Tik, where a British helicopter had just unloaded us for the three-day walk to Long Lellang.

Our first night on the trail from Pa Tik to the big longhouse at Long Lellang. The accommodations were definitely inferior to those we would find at Long Lellang. Seen here: Dapat Aran, Barbara, and Tengong Na, a Penan jungle nomad.

infrastructure typical of US military practice, and this seemed to make it easier for them to exist on familiar terms with local people.

As it turned out, the British military did not want us to walk over the first stretch of our proposed route because it meant going via Kubaan longhouse, from which, we later learned, their Special Air Services were running patrols into Indonesian territory. So they gave us a delightful helicopter ride to Pa Tik, which saved us three days' walk, and there we hired guides for the next stage.

Then came the fun part—three days of hiking along often leech-infested trails following a route once used by District Officers, but largely unmaintained since the advent of small aircraft. One night we huddled under a leaf and plastic sheet lean-to as it poured all night. Another time, we sheltered in a slightly more substantial structure which was the Appalachian Trail hut equivalent on this tropical route. And the Girl Scouts in Cincinnati thought they knew something about primitive camping!

That brought us to Long Lellang, a magnificent Kelabit longhouse where we spent several fascinating days. We were given some nice old beads, and on a rainy day Barbara taught the Long Lellang people how to play shuffleboard with old tobacco tins and wooden sticks, on their long, beautifully smooth verandah.

After Long Lellang we walked for two more days through country populated by Penans, jungle nomads in varying degrees of settlement. We traversed "rice fields" made by felling old-growth trees, requiring us to scramble over and around their enormous trunks. In other places there was evidence of much larger populations in the past, reduced by epidemic of some kind. Everywhere we were warmly welcomed.

Once we stayed in the first house that a small Penan family group had ever built; we really had to watch out as we stepped gingerly over the widely-spaced bamboo floor poles. They served us cassava seasoned with hot pig fat for dinner. But no one could beat these Penan women for the lovely mats and baskets they wove as they sat in their rickety dwellings and survived on cassava, pig fat, and the wild edibles from the forest—when they could find them.

On June 16 we reached Lio Mato, the settlement at the furthest upstream navigable point on the Baram. Sitting on a large flat promontory, its fort had an outhouse with the best view in the world—no doors, just endless forest and streams and mountain mist to gaze at. In the fort we witnessed a "*tamu*" (literally "meeting") between Penans selling jungle produce (wild rubber, monkey gallstones, etc.) and the women's woven products, and buying cloth, shotguns, Indonesian batik and other merchandise, with a government official on hand to make sure they were not cheated. *Tamu* were scheduled months in advance and the often illiterate Penan headmen were given a *temuku tali*, a string with knots in it. By untying one knot a day, they could tell when they should return to the meeting place. (It's interesting that Precolumbian Andean groups used a similar system of knotted strings to keep track of meetings and market days.)

After the *tamu* was over we hired a boat to go down the Baram, lined at long intervals by Kenyah and Kayan longhouses. This lovely trip ended at Marudi, the first Residential headquarters in the Fourth Division, which had been replaced by Miri in the 1920s. The most interesting result, from an historian's point of view, was to preserve Marudi's Charles Brooke-era layout and buildings, and Bob enjoyed comparing the current town with old photos he had seen.

From Marudi, we proceeded by air and slow boat to our last stop, the Harrissons' archaeological site at Niah Cave. Only Barbara Harrisson was there, and she showed us the current excavations as well as explaining how the local settled Punans collected guano (bird or bat manure) and birds' nests. The Sarawak Museum, at that point, regulated the collecting of both. They restricted the number of birds' nests which could be harvested, and when, to ensure the survival of the swift population in the cave.

This was important because rights to collect in various parts of the cave were heritable, and over-eager owners could have done great damage by over-harvesting as better poles (used to reach the cave ceiling where the nests were) came with more trade and more modern materials. The guano collectors, on the other hand, seemed to have an inexhaustible supply, and were limited to four days' work a week so that the local, impoverished Iban population could collect one day a week "for their own gardens," but as Bob said in his diary, probably "for their own pockets" instead.

It had rained quite a bit before our visit and the trail of boards to the cave was often submerged; we marveled at how the guano carriers could navigate them with their heavy loads. We stayed overnight in the Harrissons' little field bungalow, and Bob spent the following day interviewing the local Ibans, moved to the area several generations previously from the Second Division, and not thriving in their current home. That evening we boarded a small, rickety launch back to Miri. Crossing the bar into the Baram delta, it bumped and pitched as the waves caused it to hit the sandy bottom, and Bob wrote that he could think only of Tennyson's poem "Crossing the Bar," as a boatman stabbed his red-and-white pole into the water calling out *Lima kaki se-tengah* (5½ feet) over and over again.

When we arrived in Miri at 6:30 a.m., a former colleague of Barbara's from Batu Lintang, Mary Chua, welcomed us into her house for the day, to clean up and rest before our flight to Brunei. We were startled that she left the gas burners on her stove lighted when she went to school. Though there were no tiny children to get into trouble playing with fire, we turned them off, but when she came back, she laughed, "Oh, we all leave our burners on; it's cheaper than buying matches." It turned out that the oil company was simply providing the town with cooking gas (no question of needing to heat houses) that would otherwise be flared off at the wellheads. After treating us to a lavish meal at a Chinese restaurant, Mary put us on the plane for Brunei—a half-hour flight, but there was no road between Miri and Brunei Town.

Home via Brunei, Angkor and More

On June 29, 1966, our Sarawak stay was over, and we were in the Sultanate of Brunei, with its big Italian marble mosque, built in 1959 with oil revenues, looming over a village built on stilts. It is the only surviving example of the "water city" style typical of Southeast Asia's early coastal states based on trade, the precursors of modern Singapore. We were hosted by our friend Pengiran Sharifuddin, the curator of the new Brunei Museum, and accommodated in its new guesthouse. He was just our age, had been educated abroad, and while we lived in Kuching had been at the Sarawak Museum to reclaim the cannons captured from the Sultan in various conflicts with the Brookes and to bring them back to his country's new museum. In fact, the outhouse for the guesthouse had been constructed of ex-packing crates for the cannons, which were still labeled "Sarawak Museum." Imagine any plumbing that primitive in wealthy Brunei today.

The highlight there was an extraordinary dinner, to which Sharifuddin invited us, hosted by his uncle Haji Usop, the Chief Minister. All the other guests, including many senior Brits, old Malay-world hands serving the Sultan, were dressed formally, but we had only what we had carried in our backpacks from Bario. When we apologized to our host about our informality, he said, "Oh, don't worry, the rest of them only do it to impress me!" Then he proudly showed us his collection of cigarette lighters, many of them models of fancy cars.

We had time to drive around and appreciate Brunei's varied population, and to buy some hand-woven, gold-thread silk brocade—much more expensive though not as well woven as the sarong length of silver thread weaving we bought a few weeks later in Kelantan (Malaya) that became Annie's wedding dress. The latter was originally to have been for one of Barbara's sisters, but Jane had married Ron before our return and fashionista Susie had other ideas. So Annie inherited a lovely piece of silk that was perfect for her.

Following our instructions to see more of Southeast Asia, we moved on to Sabah, where we spent five days. Sabah was a lot more developed than Sarawak, with extensive plantation agriculture as befitted a former "chartered company." Jesselton, the capital, having been bombed flat during World War II, was a raw clutter of new buildings, so we paused there only briefly. Sabah has a narrow-gauge railroad, and we rode it between Beaufort and Tenom (there was no road), through the spectacular Padas Gorge, where the train was stopped by a landslide. We had to get out and walk with our luggage to the train on the other side; its passengers were doing the same in reverse.

We visited Charlotte Cooper, a widowed friend of Barbara's Aunt Alice, a Peace Corps volunteer nurse and "health visitor." It struck us that elderly PCVs were often more effective than younger ones in societies where age is respected; in fact, the only concession that seemed to have been made to Charlotte's age was that all her clinics were on the railroad—no hiking or jolting in 4-wheel-drive vehicles to get to them. And she baked a mean apple pie in her wood stove oven. (This was just before "Miz Lillian," President Carter's mother, served as a volunteer in India.)

We reached the east coast of Sabah and the town of Sandakan on July 9 and found it depressing. Like Jesselton, old Sandakan had been destroyed by World War II. Now it was block after block of concrete buildings, the population entirely Chinese, the harbor crowded with freighters loading logs, for Sabah had gotten a jump on the rest of Borneo in the timber business. We saw no point in lingering there, and on July 11 we flew to Singapore a day ahead of schedule. We did not climb Mt. Kinabalu.

In Singapore we stayed again with Edwin Lee's charming and hospitable family. His father knew everything about Singapore politics and society, and he treated us to more of its incomparable street food. We went on to Malacca, where we enjoyed its pretty Chinese temples and wondered how such a tiny harbor could have served as the dominant port-city of its namesake straits. (Answer: The port had probably silted up since the sixteenth century.) From there we went on to Kuala Lumpur, where we stayed with Otto and Barbara Doering, our agricultural economist friend and his wife.

Along the way Bob interviewed academics and others relevant to his research, including historian Wang Gung-wu, dean of Malaysian historians, and C.C. Too, who had been groomed by Bob's professor, O.W. Wolters, to be his successor specialist on psychological warfare against the communist Chinese rebellion, by now almost over. We visited George Elliston in the fishing village where he was doing research, and traveled to Kuantan on the solidly Muslim-Malay East Coast, where we bought Annie's wedding brocade, mentioned earlier.

Our next stop was Bangkok, by air. Barbara had never been there, so there was a lot to see. We stayed at a hotel over the railroad station, an unair-conditioned colonial relic with marble floors and potted palms, which Bob remembered from his 1961 visit, rapidly being made unlivable by the fumes and din of Bangkok traffic. We were told that we could continue into Cambodia by land, but when we arrived by train at the border a few days later, it was closed. The only way to enter Cambodia legally was to return to Bangkok by bus (the train having already departed on its return trip) and fly from there, but the next flight to Phnom Penh left in a week, so we took another train to Chiang Mai in northern Thailand to kill time.

Bob was happy to see lots of wood-burning steam locomotives, many of them American-made, still in use, and we could see a few Khmer ruins from the glory days of Angkor from the train. Chiang Mai had grown since Bob's previous visit six years earlier, but was still fun to explore, especially its famous silverwork and other handicrafts, sold in small shops all around a grassy central *maidan*. Barbara particularly admired the hammered silver work, and planned someday to acquire a large punch bowl decorated with intricate dancing figures and other Thai motifs. But she never went back, and, in truth, never had that much use for a punch bowl. Bob spent some of his time trying to learn about relations between the Thai government and the northern hill tribes.

We finally got to Cambodia by air on August 5. Our Phnom Penh flight was bound for Saigon (which we had decided was too expensive to visit due to the growing US military presence) and former Vice President Nixon was on board. Why, we wondered, would a washed-up, second-rate politician be junketing around Southeast Asia as if he expected to be president some day? After deplaning during the refueling stop, where we caught a glimpse of this has-been, he reboarded the plane and continued to Saigon.

We transferred to a DC-3 for the flight to Siem Reap, site of the biggest concentration of Angkorean ruins. Barbara was illegally carrying Cambodian currency, because that is what one supposedly had to do to avoid the outrageous official exchange rate. She was terrified, but bravely stuffed the *reals* in her bra and did not get caught, perhaps because, in order to accommodate a large tour group on the DC-3 flight to Siem Reap, the airline had left most of its luggage behind in Bangkok. The chaos upon landing, and the loud complaints of the luggage-less tourists, left the customs officials unable to worry about anything else. We had our backpack full of dirty clothes, but not the suitcase with clean ones. We won't ever forget climbing back into sweaty underwear and socks after bathing that evening. Our suitcase caught up with us on the next day's flight; Bob got a photo of it, or the DC-3 carrying it, flying over Angkor Wat, the biggest and most famous temple.

August turned out to be a good time to visit Angkor. The rainy season had started and everything was lush and green, much pleasanter than it had been during Bob's March 1961 visit, or than it would be when we returned in 2005. On both those occasions the forest was sere and dry, the tendril-covered monuments looking bare and unromantic, and it was much hotter.

We found a simple hotel room in the Chinese quarter; there was, as of 1966, no Western-style hotel in town except for the very expensive *Auberge des Temples* across from Angkor Wat.[32] The day after our arrival we rented bicycles and ended up pedaling many miles through and around the ancient Cambodian capital. When we ran out of water in those days before bottled water, we dipped water out of the stagnant irrigation canals and purified it with chlorine tablets, and got thoroughly exhausted. That was clearly not too bright, and for the rest of our stay we either rented pedicabs or cadged rides with low-end tours.

This time Bob knew quite a lot about Angkor from his Cornell studies and did not make mistakes such as skipping Banteai Srei, perhaps the most beautiful attraction, but located in an outlying area. He carefully took pictures of the famous Bayon reliefs depicting everyday life and warfare in thirteenth-century Cambodia, which were still in pristine condition. By the time we visited again in 2005 they had been

[32] For the non-cognoscenti, "Angkor" means the entire area of the ancient Cambodian (or Khmer) capital or state; "Angkor Wat" is the name of one very famous temple which was never totally abandoned or destroyed, as most other Angkorean buildings were.

badly damaged, not so much by Khmer Rouge vandalism or antiquity theft—both did occur, but not significantly at the Bayon—but by a botched Indian effort at preservation.

Milton Osborne was in Cambodia doing his doctoral research. The original plan had been to meet him in Siem Reap and tour its temples with him, but by the time we arrived, he had returned to the archives in Phnom Penh. So we headed for the capital city via a fascinating local bus ride. The driver stopped to let us photograph an ancient Khmer bridge which the road still crossed, and we bought fried shrimp cakes at the ferry crossing of the Mekong, another health risk which turned out OK. In Phnom Penh we stayed in the old colonial hotel, complete with ceiling fans and enormous bathrooms with *mandi*-style washing facilities—very pleasant. Milton showed us around, and we had a good visit to Phnom Penh's important museum. From Cambodia we flew to Laos. There we stayed at a USAID guesthouse thanks to Norm Sweet, an old friend from Korea and before, then the USAID Program Officer for Laos. We met and were taken around Luang Prabang by Tae Tong, (newly married and then Mme Sabab Bounyavong), a great friend of Kate's from the time of her exchange visits to the US.

Laos was playing out its traditional role as buffer state between contending powers, in this case the US and Vietnam (in the previous century it had been Britain and France), and there was massive evidence of the Vietnam war, from fighter jet contrails overhead to US military personnel in the bars of Vientiane. We were fascinated by the rich diversity of Laos and hoped to see more of its colorful hill tribes.

Partly for that reason we wanted to visit Luang Prabang, the "Royal Capital," further up the Mekong. Here we discovered a problem: our official American friends knew little about how ordinary people got around Laos, because they always went by Air America, the CIA-operated "airline," which non-officials could not use. So on a stormy morning we set off for Luang Prabang on the most terrifying flight of our lives thus far, by Veha-Akhat, or *Société Anonyme de Transports Aériens Lao.* (Bob kept our ticket.)

We later learned that Air America had cancelled its flight to Luang Prabang because of the weather that day, but Veha Akhat was not fazed. Our ex-Air Vietnam DC3, replete with broken, velvet-covered seats, pitched and groaned through the clouds low enough so that now and then we could glimpse mountain peaks higher than we were, illuminated by lightning flashes.

But the trip was worth it. We stayed at "The Bungalow," the only hotel in town, with a fabulous view over the Mekong, already roaring down from Tibet in what turned out to be a record flood. We saw interesting USAID projects and plenty of tribal minorities, including Meos in full regalia, many of whom are probably now living in Wisconsin or Minnesota, there better known as Hmong. The CIA was famously arming and supporting the Meos against the communists, which is the reason most of them came to the US after the CIA lost the war. And while it's a shame that the Free World may have lost Laos, it has to be said that Luang Prabang, now at peace, with its charming *wats* and interesting cultures, is much better off today. It is a world heritage site and major tourist destination, which we visited again in 2005.

Getting away from Laos was an adventure. The Sweets did not know that ordinary people needed *exit visas* to leave Laos, and neither did we. We found out too late. It was Sunday afternoon and all offices in somnolent Vientiane were shut tight. No amount of official American pleading at the airport could get us on our flight. We had onward connections from Bangkok the next evening on Pan Am's round-the-world flight, of fragrant memory.

"Well," someone told us, "that's easy: you just go down to the river and cross into Thailand by boat, and you get the train to Bangkok from Nong Khai. The Lao won't know you've left and the Thai [who didn't think highly of their rustic ethnic confreres, the Lao] won't ask for a visa." And so it came to pass that Robert and Barbara Pringle are still officially in Laos.

Norm Sweet, perhaps feeling bad about our messy departure, more than compensated—to the extent that it was his fault—by buying for us a Kha Drum, allegedly bullet-scarred while being transported down the Mekong, an authentic Great Bronze Drum of Southeast Asia. He shipped it home to us months later in his household effects and it has lived in our living room ever since.[33]

It turned out that the train from Nong Khai conveniently stopped at the Bangkok airport, the last stop before Bangkok itself. We got off, ran across the tracks, and struggled into the airport. Bob was unshaven, both of us were filthy, lugging a large green suitcase, a battered grey knapsack (veteran of the Baram trek), a large wicker basket with a paper umbrella between the handles, a basket of fruit, Bob's black camera bag (by then falling apart) and Barbara's Penan purse. But we got into the airport and found a friendly Thai Pan Am representative, who got us into the transit lounge, where there was a shower and access to a shiny, modern restaurant.

Once on the plane Bob wrote nostalgically about the train ride:

This watery world of lower Thailand still has a magic quality, with its emerald rice and teeming klongs [canals] . . . . This is the bright, clean face of Thailand seen from a train window, a land of attractive yeoman farmers with enough room to breathe and enough rice to eat. And there is plenty of real economic development going on—not just good roads (heavily subsidized by the US) . . . . No doubt the Vietnam War is pumping in a lot. A huge new US base is opening up on the Gulf of Siam and will hold the SAC [US Strategic Air Command] jet tankers which refuel fighters over Vietnam and which now land here at Don Muang [the Bangkok Airport]—we saw several come in tonight, their fuel appendages dangling, interspersed amid the bright jet liners full of businessmen and tourists.[34]

London Again, then Back to Cornell

It took twenty hours to reach Frankfort, with stops in Rangoon, Karachi, Beirut, Istanbul and Vienna. We were going to stop for a day or two in Rangoon but because of the delay caused by our unorthodox departure we had to rebook on a flight one day later than planned and had to skip Rangoon due to

---

[33] Its style suggests that the drum is not one of the really old bronze drums found all over Southeast Asia. My hunch is that it is one of the ones made in China for export to hill tribes in Indochina as late as the 1920s. The one that daughter Anne has is a modern imitation of the really old ones, from Laos.

[34] Bob Diary entry for August 22, 1966.

commitments in Europe.

After a short stay in Germany with Barbara's former roommate Helen Knoll and her husband, we split. Barbara continued home via London to see her family, acquire a car, and find an apartment for us in Ithaca. I went to Amsterdam, where I spent nine days interviewing retired Dutch colonial officials who had worked in the Iban areas of what was then Dutch Borneo. This turned out to be extraordinarily easy. I got the names of the relevant officials from the Royal Tropical Institute near The Hague, then went to the government pension office to find out which ones were still alive (most of them were) and how to call them. Language was not a problem since virtually all the retirees spoke fair-to-good English. One was a Eurasian with a son and two daughters in the US. Getting around Holland for the interviewing was also a cinch. As for the telephones, they had instructions in seven languages and seemed miraculous after the British antiquities with their thruppenny bits and saucer-sized pennies. My only complaint with the Netherlands was that I couldn't find anywhere to stay for less than $5 a night, including breakfast.

Back in London, I stayed at London House, a fancy new University of London international hostel. I visited the Isle of Wight to meet A. B. Ward, a retired Brooke official; Otto Doering and I were helping him to publish his memoirs, *Rajah's Servant*.[35] I also attended the annual Sarawak cocktail party, "a huge, noisy affair at the United Services Club." The toast was "Sarawak, coupled with the name of Brooke!"[36] I saw Brooke family members again, including Lady Anne Bryant. I wrote:

Lady Anne is very nice indeed. She says Sir Arthur [Bryant], her husband, an extremely successful historian, does make money writing books. I'll bet. She has amazing grey-green eyes. I wonder if those are Brooke? [37]

I must have given the requisite London-Cornell seminars,

---

[35] Kathy will remember helping us to proofread the manuscript in Helena's attic at 103 Prince Street months later.

[36] Covered in Bob Diary entry for September 24, 1966.

[37] Ibid.

but can't remember or find any record of them. On October 15, 1966, I flew back to the US, finding the service "drab and commonplace" after trans-Pacific travel.

Meanwhile Barbara had found us a furnished, second-floor apartment at 222 University Avenue, on the precipitous slope between the Cornell campus and downtown Ithaca and within walking distance of the main Cornell library. Kate wrote to Bob, "You do seem to have arranged your fall schedule rather neatly to be able to walk into an all-settled home."[38] Clay helped us to buy our first car, a Chevrolet Corvair, of the kind that made Ralph Nader famous. It was OK for us, but unstable at any speed when going down Ithaca's steep hills, until we put sandbags in the front.

Once moved in, which, since the apartment was furnished, involved unpacking the trunk from England, buying a few dishes and pots and pans, and dealing with the shipping crate from Sarawak once it arrived, Barbara began to work on an MA in medieval European history. The year turned out to be an entertaining exposure to what it meant to study one period in some depth, including a dose of medieval Latin, but, in retrospect, it's a good thing that Bob's career, in an age where married couples did not live separately for minor details like advanced degrees, prevented more years of study in the same field. I was never cut out to be an ivory tower scholar, and that was what medievalists in those days tended to be. I've enjoyed exploring the contemporary world in its many aspects as I lived and taught a wide range of historical topics, and even other subjects, in the US and abroad.

However, the year was not wasted. My fellow graduate students in medieval history that year were a lively group, and I enjoyed studying with them. For a while, I kept in touch with Richard Marks, who had entertained us all with his tales of growing up in an ultra-Orthodox New York Jewish family, but I gradually lost track of the others. While they all earned their doctorates, only one, John Dahmus, found a university teaching job, and he has had a distinguished career at Stephen F. Austin State University in Texas. The problem was that those World War II vets who had started college in 1947 and then gone on to get PhDs were still fairly young and occupying almost

---

[38] Kate letter to Bob, September 14, 1966.

all available history teaching jobs at the university level. I, meanwhile, with that MA and the teaching certification I had earned as an undergraduate, was well-placed to earn what then passed for a high secondary-school teaching salary.

Throughout this period Bob pounded away on his thesis at 102 West Avenue, the office of the Cornell Modern Indonesia Project. It was a creaky old fraternity house that had been condemned as unfit for undergraduate residence, but deemed safe enough for graduate study, which, in theory, never included sleeping there. At least one couple we know broke that rule. Every month or so, Bob took another chapter or two to Professor Wolters, who was unfailingly helpful. Sometime in 1967 he passed his Foreign Service orals, meaning that he would soon begin working for the State Department. In June we took a break from academics and visited the Expo world's fair in Montreal.

We entertained occasionally at our hillside apartment. On one unforgettable occasion in mid-April, we hosted a reception for a visiting London member of the London-Cornell Project. The Project paid for a gallon and a half of sherry. The guests, mostly male, had such a fine time that none of them went home at the hour that evening receptions usually end, so Barbara roasted a chicken we happened to have in the fridge. "It is amazing how many people one chicken will feed if they've had enough sherry," she wrote. "The party ended at midnight and from the looks of people the next day, Bob figures it cost the Southeast Asian History department about thirty man-hours of work."[39]

Bob traveled to Washington in mid-August, leaving Barbara to finish her own thesis as well as to get his in final. It came to over seven hundred pages of typescript and cost about $700 to type, which we were later able to deduct from taxes because of book royalties. At the time, Bob made two copies with photographs. Before long he would be working on the book version, *Rajahs and Rebels*, for Macmillan (UK) and eventually the Cornell University Press.

---

[39] Barbara letter to her parents, April 14, 1967.

5

Beginning Diplomacy: from Washington to Indonesia, 1967-1970

While Barbara stayed in Ithaca, making sure that our respective dissertations were typed and accepted, I came to Washington in late 1967 and began the introductory course for Foreign Service Officers at the Foreign Service Institute in Rosslyn, across the Potomac from Georgetown. I stayed in Alexandria at 103 Prince Street with mother, who was struggling with her latest writing project, her financial problems and her ongoing fear that 103 Prince Street was about to fall down around her ears. (At this writing in 2016, the tiny old house is still standing and has recently been on the market for over $900,000.)

Barbara, meanwhile, was perched on a hassock in front of a typewriter on a trunk in the grad-student apartment of a friend. In the typewriter was her non-masterpiece MA thesis, "The Study of History in the Middle Ages." Conclusion: there wasn't any real history, meaning the examination and analysis of events and their causes, being written in the Middle Ages. Rather, the monks, the only literate class, kept chronological lists of events they considered important, like royal reign years, ditto for abbots and bishops, and occasional natural wonders, like comets, and glorious (or not) royal battles. She also proofread and saw to the typing and binding of my thesis.

I was the oldest person by far in my Basic Officers' Course, and, lawyers aside, almost the only one with a graduate degree. There were about thirty-five of us but only five women and, as far as I can recall, no people of color. Otherwise I found the class surprisingly diverse. The ladies included Xenia Vunovich, fluent in Serbo-Croatian, and Deborah Duda, who had just spent two years making and selling papier-mâché jewelry on the French Riviera. Then there was Theodore Roosevelt IV, who was indeed a relative of TR and had graduated from Harvard after me. The Foreign Service had the temerity to send him to Ouagadougou on his maiden assignment.

First Assignment: Intelligence and Research (INR)

I was the only one in my class to be assigned to Washington. Most new FSOs yearned for an initial assignment to Paris or at least Rio, certainly not Ouagadougou, and even more emphatically not Foggy Bottom! It happened because Tom Hughes, Director of State's Bureau of Intelligence and Research (INR), had been having problems with a young staff assistant, who showed no respect for the foreign affairs specialists whom Hughes recruited from academia to serve as regional office directors. He figured that a new staff assistant with a little more gravitas, who at least knew what a PhD was, would be an improvement, and I got the job. Hughes' concept of leavening his government staff with non-government specialists was a good one, but it did not long survive his time in INR.

I was initially somewhat disappointed by my assignment to INR, but since Jamie was on the way there was much to be said for staying near Washington for two years and learning more about the inner workings of the State Department. There was no better place to do that than INR, the State Department's window into the "intelligence community." This far-flung entity, supposedly "coordinated" by the CIA, included military intelligence organizations and exotic, usually very secret, components such as code-making and breaking (the National Security Agency) and satellite photography (a branch of CIA).

INR did not plan covert action or run spies, but it did play an important role in the analysis of "intelligence" (defined as information from all sources) and the production of reports on important subjects on which everyone agreed, often only after strenuous debate. One of my functions was to accompany the Director of INR to meetings of the US Intelligence Board, which produced such reports. I learned a lot about the CIA and how it works, a subject at least as mysterious as any foreign country, and emerged knowing quite a bit about the nature of the information base that in theory supported the making of policy.

INR consisted mostly of country analysts grouped in regional offices. The analysts, usually quite junior, were divided between Foreign Service Officers (who served abroad and in Washington) and Civil Servants (who normally stayed in Washington). For FSOs focused on career advancement, INR was not a prize assignment. They felt it was preferable to be in one of the regional bureaus, which dominated the policy process and had the major say in deciding future assignments. On the other hand, many of the Civil Servants were veterans of the old World War II Office of Strategic Services (OSS). They were deeply knowledgeable and were complemented by the academic experts that Hughes recruited. The whole system was enriched by a robust system of "External Research," which recruited additional academics for specific research projects.

The INR front office, where I worked, housed the Director and three deputies. Much of my work involved helping with the production of analytic reports, edited by a team headed by Allan Evans, a retired professor of medieval economic history, plus anything else that Hughes wanted me to do. Hughes was an urbane cynic from Minnesota, immensely proud of having been a Rhodes Scholar. He was addicted to writing witty speeches, which he sent with little signed notes to friends in the foreign policy world.

He loved to convoke annual meetings of senior policy officials to quiz them about what kind of intelligence they would like to have from those who produced it. The tenor of the collective response was predictable: the policy people, mostly FSOs, had little respect for intelligence (except Foreign Service reporting), but would never agree to give up any of it. Hughes roared with laughter about this in private.

INR also provided oral intelligence briefings to the Secretary of State and his senior staff, including the assistant secretaries in charge of regional bureaus (Bureau of European Affairs, *etcetera*). The "briefers" gathered in the INR conference room at an ungodly hour of the morning to assemble loose-leaf notebooks filled with information on the latest foreign news, classified and otherwise. Then, at the opening of business, the briefers would hurry to the offices of the briefees, and go through the notebooks, explaining and condensing the contents to suit the interests of each recipient. Tom personally briefed the Secretary of State, his deputy briefed the Deputy Secretary, and the head of each INR regional office head did the same with the Assistant Secretary in each regional bureau. In this way the briefers achieved close personal relationships with senior officials and sometimes influenced policy, which made it all seem worthwhile.

Another INR specialty in the 1960s was the "briefing note." It was a short, *ad hoc* news item at any level of classification, about what in journalism would be called a "breaking story." Any analyst, however junior, could type one out on a form with many carbon copies and send it to the INR front office. Typos and cross-outs were allowed in the interest of speedy processing. If a note was approved, and they usually were, it was sent directly to the Secretary of State, with duplicates to relevant senior officials. One of my jobs was to hand-carry briefing notes to the office of the Secretary, at the time Dean Rusk, who actually read many of them. We could tell if he had because the top copy of the note was always sent back to us, and, if the Secretary had read it, it bore his initials. Success!

INR gained much of its clout from the fact that, within the State Department, it was the exclusive purveyor of "code word" intelligence, meaning something based on information obtained by intercepting and reading other countries' messages. Old-line diplomats did not really approve of this; one of them (Henry L. Stimson) had once remarked that "Gentlemen do not read other gentlemen's mail." But by my time in INR, such punctiliousness was long since a thing of the past and everyone wanted access to this ultra secret stuff. A special "code word" security clearance was necessary to read intercepted material, and the reports, along with satellite photography, which was then even more highly classified, were retained in a special INR office with a bland, meaningless title.

During my time in INR, David Kahn published *The Code Breakers*, a comprehensive history of codes and code breaking. All employees of INR were immediately required to sign a statement swearing that we would not read this work or discuss its contents, resulting in an immediate rush out the door at lunch time to the nearest book store. Disappointment resulted: very few of us could begin to understand the math involved.

By mid-October of 1967, both my and Barbara's dissertations were typed and approved and I drove north to Ithaca in our Corvair to pick her up. On the way back we stopped in New York to visit Uncle Max and his wife, Anne. He took us to a nice steak dinner in Greenwich Village and Barbara had a severe stomach upset afterwards, perhaps indicating that Jamie was on the way. Within a short time we had rented an apartment in Arlington in Colonial Village, a World War II garden apartment complex similar to Buckingham, not far away, where Clay and Charlotte had lived when Barbara was born.

Now equipped with an MA (to be awarded in January) in addition to my New York state permanent teaching certificate, I, Barbara, was hoping to teach after we learned we were staying in Washington. But there was a hitch: I was unable even to consider a permanent teaching job because by second semester, when I would have been hired, my pregnancy would "show."

I had to content myself with some volunteer work and taking a correspondence course in educational philosophy from the University of Nebraska in order to qualify for Virginia certification for possible future use. That effort was memorable only for its sad commentary on university standards in some parts of our country; the professor almost swooned in his complimentary comments about my one-page essays on Socrates simplified and other challenging topics. However, it paid off in a part-time job teaching World History and giving background lectures to English classes (the fun part of the job) at Washington and Lee High School during the first year of our new son's life.

*(Left) New dad bringing his son home from the hospital. (Right)
Barbara and Jamie in his christening gown, at 103 Prince Street
when his Grandmother Helena lived there.*

Jamie Arrives

Jamie arrived early on June 10, 1968. We had been at a party in Bethesda with friends from Bob's Foreign Service class (some of whom were still in Washington studying various languages prior to going abroad), and our host had scoped out the route to Bethesda Naval Hospital—where, of course, we had no right to go—just in case. We all teased him royally, but shortly after we arrived back in Arlington, my water broke, and Jamie was born early the next morning.

Reverend Russell Stroup christened him at the Georgetown Presbyterian Church, which Bob's father and Kate had attended and Kate still did. As an infant and toddler, Jamie was as happy and generally calm as the photos above suggest, not unlike his own son, Alexander. Also like Alexander, he walked late and he began to talk late.

Jamie took his first vacation when he was about six weeks old, in a rented cottage at Bethany Beach on the Eastern Shore which his Grandma and Grandpa Cade paid for so that they could spend time with their first two grandchildren, Heidi and Jamie. This was the beginning of a tradition that lasted right through college for the oldest four grandchildren (later including Heather and Annie). Perhaps remembering the kindness of both the Pettersen and Cade grandparents in having their own four daughters for long visits during summer and Easter vacations in the 1950s, Clay and Char often welcomed their grandchildren at Park Lane and, later, at the beach house in Pine Knoll Shores. Before that, there was one more summer, at a larger and fancier cottage, also in Bethany Beach—and then we were off to tropical beaches half a world away for the next seven years of Pringle family vacations.

Jamie, three months old when the school year 1968-69 started, spent mornings while I was teaching at the home of his "best friend" Michael, son of neighbors who worked for the CIA. Michael had been born with a cleft palate and therefore needed constant attention and several operations which precluded his mother's going back to work. For me, the three hours a day in the adult world were a great transition from complete freedom to the constant responsibilities of motherhood.

The pre-Jamie period had been marked by a big upheaval for the country and the District of Columbia. Martin Luther King was assassinated on April 4, 1968. Many government workers were sent home as rioting began in the black areas of DC, but Bob had to work late. His route to the State Department was unaffected by the turmoil, so as dusk was falling I drove across the Theodore Roosevelt Bridge to pick him up. We will never forget the sight of the Fourteenth Street corridor in flames across the river as we drove a colleague of his home to Alexandria along the George Washington Parkway.

We spent all four Christmases between Sarawak and Indonesia in Cincinnati. In 1966, special guests were Ruth Rach, the AFS exchange student who spent most of the school year with our family in Mariemont, and Henry Lian, a Kelabit student at Ohio State who was studying aviation and trying to get a pilot's license. We had fun with him over vacation, but later he had an aviation accident and unfortunately never completed the training he had come for, although he found a good career after that.[1] Presumably the Kelabits had been hoping that one of their own would set up an air service to serve the isolated area where they lived. Kathy was back from her first year at Radcliffe, and Heidi was having her first Cade Christmas.

On Christmas Day in 1967, the family assembled at 6508 Park Lane, and Heidi, at the unwrap-everybody's-presents-for-them stage, provided most of the entertainment. By 1968, Jamie had arrived, and we combined the trip to Cincinnati with a visit to Grandmother and Grandfather Cade in Oak Park—the occasion of those wonderful photos of him playing with Grandfather Cade on the floor of their Oak Park apartment.

A Major Family Change

By this time Kate had married Mark Massel, creating a major and very positive change in our family. Mark was a prominent lawyer and economist, specializing in competition, anti-trust, monopolies and government regulation. His parents were Jews who had emigrated from Russia and Belarus and had settled in Brooklyn at about the same time that Bob's grandfather, James Maxwell Pringle, was arriving in New York from South Carolina. Both of his parents were multi-talented, with a strong interest in Jewish culture but primarily secular in outlook. His father, Jacob, had run a large printing company, among other occupations.

Like Henry Pringle, Mark Massel had come to Washington during World War II and worked for a number of New Deal agencies, including the quasi-socialist NRA (National Recovery Agency). He had degrees in both law and economics, and after the war had moved to Chicago to work for a large law firm, Bell, Boyd, Marshall and Lloyd. In 1958 he had moved back to Washington to do research at the Brookings Institution, where he wrote a book on monopoly and competition.[2] He then left Brookings and began a diverse career of consultation, increasingly on international economic issues. One of his consultancies was with the Sanford Ink Company, then family-

---

[1] Personal communication from Jayl Langub, University of Malaysia (Sarawak).

[2] Mark S. Massel, *Competition and Monopoly: Legal and Economic Issues*, Washington, DC, Brookings, 1962.

owned, which he helped to expand into Mexico and Venezuela. He had become a major shareholder of Sanford and although Mark would have preferred it to expand on its own, he did well when the company sold out in 1984. When his wife, whom we never knew, died in 1965, mutual friends introduced him to Kate at a dinner party and they were married the next year. He had two daughters, Lynn and Joan, who, together with their children and husbands, became friends and family to us.

Mark was bluff and dogmatic. I remember once losing an argument with him about the pros and cons of Kodak being forced to end its monopoly on processing Kodachrome. I adored Kodachrome and the fact that it was sold only with Kodak processing included; he applauded the anti-trust action that destroyed this efficient arrangement. He was not in the habit of letting his less qualified interlocutors down gently. He could not understand or abide Margot, not least because she reciprocated his feelings, but he tried to help her deal with her own children. To be fair, he could be equally tough with his own children, especially the free-spirited Joan.

He realized that Kate, the ultimate lady, was just what he needed to compensate for his own rough edges. They shared passionate interests in music, theater, travel, canoeing, hiking and a wide range of good causes. He liked California, and when they moved to Carmel, he totally appreciated that she was that rarity, a true native Californian with a deep and abiding knowledge of its varied beauty. More importantly, he gave her a degree of security, both emotional and economic, which had been sorely lacking during her years with Henry Pringle.

After Henry died in 1958, Kate had sold their house at 3319 N Street, and bought a smaller one at 2911 O Street. This is where she gave the party to introduce Barbara to our friends, where the episode with Arthur Schlesinger, Jr., and the exploding cherry tomato took place (see Chapter 3). She had joined the State Department's Bureau of Cultural Affairs, where she worked on exchange programs and traveled widely, especially to Latin America, until after she married Mark.

She eventually sold the O Street house, but kept the proceeds in a separate account, which, in a typical act of generosity and kindness, she willed to Margot and me. It is no overstatement to say that the 2911 O Street money has enabled us to live comfortably in retirement, and to set some aside for our own grandchildren's college educations. The house is a stylish little number on the edge of Rock Creek Park and is obviously being appreciated by its current owners.[3]

Vietnam War-era Washington

When we first discovered that we would be staying in Washington and were just settling in to our apartment in Arlington, we were flummoxed by a request from Helena to borrow $200. That was a third of Bob's bi-weekly take-home pay, and we were living paycheck to paycheck at the time. When it became clear that she was behind on her mortgage payments, Barbara's father Clay offered to help, and the upshot was that we took title to 103 Prince Street in return for a promissory note ($5000 after five years or upon sale of 103) to Helena and an agreement to support her housing expenses in future.

At the time, the remaining mortgage was $18,000; she had bought the house for $10,000, so she must already have been borrowing against it.[4] Clay agreed to loan us the mortgage payments (interest-free) until we could manage them ourselves, and Helena remained in the house while we stayed in Arlington. We eventually paid him back in full, but we could never repay fully his kindness in paying that $200 plus monthly mortgage payments at a time when he and Char still faced college expenses for Barbara's two youngest sisters as well as, undoubtedly, continuing payments on the mortgage for 6508 Park Lane.

At about the same time, we discovered that Helena owed the tax man substantial payments for capital gains taxes on stock which she had inherited from her father and which she had been selling off over the years to support herself. She had not filed returns in about ten years, because, she said, she

---

[3] This account of Kate and Mark is based in part on "Memories of Mark Massel," which Kate wrote for a family gathering on June 17, 1989, after his death.

[4] Records labelled "HHS" in family file drawers; see especially "HHS Support," "HHS Support (misc)," and "Records Directly Relevant to HHS Support."

never had any income. But she had kept all records that she considered relevant stuffed into old shoe boxes. Barbara set about straightening this out, necessary in order to qualify her for Social Security, and even more important, though we had no inkling at the time, making her eligible for Medicaid when it was created shortly thereafter. It was Medicaid that paid for her long stay in Woodbine Nursing Center, when round-the-clock care became necessary and we were headed abroad again.

We had a lively time in Arlington. Besides the Freemans and other neighborhood friends, Kate's younger stepdaughter, Joan, and her first husband Steve Silard, lived in Washington and had a son, Tony, about a year older than Jamie. He later went on to head an NGO working to provide Kenyan schools with desks and textbooks, a follow-up to Peace Corps service there. We visited Joan's beachfront condo several times, during one of which the first astronauts landed on the moon. Jamie watched this historic event on TV; it happened shortly before midnight but, little dickens, he wouldn't go to sleep and let the grownups watch in peace.

Although still an infant, Jamie also participated in a major historical event—one of the biggest protests in Washington against the Vietnam War. His birth coincided with the groundswell of opposition after the Tet offensive, and he marched, riding in his baby carrier on Bob's back, down Constitution Avenue with an estimated 600,000 people (according to Wikipedia) on a cold, rainy day. Barbara remembers being horrified to notice soldiers with automatic weapons stationed on top of the old World War I temporary buildings on the Mall, apparently pointing them at the crowd. What did they mean, aiming weapons at a peaceful crowd that included children!

Beginning in the fall of 1968, we had the pleasure of visits from sister Susie, who started as a freshman at American University that fall. She and Kathy had traveled together, with backpacks and *Europe on $5 a Day*, which you really could do then, all summer, and we enjoyed having her over for a meal now and then. Later, as Jamie grew older, Susie filled in as an occasional babysitter—but she didn't have too much time for that.

Our many visitors included Benedict Sandin, by now the Curator of the Sarawak Museum. Barbara wrote:

Benedict was the perfect house guest, totally able to look after himself by systematically looking through all our books, mine included. Last night he read one I have about the ancient Hebrews. In addition to touring the Capitol and the White House, Bob took him and Barbara Harrisson over to see Helena one evening (the one Jamie was sick, so I didn't go) and we had Kate and Mark as well as Susie and two of Bob's State Department friends over last night for dinner. Benedict amused us by recounting the heroic exploits of a very strong warrior named Baka, whom the Rajah couldn't keep in jail. Then he sang Iban pantuns (historical poems or ritual ones), and I imagined what anyone walking by our open windows thought was going on.[5]

Bob's job entailed long hours, but after rush hour our apartment was only a few minutes away across the Theodore Roosevelt Bridge, which made it easy for Barbara to pick him up after work as she often did. By this time we had acquired a new, bright blue VW bug. Jamie enjoyed the view from his car seat in the front, and one of us sat in back on the way home.

As always, having a high-ranking boss (Tom Hughes) helped Bob to secure what he wanted for his next job, an assignment to Indonesia, preceded by six months of language training at the Foreign Service Institute. He had already learned a little Indonesian at Cornell and Yale summer language school, but nowhere near to the point of fluency, so he started the course partway through, while Barbara began at the very beginning. It was a great course. The supervising "linguist," Joe Harter, was not a PhD linguist, but he was an inspired teacher with a bottomless repertoire of effective gimmicks, from translating clippings from the Indonesian press to singing catchy songs from the Indonesian Revolution ("Hallo, Hallo Bandung!" and the like). He had a book of these songs, which we assumed would be available in Jakarta, so we never Xeroxed his, but alas it was not! In a fit of bureaucratic shortsightedness, FSI later let Harter go for being insufficiently "qualified." Our

---

[5] Barbara letter to Dear Family, n.d., Autumn, 1968.

"native language" instructors were Andang Poeraatmadja and Jijis Chadran, who for many years showed up at the same Indonesian Embassy functions and other Indonesian get-togethers that we did.

Jamie survived his parents' language lessons, but not easily. At age fourteen months he started day care at the Fort Meyers nursery, a military facility also open to Foreign Service children. But he had never had wide exposure to various childhood germs, and he kept getting sniffles, fevers, and so on, to the point where his mother was getting behind in her Indonesian classes and various friends' good will as emergency sitters was used up. So he spent the second half of the course at the home of a Navy enlisted man's widow, who took in a few children, some sewing, and did other minor projects, often at the same time—not an arrangement which might pass muster today, but she was generous and had had her own children, and Jamie did much better with her.

As we prepared to leave, Helena was finding that 103 Prince was no longer practical for her, so we agreed that she would move to a nearby apartment on Bashford Lane and that we would rent out 103 Prince Street. The rental income would cover both Helena's apartment rental and the mortgage on 103, although it would still be a while before we could start paying Clay back for his loan to us.

Using only 1000 pounds of our shipping allowance (one crib, one highchair, summer clothes, and a few dishes), we left for Jakarta in March, 1970. Our route took us from Cincinnati to Chicago (where we visited the grandparents Cade, the last time we were ever to see them) and then to Tokyo via Alaska. The trip was memorable in two baby-related ways. As we took off from O'Hare, we celebrated by ordering Bloody Marys. Bad choice! Jamie promptly kicked Barbara's up in the air and all over her travel outfit. Whatever it was, it was washable, but from then on she must have looked like a harried mother. After that auspicious start, he slept through the night, Eastern Standard Time, in a little baby bed hooked to the bulkhead. We didn't even have to use the tranquilizer which the pediatrician had prescribed in case of need. But when, after a very long flight, we arrived in Tokyo in the evening, Japan Standard Time, and wanted only to sleep for hours, that potion proved very valuable.

I wanted to show Barbara a little of Japan, so we added several days to my official business time. I booked us at the old Sanno Hotel in Tokyo, still operated by the US military. Located in a prime downtown area, it was a drab, blocky building already surrounded by shiny, much newer glass towers. It was famous as the site where Japanese military officers had plotted the coup that overthrew democratic rule in 1936, a major cause of subsequent Japanese aggression. Much later, when I was in Korea, it had housed the US military press liaison office, and I had often worked with its staff when I was a GI in the Eighth Army public affairs office in Seoul.

Needless to say, it was an experience having a blonde toddler in Japan. The Japanese could not believe that his dad carried him around in a frame baby carrier on his back, and every expedition, especially on public transportation, elicited endless friendly curiosity. Dinner at a fancy Japanese restaurant was daunting because of course Jamie wanted to wander into every other dinner party, easy enough since each was ensconced in a separate tatami-floored cubicle at toddler-eye level. Even though everyone was super-friendly and the waitresses would have loved to carry him around, he was at the clingy stage and refused their kind overtures. So much for our elegant dinner.

The next night we ate at a much less elegant Korean place with Western-style tables and chairs and an unobstructed view from Jamie's highchair; he couldn't have been a better meal companion. We also had dinner with friends from Cornell, historians Akira and Yoko Nagazumi, in their traditional home; we have no recollection of problems with sitting on the floor there. Perhaps their older children amused Jamie.

Our next big event was a trip to Kyoto on the bullet train, high-speed rail service being already well established in Japan by 1970. Whooshing in and out of tunnels at 175 km per hour was fun, of course, as was staying in a small but elegant *ryokan* in the old city. It turned out that Jamie did not like rice (oranges and eggs were fine, and readily available), but he didn't mind the March chill of unheated Japanese tradition, or the beautiful accessories such as the ancient jar with a big water dipper, a most amusing toy but a real danger to his blanket sleeper which he had to wear because it was so cold. We then rented a car and set off for the ancient temple complex at Nara, threading narrow roads through a congested jumble of factories, towns and rice fields. Whenever we seemed to be hopelessly lost, we would finally encounter a sign in Western script, one of not very many being installed for forthcoming Olympic Games.

Proceeding onwards, we flew to Manila in order to connect with Pan Am (regulations required us to fly on US-flag carriers wherever possible) for the last leg via Singapore to Jakarta. We went on a city tour of Manila and lamented the very visible income disparity, not imagining that four years later we would be back on assignment to the Philippines. In Singapore we again took a few days to look up Cornell acquaintances, Chan Heng Chee and Edwin Lee, both then on the history faculty of the University of Singapore. As always, we met Edwin's delightful family and had a fine time enjoying the sights and cuisine of the city, and hearing all about its politics from Edwin's father.

Hallo, Hallo Jakarta!

On our arrival in Jakarta, where we would live for four years, we were greeted at the airport by most of the political section: Skipper and Til Purnell, Dan and Margaret Sullivan, and Bob and Rose Slutz.[6] Bob was carrying Jamie in his backpack, and later Til Purnell, an exemplar of Old Foreign Service values, confessed to Barbara, "I saw that and thought you might be another of *them*." She was probably referring to the Sullivans, who had four children and were a little too unbuttoned and outspoken for Til's taste, Margaret especially. All of them became our good and lasting friends.

Our first dinner in Jakarta was at the home of the Sullivans, where Bob made his Jakarta social debut by collapsing one of Margaret's cloth-and-wire patio chairs and landing on the floor. The episode, given that no lasting damage was done to Bob, was funny because the chair was on its last legs and

---

[6] Ann Swift, to become one of our best friends, and much later one of the Iran hostages, was out of town when we arrived.

Margaret had insisted that Barbara, visibly quite pregnant, should not sit in it.

Before long we were installed in a typical late-colonial-era house on Jalan (street) Kiai Madja, previously inhabited by Ann and Al Laporta, who had left before our arrival but became good friends later. The neighborhood, which was known as Kebayoran, had been the last word in Dutch colonial chic when it was established just before World War II. In its center was a small collection of shops known as Blok M, which is today much expanded, although seen as almost antique. Our house was one of the modest ones—one storey masonry, with two air-conditioned bedrooms and lots of screened windows in the living and dining room area. As in early Virginia homes, the kitchen, generator of heat, smoke and cooking smells, was separated from the house by a short walkway. There was a narrow screened front porch, of limited use because Kiai Madja was a busy street made even noisier by the construction of a huge new hospital right across the way.

The establishment was run by five servants: houseboy, nanny, washerwoman, cook, and guard. Our first houseboy was angling for a job elsewhere when we arrived (although we did not know that) and soon after receiving a loan from us, disappeared. We then employed Supari, a gentle soul who took good care of Jamie once beloved Sumila, the nanny we hired with Annie's arrival in mind, became occupied with her new charge. We can't remember the cook's name, but she was quiet and capable, and the guard was Jani, who guarded us all four years we were in Jakarta, but whose signal achievement occurred early on, still in Kebayoran. One night, he and other nearby guards apprehended and "beat up" (*pukul-pukul*) a hapless thief who tried to enter one of the houses. Since *pukul-pukuling* can be rather harsh, as on drums or in hulling rice, we never dared ask what exactly had occurred, but Jani, despite his constant financial troubles (big family and many obligations back in the village), had firmly earned his position.

Jakarta in 1970 was a sprawling city, a series of huge villages that had grown together. There were no tall buildings until shortly before we left and only one big, modern hotel. I wrote home that it was a city of 4,500,000 people, 500,000 pedicabs (or *becaks*) and one traffic light, tied together by a few major roads and Dutch-era canals clogged with trash.[7] The main traffic problem was pedicab congestion, but it was trivial by comparison with the motor vehicle congestion that plagues Jakarta today. To the north, on the coast, was the seaport of Dutch East India days and the huge Chinatown. The modern port at Tanjung Priok, where we would keep our sailboat, was east of the old port.

To the south a couple of big volcanoes loomed, visible even then only on clear days, to remind us that we were on the island of Java. Most US Embassy staff lived in Kebayoran and commuted about half an hour to the heart of the pre-World War II city in Menteng. It was the site of important government buildings and monuments, most embassies (including ours), and many diplomatic residences, as well as the high-quality public elementary school that Barack Obama was attending at about the time that we arrived.

By 1970 Jakarta had been under military rule headed by President (and General) Suharto for four years. It was a dictatorship, but a moderate one, except insofar as the communists were concerned. Once the largest communist party in the world, the PKI (*Partai Kommunis Indonesia*) was never forgiven for its bungled effort in 1965 to destroy the army, enforce land reform (which had set off an army-supported bloodletting on Java and Bali) and perhaps seize power. Communist leaders had been executed and jailed or (imitating Dutch practice) sent to a remote island, Buru, in eastern Indonesia.

Indonesia's former president, Sukarno, was under house arrest, where he died in June, three months after our arrival. Those who had belonged to the PKI's numerous front organizations had been fired and blacklisted. Later we would employ several extraordinarily capable servants who we now know (and always suspected) were former teachers in East Java, where our friends David and Helen Kenney had first hired them, and had belonged, as most teachers did, to the communist teachers' union.

---

[7] Bob letter to Dear Mark and Kate, n.d. but must have been May, 1970.

Low Man in a Big POL

Bob's assignment turned out to be fascinating, despite unavoidable bouts of annoyance with bureaucratic routine. I was the most

junior person in a five-person political section, abbreviated "POL." I was so junior that I did not have my own office, but a desk in a space between two others. Our main job in POL was writing reports on both foreign and domestic developments, by cable, memo and, for long, non-urgent analysis, reports known as "airgrams." Since most of the latter were not directly policy oriented, but rather intended as background, one could go into interesting detail and express opinions that were not necessarily those of the ambassador,

Bob at his desk in the hall. even though his name appeared on them, along with that of the author.

The idea of all this was to inform Washington officialdom about important political and economic trends. Were the communists really finished? (It was the height of the Vietnam War, and that still interested Washington a lot.) Was General Suharto going to succeed, or would Indonesia fall into a chaos that our Cold War adversaries could exploit? Traditionally, political sections reported on elections, even in countries where they were less than free, as was the case in Indonesia, and we did rather too much of that. Junior officers, especially those who spoke Indonesian, were encouraged to visit remote areas and report on what was going on politically and economically.

This was still the old Foreign Service, which for all its occasional bouts of stuffiness, prized good, concise writing and analysis. The assumption was that one learned by research and writing.[8] Official reports had to be honed and rewritten if necessary. E-mail-itis—the rapid production of

---

[8] There will be more about learning by reporting in later chapters.

unverified verbiage—was still in the future. State Department reporting was much like journalism. Sources were usually named, and of course they were not paid, in contrast to the "covert" intelligence model, where sources (aka "spies") were paid but never named. The reason was—and still is—that the latter were being paid by a foreign government, which in most countries made them liable to unpleasant consequences if caught. This distinction has not changed.

My first ambassador was Frank Galbraith, a handsome South Dakotan born on the Standing Rock Indian Reservation, although not a native American himself, and not related to the famous economist. He was an old Indonesia hand, having served in Indonesia (and worked in Washington on it) several times, in addition to being the first US ambassador to Singapore.[9]

He was also a very nice guy, as I discovered the first time I served as his note-taker, for a meeting with an elderly leader of a Muslim political party, the Java-based Nahdlatul Ulama (or NU). Our visitor spoke Indonesian with a strong Javanese accent, quite different from what I had learned at FSI, and I couldn't understand half of what he was saying. I left the meeting perspiring, but Galbraith, who had obviously noticed my concern, called me back. "That was interesting, wasn't it?" he said pensively. "Now this is what the main points were," and he proceeded to tell me, without saying so, what to write. I remember thinking, "Now there's a real gentleman!"

I should explain that Indonesian (a variation of Malay) is the national language, but a second language for most Indonesians, who grow up speaking regional languages and learn Indonesian only in school. This may have been truer in the 1970s than it is today, but one happy result for us was that Jakarta's residents were used to rather badly spoken Indonesian. Ours was as fluent as that of many less educated Indonesians, including most of our household staff. However, we did have trouble with local accents, not least the Jakarta patois, influenced in part by the language of Bali, because in the seventeenth century the Dutch had had a taste for Balinese slaves. And of course we didn't speak any of the regional languages at all.

[9] His tour there began in December, 1966, after we had left Sarawak.

Frank's wife, Martha, was a little less forgiving than he was. It was my job as the junior officer in POL to be the protocol officer. This mainly meant doing seating plans for ambassadorial functions, assigning each guest a place according to rank, with the most senior female on the right of the male host, and so on around the table, with more junior attendees in the middle, farthest away from the host and hostess.

I had two big problems with these responsibilities. First, I have no sense of spatial relations; my mind turns to mush when confronted with a seating plan. Second, Mrs. Galbraith, who had a warm heart but was very stubborn, was convinced that the Indonesians possessed a system for determining rank even among different categories of guests: diplomats, military officers, civil servants, etc. Moreover, she *knew* that every embassy in town except ours understood this plan. Why couldn't *we*— meaning *me*—get it?! In desperation, I usually took my seating assignments home to Barbara, but nothing seemed to work.

We survived and enjoyed various other Galbraithian virtues. Annie received a handsome engraved cup, made of shiny Bangka tin, upon her birth. Martha noticed that Indonesians adored caged birds, and she built a sizeable aviary full of beautiful examples at the ambassadorial residence. Some of them may have been endangered species, but, not yet well informed on matters of avian conservation, we enjoyed them. We ourselves bought a saltwater aquarium midway through our stay. Keeping one was totally painless because the aquarium service cleaned it and replaced any fish that died, which of course they did from time to time, and we had no idea as yet of the environmental downside; it was just something to be enjoyed along with the cheap orchids sold in Jakarta's street markets.

Lewis "Skipper" Purnell and his wife Til were at least as important in our lives as the Galbraiths. When we arrived, Skipper was the Political Counselor, and as such approved my efficiency reports (his deputy, Bob Slutz, wrote them). Later Purnell became the DCM and his replacement, Dick Donald, became a good friend as well. In due course the Purnells moved to Manila, to which Skipper arranged my assignment in 1974.

Skipper was gruff and sometimes arbitrary, and he didn't

get along with everybody, a serious matter in an organization as hierarchical as the Foreign Service. As for Til, she was definitely living by old Foreign Service rules and customs. To give you an idea, until shortly after we arrived in Jakarta, it was still the rule that any female officer had to resign if she got married. The very existence of such a rule dissuaded many women from even considering a Foreign Service career, including Barbara before she met me. It should be noted that at that time our military was even worse.

Our good friend Ann Swift, a Radcliffe graduate, was nothing if not both a free spirit and determined, and she famously collided with Til when, at a formal lunch, the women were directed one way and the men the other, the men to smoke cigars and get down to business and the women to do unimportant female things. Ann refused and when Til objected, she said that for the purpose of the lunch she was, being a member of the Political Section, a man. She got away with it probably because Skipper, who thought the world of her, was on her side.

On another occasion, both we and Ann were late to a dinner at the Purnells because we were caught out sailing after dark in a serious storm, but Ann, a highly experienced sailor, in her own boat, was delayed more than we were. When we finally arrived at the dinner and she had not, Skipper acted like an aggrieved father whose daughter has done something foolish, and blamed me for letting it happen. Despite his nickname, he was not a sailor.

Until we moved to Menteng, my daily routine began with a carpool from Kebayoran to the embassy. Even in 1970 traffic was often a problem on the main road, especially when it rained and motor scooters took shelter under overpasses, clogging all lanes until the police shooed them away. My carpool had a rolling debate about the Vietnam War, which some supported and I opposed—and was glad to be in Indonesia avoiding it, an avoidance made easier by prior military service.

Once at the office, I read (or scanned) about a dozen newspapers. There was *Kompas*, the *New York Times* of Indonesia, Roman Catholic owned; *Sinar Harapan* (Ray of Hope), the Protestant newspaper; the *Jakarta Post*, the only English language daily; *Abadi* (an Arabic word meaning "eternal"), the only explicitly Muslim paper; *Merdeka*

(Freedom), the Sukarnoist paper; and *Harian Kami* (Our Daily), representing students and ex-students, to name a few. My favorite was *Abadi*, usually only four pages and obviously printed on an aging flatbed press similar to the one familiar to me from the *Harvard Crimson*; its handset type dented the pages, and impressions ranged from inky black to light gray.

I would then consult with Indonesian staffers who prepared a daily press summary in English for the embassy. More than 30 years later one of the translators, now retired, Tatu Maulani, remembered me and was a major help in writing my book on Islam in Indonesia. Attention to the press was important because despite military rule it remained lively, able to express opinion and even criticize authority through innuendo and double meaning. If a headline read "Corrupt dictatorship threatened with popular uprising," you had to read to the end of the story to discover that it was about some place in South America.

Abadi was of special interest because one of my "beats" was to cover political Islam. Then as now, less than a quarter of Indonesia's Muslim majority believed that Islam should engage directly in politics. The rest favored a primarily nationalist approach based on the multi-religious (not "secular") founding philosophy created by Sukarno before independence. During the upheaval of 1965-66, Muslim youth groups had helped to carry out the anti-communist crackdown led by the army under Suharto. But Suharto, who became president, distrusted Muslim activists almost as much as he did the communists.[10] For their part, the activist Muslims felt betrayed by Suharto's refusal to reward them for their support in destroying Indonesian communism.

Most Indonesian Muslims are Sunnis; there were only a few Shi'ites and few formal doctrinal differences.[11] Indonesia's Islam is nonetheless marked by two broad but important divisions—between Traditionalists, conditioned by tolerance

---

[10] Much later, toward the end of his three-decade rule, and under changing circumstances, Suharto decided he needed Muslim support and became a more observant Muslim himself.

[11] The number of Shia, or Shi'ite, Muslims in Indonesia was apparently increasing slightly, for reasons never clear to me, at about the same time I was writing a book on Islam in Indonesia published in 2010.

of Indonesia's pre-Islamic traditions, and Reformists or Modernists, more oriented toward a scriptural if not fundamentalist base. At the time of my service in Indonesia, the well-educated leaders of the Reformist wing were still excluded from politics due primarily to their involvement in a regional rebellion in 1958, which the US briefly supported, and their former political party, Masjumi, remained banned. This situation was to persist, in time encouraging a swing toward Islamic politics more radical than the kind espoused by the old leaders.

That change lay in the future. My job was to meet the existing leadership of political Islam and assess what was going on. This was easy because according to local custom it was perfectly normal for a diplomat to call a political leader, even a total stranger, and ask for a meeting. Such visits typically took place at the leader's home, around 5 pm. They enabled me to meet a number of senior Reformist leaders in an informal setting and to form real friendships. It was also normal for Barbara to accompany me, and when she did we also met their wives.

These people were quite unhappy about their continued exclusion from politics and were equally upset by Suharto's ongoing efforts to establish a new government-controlled Muslim party, which were to continue for some years. The fact that as a very junior officer I was assigned this job shows that the subject was not a high priority for the US Government. We were still far more concerned about communism than about Islam, which after all had been the most active anti-communist force in Indonesia.

My travel was sometimes keyed to my coverage of religious politics. At one point I went to Central Java to assess a revival of Hinduism, which had been Indonesia's first world religion, before Islam. For a time Suharto and his strategists toyed with supporting such a revival in order to attract the nominally Muslim peasantry, which had provided the communists with a mass base, and had been harshly punished in 1965-66 for so doing. The idea was soon abandoned because it was highly offensive to more fervent Muslims.

But much of my travel was simply to take the pulse of Indonesia's varied countryside. I couldn't go everywhere, for bureaucratic reasons. Our consulate in Medan was responsible for reporting on developments in most of Sumatra, and our other consulate in the great port city of Surabaya covered East Java. That left the rest of Java, the southern tip of Sumatra, Borneo, Sulawesi and all of Eastern Indonesia for me to explore and write about.[12] Barbara accompanied me on most of these trips, especially after Annie was old enough to be fed from a bottle and therefore left in Sumila's (or later Munarti's) capable care. I wrote dozens of travel reports. Most have been declassified (or were never classified in the first place) and are now in the public domain.

In May, 1970, we made our first trip, the only one before Annie's arrival, by train to Central Java. In order to see the countryside, we took the unair-conditioned day train. These were the days before bottled water; the train car was too hot for beer, and we were thoroughly sick of sugary, neon-colored pop by the time the train pulled into the station in Jogja. We explored the twin royal capitals of Jogjakarta and Surakarta (Solo), staying in dilapidated hotels; we avoided the only modern one, the Ambarrukmo Palace, in order to be in the center of Jogjakarta. "There isn't a single toilet in Indonesia that works," I wrote in my diary.

We saw the great temples, Borobudur and Prambanan, Buddhist and Hindu respectively, for the first time, and noted the lyrical sweetness of much of Indonesia's great Hindu-era art and architecture. In Solo we bought our big, beautifully framed *wayang* painting. In Indonesia, the great Hindu epics of the *Mahabharata* and *Ramayana* as presented in dance, drama or puppetry are referred to as *wayang*. The most familiar and most popular form is the *wayang kulit* puppet theater, in which flat leather puppets cast shadows on a screen

---

[12] Practically speaking, there were limits to where one could go. Many places had no air service, and cargo boats—mostly battered hand-me-downs from Dutch times—did not travel on schedules, so there was no way to visit most of the numerous islands east of Java, like Sumba, Komodo (of dragon fame), Timor (then still divided between Indonesia and Portugal), Sumbawa, and Roti, which trail off toward Australia. Bali, already a famous tourist site, was an exception. Others, including Ambon, Ternate, and Tidore, as far as we ever got among the fabled Spice Islands, are in a province (Maluku) that is nine hundred miles from north to south. Check out a map if you don't believe this.

while the puppeteer, called the *dalang*, recounts the story. Our painting, however, was done by an artist who was one of the last to work in the style of *wayang beber*, an antique variant of illustrating the story which consists of successive paintings on scrolls, slowly unrolled as the tale unfolds. Although much larger than the scenes on the scrolls, our painting shows the "good" Pendawa family of the *Mahabharata* holding a strategy council in their palace. It would later suffer water damage en route to the Philippines, but it was lovingly restored there.

Annie Arrives

Annie was already making her presence known. In fact I, Barbara, was somewhat concerned when a horse and buggy ride to Kota Gede, the silver-working village near Jogjakarta, turned out to be far bumpier than anticipated, but it didn't provoke premature labor or any other complications. That may have been because, as I wrote home after the trip, "The baby is much more active than Jamie was—portent of things to come?"[13] I decided to go to Kuala Lumpur for the delivery, rather than Singapore where most Jakarta moms went, because our good friends Otto and Barbara Doering were there, and both their children had been born at Assunta Hospital, run by American Catholic missionary nuns in that city.

Jamie had been born well before the expected date, so I left early in August, just in case. Annie, of course, did it her own way and didn't arrive until the 26th, which is Malaysian Independence Day. Otto Doering was away doing field research, so Barbara Doering and I decided to leave for the hospital at the first sign of labor pains on the evening of the 25th. This resulted in my having the only air-conditioned delivery room in the hospital (thank goodness!), but also gave me time to read the better part of Han Su Yin's classic, *A Many Splendored Thing*; the nuns are probably still talking about my unusual behavior.

I found the book on one of several shelves of books in the delivery room; I'm not sure what else they were supposed to be for. Perhaps it was the nuns' library, but they also

---

[13] Barbara letter to Dear Family, June 6, 1970.

liked American movies for relaxation, and later even invited me to watch *Flipper* (about a dolphin) with them while I was recovering. Annie came quickly the next morning, no anesthesia, thank-you, but a much faster recovery for Mom than with Jamie, which was a big plus. I even had the energy to go down to the embassy to collect a passport for Annie before we left for Indonesia, when she was about ten days old.

Back at home, Bob kept working, more or less as usual. Jamie had already been moved into a bigger bed in anticipation of a sibling. He was happily attending a playschool, activities at which included painting "murals" on the white wall in the head teacher's garden. Each afternoon, the gardener turned the hose on the wall and created the next day's pristine canvas.

On August 16 Bob climbed Gunung Gede, one of the big volcanoes visible from Jakarta, with an Australian acquaintance, George Hicks, and a friend of his, a Dutch botanist named "Ahmed" Costermans,[14] who had been director of the world-famous Bogor Botanical Garden. Costermans had been interned by the Japanese and sent to work on the Death Railway in Thailand. He had returned to West Java after the war and spent the tumultuous times that followed in Bogor on the front porch of the herbarium, armed with a machine gun to repel bandits.

He said he was sixty-four years old and had forty-six Indonesian "sons," all adopted, fourteen of whom had PhDs (their fees paid by him). He had been recently charged with homosexuality, possession of an illegal weapon, and inciting one of his "sons" to murder another son. He said the charge had been trumped up by an official trying to extort money from him, but the US Army, which had been helping to pay for a three-volume study of economic plants of Indonesia which he was writing, withdrew from the project.

On the way to the 10,000 foot summit of Gede, Costermans delivered a running commentary on the flora and told us about his life of collecting orchids and other exotic plants in the rainforest. He would go to Borneo (and elsewhere) with a substantial crew and fell huge trees so he could gather specimens from their canopies. One of his best stories was

[14] "Ahmed" was obviously not his original name; he took it when he decided to become an Indonesian citizen (from George Hicks).

provoked by a concrete, bunker-like structure we noticed across the valley from our trail. He said it had been built to produce seed potatoes. Needed by local farmers, they had previously been imported from Holland because potatoes require a cold spell to become dormant in order to sprout. It was hoped that Gede's high elevation and resulting cool temperatures would end the need to import them, but it hadn't worked and the project had been abandoned.

Decades later an enterprising local imam discovered the abandoned concrete structure and, hoping to attract pilgrims and commerce, announced to his followers that it was the ancient tomb of a famous Muslim holy man. "Ha, ha, Saint Potato!" Costermans laughed.[15]

Barbara called me soon after Anne's birth; it is a good thing we had already chosen her name because the connection was so bad that we couldn't have discussed it then. The cable sent from Bukit Bintang (Star Hill), Kuala Lumpur, to Clarence Cade read *"Anne Elizabeth arrived 26th August 6 pounds eleven both fine call Kate Helena Margot Love Barbara."* Our plans were already set. After a few days' rest, mother and daughter would travel across the Straits of Malacca to Medan from Kuala Lumpur, a very short flight. Bob would get a free ride from Jakarta to Medan to meet them by escorting the classified diplomatic pouch to our consulate there. All went well on the flight from KL to Medan until, as Barbara tells the story . . . .

In those days before paper diapers and roll-aboard suitcases I felt like a pack mule with all my carry on, plus Annie in the soft baby carrier, worn on the front and never used again once she got home to Sumila. Then it occurred to me that I had forgotten all about the possibility that even an infant might need a visa, as well as a passport. (How could anyone so small need a visa?) Fortunately Mark Dion, our newly arrived consul in Medan, easily persuaded the relevant immigration official to let her go home with us, but not until he had put a note in her passport saying that her father must get her a visa asap in Jakarta. (This story explains why diplomatic missions send little presents like bottles of scotch to their official friends at holiday time, but one must also

---

[15] Bob letter to Dear Mother, August 17, 1970.

consider what the official thought he might do next if he did not grant this infant entry.)

Indonesians are not accustomed to important men being bachelors, as Mark was. By the time we got to his official residence, the news was already all over town that *Mem Besar* (literally "Big Madam") had finally arrived with a cute daughter, and everything was going to be all right. Bob had not yet come from Jakarta.

After he did, Mark lent us a vehicle and Bob and I and the new addition to the family spent a day driving up to see Lake Toba, the huge volcanic lake in the middle of Sumatra, which we had to see because it figured in the ending to a famous novel by Mochtar Lubis which we had read in Indonesian class. The unair-conditioned jeep was so hot, however, that Annie began to throw up on the way back to Medan, and I wondered again whether our travel was too much for her. Again, not a bit, and she was well taken care of—spoiled— by Mark's staff the whole time we were visiting. So was her mother; this was definitely better than coming home to an apartment in Arlington with a new baby, even though on that occasion Grandma had arrived after a few days.

We headed home with the bright orange sack (aka diplomatic pouch) supposedly full of secrets on the plane seat next to Annie, both about the same size, a scene duly photographed. Jamie got along fine with her from the beginning. In fact, we

Jamie discovers that he has a baby sister.

brought him a present—a set of plastic nested eggs—and he didn't really notice her until the next morning, when she was still there, and moving. He had already discovered that it was great fun to play with the servants' children, in this case a five-year old belonging to Sumila, his nanny, perhaps one reason why he didn't miss being the sole focus of Barbara's attention. When Annie was only a few months old, she accompanied us on what may have been our first family outing, to the botanical garden in Bogor that Dr. Costermans had once defended with his machine gun. That was the occasion of the photo with Barbara sitting at the foot of a banyan tree

No more baby front- or backpacks. Sumila, Annie's nanny, carries her in a folded and tied sarong called a gendang. Sriah, the wash lady, also helped look after her,

with Annie on her lap, still unable to hold her head up, and Jamie on another root next to them.

Jakarta was officially a hardship post, meaning that there were no supermarkets, no American movies (and only one government-controlled TV station), and water had to be laboriously filtered and boiled before it was safe to drink, a major reason why servants are not a luxury in such places. Hospital sanitation was medieval, mothers were strongly advised to have their babies in Singapore or Malaysia, as Barbara had done, and any serious illness required medical evacuation. We did have three good doctors in the US Mission, one from the State Department; another, technically employed by our USAID program's very successful family planning project and often a source of superior medical advice, especially for the children; and a third, working with a US Navy research project on tropical diseases. But they ran only a small embassy clinic, which gave inoculations and treated minor health problems. Perceived risk of political instability was another hardship factor, even though we sensed little of it until the very end of our stay.

The real hardships, given that we both spoke Indonesian so that communication was not a problem, were really just minor challenges, requiring American residents to expend effort in areas not usually matters of concern. Servants were great, but they had to be trained, for example to buy into the likelihood that water, even though sparkling clear, might have germs in it. They needed help to survive financial woes, and their American employer became a banker, as well as a medical insurance company. And while the markets held all sorts of pleasant surprises, they didn't have certain "essentials" for coping with daily life.

Contrary to what we had been led to believe, we could buy supplies like paper and crayons and some children's toys, which had not been available immediately after the 1965-66 coup. These were, after all, the Spice Islands, so spices were no problem, but what about herbs? They are not part of Indonesian cuisine, and many of the ones we know don't grow well in the tropics except at high altitudes. (Mark Dion found it was part of his unofficial job description to keep certain high-ranking cooks in Jakarta supplied with green peppers, which thrive best in the highlands around Lake Toba. They got from Medan to Jakarta the same way Annie had.)

Though talented tailors could sew lovely dresses and shirts, men's shorts and trousers were difficult, both finding appropriately sturdy fabric and fitting the Western bottom. So letters home were full of requests for such items, and we felt very lucky to be part of the US Armed Forces mail system, that brought us packages safely and without import hassles. We also felt lucky to have purchasing agents, named Char (for most items) and Clay (sailboat fittings), in the US to buy the trivia we constantly asked for. Both Sears and Monkey Wards still had catalogue operations, and they were a major source of desired American products too, especially in the clothing department— despite all the batik shirts and dresses that we loved.

Hardship status meant that Bob received a 25% salary bonus, or "differential," and every year all sections of the embassy joined forces to compose a document describing the fearful perils of living in Indonesia, so that we would not lose it. All this would be repeated with variations at our four other hardship posts.

The Soft Side of Hardship

In fact, even allowing that first postings often seem idyllic in retrospect and leaving aside Bob's professional interest in Indonesia, we had a ball, as did most of our colleagues. For all Jakarta's pedicab-clogged streets, we could get down to the old port area easily, especially on Sundays, and driving to the cool mountainous interior or "*puncak*" (peak of a mountain, no matter its height), where many expatriates rented cottages, was almost equally painless. But there was more.

Soon after our arrival we were sitting at the embassy Recreation Club pool, making sure that Jamie didn't fall in, when Barbara heard an AID contractor named Marilyn Zak, soon to be leaving Indonesia, say she wanted to sell her half-share in a seventeen-foot sailboat, a Dutch NN class. With a five horsepower outboard motor, the cost would be $300. We couldn't pass that up, and the sailboat became our major source of recreation. Soon afterwards, a cheerful Scot named Lachie Macintosh bought the other half, which he used only occasionally.

We did not like the boat's name, *Ichi Ban* (Japanese for "Number One"—a tired bit of old GI slang) but we did not change it. Designed for the North Sea, it featured a gaff rig, mainsail plus jib, and an enormous iron keel—not so great for getting into beaches fringed with coral reefs, but making the boat extremely stable. Although the design was Dutch, the hull construction was Indonesian, featuring, rather than planks, narrow horizontal strips of wood caulked together, and laboriously replaced piecemeal when rot set in.

Fortunately we had a "boat boy," an atypically grumpy individual named Sudin, who supervised the pulling and repairing of the boat whenever necessary at the Dutch-founded boat club, located in the "new" port of Tanjong Priok. He also prepared *Ichi Ban* for day sails before our arrival and put her away when we returned. Hardship indeed!

This acquisition ushered in many a day of weekend sailing. We discovered that except during the storms of the northwest

A Buginese schooner with sails reefed because of an approaching squall.
Although we saw these all-sail vessels frequently from our own dinky little
craft, this was the only time we saw one moving fast and close to us. The
crew was obviously enjoying it.

monsoon, the morning breeze was offshore, from the south, often feeble and fickle, but we had our little motor. In the afternoon the wind freshened and came onshore, from the north, perfect for a brisk sail home. Handling our own boat was great fun, but we also enjoyed seeing the world's last great sailing fleet, mostly big two-masted Buginese schooners known as *pinasi,* from "pinnace," and almost equally large dhow-rigged ships from Madura, a large island at the eastern end of Java, coming in and out of Jakarta from around the archipelago.

They had no auxiliary power and no rudders, using steering

oars instead. Their sails were often a colorful patchwork of used fabric, and they usually had messy deck cargoes of lumber and all kinds of consumer goods, like Chinese produced plastic buckets and basins, and even plastic chairs, piled high. They were almost always badly overloaded. They had a special port of their own, appropriately enough near the old Dutch port, where the Batavia Castle, long since razed, had stood.

Once as we were heading home in the afternoon Bob was able to take a several photos of a fresh-painted, blue-and-white schooner as it came by us going fast under reefed sails during a squall, one of the great sights of our stay in Indonesia.[16] We never saw anything like it again. The painting that hangs in our living room, commissioned after we got home, is based partly on those photos, one of which is on the previous page.

Jakarta's harbor is located on a shallow indentation on the coast, and we could never quite figure out why the Dutch chose this place to locate their main base on Java. To keep the docks safe, a huge seawall had been constructed, with a narrow entrance, indicated at night by what seemed like two 40-watt bulbs, one on each side, visible only from uncomfortably close range. A small archipelago, the *Pulau Seribu* (Thousand Islands), was strung out about thirty miles north of the harbor, too far for us to reach on our own. But only a few miles away there was a smaller scattering of islands, several of which were great for snorkeling and swimming.

One particularly nice island belonged to the President of the Republic. Suharto, president during our time, never used it, but no one dared despoil it or its fringing coral reef. If no one was around, which was almost always, we sometimes stopped at it. It had a resident cassowary, a huge flightless bird from New Guinea, a present to the president from someone, which often came down to the beach to greet us. We didn't know then that cassowaries can be lethal: they have long, sharp toes, which the natives of New Guinea use for spear points, and have a nasty habit of charging at intruders through thick bush, feet first.

Then our friend Judy Bird taught us about shell collecting

---

[16] There are six pictures altogether, taken with a Leica M-2 camera with a fast film advance lever. The Kodachrome colors have not faded at all thus far.

and the malacological treasures that could be gathered by following tracks in the offshore sand or turning over hunks of dead coral, which you had to be careful to replace. Some of the closest islands had once been part of the oldest Dutch harbor, the one that made Batavia famous, and the adjacent waters were littered with ancient trash, including shards of Chinese porcelain and Dutch Gin (Genever) bottles. There were no healthy coral reefs close to the harbor, but enough interesting terrain to encourage shell collecting by beginners. A little further out there were huge square fish traps made of bamboo poles, on which lights were hung at night to attract small fish, *ikan bilis*, to be dried and salted and greatly savored as cocktail snacks by old Indonesia hands. All this opened a whole new world of masks and snorkels and made us eager to

A sail on Ann Swift's sailboat, which was the same model as our Ichi Ban. Apparently a grown-up party, because Annie is not with us. Under the sail is Mark Dion, with Jamie. On the starboard side toward bow sit Helen Kenney, then Barbara, then David Kenney and Ann at the helm.

learn to scuba dive, not yet possible in Indonesia.

Much of the old harbor area has since been filled in for residential development, and the offshore sea within day-sailing distance of Jakarta is now very polluted. The *pinasi* are still there, but they all have auxiliary motors. The yacht harbor from which

During Ambassador Galbraith's visit to Irian Jaya, local missionaries flew us to the Baliem Valley, home of the Dani people, who are famous for their penis gourds, not to mention their spectacular airports. That's Galbraith with the checked shirt and white sideburns.

we sailed has been relocated farther west along the coast.

A Glimpse of Indonesian New Guinea

As time passed, Barbara would accompany me on most official trips beyond Jakarta, but she missed one of the most interesting due to Annie's tender age (and also not being invited) when, in October 1970, I accompanied Frank Galbraith on the first visit ever by an American ambassador to the Indonesian half of New Guinea, then known as West Irian (today as Papua). Indonesia's long squabble with the Dutch over this territory had just ended with a widely distrusted "Act of Free Choice" in which the New Guineans ratified joining Indonesia. (The Dutch had argued, with some reason plus a lot of righteous self-interest, that it should be independent because it had little in common historically or ethnically with the rest of their old empire.) I traveled with the ambassador by commercial air, which took only one day. Other staffers came in the DC-3 assigned to our military attachés, and it took them two and one-half days because our pilots were leery of flying their World War II workhorse to islands infested with thunderstorms, so they didn't fly after noon.

We spent a week in New Guinea, hosted by American Protestant missionaries based in Sentani and taken around by their air service, Missionary Aviation Fellowship (MAF), still operating as I write. It was a memorable experience. We visited Jayapura (Hollandia in Dutch times), the territorial capital. General Macarthur's headquarters was located in this place for a time during World War II, on a suitably Olympian hill. Jayapura's vast, mountain-ringed harbor, now almost empty, is shown in old photos with hundreds of US warships, many of them aircraft carriers, preparing for the invasion of the Philippines. On land there had been three airstrips; half of one of them now served as a civil airport with room to spare. We stayed at Lake Sentani, the mission headquarters. The mainly Christian population lived in villages built on stilts over the lake, an entrapped arm of the sea filled with exotic species, including fresh-water sharks.

Then came the biggest adventure, visiting the highlands of the New Guinea interior. I wrote to the family, which was already getting used to such travelogues:

There are about 160,000 Dani people in the western highlands . . . divided into two main language groups. Until recently the place has been an anthropologist's dream—for some reason the people are remarkably unmoved by cameras, and it was possible to move around in a full-scale cannibal battle taking pictures and jotting notes—but now most of the population has either become enthusiastically Christian or decided that war isn't worth the village-burning retaliation that is eventually meted out by Indonesian police patrols. There are still some smaller, untouched valleys, and two American missionaries were killed and eaten in the area east of the Baliem [Valley] only two years ago.[17]

---

[17] Whoever told me this story may have been pulling my leg. I later learned that while ritual cannibalism was practiced in some areas of New Guinea, as recounted later in this chapter, it was never typical of the highly varied local ethnic groups, and not the well-studied Dani.

The Danis live by growing sweet potatoes. The surplus is used to accumulate pigs and wives, both important for wealth and status. They are great gardeners, and the missionaries have now gotten them started on everything from dairy cattle to tomatoes. Unlike the south coast people [the Asmat], who go naked, Dani men wear penis gourds (only) without which they feel improperly attired. The gourds are sometimes a couple of feet long, bent into interesting loops and curves, and decorated with feathers, etc. The Danis, who are bright and practical, enjoy getting out of the highlands when they get a chance, and a while back the missionaries took some of them down to the south coast to help on a construction project. They were shocked at the nakedness of their Asmat brethren, and after they got back a delegation came to see one of the missionaries and volunteered to collect a planeload of gourds if he would see that they were flown down south! I should have mentioned that female Danis do wear pandanus-leaf mini-skirts.

We flew around with the missionaries for two days, which I assure you is an experience never to be forgotten. [MAF has] a fleet of nine planes operating into about ninety strips. The pilots are trained at a flying school operated by the Moody Bible Institute; all are missionaries and mechanics as well as pilots . . . . They are the only people who are there year after year, really learning the exceedingly difficult and highly structured local languages, and providing education and medical services which the Indonesian government won't be able to match for years. This of course puts them in a very tricky political situation, but by some kind of miracle they survived the Sukarno years, although only by a hair, and they have learned to behave with great tact toward the local authorities.

In West Irian you fly through the mountains, not over them, always with an eye on clouds which can sock in a pass in a matter of minutes—but as long as there's a hole in the weather ahead, and as long as you can still keep an eye over your shoulder and see a way out behind, you go! This is facilitated by a very efficient radio net manned by other pilots, missionary wives, etc., which provides more or less instant weather information. It's all done in Indonesian, albeit with strong California accents, to avert any possible suspicion on the part of the authorities, who may be listening in. Interestingly enough there seem to be few southerners among the American fundamentalists.

The strips are frequently built on horrendous slopes, which are hard on the nervous system at first, but not so scary once you see that this really does make it easier to land (uphill) and take off (downhill) in a Cessna loaded with a thousand pounds or so of people, vegetables, etc. Every mission has an air strip but we also landed at one place where the station had been pulled out because of constant warfare (they unwittingly located it on the border between two rival groups) and our pilot had to fly in several times in the last few months to crack down on the local people.

Wherever you land, the Danis come crowding around the plane, smelling rather strongly of pig fat and wood smoke, but after you get acclimated to the gourds (only), which takes awhile, they seem very ordinary people. This impression tends to be confirmed by their villages, mostly made up of round huts with wooden walls (double plank walls with pandanus insulation to keep out the cold) which at first glance seem totally savage, yet once you get inside they are quite cozy except when the fire is starting up. There are no chimneys or even smoke holes so it's a bit close until the fire works down to a good bed of coals.[18]

Living with the missionaries was extremely pleasant even though some of us missed our cocktail hour and others were constrained to sneak outdoors now and then for a cigarette. The wives all seemed to be excellent cooks, and in addition to eating well from the produce of Dani gardens, the missionaries had over the years fixed themselves up with snug homes including good plumbing and wood stove-heated hot water. In the highlands they had on-demand electricity, rigged from P-38 (World War II fighter plane) turbochargers, easily scrounged from crash sites or from the vast stores of "war surplus" left by our departing troops. Turbochargers compressed air so that the reciprocating engines of that time could function better at high altitudes, but they also made good mini-hydroelectric turbines when water was run through them backwards. All you needed in addition was a water supply on a nearby hill, easily

---

[18] Bob letter to Dear Family, October 25, 1970; also Jakarta A395, "Rendering unto Caesar in West Irian: The Foreign Missionaries and the GOI," December 4, 1970.

available in highland New Guinea, and of course the resulting electricity didn't cost a cent. We were quite jealous, not having anything like that in Jakarta.

I should note that embassy officers had another extraordinary source of information on New Guinea, a medical researcher named Carleton Gajdusek, pronounced "guide a check." Unlike almost anyone else, he worked on both the Australian (as it then was) and Indonesian sides of the border. He loved coming in to chat with us, especially with our statuesque blonde consular officer, Harriet Isom, about his latest travels.

A raving polymath, he was, among other things, an expert on New Guinea languages. In an exceptionally remote area even for New Guinea, he had studied a rare form of ritual cannibalism which led to *kuru*, a disease of the brain. We all thought he was delightful, but more than slightly nuts; however, his *kuru* research would help lead to the discovery of the retrovirus, eventually winning him and his co-researcher a Nobel Prize. He certainly had the last laugh. He later worked for the National Institutes of Health and, while there, after pleading guilty to child molestation, was effectively hounded out of the USA. His is a long story. There is a good Wikipedia entry on him.[19]

We all flew back to Jakarta together in the DC-3. It was a lazy, gorgeous flight. The archipelago westward from New Guinea was magnificent from our modest altitude: volcanoes, coral islands, sapphire smooth seas and lots of lovely thunderstorms, which we prudently flew around. Our plane, which I got to fly for a few minutes, was relatively young in airborne hours for one so old in years, but not inclined to acrobatics or undue turbulence. She had had a rather humiliating accident just before the ambassador was supposed to leave on a previous trip, when a Pan Am Boeing 707 somehow got too close to the place where she was parked at the Jakarta airport, and blew both her elevators clean off. They were hard to replace, as DC-3 parts were already getting scarce.

Our first overnight stop was Portuguese Timor, the eastern half of the island (now independent Timor Leste); the other

---

[19] https://en.wikipedia.org/wiki/Daniel_Carleton_Gajdusek .

half had belonged to the Dutch and was Indonesian. The attachés wanted to go there because you could buy Portuguese wine, *vinho verde*. Timor was almost as psychedelic as West Irian. In Dili, the capital, the governor had a white palace guarded by picturesque, spear-carrying Timorese troops in short skirts made from the *ikat* (tie-died) fabric for which the region is famous. There were only one or two paved roads, which ended at the edge of town. The hinterland was reported to be even poorer than Indonesian Timor. The shops were full of Colgate toothpaste made in Angola and other such oddities. There was one quite pleasant little hotel.

The Australians had a consulate with a thatched roof to deal with the numerous backpackers who globe-trotted through Dili because of a cheap air fare ($70) to Darwin, in northern Australia. The consul was irked at the US because, although most of his clients were Australians, quite a few were Americans, and he was supposed to take care of them as well when they ran out of money, etc. I wrote a report entitled "Old Wine in New Bottles: A Glimpse of Portuguese Timor" [20] which drew praise from the Assistant Secretary of East Asian and Pacific Affairs. (It must have been a slow day in EAP, as the Bureau was known.) After Portugal's dictator was overthrown in 1974, the Indonesians, fearful that communists would take over, invaded Portuguese Timor late in 1975, with tacit US encouragement. That led to a long-drawn-out political nightmare and eventual independence for East Timor in 1999.

We continued on to Lombok, the island just east of Bali. The Hindu Balinese conquered most of mainly Muslim Lombok in the seventeenth century. The western side had remained culturally Balinese, but, unlike Bali itself, it was still largely untouched by tourism in 1970. We must have landed and spent the night in Mataram, the major town in western Lombok, but I don't remember anything about it. I do remember seeing a beautiful water temple where the Hindu priest put a hard boiled egg in one of the water outlets, inducing an enormous eel to emerge from inside the temple wall and gobble it up. Today Balinese Lombok is almost as heavily touristed as Bali

---

[20] Jakarta A-398, December 4, 1970.

itself. We returned to Jakarta the following day.

Back at home, we spent our first tropical Christmas with both children. We cut a tree in the mountains and gathered some pine cones to paint for it, and with those and a few ornaments sent from home the tree made a big hit. When Jamie saw it he came running to find Barbara and announced, "Look, Mommy, *tree!*" Having spent previous Christmases of our married life in London, upriver in Sarawak or in Cincinnati, we did not have a great collection of ornaments. So we decided to make gingerbread men and hang them on the tree—old-fashioned decorations. However, not old-fashioned tropical Christmas decorations: the next morning, we found them all on the floor, having absorbed enough moisture from the ambient humidity to become heavy and fall off their strings.

We attended a Christmas service at the old Batavia Anglican Church, where Jamie, who had been released to wander around after he decided to comment on every scripture passage, suddenly appeared in the chancel beside the talented British soloist, gazing out cherubically at the congregation while she sang. On her first Christmas, Annie was "a delightfully cheerful three and one-half month old; she's all kinds of fun to play with because she reacts so much; she plays and laughs with abandon."[21]

On Christmas morning we celebrated with the servants and their children, and there were plenty of presents for all the kids. Jamie opened Jane's magical circus box first and could hardly be persuaded to pay attention to others, which he kept trying to give to our houseboy's daughter. Barbara got a handsome teak desk, which Bob found at the last minute—the one that now adorns our living room, under the Bugis schooner painting. The prospects for Christmas dinner looked grim because the state oil company had run out of bottled gas, leaving us with a balky, back-up kerosene oven, but a full gas cylinder arrived at the last minute, sparing us a kerosene-flavored turkey.

We invited Indonesian friends and their wives, including Umar Kayam, the Director of the Jakarta Arts Center; Abu Ridho, the elderly curator of the ceramics collection at the National Museum, with whom Barbara was working as a

---

[21] Barbara letter to Dear Family, December 21, 1970.

museum volunteer; and a Navy commander, Pandam Guritno, officially charged with fleet maintenance, which, since there wasn't any money for it, left him largely free to pursue his passion, writing about and producing wayang shadow plays and making leather puppets.

He brought us a suitable present: a puppet of Kresno Duta (Krishna), the wily diplomat who negotiates between the warring families of the Indian-origin *Mahabharata* epic, the core of the wayang repertory. We framed it, mounted on blue velvet, and it adorned many walls over the years, an example to all diplomats. All our guests brought their wives except Abu Ridho; she stayed home because she feared that we might have a dog. Barbara wrote: "Abu Ridho was the only old-school, not really westernized guest, but all our more sophisticated friends were very respectful of him— an interesting comment on how strong old mores still are beneath the obvious changes."[22]

---

[22] Barbara letter to Dear Family, December 27, 1970.

6

Indonesia (2), 1971-1974

Before long we were thinking about how to spend our "Rest and Recuperation" (R&R), a special kind of leave available only at "hardship posts" like Jakarta. We decided that we would like to visit Burma, but our administrative officer found this questionable. "R&R is supposed to provide a *complete* change of scene," he objected; "Isn't Burma even worse off than Indonesia?" Putting on my PhD face, I said, "No, of course not, it's a Buddhist country. Indonesia is Muslim, so Burma is *completely* different." He looked dubious but authorized us to go (meaning that the USG paid the international air fare and the time spent was not charged against my regular leave allotment).

Resting and Recuperating in Burma

On the way to Burma we spent one night in Bangkok, at the Oriental Hotel, in the colonial-era wing overlooking the river with its splendid vista of royal palaces and endless boat traffic. In Rangoon we stayed with Peter and Joan Smart, British diplomats I had known in Korea. We had seven days to explore Burma, the longest visa the government, already a military dictatorship, would allow. We got our Burmese money (*kyat*, pronounced "chat") from friends assigned to the US Embassy, which had mountains of the stuff generated by sales of surplus US food to Burma after World War II. We received it at or near the (black) market rate, whereas most diplomatic missions were paying the absurd official rate, which made Burma extremely expensive. However, at our rate it was absurdly cheap. We changed $100, and with our wads of *kyat* we got tickets on Air Burma for all the travel we could do in one week in the Texas-sized country, plus food, a couple of hotel nights, and all the handicrafts we could carry, and we had *kyat* left over.

We spent two days in Rangoon, one arriving and one departing, where we visited the great Schwedagon Pagoda, encircled by shrines and vendors, worth a trip to Burma by itself.[1] We then proceeded to Pagan, one of the most spectacular ancient sites in Asia, with hundreds of thousand-year-old temples scattered across an arid plain on the banks of the Irrawady River. After that, we stayed for three days with Carl and Ching Wen Taylor in Mandalay, where Carl was the US Consul, surrounded by the remains of four other ancient capitals and a wealth of traditional craft centers.

In Pagan, we overnighted at a "temporary" guest house built for the visiting Prince of Wales in the 1930s and scarcely renovated, not to say cleaned, since then. A crew of villagers cooked for us on an open fire in the back yard; the food was almost inedible. The water came from the Irrawaddy, mud came out of the showerhead, and we brushed our teeth with tea. We had brought seltzer water in glass bottles from Rangoon to drink.

Work was just beginning on the first real hotel. A very good guide plus his World War II jeep cost five dollars a day. Two days at the guest house cost $7.50. A cash-strapped backpacker also staying in the guest house found that he could sell his shirt and a pair of blue jeans for enough money to fly back to Rangoon, giving him an extra day in Pagan.

Barbara was reminded of medieval Europe:

> . . . *[Burma] is steadily, and consciously, progressing backward into the Middle Ages. The name of this process is "the Burmese way to socialism . . . . " Religion pervades everything; people are always at the temples praying (medieval cathedrals must have been like that) and they also spend a major portion of their*

---

[1] Note that our photo of Jamie and Annie on the Schwedagon terrace was taken in 1974, when we stopped over briefly, again staying with the Taylors, who by this time were in Rangoon, on our way home from Indonesia.

resources on it . . . .[2]

The temples of Pagan stretched in all directions, most built from the eleventh to thirteenth centuries, some of them whitewashed, others sinking into piles of brick rubble. We met the conservator of monuments, U Bokay, in his village house-cum-office, piled high with books. He talked our ears off about how the Buddhist religious leaders made conservation almost impossible, because they assumed that conservators were really hunting for treasure. No surprise why Burma was covered with rotting pagodas: if you fixed one you didn't earn any merit; it all accrued to the original builder.

The best maintained temple was the very active Schwezigon (not to be confused with the equally impressive Schwe*da*gon in Rangoon). King Anawrahta (1044-77), the great monarch credited with unifying Burma, had built it to demonstrate his control over the principal *nats* (spirits) of Burma, thirty-seven in number, and their subordination to Buddhism. He had statues of all the *nats* carved, painted, and put inside the sanctuary, which immediately made this temple the most important and among the most visited in the country.

The weather was hot and sunny, but frequent thunderstorms and shifting cloud masses made for gorgeous lighting, and I took hundreds of Kodachrome slides which, at this writing, are still unfaded. All the temples had signs saying "footwearing prohibited," and visitors had to hop fast over scorching brick plazas to reach the shady interiors. We began to sympathize with the British, whose stubborn refusal to shed their shoes helped bring on three Anglo-Burman wars and their eventual conquest of Burma.

Mandalay (landlocked, no flying fish) has a huge royal compound and one remaining wooden palace with gorgeous carved wooden decoration. Most of the other old wooden buildings were burned by the British or carried off to the Indian Museum in Calcutta, Burma being then part of India, where we later unsuccessfully tried to see them. We visited thriving handicraft centers: silk weaving, wood and marble carving, production of lacquer ware, and bronze casting. The latter featured a giant statue of independence hero Aung San being cast in bronze. Not far away

---

[2] Barbara letter to Dear Family, June 8, 1971.

were massive brick ruins of a pagoda started by a megalomaniac eighteenth-century king that, had it been finished, would have been as tall as the Washington Monument and much wider.

Barbara wrote, "Here's one country where you don't have to buy antiques to get the workmanship that unmeasured time produces."[3] We acted on this observation, and came home loaded with lacquer ware, wood carvings, and even a tiny marble Buddha. The wood lions in our bookshelf and the black-and-gold lacquer birds that Charlotte always kept on her mantelpiece are both products of this trip. For all its hermit kingdom failings, Burma struck us as one of the most interesting places we had ever visited.[4] We returned to Jakarta wishing we had had more time there.

Children, Servants, Travel

By this time we had learned to trust our household staff with the kids when we were away, making sure that friends kept an eye on things, and not getting too excited when minor colds and illnesses popped up in our absence (though this trip was postponed a week because Annie had a fever, which turned out to be nothing after a couple of days, on the first scheduled departure date). As Barbara put it, ". . . the availability of $20 a month servants does take the edge off raising children. We have freedom to travel and to entertain, without sacrificing sanity."[5] There was no malaria in Jakarta and no crime worth worrying about. Of course servants also made frequent official entertaining possible, not to mention a never-ending stream of houseguests, many of them old friends from academia, some of whom would repay the favor with interest in later years.

Despite this unusual situation, our fairly frequent absences were probably hard on the children at times, although they were too young to complain. Writing of our trip to Burma, Barbara noted that her first night away was the first whole night's sleep she had gotten since Annie was born nine months previously. "When I got back she was so glad to see me she didn't want to

---

[3] Barbara letter to Dear Family, June 8, 1971.
[4] The dates were May 26-June 3, 1971; see insert in Bob's Diary of June 3 on Thai Airways stationery and Barbara letter to family cited above.
[5] Bob letter to Dear Mother, September 20, 1971.

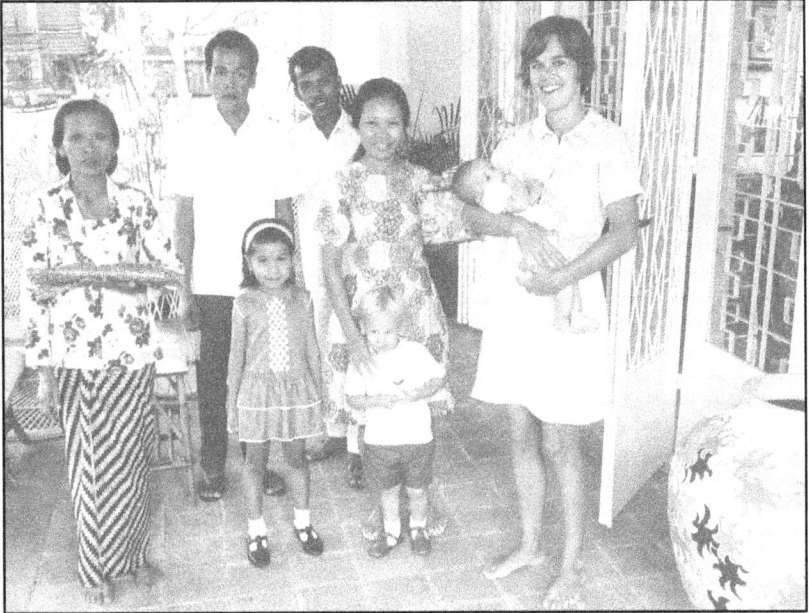

Staff at our first house on Jalan (Street) Kiai Madja in Kebayoran: Sriah, Supari, Jani, Sumila, Barbara with Annie; in front, Sumila's daughter and Jamie.

Staff at second house on Jalan Mangunsarkoro in Menteng: Sujadi (Pak Di), Munarti, Jani, Yuda with Annie, Idja; in front, Djoko, Jamie, Budi. The Indonesian children were Sujadi and Munarti's family.

go to bed, and when I put her in her crib anyway, she threw up all her dinner—that's our littlest angel." [6]

Our letters home are full of comments on the children and their development, all of which would probably have been lost in a later, e-mail age:

April 5, 1970:
Jamie is slowly, but very slowly, adapting to the servants. Last night he waved goodbye to us without a tear; but he was a bear all today. He's got a bad case of Asian tummy, which doesn't help. [7]

June 16, 1970:
Had a great sail out to one of the nearest islands today for a swim & a picnic. Now we have a little beet running around the house; despite his hat, Jamie's cheeks are very rosy. He loves the boat and swimming in the ocean. Our little beet and his daddy have different temperature gauges, and the air conditioning is a bit much for Jamie, who won't stay under blankets. Could you see if Swallen's has any of those flannel sleepers like the one you got [him] last August and send us a bigger one?

June 23, 1970:
[Another] day-long sail . . . .He can't swim yet but will have any amount of being swished around by Bob and me. The island we visited yesterday had sand, which Jamie is now old enough to enjoy thoroughly—he found an old bicycle handle which he filled and emptied. He's at the pouring stage now, drives the lifeguards at the swimming pool crazy because he likes to take a cup of water from the baby pool and walk over and dump it in the big pool. The lifeguards panic when he approaches the edge but Jamie has no thought of going in . . . [future physical oceanographer].

---

[6] Barbara letter to Dear Family, June 8, 1971.
[7] This excerpt and the following ones are all from letters written to Mother and Daddy Cade, mostly by Barbara, from April, 1970, through New Year's Eve, 1971.

July 4, 1970:
Jamie's Sumila has her own five-year old living here now, and the two of them keep him on the run. They have just finished a mighty romp in his plastic swimming pool in the back yard . . . . He still isn't talking more than a handful of words (plus one or two in Indonesian) and I suppose it is likely that the transition into a bi-lingual world is going to slow him down considerably. We aren't worried—he is an exceptionally happy and self-contained little boy, and that in itself would probably make him a slow talker. He has been moved into the other bedroom in anticipation of the new arrival in August.

July 30, 1970:
Junior #2 is kicking around lustily—Barb thinks it must be a girl since they are supposed to be more active.

January 14, 1971:
I'm somewhat exhausted at the moment. My dear darling daughter has taken to getting up 2 or 3 times each night for a drink of milk—just likes it, I guess, and we were out every evening last week except Sunday (all fun—but still) and also Mark Dion was down for three days, so that meant both kids in our room at night. Now I'm trying the water at night routine, equally non-restful; Anne [sic] hates it and I feel like an ogre when all the sleepyhead wants is a little cuddly nursing. But this can't go on.

January 25, 1971:
Request for Daddy. Jane sent Jamie a Mattell "Mr. Circus Says" for Christmas. Unbreakable, no child can open it. Nor can any parent. Jamie, who shows real signs of mechanical genius, managed, by taking the battery in and out about fifty times Christmas day, to break off the copper contact. So I need to open the toy. But the screws have three indentations coming in from the edge, as pictured . . . .[Rest of letter is an illustrated request for the right tool to open the toy.]

March 15, 1971:
Anne is happily scooting all over the place these days in her walker. She can push herself up on all fours and can almost

sit, altogether a strong and very supple little girl. But she's still getting up in the middle of the night; tonight I'm going to try cereal at ten, and see what happens. Jamie, bless his heart, is almost trained; he requires an audience when he performs but when he's awake manages to make the toilet most of the time. . . . He really is fun now that he is talking. Kate gave him a book about a Dutch cow that fell into a canal and floated to Amsterdam. Every time we cross a canal when we are out driving, Jamie announces: "Canal. Cow there. Brown one." The first time he said it I couldn't imagine what he was talking about. His analysis of bath water going down the drain is "Water going tunnel" [incipient oceanographer again] and of our new quiet air conditioner, "Broke." His teacher at school is English, and "naughty" has become a favorite descriptive word. Cars are naughty if we have to honk at them, the floor is naughty if Jamie falls down; the puppy is naughty if he wets in the house, which is true.

Date uncertain, sometime between March and July, 1971, or, more likely, 1972:
[Jamie] really enjoys his books; . . . [his] favorite ones are the ones about things he's familiar with, the one exception being the book about the sun and the stars. The all-time hit was the book about the sea which we borrowed from Erica Gibson . . . .In the morning before I leave for school, at 6:45, Jamie and I read our nature books; there may be a scientist yet in the family, Daddy.

July 31, 1971:
As for Anne, that little miss has just begun to walk and thank heavens. She's wearing herself out so much that she has started to sleep through the night from seven to six, and what a relief! Character that she is, she never looks where she is going, but careens from one obstacle to another and has several bumps a day to howl over. We discovered that fruit loops are very comforting after a fall.

New Year's Eve, 1971:
The great event of today was that the man who maintains our saltwater fish tank came with a long-promised sea horse—Jamie is fascinated. The aquarium has been a great source of pleasure

ever since we got it a month ago. It's gorgeous, and interesting for Jamie—he's fascinated with the starfish and a big fish that Bob named Freddie, and he's getting a real nature lesson from watching the fish eat the prawns and smaller fish that are their food.

Freddie was named after Bob's recently arrived boss, a truly weird albeit cheerful character named Fred Flott, a CIA analyst who gained notoriety by making speeches praising the Vietnam War. For this he was offered his choice of overseas assignments, and picked the Political Counselor position in Jakarta, normally a sought-after State Department, not CIA, position. Why he wanted it was never clear—he was fluent in Chinese and Russian but knew no Indonesian and made no effort to conceal his disinterest in the country or its internal politics. The main thing he seemed to enjoy was talking to Russian and Chinese diplomats at cocktail parties, although he seldom gave one himself. He lived immediately in back of us in a nice embassy house, where he proceeded to isolate himself in one room with its air conditioning turned up full blast, equipped with a safe where he could keep classified papers and his pistol—he was also a gun nut. The rest of the house was barely furnished during his stay.

Despite all that, he was pleasant enough, and one night when we had him to dinner Jamie met him at the door and showed him the aquarium. "Look," he said, pointing to the fish in question, "That's Freddie."

Ramblings around Java and Sumatra

Then there was the memorable expedition to Central Java in August, 1971, Jamie's first long car trip with us, in our own little Toyota Corolla. The only road maps available dated from Dutch times, and they often showed bold red lines indicating the 1930s equivalent of superhighways which no longer existed, their "paving" now reduced to jagged chunks separated by large holes. To quote a marvelous book about Sumatra in the 1960s, "Every time it rained, another fragment of the colonial past slid toward the sea."[8]

We had hoped to make it through the mountains between Jakarta and Central Java in one day, but we began to think it might be better to turn around rather than risk wrecking the car, a not infrequent dilemma in Indonesia. The map no longer made any sense. At one stop, a villager had advised us that the road ahead had deteriorated seriously. It was a *"jalan jelek,"* meaning "bad road" in Indonesian, he said, but concluded that we could probably make it. What did that mean? Experience based on his oxcart or the local jitney? More deadpan Javanese revenge for the sins of the Dutch?

As we crept along the road, the slabs of old paving kept getting bigger and sharper, the potholes deeper and more liquid, and the darkness darker, but Jamie remained cheerful. He was by this time toddler-bilingual; he had overheard our conversation with the villager, and he bounced up and down on the back seat repeating over and over, *"Jalan jelek! jalan jelek!,"* a language lesson we didn't need.

When we got out of the hills there was a fairly large town, almost as lightless as the surrounding countryside. We were famished and finally found a modest Chinese restaurant, which we settled into. About five minutes later an extremely angry policeman came peddling up the road on his bicycle. Apparently we had gone by his booth at the town's only traffic circle, not even noticing him, much less stopping as we were supposed to. We finally got him calmed down by repeating at length that we, ignorant foreigners, were deeply sorry for having thus insulted duly constituted authority. He really did not seem to be asking for money. We ended up having a great trip, visiting the seventh-century Hindu ruins on the Dieng Plateau and later attending the Ramayana Ballet performances at the great Prambanan Temple.[9]

We needed an excuse to visit Palembang, site of a previous city famous in Indonesian history as the assumed capital of the maritime empire of Srivijaya, powerful from the seventh to the fourteenth centuries, and, since it lived by controlling trade through the nearby Straits of Malacca, the geopolitical

---

[8] James Mossman, *Rebels in Paradise: Indonesia's Civil War*, London, Jonathan Cape, 1961, p. 122.

[9] Barbara letter to Dear Mother and Daddy, August 13, 1971.

ancestor of modern Singapore. Because it had been a "water city," an assemblage of wooden buildings on stilts over a big river, it had left few physical remains and there was debate for years about where it actually had been. The verdict is now in that it was indeed at the site of modern Palembang.

My professor at Cornell, Oliver Wolters, was the world's leading expert on Srivijaya history, and I persuaded the embassy to commission me to deliver a copy of his latest book on the subject[10] to the Rector of the University of Srivijaya, which Barbara and I duly did. In the process we were able to see some of the famous silk weaving done in this heartland of the Malay people. It was gorgeous, but only very wealthy people could afford it, mostly for weddings.

Our trip home was a combination of awful train and even worse ferry across the strait separating Sumatra from Java. The ferry was sweltering and we were stuck in the same small cabin with an Indonesian couple who did not want to open the porthole because they were afraid we would be robbed. After several hours of suffering, diplomacy took a back seat and we finally opened it anyway.[11]

Wading Back to Sarawak

In late 1971 we made our first and only trip to Indonesian Borneo, and then crossed the border into Sarawak (Malaysia). Serious unrest among the ethnic Chinese along the Indonesia-Malaysia border was just subsiding, and the Indonesians would never have allowed us to go there had our extraordinary military attaché, Colonel George Benson, not pleaded our case with his army friends. I had always wanted to make such a trip because the border area figured heavily in Iban and Sarawak history and I had read a lot about it, but had not been able to visit the Indonesian side during our stay in Sarawak due to "Confrontation." As on most of my official trips, the children did not come with us.

We flew to Pontianak, a river-mouth port and the biggest

---

[10] O.W. Wolters, *The Fall of Srivijaya in Malay History*, Cornell University Press, 1970.

[11] Barbara letter to Dear Mother and Daddy, September 1, 1971; Bob letter to Oliver Wolters, September 11, 1971.

city in the Indonesian province of West Kalimantan, spang on the equator and the site of a Sultanate founded by an Arab adventurer in the eighteeth century. We visited the nearby Sambas area, where many Chinese were still detained in camps, then headed about halfway up the 700 mile-long Kapuas River, longer than anything we had seen in Sarawak. Even with a Missionary Aviation Fellowship Cessna it took us three hours to reach our destination, the district capital at Putussibau, where we chatted with local officials and American missionaries. Then back downriver a ways by speedboat, with a burp-gun toting government bodyguard supplied by the *bupati* (District Officer, or Regent in Dutch terminology).

I wrote: "The mighty river flows, not as the crow flies, but in majestic, mile-consuming meanders. Here and there nature or some long-forgotten Dutch regent has punched a channel across the neck of a loop."[12] We thought it would make sense to dig many more of them. It took a full two days more to reach the Malaysian border, with a stop to check in with local officials at Semitau, then to return a bit upriver to where we turned up a side stream and headed north toward the border by way of the Kapuas lakes.

These lakes are great, shallow depressions, seasonally variable in depth and number, in a sea of swamp forest. Each year in the rainy season, the streams linking them with the main river reverse course and the lakes refill, in the same way as does the better known Cambodian Tonlé Sap, which supported the ancient Angkorian Empire. Our trip took place during this seasonal refilling. Traditionally these lakes, like the Tonlé Sap, produced huge harvests of fish, caught as they were trapped by the receding water, then smoked and exported by the locals. (Later we would see something very similar in Mali.)

Today this area has been heavily damaged by deforestation,

---

[12] "Kalimantan Diary," Jakarta A-011, November 26, 1971. The Kapuas Lakes area now includes a large national park, Danau Sentarum, the subject of eleven essays in the *Borneo Research Bulletin*, Vol. 41, 2010; the report cited here has also been published in the *Borneo Research Bulletin*: Robert Pringle, "West Kalimantan Diary—November 29-December 14," 1971, Vol. 42, 2011, pp. 111-126.

On our hike from Indonesian to Malaysian Borneo (Sarawak) we were escorted by troops from the Siliwangi Divison along an often watery trail. (Note soldier wading in back of Barbara's shoulder.)

partly for oil palm plantations, leading to unprecedented fires in both forest and desiccated swamp, and blanketing the entire region with smoke, as far as Singapore and beyond. All that was still in the future. We had to cross one of the lakes in an overloaded, *bupati*-supplied boat, which needed its sparkplugs cleaned every five minutes, and we were caught by a thunderstorm that suddenly stirred up big waves in the shallow water. We did make it to a small army base at Pulau Madjang, not a minute too soon, but this lake-crossing remains one of the scariest experiences I can remember in my Foreign Service career.

After spending the night at Pulau Madjang, we picked up escorts from both the "crack" Siliwangi Division and the Indonesian Special Forces (RPKAD) for the rest of the trip by foot to the border. They were veterans and professionals, but seemed more like friendly kids. They were armed with everything from US World War II carbines to AK-47s. Their uniforms were anything but uniform. They enjoyed having their pictures taken and obviously found it quite fun to have a pretty lady to escort. Some of them were living in a big Iban longhouse, which we saw, and seemed to be getting along

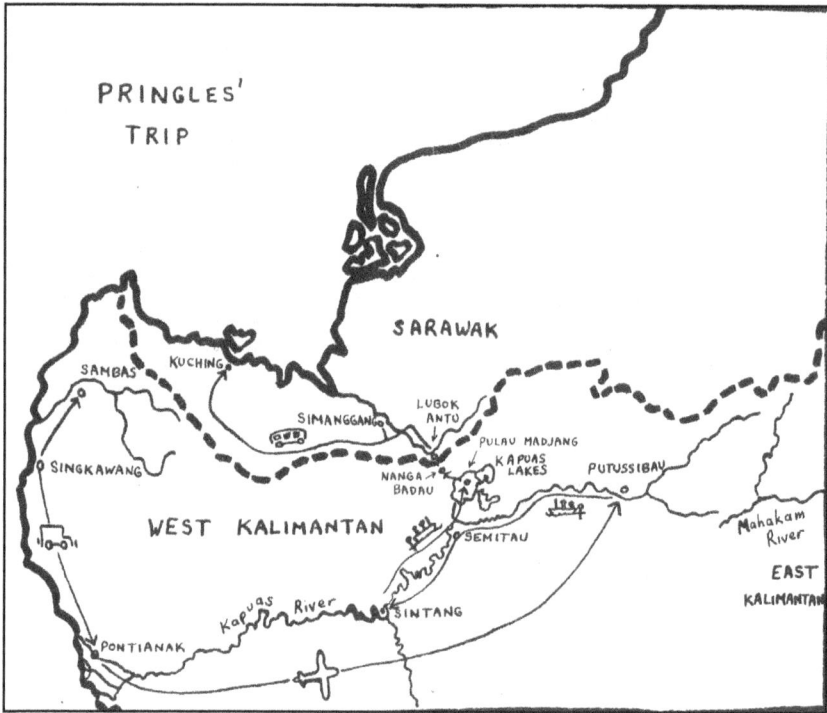

Barbara drew the map for the report Bob did based on this adventure.

well with their local hosts, the Ibans being famous for their hospitality, not least when it comes to boy-girl stuff. The trail alternated between deep mud and water. It led to Nanga Badau, a small military outpost only a short distance from the Sarawak border.

But there we sat for several days. Messages flew back and forth between the Indonesian and Malaysian border posts. The Indonesian authorities would not let us go further without confirmation that the Malaysians would meet us at the border. The Malaysians didn't think we needed to be met—there was a well-worn trail into Sarawak used by Iban traders. Meanwhile, our Siliwangi/RPKAD escorts had departed, and we shuddered at the thought of trying to get back across the lakes on our own.

Finally a squad of the Royal Malay Regiment arrived to pick us up. The contrast between these troops and the Indonesians was dramatic—the Malaysians had new uniforms, all the same kind, no long hair, no tennis shoes, no bare feet. They all had the same kind of rifle, even a field radio. In a few hours we were at the Sarawak border post of Lubok Antu, which, with its running water and profusion of well-stocked shops, was quite a contrast to what I had seen there in 1966. Compared to adjacent Indonesia, everything about the Malaysian side struck us as prosperous. Local school teachers were earning the equivalent of $100 a month, at least five times the Indonesian average.

Soon we were on our way to Kuching by bus, over a new road. We spent four days seeing old friends, and the local paper ran an interview with me, "Author Returns to Sarawak." We came back to Sarawak from Indonesia once more, by plane via Singapore on our way home in 1974, to visit Kuching and Benedict Sandin's longhouse with the children, but after that not again until 2004.

Home Leave via Fiji

Since we were going to be in Jakarta for a second two-year tour, we were entitled to two months of home leave with the children, which we took in May-June 1973. We spent most of the time at Pine Knoll Shores, going fishing, helping Clay to install a new swing set, and generally relaxing. The pictures of Annie as a toddler on the deck and "helping" to install the swing at PKS were taken at this time.

When we departed on leave Jamie was already speaking fluent Indonesian with a slangy Jakarta accent. When we got back, he had forgotten it—until it suddenly clicked back on again. We had already discovered that the psychology of bilingualism is tricky. Jamie would not speak Indonesian with us, because that was not our language. But he conversed with Sujadi and Munarti and their children in *Bahasa Indonesia*. Another time he refused to respond when an Indonesian friend, Filino Harahap, tried to use the language with him, apparently because he had observed Filino talking to us in English the night before.

We traveled home on leave with Moertini, who had worked for our embassy colleagues and later close friends, David and Helen Kenney, as their *babu anak* (nanny), and they had hired her to continue that job for them in the US. She never worked for us, although we knew her well, but she did accompany us

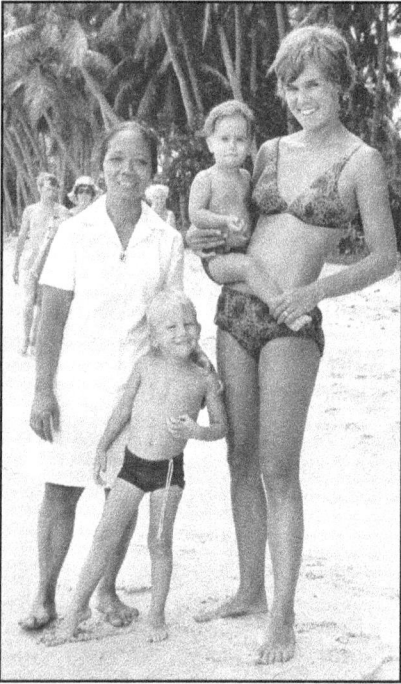

*Barbara with Moertini and the children
at our stop in Fiji.*

home on this trip, acting as *our* nanny. That, dear reader, is the way to travel with small kids, we assure you.

The trip generated several memorable moments. Our first stop was Australia, where we saw academic friends and had a first glance at the country. As we settled in our first hotel, in Melbourne, Barbara asked Moertini to give the kids some Tang (instant orange juice). When Barbara came back a few minutes later, Moertini was just sitting there, no Tang prepared, which was not like her. "Moertini," Barbara said, "why don't the kids have their drink yet?" "*Mem*," she replied, "I'm waiting for the hotel to send us some boiled water." She had never previously encountered tap water that was safe to drink.

Our next stop was Fiji, where we intended to drive across the island to the capital, Suva, from the international airport at Nandi. We did not realize that the road was unpaved until, only halfway to our destination and already flagging, we stopped for refreshments at an unexpectedly deluxe beach hotel on the "Coral Coast." There we noticed a calendar turned to April 17, Barbara's thirtieth birthday, which we had totally forgotten in all the excitement. So we decided to cede to *force majeure* and celebrate. We rented a room for the night, and enjoyed the pool, beach, and snorkeling, not to mention Moertini's all-expenses-paid, child-supervising talents. We never did get to Suva. Fiji's tiny airport was the first place we had ever encountered a 747 jumbo jet, which we boarded for the rest of our flight to the US by climbing an amazingly tall set of rolling steps.

Visiting Margot and Paula and Henry at the University of Nebraska.

Jamie and Anne, with Theobald cousins Heidi and Heather, on a cannon at Fort Macon near the family summer home in Pine Knoll Shores, North Carolina. This was the go-to holiday venue, especially for the children, every time we had home leave.

We transited customs in Hawaii, as one did in those days. The officer on duty thoroughly, but thoroughly, inspected Moertini's baggage, remarking in an aside to Barbara, "You know these Asians, they are always trying to bring in plants to cook with." Guess who it was that was not scrutinized at all but had all kinds of questionable things needed to prepare a promised Indonesian dinner for the family at Pine Knoll Shores? Not Moertini!

Moertini stayed in Washington for many years but, being widowed, decided she would return to Indonesia rather than remain where she had no family or other ties. With this in mind she bought some land in East Java with her American earnings and paid for her children's education, so they would be able to take care of her later, which is what has happened. We stayed with her in her comfortable house in the pretty town of Malang on a trip back to Indonesia in 2007, and Annie has also visited her there.

Jalan Mangunsarkoro

In the summer of 1972 we inherited the Kenney's house in Menteng, the high-end residential area of Jakarta, at No. 3 Jalan Mangunsarkoro, formerly Jalan Jogja, the way most Indonesians still knew it. This house was much closer to the embassy than our first residence in Kebayoran Baru. Even more important, a superb Indonesian staff came along with the house. Several of these people remained lifelong friends, not least after they accompanied the Kenneys back to Washington, as Moertini already had.

A story came with these people. They struck us immediately as intelligent and talented. They had worked for the Kenneys in Surabaya before they came to Jakarta, and we learned that several of them had been teachers. That meant that they had (no choice) been members of the communist-affiliated teachers' union. Along with thousands of others, they had lost their teaching jobs and been blacklisted after the failed communist coup d'état of 1965-66. They had been fortunate, under the circumstances, to find work as servants with an American family, especially a caring and generous one.

The house was a narrow, one storey structure, a short distance from the US ambassador's residence, and only a few blocks from the elegant new central Jakarta mosque. The mosque boasted a hi-fi sound system which made the calls to prayer seem quite lovely, even at dawn. The Canadian ambassador, who lived closer to the mosque than we did, was the father of new baby from a late marriage and did not find the calls lovely at all; he complained about the noise to the mayor, to no avail. The school which Barack Obama was attending at about this time, as well as his home, were also close by, although we never met his now famous mother. Many Indonesians were familiar with our new house because it had been the residence of Colonel Benson on his first tour as Army attaché in Jakarta.

There were servants' quarters and a modest but very pleasant combined garden, courtyard and utility area. Only our and the children's bedrooms were air-conditioned, but that was enough, the servants being used to room temperature in Jakarta. The house has survived until now and a second storey has been added; the much larger property next door, once the home of the American Caltex oil company director, is now the official residence of the Vice President of Indonesia.

Despite its modest size, we could do a lot in this house. Thanks to our friendship with *wayang* expert Pandam Guritno, we were able to stage a full-scale shadow puppet show with a top-notch *dalang* (puppeteer) as a departure party, with many guests, for our good friends Peter and Susan Purdy. And the back screened-in play area was large enough to show movies. Our biggest film hit ever was *Lawrence of Arabia*, then quite new. Quite a few of our student and ex-student leader friends, people like lawyer Nono Anwar Makarim and journalist Fikri Djufri, were the descendents of Arabs who had immigrated from the Hadramaut region of Yemen in the nineteenth century. These people were mainly Indonesian by blood, but they could trace their descent from the Prophet, and as a community they were an influential, many-faceted Islamic elite. Such was the appeal of T. E. Lawrence that all of them invited friends and relatives, or so it seemed, and at that movie night we had a scene best described by the Indonesian word *ramai*, which means pleasantly crowded and exciting.

At the front of No. 3 Jalan Mangunsarkoro, there was a small garden separated from the street by a chain link fence. On the sidewalk was a cigarette kiosk, about eight feet by three feet, manned by three brothers who rotated up from their home in Central Java and slept in the kiosk while in Jakarta. From them we got a lesson in security, real versus theoretical. We had a deal: in return for allowing them to use the servants' toilet facilities and our water spigot, they opened our driveway gate when we came or went and kept an eye on things in front of our house during the day. (Jani, the guard who had *pukuled* an intruder earlier at our first house, worked at night.) On one occasion when everyone was busy, toddler Annie wandered out the gate, which someone had left ajar, and for a while nobody missed her. After a moment of panic, she was found safely sitting in the kiosk with the on-duty brother, no doubt promoting the sale of clove cigarettes.

Toward the end of our stay Ali Sadikin, the Mayor of Jakarta, a retired Marine Corps general and otherwise excellent mayor, ordained a rigorous clean-up of street stalls in the central metro area. One of the kiosk guys came to us in desperation: would we allow them to cut a hole in our chain-link fence sufficient to allow his family's source of livelihood to be pulled a few feet back into our garden? Being thus on US Embassy property, it would avoid being "cleaned up" by the mayor's campaign. We thought about it and said yes, and simply never told the embassy what we had done, trusting correctly that the move would not be noticed. After that, I think, the kiosk trio would have died for us.

We traveled with complete confidence after we inherited the Kenney servants, including the former "communist" teachers mentioned earlier, Sujadi ("Pak Di"), his wife Munarti, and our elderly wash lady Idja (with her wringer washing machine), all of whom lived with us. Their children made wonderful companions for ours, and we included them in family celebrations. Later we kept up with Sujadi and Munarti when the Kenneys brought them to Washington (in addition to Moertini), and sometimes they did favors for us in their new country. Pak Di, for example, laid the brick patio in the garden at 216 Wolfe Street, the same garden with a copper plaque on the side wall reading: "*Barbara Cade Pringle hunc murum aedificavit AD 1979.*"

Sumila, who had been Annie's *babu anak* (nanny), the one who "gendanged" her in a baby sling (*gendang*), did not make the move to Menteng with us because the new commute would have been too far for her and she had just become pregnant, with twins it turned out. In any case, Annie was getting old enough so she did not need a nanny, especially with Munarti available, although Munarti was primarily our cook. But Sumila remained good friends with our driver, Sulomo. When we left for home leave, not only Sumila but also Sulomo's wife were expecting twins, to arrive during our absence. Sumila's delivery was normal, but Sulomo's wife went back to their village, probably to save money, and her babies died. What happened next was a typically Javanese arrangement: Sumila's family shared one of her twins with Sulomo and his wife, who adopted the child as their own. Feeding both could well have been a burden for Sumila and, undernourished, they would have become more susceptible to illness, illustrating why in so many societies twins are considered to be bad luck.

The Hotel Pringle

Especially at the house in Menteng, we had a constant stream of visitors, old friends from academe, graduate students often grateful for a free place to stay, Foreign Service colleagues, and of course family. Our superb staff made it possible to be so hospitable, and it was a huge benefit to me professionally because I learned much from experts doing research in Indonesia. We could visit them in return at their research locales, and some became life-long friends.[13]

When we traveled, the Hotel Pringle kept right on attracting visitors, to the point where, before we left on home leave, Barbara had to send out a joint letter to an incoming contingent informing them who would be there when and referring them to a "Den Mother," an NGO employee staying with us for a longer period, who could answer further questions.[14] One of our repeat guests, Ron Hatley, arrived on our doorstep to recuperate from the removal of a ruptured appendix when his British doctor decided he would be better off with us than in one of the notoriously unsanitary Jakarta hospitals. Hatley seemed to be on death's door and Idja, our wash lady, was kept frantically busy laundering his filthy bandages in

---

[13] A partial list would include Jim Fox, Birute Galdikas, Bill Liddle, Milton Osborne, George Kahin, Mark Dion, Barbara Harvey, Stephen Morris, Barbara Harrisson, Filino Harahap, Margot Lyon, Bill and Muriel Frederick, and Den Mother Barbara Koch.

[14] Barbara's letter to some of them re: the "Pringle Hotel" is "Barbara to Barbara Harvey, Ron and Barbara Hatley, Bill and Muriel Frederick, March, 1972."

our wringer machine and hanging them out to dry and sterilize in the tropical sun, and he did recover.

Besides the move to Menteng, another big change in family life occurred early in the second half of our Jakarta posting— Barbara went to work. A position opened at the new campus of the Joint Embassy School in Cilandak when the junior-high Indonesian language teacher was fired. He was a nephew of the mayor, Ali Sidikin, and had perhaps been a "nepotism hire" in connection with obtaining the land for the new school. In any case, whatever his training, it had not included maintaining order in a room full of American adolescents, and by Christmas, when I was asked to evaluate the students' progress, they had learned nothing but a few politeness phrases in Indonesian. I was asked to take over the classes for the rest of the (American) school year, until in September, 1973, I switched to a position teaching World History during our final year in Jakarta.

This re-entry into the professional world did not preclude continuing with an increasing number of volunteer activities which I had taken on. The most important was leadership of a large group of foreign wives who volunteered at the National Museum, also known as the *Gedung Gadjah*, or Elephant Building, because of a large statue of an elephant, a long-ago present from a famous Thai king, Chulalongkorn, which stood in front of it. The volunteers worked under the aegis of the Ganesha Society, named for a famous Hindu god in the form of an elephant who is the patron of arts and sciences.

The society had been founded by Zainal and Rukmini Abidin, a wealthy couple who had made their fortune in pharmaceuticals and wanted to preserve their country's heritage. One of their targets was to improve the security of the collection at the National Museum where, in the period of economic hardship at the end of the Sukarno era, items, especially valuable ceramic pieces, had begun to disappear, or so everyone thought.[15] Besides improving the salaries of the

---

[15] In fact, the pilferage problem was perhaps not nearly as serious as everyone thought. Stories to that effect may have gained currency because dealers hawking antique ceramics were allowed to do so on the steps of the Museum, and foreigners concluded that they must be from the Museum's collection, which was still dusty and badly lit. By 2006, when Bob returned to do research on the Bali book, it was clear that the wonderful collection of Chinese and other export ware, now much more visible, was still in good shape.

guards at the museum, several years before we arrived they had persuaded a small group of expatriate volunteers to begin translating the museum records, all in Dutch, which fewer and fewer Indonesians could read, into Indonesian and English.

From that beginning, a program of guided tours for foreign-language speakers was developed, periodic lectures for overseas residents were presented, and the volunteers even organized a small exhibit of bronze statues and produced a homemade guidebook for it. Barbara maintained her friendship with Rukmini Abidin into the twenty-first century, thanks to Christmas (holiday) cards over the years and two visits when Bob returned to do research after his retirement. She was a remarkable lady, and the pharmaceutical factory, now managed by her children, is still a leading producer of trusted medicines.

Bob's work at the embassy had taken a new a turn after Ambassador Galbraith asked Colonel George Benson to return to Indonesia to be the Defense Attaché. Benson was already well known locally because he had attended the Indonesian Command and General Staff College in the 1950s, where he made friends with many of the rising officers in the Indonesian Army. He was serving at Embassy Jakarta when John Foster Dulles decided to support the Outer Islands Rebellion of 1958—Dulles thought Sukarno was becoming a communist—only to reverse course when the Indonesian Army rapidly began to win.

Colonel Benson had made clear his outrage about the US intervention. Before our role was known, he had even supplied the Indonesian Army with maps of Sumatra to help them stop the rebellion, as his Indonesian Army friends knew and never forgot.[16] At a time when the army was running the country, this level of camaraderie was priceless; I knew that if you wanted to find out something about Indonesia's army rulers, our large CIA station was often not much help. What you did was to ask George Benson, who would pick up the phone and call the Chief of Staff (or whomever) and ask him directly.

---

[16] On the Outer Islands Rebellion and especially U.S. support for it, see Paul F. Gardner, *Shared Hopes, Separate Fears: Fifty Years of Indonesian-U.S. Relations*, Boulder, CO, 1997, pp. 133, 139 and 151. I served under the author when he was the US Ambassador to Papua New Guinea in 1985-86.

Benson was an Irish Catholic from Philadelphia, of the big-hearted, blarney-endowed variety. His people-to-people skills transcended language; he never did learn Indonesian well, which in his case didn't matter. But he rarely wrote anything. So I decided that I would talk to him the way my mother had talked to Teddy Blue, and then wrote a stream of embassy reports on what was going on in the army, one of the key questions of the day. Someone once asked me about these reports and I fliply replied that they were "the Gospel According to St. George." This got to him and he loved it, quoting it back to me for years afterwards. He became the representative of the Indonesian State Oil Company (Pertamina) in Washington after his retirement. His wife Barbara was also a good friend, and we have a great photo of her carrying Jamie in a Halloween parade at the American recreation center in Jakarta.

I learned that to understand Indonesia's ruling military, you had to parse the interrelationship between modern military mores and the traditional cultures, especially Javanese. President Suharto was a case in point. Certainly his army experience was the primary factor in his background. He easily grasped the self-serving belief that only the army's martial discipline could keep Indonesia's diversity from destroying the nation. He had spent much of his early career pursuing Muslim rebels and, as mentioned earlier, once the communist party had been destroyed he saw Islam as the primary threat facing Indonesia, as well as a useful justification for continuing military rule. But his political instincts were no doubt informed by his love of the *wayang* theatre—the endless struggle between two families, the absence of "good" and "evil" (only left and right), and the almost invisible primacy of the crude, farting clowns, representing the pre-Hindu spirits of Java. Both sides resorted to duplicity and cunning. It was a "stable world based on conflict,"[17] and that is the way Suharto envisioned Indonesia.

I was amazed to learn soon after our arrival that all-night *wayang* shadow puppet plays were frequently performed at the presidential palace. Any diplomat, no matter how junior,

---

[17] The quotation, attributed to Claire Holt, is from Benedict R.O'G Anderson, "Mythology and the Tolerance of the Javanese," Monograph Series, Cornell Modern Indonesia Project, 1965.

could attend without being patted down at the door—all you
had to do was call and say you were coming. Rows of chairs,
with sofas in front for cabinet ministers, etc., were arranged.
Suharto and his wife seemed always to be there. Needless to
say, only the top puppet-masters performed. If you stayed all
night—which I confess we never did—breakfast was served
by dawn's early light.

The richness and humor of Indonesia's culture and history
enriched our everyday lives. We learned that one of the first
things you asked a new friend was *"Berasal dari mana?"*
literally "Where are your roots?" rather than "Where are you
from?" in a geographic sense. Indonesians loved their un-
melted cultural pot, with all its stereotypes—the Acehnese,
too Islamic by half, but what could you expect from people
who season their food with marijuana? The Balinese, so
adored by western tourists for their flashy art and drama,
but more than a bit too noisy for the obsessively understating
Javanese. The Minangkabau, matrilineal and devoutly Muslim
at the same time—but some of them were behind Indonesia's
first communist (!) revolt in 1926-27.

Sukarno, Indonesia's first president, was a great source of
political humor. He ordained a National Monument (MONAS),
inspired by Indonesia's Hindu-Buddhist past and obviously
reflecting Hindu symbolism. It was a Washington Monument-
size *lingam* (phallus) with a giant flame at its towering tip, on
a flaring *yoni* (female) base, with a diorama of the Revolution
inside. The monument immediately became known as
"Sukarno's Last Erection."

The Father of his Country sponsored revolutionary statuary
on nearly every traffic circle. One, a screaming figure with his
hands flung toward the sky, was said to be yelling *"Uang Habis,"*
meaning "The money's all gone," in reference to the economic
results of Sukarno's quasi-socialism. (The statue was supposed
to be throwing off the chains of colonialism.) Another, of a
running youth, was "Tukang Tjopet," "The Pickpocket." Yet
another, a peculiar figure with a cloth flying around his loins,
caused Jamie and his friends in the kindergarten carpool to
comment, "His pants are falling down!" Thereafter, he was
known in our crowd as the pants-falling-down statue.

My favorite example of political humor concerns the

great Istiqlal mosque, located near Sukarno's Last Erection. In this case Indonesia's founding President, a less than fundamentalist Muslim, had hired to design it a genuinely distinguished architect friend who happened to be a Christian Batak. As it neared completion, wags discovered that it had twelve columns holding up its vast dome. Presto, the pillars obviously represented the Twelve Apostles of Christianity. Not many people believed that the architect had any such intent, but everyone got a laugh out of it. Such humor, including the ethnic stereotyping, was and is the lubricant of Indonesia's diversity, but it is not a guarantee against ethnic unrest, as subsequent history has shown.

A lot of the ethnic humor was only quasi-humorous, as in "We don't quite believe this, or do we?" A good example involved the Badui people of West Java not far from Jakarta. They are a small group of Hindu-Buddhist-animists who at some point withdrew into isolation, perhaps to avoid conversion to Islam. There were two categories, about three hundred "Inner Badui," at the center of a roughly circular area, who wore only white clothing and were allowed no contact with the outside world, and roughly ten times that number of "Outer Badui" in thirty villages on the periphery, who could go into town on necessary business. You couldn't mention the Badui to anyone without being reminded that, due to magical powers which generated heat, they could fry eggs on their heads.

We visited them in October, 1972, and discovered that the reality was not so funny. You had to hike in and wade across a river to reach the Outer Badui; you could not go beyond that to the Inner settlement. One of the Inner Badui children was sick; did we have anything that might help? Barbara found an aspirin, carefully cut it into two child-sized halves, and provided it to the family by messenger. Later, both halves were returned; the child had died before they arrived.

As a result of our visit, Outer Badui sought us out when they came to Jakarta to buy the distinctive blue-and-black batik fabric that they wear. (Bob still has a well-worn sample which he wore as a sarong for years). They asked to stay with us, and we gave them a place on our screened-in back porch. Our servants were not amused (and perhaps a little frightened), and we were concerned that the Badui might scald themselves using our showers, especially if they visited while we were away. So after the second visit, we gently, we hoped, explained we could not host them again.

Texas Comes to Bali

By our third year in Jakarta, I had become an "old Indonesia hand" although still the most junior officer in the Political Section. We continued to travel often. Almost everyone went to Bali because (how sad!) we all had to be ready to escort high-ranking visitors who managed to spare time for the Island of the Gods during "official" visits. The biggest such visit by far occurred in November, 1972, when Treasury Secretary John Connally dropped in. As Governor of Texas, Connally had been sitting next to John F. Kennedy at the time of his assassination, and he himself had been seriously wounded. He was still deemed possible presidential material. A large part of the embassy decamped to Bali to look after him and his official entourage plus family, hauling everything from Xerox machines and communications gear about eight hundred miles across Java to Bali by road. Everyone stayed at the Bali Beach Hotel, then the only big one.

The Balinese had spent much time locating the best cars on the island, all of them old Chevrolets with big tail fins, to meet the official party at the airport. The vehicles were duly lined up in order of perceived elegance in front of the hotel, but when the Secret Service inspected them, they were all found to be wanting, especially in the tire department. When the Balinese explained that these were the least bald tires as well as the most presentable cars on Bali, the head agent grumbled and redid the motorcade so the best, in his opinion, were assigned to the Secretary and his family, and so on by order of importance, and that is how they arrived at the hotel.

As part of her unpaid spousal contributions, Barbara got to plan the cultural side of the program and scored what should have been a bull's eye, thanks to her friendship with an expatriate Australian husband and wife team who had founded a small travel agency, PACTO. Through them she learned that one of Bali's eight kings had just decided to go into the tourist business (many of the others already had) and he agreed to put on a Balinese feast and a special dance-drama performance for the Connally party in his *puri* (palace). This was a spectacular opportunity, but they decided they were too tired after all their travel, and the poolside buffet with a short dance presentation at the hotel was more tempting.

We were extremely relieved when Connally's plane crew was delighted to get out in the countryside and see a real cultural event. Never again in many future visits to Bali would we see anything as elegant and genuine as this. The audience consisted of the entire village, including enthralled children, and, as far as we could tell, having the pilot of a big American jet was at least as important to our royal hosts as having a politician from Texas.

By the next morning, the Connally family had recovered sufficiently to go shopping. What they seemed to notice most about this fantastically artistic island, though, was the quality, or lack thereof, of the Zebu-derived cattle originally bred in hot, humid areas of Texas. We have always wondered exactly what memories the official party took home of their visit to Bali.

In early 1973 we had a second, but far less colorful, VIP visitor from Washington—Vice President Spiro Agnew, who, we were convinced, was the most obnoxious person in US politics. Bob was assigned the exalted role of "gifts officer," and suffered through a row between the VP's advance team and the Indonesians. The advance team insisted on knowing what Suharto's present to Agnew would be, and the Indonesians flatly refused to comply. But the great moment arrived, and there is a photo of Bob, obsequious in the background, holding the American gift while the two principals converse prior to the exchange. We were all greatly amused when the much-debated Indonesian present turned out to be, in addition to a vast silver tea set, a portrait of Agnew executed in chicken feathers.[18] We had no idea if the Indonesians realized the symbolic implications of the chicken in American culture.

Dance, Painting and Architecture: Bali and Sumatra

The Pringles had many more memorable visits to Bali, three

---

[18] Bob letter to Dear Mother, February 12, 1973. As I recall, it was not as nearly nice as the chicken feather portrait (of me) that I later received in Mali.

of which stand out. The first was Annie's introduction to the Barong dance, in which the blood-dripping witch Rangda fights the benevolent, lion-like Barong to a standoff, while villagers in trance try to stab themselves with their krisses. Our daughter did not like Rangda one bit, and when the witch made her grand entrance down the steps of the temple, she hurtled into Barbara's lap, looking resolutely away from the dancers.

Annie's next adventure took place at Campuan, site of a small hotel in Ubud which had been the home of Walter Spies, a famous German artist who did much to introduce Bali to the world in the 1930s. There was a pet monkey in the hotel and it bit her. Luckily the monkey could be kept under observation, so she did not have to undergo the fearful rabies shots.

Then there was the visit to Tom and Yanti Spooner, who were living on the road to Karangasem in eastern Bali, one of its eight old kingdoms. Tom had just finished his tour in our Public Affairs (USIS) section and taken a year of leave to write about a famous Balinese Governor of Bali who belonged to a family that had adopted him. By the time we stopped by, however, he had discovered how corrupt and cruel traditional Balinese politics could be and was quite ready to abandon his biography project. His wife Yanti, from an aristocratic Javanese family of the kind that regarded the Balinese as more than slightly too noisy and demonstrative, was not surprised.

We also remember a fourth Bali visit—the time we went down to meet Charlotte and Clarence (aka Char and Clay, also Grandma and Grandpa Cade) when they decided to visit us in Indonesia and make it the major stop on a round-the-world trip. (Thank you Pan Am, which in the days of frequent refueling stops still had a daily round-the-world flight, with slightly different cities served on each day of the week.) There is more about this visit below.

On all our visits to Bali, we especially enjoyed just driving around the island, with its spectacular views of meticulously terraced rice fields and the never-ending ceremonial life. One could usually find out from the hotel when and where a really big cremation was taking place, but village festivals were too numerous to be plotted; one just blundered into long lines of women processing along the road with offerings on their heads.

The art remains impressive today, but in other respects

Bali is less attractive than it used to be. Tourism multiplied by a factor of ten from 1970 to 1980 and has continued to grow at a pace that has overloaded the small island. The income has stimulated endless strip development along the narrow roads, obscuring once incomparable views. Few Balinese in the heavily touristed areas are still real farmers. They now run small hotels and businesses and work their land with labor imported from Java. Where every square inch was once worked for something, the steep gorges that cut through the slopes of the central volcano are now overgrown with weeds. Bali is marred with too many non-traditional buildings and the days are gone when every scene begged to be painted. Fortunately the Balinese people are still charming and most visitors don't miss what they never saw.

In July, 1972, we traveled through the middle of Sumatra with Mark Dion, our Consul in Medan, where Barbara and Annie had arrived almost two years previously. We drove from Padang (home of the matrilineal Muslim Minangkabau people) to Medan. It was a two-day trip over a road that often verged on impassable. Mark had taken a standard Consulate sedan with his driver on this marginally "official" trip. He was worried that if the vehicle was damaged, his driver would be blamed. At one particularly awful spot, he drove the car himself while the rest of us walked. We could hear the big, black official car screeching and banging over the rocks and ruts, each bang louder than the last, but it survived. (This was in the days when, military vehicles aside, four-wheel drive, high clearance vehicles did not exist except for British Land Rovers, and of course we had to use US-made vehicles.)

The West Sumatran scenery was in places Bali-like in its beauty. I spotted one particularly wonderful antique village mosque beside an emerald rice field, built in the Hindu-Buddhist pagoda style, its spire tilting precariously. When I got out to photograph it a very upset villager ran up and tried to stop me. I attempted to explain that I was doing it because the mosque was so beautiful, but he didn't speak Indonesian or didn't understand mine. I could imagine what might happen next: an urgent village meeting to deplore the lamentable state of the old mosque, so bad that foreigners were stopping to take pictures of it! It would have to be torn down and a new one built immediately!!

We skirted the West Sumatran Minangkabau highlands, missing the much bigger and very well cared for pagoda-style mosques there, which we became aware of only on another visit thirty-five years later! We spent one night at Sibolga in a *"losman"* (Dutch for barely survivable hotel) from which a picture survives of Barbara sitting on the porch, dressed quite elegantly, reminiscent of Victorian travelers in frilly blouses and long skirts in Darkest Somewhere. Note from Barbara: The reason was that in order to travel modestly in a Muslim province, I wore long skirts and long sleeves.

Back in Jakarta, the summer of 1972 was less than cool. Jakarta's electricity supply depended on a French-built dam, which developed a crack so the water behind it had to be drained. This occurred right at the end of the rainy season, and the dam could not be sufficiently refilled to provide power for the entire dry season. By the time the rains started again, ordinary houses in Jakarta were receiving power on a 36-hours-off and 12-hours-on schedule. This is not enough to hold ice or food in the freezer, nor to keep items that will spoil easily, like milk and mayonnaise, in the fridge.

This meant shopping every day for that day's food, and mixing all milk from powder just before meals. With Munarti handling most of the food issues, the biggest nuisance for all of us, servants included, was the immense, very noisy, antique generator of the Iranian ambassador's residence next door. His government, the Shah at that time, had apparently, unlike us, thought ahead.[19] We had to have our windows open because our air conditioning, of course, did not work. Cables went flying asking Washington for back-up generators, which, at vast expense, did not arrive until after the dam was fixed.

Not Seeing the Javanese Rhino

In September we embarked on a quest for the Javanese Rhinoceros, an almost extinct species confined to the southwest corner of Java. It is an enormous animal, almost as big as its cousins in India and much larger than the more

---

[19] Bob letter to Dear Family, September 8, 1972.

common Sumatran Rhino. They are found in a reserve at Ujung Kulon, on the Java Strait at the southwestern tip of Java. The Dutch established a game reserve there after the huge tsunami from the famous eruption of nearby Krakatoa in 1883 wiped out the only existing village. The soil is non-volcanic and poor (unusual on fecund Java), accounting for the lack of population, so the Dutch moved the human survivors to a new location to make way for rhinos.

We and a few friends (including Stephen Morris from LSE, the Purdys, and several other couples) hired a small coconut boat, a crude little coaster with a putt-putt 1952 truck engine and an apparent top speed of 0.1 knots, to get there. There was a rest house at Ujung Kulon, sometimes occupied by a Swiss researcher and caretaker, on a small offshore island with a sparkling coral reef. To see the rhinos you had to go to the mainland and follow bad trails through dense undergrowth. The tidal wave from Krakatoa had picked up the fringing reef and pitched it a mile or so inland, where it lies around in large bleached lumps.

The displaced reef was spectacular, but the rhinos are almost impossible to see. A famous photographer, Eliot Elisofon, had visited the place a few years previously (accompanied by our friend and fellow FSO Ed Barber) and not gotten a single photo, although he wrote a book about his effort anyway.[20] Population estimates were arrived at by counting the tracks and dividing by four, someone joked. Quite a few photos have been taken since then with the aid of motion sensors, and at this writing the Javan Rhino seems to be hanging on, but just barely. According to *Wikipedia* there are now seventy of them at Ujung Kulon, a slight increase from the time of our visit.

Nevertheless, a great time was had by all and we headed back to Jakarta in fine spirits. The ladies cooked a gourmet pancake breakfast over a wood fire on a little platform in the stern of our putt-putt. We had just finished eating the first servings, and the cooks were preparing to offer seconds, when the boat rounded a corner and headed north into the Java Strait. Immediately we hit waves and a strong headwind, which literally blew our cooking fire overboard.[21]

---

[20] Eliot Elisofon, *Java Diary*, New York, 1969. A good update on the Javan Rhinos is available on *Wikipedia*.

[21] Bob letter to Dear Family, September 8, 1972.

In April, 1973, we took our second R&R, this time to the Philippines, where we stayed with Dan and Margaret Sullivan in Cebu, to which Dan had been assigned as Consul. We don't remember much about this visit except the funky charm of the Sullivan's house and a visit to Mactan Island and the beach where Ferdinand Magellan had been assassinated by the natives in 1521, while wading ashore in full European armor like something out of Monty Python. Three different monuments, erected by the Spanish, the Americans and the post-Independence Philippine government, mark the site. The first tells how Magellan paved the way for Christianity and Civilization, the second is fairly factual, and the third glorifies Chief (Datu) Lapu-Lapu, the warrior who did the deed, as a progenitor of heroic nationalism. Score one for the Filipinos, for not tearing down the other two.

A Taste of the Spice Islands

In July Barbara and I visited Maluku, the fabled Spice Islands, returning by way of Sulawesi. One thinks of Indonesia as a 3000-mile archipelago from west to east, but in the east it is also 900 miles from north to south. This huge expanse is dotted with islands, most of them volcanic. Some of them produce the cloves and nutmeg that helped stimulate the Age of Exploration. We visited a spice factory on Ternate that sold cloves for seventy-five cents a *kilo*, rather lower than the retail price in the US. We also made the acquaintance of mace, the flower of the nutmeg tree. As usual, I interviewed local officials and missionaries, one of whom, a German Catholic priest on Ambon, provided rare information on conditions in the prison camps of Buru Island, where allegedly communist prisoners were interned.

We flew minor Indonesian airlines using DC-3s, one of which had its original World War II bucket seats (metal frames with canvas covers). As we tried to leave Ambon, where the airport was twenty miles of coral road after a sail-powered ferry ride from town, our scheduled flight was filled with a soccer team from Biak (in Indonesian New Guinea), so it overflew us without stopping. We had no advanced notice of this (if airports had radios, they rarely seemed to work), so

we had an extra day there. Bob had already lost his glasses—
some village kid (probably) stole them while we were looking
for olive shells in the sandy interstices of a mangrove swamp.
But we used the extra day for more snorkeling, and found
some lovely grey bonnet shells in the sand.

On this trip, we also spent a few days on the twin islands of
Ternate and Tidore, the two original Spice Islands, laced with
old forts and other relics of the Sultans of each island and still
slightly scented with cloves. It was there that we had our first
taste of using scuba equipment, fortunately in rather shallow
water, courtesy of a cheerful American missionary with no
clue about safety requirements for diving.

In Ternate the airport was at the base of a perfect volcanic
cone, usually swathed in clouds. Our outbound plane landed
anyway, but so late that we missed a connecting flight in
Menado (North Sulawesi). So we added another night to our
trip there in what turned out to be lovely hotel with hot water,
air-conditioning and even a typewriter on which Barbara
typed a letter home describing our adventures.[22] Menado is
a Protestant area and is famous throughout Indonesia for
its beautiful women and relative prosperity. Our last stop
was Makassar, in South Sulawesi, where we stayed at the
old colonial hotel, decrepit but overlooking a spectacular
waterfront crammed with shipping of all kinds, including
many sail-powered craft.

The Parents Visit

Throughout this time we were planning for the long-
awaited visit from Barbara's parents. Charlotte had famously
proclaimed that if she had enough money to visit us in
Borneo, she would go to Europe instead, but eight years later,
when it was clear that we might be in Asia forever—not to
mention that she would have a chance to see her two darling
grandchildren before our next home leave, she relented. Of
course, having decided to come, she and Clay tacked on Hong
Kong, Thailand and India plus Iran and Portugal as well. It
was their round-the-world trip. At our end, Barbara had

---

[22] Barbara letter to Dear Family, July 9, 1973.

a brainstorm: instead of flying to Jakarta, why not take the weekly Pan Am flight from Hong Kong to Bali, which could be done relatively inexpensively as an extension of Pan Am's round-the-world route. Then we could send our car and driver to Bali to meet the parents and take them to major sights there until we could get free and come to Bali ourselves. After that, we would all drive home together across Java.

All went according to plan, more or less. Charlotte and Clay arrived in late October and got along swimmingly with our driver, Sulomo, despite his almost non-existent English. They managed to get quite an introduction to Balinese culture with the help of an itinerary we had given to Sulomo. They loved their thatch-roofed beachfront cottage, as well as the beach, and before we came Clay collected shells. He put some of them on the back of the toilet to save, but was startled to find, when using the bathroom the next morning, that some of his shells were walking around on the floor. Hermit crabs!

After four days we arrived, and spent several days exploring art and dance in the mountainous Balinese interior together, with Bob now the driver. Charlotte, of course, loved Bali's painting, carving, and silver work. Several of the family have paintings she bought while there, and I have kept one of her purchases, a gold washed silver pendant of a barong mask. When she found it in Celuk village, it was silver, and she was looking for something gold. That, said Celuk's craftsmen, was not a problem—it could be given a gold wash and we could collect it the evening of the next day. Grandpa and Bob thought it would be crazy to drive up into the mountains from our beach accommodations just to get it, but Barbara offered to take her back.

Which I did, threading traffic in the late afternoon down the narrow road, lined by drainage ditches on both sides and crowded with farmers walking home with buffalos, older people or kids herding flocks of ducks, and other children in school uniforms on the pavement and very narrow shoulders. Mother was terrified, but we made it, at the cost of an overheated engine. No problem: just dump a bucket of cold water on the engine block. My turn to be appalled. But no more damage was done than the leak we already had, to make driving back across Java an adventure. And Mother always loved that pendant, which she wore often.

Then we set off for Jakarta by road. The parents were impressed by the World War II landing craft-converted-to-ferry across the Bali Strait to Java. Its one-lane hold was for cars and trucks, while passengers perched precariously on the sides above them for the short trip.

Next stop: a coffee plantation named Kaliklatak on a hill above the Java side of the Strait, owned by Colonel Soehoed, whom we had met through David and Helen Kenney. We never asked how he obtained the plantation, but after the Indonesian Revolution many Dutch landholdings somehow ended up in the hands of army officers. The Soehoeds adored having visitors and Kaliklatak was a very comfortable place to stay, but we had failed to explain adequately to Charlotte how things worked. At first she suffered in silence, assuming that to ask for hot water would be an imposition. The staff brought it to her anyway.

It was at Kaliklatak that we discovered that there really is such a thing as a *luak*, an Asian civet cat with a very sensitive nose that sniffs out the best of the coffee berries at their peak of ripeness. It then excretes the seeds, or "beans" as we call them, and from these are made *kopi luak* (luak coffee), which today sells for outrageous prices to the most sophisticated coffee lovers worldwide. It was not yet world famous, however, and we had assumed that the *luak* tale was a put-on to nauseate gullible foreigners, until we actually saw little *luak* turds under the coffee trees. However, the resulting coffee was not served to us.

Onward, then, westward through East Java. As we were driving along, Clay announced plaintively that he sure would like to see a banana tree before he left Indonesia. We explained that we had been driving all day on roads lined with banana trees, and we stopped to examine one. From one of Bob's much later research trips, we brought home an elegant, carved Balinese banana tree for him. Newell, who adored it, had it until she died.

We had had one flat tire, hence no spare, and as our first day of trans-Java driving waned, we began looking for a place to stay. We had heard about something not far from Malang, an easily recognized multi-story hotel—there was nothing else like it—sticking up in the middle of the rice fields. It was operated, we were told later, by an eccentric Chinese Indonesian. Nothing ventured, etc., so when we saw it, we pulled in to this place and the desk clerk gave us a room in the tower.

It gradually dawned on us that we were the only guests. We asked if there was a swimming pool, and the desk person said "of course," but when the first would-be bathers came down ready for a swim it turned out that there was no water in it. We had left our flat tire to be fixed when we checked in. Sure enough, a few hours later it had been patched and was duly delivered to our seventh-floor room. About this time Charlotte decided to wash her hands and face and was startled to find that the washbasin had no drain pipe attached; the water flowed out onto one's feet and headed for a drain in the middle of the floor. This was standard Indonesian procedure, along with squat toilets, but she had not encountered it yet. We did have some sort of dinner in a cavernous dining room, which we had to ourselves.

Thus far the parents were being excellent sports and we made it to our next destination, Jogjakarta, by the next evening. On the outskirts of town we sailed past the new, modern Ambarrukmo Palace Hotel, known to the kids as the Ice Cream Hotel because it was the only place in Jogja that served ice cream. Charlotte said something like "Is that our hotel?" and we replied that, no, we were going to a really nice garden-style hotel with lots of Indonesian character, not just a sterile imitation of something western—you'll love it. And indeed it was and she did, and it worked out fine, but she said later that if it had looked anything like the Malang Monster, she had been ready to put her foot down and demand that we head back to that Ice Cream Hotel as fast we could go.

Both parents were nonetheless very happy to arrive at Jalan Mangunsarkoro after their adventures, not least because Jamie and Annie were there. It had been a year and a half since our home-leave visit. Char waxed lyrical in a letter no doubt designed partly to reassure other family members. She wrote:

Happy Thanksgiving, darlings. I don't know exactly where we'll be for the holiday; we are planning to leave here Monday the

19th for Bangkok . . . .

We live in the lap of luxury. I keep telling myself to enjoy it. We have found Jakarta a surprisingly attractive city; we expected a crowded, teeming place like Hong Kong, and, of course, in the native sections it is just like that, but the Dutch laid out the city years ago with wide boulevards for their carriages and the European sections are attractive with large houses and gardens. B and B's house is charming, an old Dutch one, one storey, but with high ceilings and much open space. One enters a screened porch conservatory with Maharani chairs, then double parlors with beautiful antique Chinese pieces that B and B have collected. The walls are white throughout the house, which heightens the airy effect, and which also displays all their Indonesian crafts very well. The parlors are followed by the dining room, which opens out into the garden. Parallel to these two rooms are two bedrooms and bath. Offset to the right is a long playroom opening to the garden, and off of it are the guestroom, bath and kitchen. All three bedrooms are air-conditioned so we sleep comfortably at night; the rest of the house has ceiling fans and is surprisingly pleasant, although at midday it is hot.

We decided Charlotte would have made a world-class real estate agent. The letter continued:

Barb has her staff very well organized; her cook [Munarti] is marvelous—we eat very well. Everything is done silently; meals appear as if by magic; dirty clothes disappear in the morning and reappear clean at night—it is a way of life that has disappeared at home and even in Europe today, except for the very rich. Here it is an accepted pattern; in Jogja we met three young wives, friends of Barb's, that were off for a week of visiting all the batik centers, while the children stayed home with Daddy and the servants; one hopes that all these intelligent young women make good use of so much leisure. Your sister certainly does; everyone we meet sings her praises as an organizer, hostess, writer, speaker, etcetera. [23]

---

[23] Charlotte letter to "Dear Janie and Ron, Kathy, and Susie and Bennett," November, 1973.

Charlotte closed her letter with a description of our outing to the Thousand Islands, about thirty miles off the coast. This time the children came along; they had not been on the Bali-Java adventure. The main point of this trip, besides enjoying the beach, was to see the beautiful coral reef just offshore. Char was not up to conventional snorkeling, so we got her a buoyant frame with a glass bottom and took turns propelling her around over the reef in a little rubber dinghy and she was fascinated. With typical tact she did not mention in the letter that as a result she got badly sunburned on the back of her legs. She also noted that we had just learned that I was being assigned to Manila. This posting was largely thanks to the efforts of my friend and first boss in Jakarta, Skipper Purnell, who had become the Deputy Chief of Mission in Manila. I thought it was a great idea because, added to my Sarawak fieldwork, it would round out my experience in island Southeast Asia.

Almost Glopped, and a Whiff of Real Hardship

In fact, the assignment to Manila almost did not happen, all because of a meeting between Secretary of State Henry Kissinger and US ambassadors serving in Latin America. Kissinger was urging them to implement a policy change—I don't remember what it was, but it reportedly involved more support for our Vietnam War—and he kept getting a litany of resistance, which went something like "Oh, but Mr. Secretary, that approach will simply not work in my country!" He went home seething, convinced that his men south of the border had spent too much time there and that something had to be done to keep ambassadors from becoming parochial advocates of their host countries' interests. So he announced a new Global Outlook Policy, immediately reduced to GLOP, which ordained that no Foreign Service Officers could serve more than one tour sequentially in the same region.[24] My assignment to Manila had been "paneled," or formerly approved, only a few days earlier; if it hadn't, since the Philippines was clearly in the same region

---

[24] The origin of GLOP is based on what I was told at the time; other accounts differ in detail, but not substance.

as Indonesia, I would have been "GLOPPED" and assigned perhaps . . . to Paris ??—no way!!!—but maybe to Panama City or Kabul, which in 1974 was in fact not such a bad place.

We still had almost six months left to go in Indonesia, and some of this time was exciting. On January 15 Jakarta erupted in demonstrations sparked by the visit of the Japanese Prime Minister, Kakuei Tanaka. The students were protesting growing Japanese economic dominance and the corrupt relationship between the Japanese, local ethnic Chinese businessmen, and the military. The protests quickly turned into riots aimed at visible manifestations of the Japanese presence, especially Toyota automobiles. The Toyota agency, PT Astra, part of a much bigger Sino-Japanese commercial complex, was sacked, and the rioters went after Toyota cars wherever they could find them, setting fire to most and dumping others in the nearest Dutch-era canal.

By this time we had a sweet little yellow Toyota Corolla station wagon, which had finally arrived to replace the one that had been lost when, enroute from Japan, the ship it was on caught fire and sank in Manila Bay. On the day the demonstrations began, Sulomo, our driver, was out with this vehicle, returning a film that Barbara had used in her classroom, to the Canadian Embassy. He ran into a traffic jam, somehow found out what was going on, and made a beeline for the US Embassy compound parking lot, where the car would be safe. He then called Barbara, typically apologizing because he had not completed his errand and asking whether he should try to make it home. Since he reported that a Toyota vehicle had just been turned over and set afire in front of the embassy, she thanked him copiously for his fast action, which probably saved the car, and instructed him to catch a bus as soon as he could for his own home. His display of quick thinking on this occasion was one reason she was able to find him a good and lasting job driving for the Joint Embassy School (later the Jakarta International School) when we left Jakarta. Later we heard that he had risen to the position of the JES Superintendent's driver.

Everyone, including the US Embassy Political Section, was caught off guard by this eruption, not by the rioting so much as by Suharto's failure to get things under control more quickly. Up to this point his military rule had been restrained but effective. Was he losing it already?

In a letter home Barbara and I wrote, a little more candidly, perhaps, than what we were doing in the Political Section:

All is quiet; there are armed troops all over, and it looks like tonight they will enforce the curfew. The TV has just announced that anyone demonstrating tonight or tomorrow will be arrested. However, the damage has been immense; they didn't just burn cars at Senin, they burned the whole shopping center. If order doesn't come tomorrow, there is going to be a real problem with food supply; it took Ponidi[25] an hour to find ten kilos of rice this evening. I decided we had better stockpile a little. As for us, school is out for the indefinite future....

Of course the vast majority of demonstrators were not students, university or high school, but rather the unchallenged, bored, futureless teenagers of Jakarta. In tonight's paper the University [of Indonesia?] Student Council President is loudly proclaiming that the university students had a rational program, etc., etc., but still they organized the first march, they started things and then couldn't control them. I think our student leader friends should have known better—demonstrations can't be controlled in a city of 500,000 privileged and 4 million poor.[26]

The protests were dubbed "Malari," an acronym for *Malapetaka 15 Januari*, the Disaster of January 15. It was the closest we would ever come in the Foreign Service to being at risk from political violence. After his initial hesitation, Suharto reacted by firing the general in charge of domestic security, closing six newspapers, and trying to depoliticize the universities. He would go on to rule for another quarter century, until 1999. We also learned a few things, including how easy it is for a mob to burn a car. Just flip it on its back and drop a match in the gas tank.

---

[25] Ponidi was Pak Di's brother (or cousin), who first replaced him in our Jakarta household when he left to work for Kenneys in Washington, later followed him there, and ended up working for the Kenneys until, following Moertini's example, he retired in 2014 and went with his American savings back to Indonesia.

[26] Barbara letter to Dear Family, January 16, 1974.

A Blot on Bob's Crystal Ball

Historians like to think that what is past is prologue. Liberals trained as historians tend to assume that authoritarian regimes will end badly.

At about the time of the Malari violence, I was working on a long report about the possibility of serious agrarian unrest on Java. Little of the thinking in this report was original. It drew on the research of William Collier, an American student of Javanese agriculture. Collier feared that the peasantry of Java would react violently to the Green Revolution, which we and our allies were strongly supporting. By introducing new, higher-yielding varieties of rice, we assumed that the poor peasants who had been the backbone of the Indonesian Communist Party, once thought to be the largest of in the world, would prosper and begin to see the bright side of market-based capitalism.

Collier's findings, which I found persuasive, found no fault with higher rice yields *per se*. But the new varieties were coming with new marketing methods favoring middle-men, more use of small, mechanized rice mills, hence reduced employment, and an uptick in rural land sales. About half the peasants on Java were already landless, and these innovations would create more. They were heightening economic inequality, endangering a traditional, supposedly benign pattern of "shared poverty," a term popularized by anthropologist Clifford Geertz.

I was reporting on Collier's conclusions, but my report was provocative: the "dilemma" of Javanese agriculture was "a millstone around the neck of the entire nation" and "seems likely to explode in massive violence, for which there is ample precedent in Javanese history." The title of the report was "The Wrath to Come: Rural Welfare on Java."[27]

This sounds like great, prescient reporting, and I was quite proud of it, the only problem being that it never happened. That wicked Old Lady History refused to repeat herself. And the equally wicked dictator, President Suharto, has to get some of the credit. No one anticipated the rapid increase in Indonesian

---

[27] "The Wrath to Come: Rural Welfare on Java," Airgram A-78, May 7, 1974.

oil revenues in 1973-74, or Suharto's decision to channel some of this money into small rural development projects around Java.[28] His "Inpres" (for "Presidential Instruction") Program is widely thought to have blunted the negative impact of globalization, in this case in the form of more efficient agriculture. In other words, enough of the oil money apparently trickled down to forestall the wrath to come.

At about this time David Newsom replaced Frank Galbraith as Ambassador. Unlike Galbraith, Newsom was not an old Indonesia hand, but he was a master of skilled diplomacy with wide experience, including serving as Ambassador to pre-Qadafi Libya. He also had an MA from the Columbia School of Journalism, where he had been one of my father's students, although I did not know that until many years later.

We were by this time the reigning Indonesia experts in the embassy, and in mid-April Barbara and I took it upon ourselves to invite the new ambassador and his wife, Jean, plus four other couples, to see Krakatoa. We thought we knew just how to do this, based on our trip to Ujung Kulon. We hired the same kind of grungy cargo boat we had used then, partly because that was all there was. However, the Newsoms took one look at it, contemplated the several hours needed to putt-putt out to Krakatoa, and politely demurred on going that far. Luckily it turned out that there was a pretty little island in the middle of the Java Strait, only a few miles out, so we went there instead. It was a beautiful day, the reef was gorgeous, and everyone had a great time snorkeling and sunbathing. I sometimes wonder if the reef around that little island is still pristine; it seems unlikely. We never did make it to Krakatoa.

Our departure was looming. Barbara noted that two days after the aborted Krakatoa trip we would be going to the Thousand Islands with the Joint Embassy School Oceanography Club, of which she was faculty adviser: "The house will have to pack itself."[29] Because we had had such

---

[28] R.E. Elson, *Suharto: A Political Biography,* Cambridge University Press, 2001, p. 210. Elson is careful to emphasize that the dramatic increase in revenues also greatly benefitted the wealthy, especially those with favorable political links. Indonesia's annual economic growth in the later part of Suharto's rule reached almost double-digit levels.

[29] Barbara letter to Dear Family, April 26, 1974.

a good time buying antique furniture—the Chinese bed/ bookshelf, the altar and desk, both now in our living room, the long carved Chinese table and more—and even though we had given away our baby furniture to local friends, we were over the 12,000-pound limit for sea shipments to and from a tropical "hardship" post. So despite her cheerful remark, there was a ton of packing, mailing, and deciding what could be sent to the grandparents separately from what we would take to Manila. Meanwhile there were also constant farewell lunches and dinners. We will never forget arriving home after one lunch to find that Jamie and Annie had built a fort out of two piles of books which had been carefully separated, one for sea and one for air transport.

It was at this time, on April 22, that the parents of a good embassy friend, Paula Causey, died in the crash of the weekly Pan Am flight from Hong Kong to Bali. It was the same flight that Barbara's parents had taken the previous November with such success, and we had told Paula about it. The plane had begun making its descent to the Bali airport at Den Pasar, on the south side of the island, and had requested permission to land. The Indonesian flight controller could not see the Boeing 707 on his radar, but he assumed that the American pilot flying for a famous international airline must know what he was doing, and granted permission.

In fact the flight was still on the north side of the island, with two very tall volcanoes, totally unlighted of course, between it and the airport. The pilot may have mistaken the lights of the bamboo-frame fish traps off the north coast of Bali for runway landing lights. In any case he flew into one of the volcanoes near its summit and everyone on board was killed. I went to Bali to help with what needs to be done after such a disaster, primarily as an interpreter and because I was a backup consular officer.

Farewell to Indonesia (*Sampai Nanti*)

The packing and the farewells finally ended and we departed Indonesia on May 15, 1974. The four years we spent there were unforgettable, and we have always kept up Indonesian friendships and connections. One life lesson we learned was that when you do decent things without expecting recompense, you sometimes get repaid with interest. Thus it was with our friends Emywati and Dorodjatun Kuntjoro Jakti. When we met Dorodjatun, he was a young instructor on the economics faculty of the University of Indonesia. In the wake of the Malari riots he was jailed, leaving Emy with a new infant. We gave her most of our no longer needed baby paraphernalia. I still remember threading the maze of streets around the university with Sulomo, trying to find her house.

Fast forward to 1999: we had just returned from South Africa, and guess who, long out of jail, was enjoying a very successful tour as Indonesian Ambassador to the US. We had completely forgotten about the baby crib, etc., but the Dorodjatuns never forgot it or the friendship it represented. That is why, among other reasons, the Indonesian Embassy staged a traditional coconut-splitting ceremony for Anne and David to ascertain the sex of their first child without a sonogram, and Zoe was, as the ritual foretold, a girl!

More important was the beneficial, long-term fallout from having hosted and helped academics and journalists in Jakarta. I knew that I could learn much of value about Indonesia from such people, and that the hospitality extended might benefit my future career, and that was certainly true. But we did it primarily because both of us enjoyed having guests (especially easy when there were five servants to help), not because it was reflected in my embassy "efficiency reports," although it sometimes was.

This kind of thing could be stressful. Jim Fox, an anthropologist doing research on the island of Roti, in eastern Indonesia, asked me if he could send some of his equipment to me through the official embassy pouch. I said yes, not anticipating the weight and volume of cameras and whatnot that arrived, quite illegally. But I didn't get caught, and three decades later Jim was running the most important Indonesian studies department in Australia and probably in the world, and was able to help me generously with research for my book on Islam in Indonesia.[30]

We enjoyed Indonesia's rich cultural qualities, its diversity,

[30] *Understanding Islam in Indonesia: Politics and Diversity*, Éditions Didier Millet and University of Hawaii Press, 2010.

and its natural beauty, and we had a wonderful time. The list of memories is a long one: visiting Bali before it was drowned in tourists, snorkeling on magnificent coral reefs, sailing back to Jakarta before the wind with volcanoes in the distance and Bugis schooners on the horizon, Barbara's teaching and her work as a Central Museum volunteer, and our servants who were friends as well. Our house in Menteng was not as fancy as Charlotte's letter made it sound, but where else would you have a sidewalk vendor who would die for you, or the chance to stage a *wayang* shadow puppet play in your home, or a screening of *Lawrence of Arabia* with an audience of enthralled Indonesian "Arab" friends? It was going to be a hard act to follow.

We have a painting to remind of us our second and favorite Jakarta house. There is a caption at the top of the panel, reading "PRINGLE" in quotes, with the first quotation marks, Spanish-style, low and upside-down before the "P". The address, "Jln. Mangunsarkoro 3," is at the bottom. It is signed "S. Toemon 24.9.1972".[31] We bought it, and one for Margot, thanks to some expatriate wives who became fascinated by the paintings that adorned the wooden panels supporting the back seat cushions in Jakarta's thousands of pedicabs, much better known as *betjaks*.

These ladies started commissioning them to use as address signs or just to display as folk art. Most, like Margot's, were of village scenes, but because we loved the ocean we asked for a sea scene, and this was the result. The red border, decorated with imaginative fish, frames a Javanese fishing village with a black, volcanic sand beach at the edge of a bay with boats coming and going. The painter had real talent, and his work has always been one of our favorite examples of Indonesian art, a constant reminder of the charm and skills of the Indonesian people.

---

[31] I learned in 2015 from Amir Sidharta, an art auctioneer who writes an art column for one of the Jakarta newspapers, that Toemon was a fairly well-known Jakarta artist who did portraits of houses for foreigners as well as *betjak* paintings; Sidharta had written an article about Toemon in his column.

7

The Philippines, 1974-1977

We arrived in the Philippines in mid-July, 1974. The country was under "Martial Law," better described as rule by President Ferdinand Marcos, his wife Imelda and their friends. My job in the embassy's Political Section, working on the internal affairs of the country, was completely compatible with my training in Southeast Asian history and my previous experience in Malaysia and Indonesia.

In Manila we inherited half a large old house not far from the embassy, avoiding, as we had hoped, the wealthy gated communities in Makati (Forbes Park, etc.) where most affluent foreigners lived. It came to us with a good cook, Marina, bequeathed by Bob's predecessor in the house, John Forbes (no relation to the former US Governor of the Philippines). She was very skilled and our kids enjoyed playing with her two children.

Then—poof!—one fine day about six months after our arrival, Marina, her family, and all her possessions just disappeared. Mr. Forbes, after highly recommending her, had obtained a visa for her to work for him in Washington, and off she went, with nary a word to us from her or him. We didn't fully appreciate that for many Filipinos going to the US was the secular equivalent of ascending to heaven. Indonesia had not fully prepared us for the hang-ups of a post-colonial relationship. However, this story had a happy ending, when we hired Lita Felisilda as cook and person-in-charge of the household. With her came her husband, Abdon, a part-time gardener, and two more wonderful playmates for the children, their daughter Bheng and son Jun-jun.

Our transition to the Philippines was not without the usual bumps and scrapes, as well as the pleasant aspects of Foreign Service life. We had another adventure with the hazards of moving when one of the big wooden crates in which our personal effects were shipped showed up damp, the lift van which contained it and several other crates having been left out in the warm tropical rain somewhere between Manila and Jakarta. All might have been OK had the apparently inexperienced packers in Jakarta not laid all our paintings flat on top of everything else in the crate. In the event, the only important damage was to our big shadow puppet painting, the one now on the third floor at 216 Wolfe Street. It and several framed gold painted Balinese cloths emerged stained and mold infested.

But this story too had a happy ending. It turned out that the Government of Spain, anxious to help the Filipinos safeguard their colonial heritage, had paid to train some artists to learn restoration techniques in Italy. The Italian skill at post-flood restoration had been honed repairing the damage from a catastrophic 1966 flood in Florence. The Filipinos trained by this project were supposed to go to work on some of the many decrepit old churches in the Philippines, but the project ran out of money, they were left unemployed, and one of them gladly undertook to restore our painting. He worked on it for over six months and did a superb job for a little more than $100.

Perhaps the water damage on the paintings had occurred somewhere in the Philippine archipelago, for we arrived at the early beginning of one of the worst typhoon seasons in decades. A letter home announced, "We had a typhoon the first weekend; the center passed 100 miles north of Manila, so we've been inaugurated." Two weeks later, this followed:

The true Southeast Asian monsoon—we've had it at last. [A reference to the fact that in Jakarta, the rainy season meant a half-hour downpour every few days] .... It has been raining without letup in Manila and Central Luzon since Monday or Tuesday last week. Now all the rivers are flooding, most of the drains aren't coping, and you can't get anywhere in or outside

Manila unless you have an amphibious vehicle . . . ."[1]

But there were many things about the Philippines that we liked from the start. A colleague of Bob's from the Political Section who met us at the Manila Airport had just completed a scuba diving course, and we signed up for it as soon we could. Such training had not been available in Indonesia, and although we had snorkeled happily for four years, the idea of exploring the sea at greater depth was irresistible.

Our instructor was a retired US Army Colonel, E.H. Gilleland, married to a beautiful Filipina and settled in Manila. Such arrangements were rare to nonexistent in Indonesia, where the vast majority of Dutch and Indo-Europeans had been expelled in the mid-1950s, but they were almost normal in the Philippines. The US-Philippine colonial relationship had been exceptionally close in many ways, but, as we soon learned, complicated. We had experienced nothing like it elsewhere.

The "Fil-Am" Relationship

After seizing the Philippine islands from Spain in 1898, the US fought a bitter guerilla war against nationalist rebels and tried to pacify the perennially restless Muslims in the south. But the ill will generated by these wars was gradually outweighed by American promotion of widespread English language education, and later by the appeal of American popular culture. After Pearl Harbor, Filipinos were the only colonized people in Asia to resist the invading Japanese, partly because they were already a self-governing commonwealth and well on their way to full independence. They paid bitterly for this loyalty both during the Japanese invasion and in the course of General MacArthur's reconquest of the Philippines at the end of the war. It was at this time that Manila suffered some of the heaviest damage of any city in World War II, inflicted mostly by American bombers, but few if any Filipinos held this against us.

We were aware of the history. We expected to get along well with the people, who are part of the great Malayo-Polynesian

---

[1] Barbara letters to Dear Family, July 31 and August 18, 1974.

family and whose islands form the northern peak of the Malay Archipelago. Most of them knew English, and we both knew Indonesian, which was related to their languages. Nevertheless we sensed a degree of malaise in the "Fil-Am" relationship, and it took us a while to figure out where it came from.

Our personal malaise was partly homesickness for Indonesia. It is a Foreign Service truism that people tend to fall in love with their first assignments. We loved Indonesia partly because it stood robustly on its own cultural feet. The Indonesians welcomed our interest in them, which they found understandable, but they were not particularly interested in us, certainly not in emigrating to the US.

In Jakarta, we had a one-person Consular Section, the office that handles visas and immigration issues. In the Philippines, there was an entire consular office building with over thirty American officers at work, a long line of visa seekers at the embassy gate every morning, and a row of commercial visa "facilitators" just across the street. Next to the consular building there was a bigger building that did nothing but manage the payment of US Government pension benefits of various kinds— Social Security, military, and so on—to Filipinos who had worked in or for the United States. Management was required because fraud was rampant: pension recipients resident in the Philippines (where an American pension income went a long way) tended to live forever, especially in remote areas, unless someone checked up on them.

The visa thing was a major annoyance. It was almost impossible to have a normal friendly relationship with a Filipino without a visa request popping out of the woodwork sooner or later. About a year after we arrived, the Indonesian airline Merpati Nusantara started running charter trips to Bali from Manila at ridiculously low prices, and Barbara and I leaped at the opportunity to return to one of our favorite places. It was about a three-hour flight, and after checking into our hotel in Sanur we made for the nearby beach, which we knew well. As we were relaxing with a drink and watching the sun sink, a Filipino gentleman who recognized us from the flight wandered over and jolted us out of our reveries by and asking if we could help him with a visa.

We were beginning to realize that almost every middle or

upper class Filipino had more relatives in our country than we did (or that we knew about), and these family links stoked the demand for visas. So casual friendships were easy to make but often tinged with wariness. As in most traditional societies, Filipinos depended on reciprocal relationships of all kinds, but we were not used to this kind of thing.

Underlying this and other irritants was a fundamentally different view of our colonial relationship. We saw ourselves as model colonialists compared to the feckless Spanish, who were in truth not all that bad compared to many others. We had demonstrated our enlightenment by eventually acquiescing gracefully to the demands of Filipino nationalists for independence, which was duly scheduled for 1946, a date we honored. The Filipinos had responded by their wartime loyalty and (we thought) loved us even more.

The reality was more complex. To begin with, our colonization of the Philippines was never wholly popular with Americans, with opinions about it divided along party lines. The Republicans were generally enthusiastic about shouldering the White Man's Burden; the Democrats saw imperialism as a betrayal of our values. When the Democrats took over the White House in 1916, they began a well-publicized effort to get rid of the Philippines, a move favored by organized labor, which feared an influx of low-priced Asian workers, and by American sugar interests, mostly in Cuba, which did not want Philippine sugar coming into the US duty-free.

To further complicate matters, Filipinos had doubts about independence. The Filipino upper crust feared that the end of access to our markets would mean ruination for them. And, because we had succeeded almost too well, most Filipinos were entranced with the idea of US statehood. This was of course impossible: having passed the Chinese Exclusion Act in 1882, we weren't about to open our borders to millions of Filipinos.

Admiring your overlord was also absurd in the global context of the 1930s. Colonized peoples were supposed to hate their colonizers, not love them. Loving them vastly complicated the task of those Filipino nationalists who sincerely wanted independence. The most prominent of them, Manuel Quezon, was put in the awkward position of advocating independence while working behind the scenes to delay it. "Damn the Americans!" he famously said, "Why can't they tyrannize us more?"[2]

After World War II, the result was a special relationship tinged with love, resentment and constant misunderstanding. Love spurned led to paranoiac resentment, all the more insidious for being repressed. Underneath their cheerful familiarity, many Filipinos felt that we had betrayed them and underappreciated their sacrifices on our behalf. Their fluency in American English often led Americans to assume that they were just like us, a serious mistake.

The "Fil-Am" relationship was symbolized by our embassy, a stately white building overlooking Manila Bay, which had been the office of the US High Commissioner before World War II. The official American presence remained huge. Its most visible element was military: our two big bases at Subic Bay (Navy) and Clark Field (Air Force). The two base commanders used their personal helicopters to visit the ambassador, landing noisily outside my office window, a spectacle our children enjoyed watching.

By the time of our arrival the bases were useful primarily as symbols of American commitment to the defense of the Western Pacific. But as part of their ongoing quest for more credible independence from us, the Philippine Government, having placed conditions on their use during the Vietnam War, also wanted them back. Fractious negotiations over their future had been going on almost constantly since the end of World War II. Ironically enough, when we finally relinquished them to Philippine control in 1991-92, we discovered we could get along quite well without them.

What was left of Clark was destroyed by the enormous eruption of nearby Mt. Pinatubo in 1991. Subic Bay, where a

---

[2] Robert Pringle, *Indonesia and the Philippines*, p. 10. Peter Stanley, author of *A Nation in the Making: The Philippines and the United States, 1899-1921*, Harvard University Press, 1974, was instrumental in helping me to understand the unique character of the US-Philippines relationship. The Quezon quotation is, however, from Theodore Friend, *Between Two Empires: The Ordeal of the Philippines, 1925-1946*, Yale University Press, 1965, p. 4.

skilled labor force could repair any ship in the US Navy, was successfully converted to a free trade zone. Its catchment area, built to serve the Navy's need for clean water, was the largest remaining area of old growth tropical forest on the island of Luzon, and became a center for forestry training and research.

Settling In

My job in the embassy's Political Section was in many ways a continuation of what I had been doing in Indonesia. I reported on ethnic minorities, most importantly the Muslim minority in the southern Philippines, which had been in more or less constant rebellion since the arrival of the Spanish.

I also covered the minorities of northern Luzon, who had remained unconverted by Spanish missionary priests and friars because of their warlike talents and mountainous homeland. That changed under the Americans, when Episcopal missionaries did achieve substantial success among these people. However, at the time of our arrival in Manila, the government had stirred up trouble by constructing a controversial dam, and the resulting unrest was stimulating a "communist" insurgency, which was of considerable interest to us. Both of these beats resulted in a lot of travel, although, due to security concerns, not as much to the Muslim south as I would have liked.

I also spent a lot of time escorting visiting VIPs and doing odd jobs, the oddest of which was serving as embassy liaison to the American Association of the Philippines. It was composed of senior members of the 60,000-strong resident American community who gathered periodically to reminisce. Many of them were veterans of the notorious Santo Tomas Japanese prison camp, and I will never forget one meeting which ended with an argument about who had gotten what in their Red Cross packages—and who had refused to share their goodies with others. Another meeting took place at the home of a member who had acquired it during the very early post-war period. His garden included a Japanese artillery piece left in place when the shooting stopped. There was a serious side to this organization; it had a major collection of books, documents and other memorabilia and still published a quarterly journal under the leadership of Lou Gleeck[3] who, although by this time retired, had served for decades as the embassy's powerful Consul General.

I was still a junior officer, and because the embassy was larger than the one in Jakarta I was subject to an extra supervisory level. My immediate boss, Charlie Salmon, headed the "internal" half of the Political Section, meaning Philippine as opposed to foreign affairs. Then, in order of seniority, came the Political Counselor, Frazier Meade. Above him was the Deputy Chief of Mission, Lewis "Skipper" Purnell, our friend from Jakarta and the person responsible for getting me to the Philippines (and also the biggest worry wart about letting me travel to the south).

Finally there was the Ambassador, William H. Sullivan, who had vaulted to the top of the Foreign Service for his role in the Vietnam peace negotiations. Following his tour in the Philippines he became ambassador to Iran until not long before radicals seized our embassy[4] and took fifty-two American hostages, including our good friend Ann Swift.

Sullivan was a great boss because he was extremely bright and self-assured. It was his rule that only he could write diplomatic reports—and he wrote a lot—using the first person. Anything not written in the first person was therefore the work of a subordinate, regardless of the fact that Sullivan, as ambassador, still signed all cables, in line with State Department-wide practice. What the rest of us wrote might be interesting, but it wasn't infallible, hence no need to get upset by minor differences of opinion between us and him. However, he read everything we wrote immediately and gave us frequent feedback, almost always complimentary, written with his signature red pencil. His wife was charming and considerate,

---

[3] *The Bulletin of the American Historical Collection.* The collection itself has been moved from the US Embassy to the Ateneo de Manila.

[4] According to what seems to be an accurate Wikipedia article (http://en.wikipedia.org/wiki/William_H._Sullivan) Sullivan left (read was probably fired from) his Iran ambassadorship because he favored negotiations with Ayatollah Khomeini, contrary to US policy. In his memoirs President Carter described him as "specifically insubordinate," which does sound like a bit like him. Sullivan died in 2013.

not always the case with pro-consular officers' wives.

Sullivan needed his lordly self-confidence because in Manila his ambassadorial supremacy was always in danger of being overshadowed by certain of his subordinates. In theory, the ambassador works for the President, and has authority over all US personnel in his country of assignment except military officers under the command of a regional commander-in-chief, or CINC. However, the two US base commanders, with all their stars, helicopters and PXs, were easy to regard as the most powerful Americans on the scene.

There was also a tradition of allowing other powerful officers to remain in Manila for long tours. In our era, that included the USAID Mission Director, Tom Niblock, and the Consul General, with all those precious visas to issue. Niblock was autocratic and ambitious, and, very publicly, a close friend of the Philippine First Couple, Ferdinand and Imelda Marcos. But when these people sometimes acted as if they were more important than the ambassador, Sullivan simply ignored the resulting gossip.

Barbara, as usual, had plenty to do besides meeting Bob's colleagues and their families. Getting to know any new city is always fun, and Manila had plenty of cultural and historic attractions, despite having been flattened by the US Air Force during World War II. Used to volunteer activities and freed from formal obligations as the wife of an FSO due to the regulation change of 1971, she was able to participate in activities of her own choosing, such as helping on the embassy committee which awarded Fulbright scholarships to deserving Filipinas. Another job, taken largely because no other woman at our church was brave enough to run a meeting, was to be president of the ladies' association of Holy Trinity (Episcopal) Church, which we attended. That turned out to be loads of fun when she got to go to meetings in Mountain Province, where almost all other delegates were tribal women from Central Luzon.

Our large half-house was on Agno Street, located off Taft Avenue, named after William Howard Taft, the first US Governor General of the Philippines. Taft Avenue was inhabited by swarms of smoke-belching "jeepneys" and busses, so the house was distinctly grimy even though well set back from the main thoroughfare. It was (and may still be) owned by Eduardo Cojuangco,[5] close friend of President Marcos and scion of a famous family which was principal owner of the enormous San Miguel beer conglomerate.

Our surroundings included a patch of slum as well as the main campus of De La Salle University, one of the largest in the Philippines. Behind our house there was a wide, partially roofed-over patio looking out on an ornamental garden and a pond with an arching, Chinese style bridge overhung with bamboo trees. The kids adored this arrangement and it was useful for other purposes, such as accommodating tribal visitors from the north who were uncomfortable inside western-style houses. A panda would have fitted in nicely, but instead we had, within a month of our arrival, six fish, three turtles, five ducks, four cats (belonging to the cook), a black-and-white puppy named Boots (a "darling local mutt with personality plus") and two parakeets on the way.[6] We soon discovered that during the torrential rains of typhoon seasons our pool overflowed and the goldfish escaped and had to be immediately hunted down or replaced.

The Children: New Schools and Adventures

As the kids grew there were new opportunities for us to share experiences with them, including weekend trips to beaches and islands. After we became proficient at scuba, Jamie and Anne, equipped with full-foot flippers and little masks, came with us on diving and snorkeling expeditions. They left the Philippines as self-confident salt-water fish. Later, in Papua New Guinea, they became certified divers themselves, and both have felt a special bond with oceans and coral reefs ever since.

Another big family milestone was reached when both children began "real" school at an English-language Philippine Montessori school recommended by friends. It was close to our house, and we wanted to expose the children to a cross-cultural educational experience. They began school right away, at the end of July, in the middle of the Philippine school

---

[5] From Nita Churchill, Filipina scholar and wife of Foreign Service Officer, Malcolm Churchill, both friends since our days in Manila.

[6] Barbara letter to Dear Mother and Daddy, August 14, 1974.

year, which began in late January and ended before Christmas. For four-year-old Annie this made no difference, and Barbara wrote to her grandparents:

Annie has taken to this school like a duck to water; after three days her teacher told me she was the most popular girl in her class. I'm not surprised; she always liked Mrs. Smith's pre-

A Philippine Christmas: a carving from Mindanao for Bob and a new hand-sewn pinafore for Annie.

Annie is off to her Montessori school in the school jeepney.

school [in Jakarta] and regarded home leave as an unfortunate hiatus in being entertained every morning at that interesting institution called school.[7]

The only academic glitch she ever ran into, as far as we can remember, was not knowing that in Filipino English a purse is a "bag," so she couldn't finish a reading puzzle.

Jamie was less fond of the Montessori school, though he loved Cub Scouts, which was run by the school and included overnight camping on the school grounds. We became increasingly concerned about his failure to learn to read in what was his first-grade year. We told him not to worry; it must be because he had missed the first half of the year, but Barbara went ahead and ordered a series of reading books and workbooks via the APO[8] so that she could teach him at home too.

First Mindanao Experience: Pineapple Land

In September 1974, Bob embarked on his first major official trip, one of several on which Barbara accompanied him. Our destination was the big southern island of Mindanao, where most of the Philippines' Muslim population lives, although we encountered none of them on this trip. Instead we went to two rich agricultural areas, Davao in the southeast and Cagayan d'Oro in the north, flying on a Defense Attaché plane, another DC-3 similar to the one Bob had used on returning to Jakarta from West Irian in 1970. He wrote,

We went down to Davao on the attaché plane, which turned out to be a little too exciting for my taste. Halfway down the port engine began to burp and splutter—it's a vintage 1943 DC-3—and our friendly crew chief, Sgt. Dobbs [whom we knew from taking scuba lessons with him] announced that it might

[7] Barbara letter to family, original and exact date missing.
[8] Originally for Army Post Office, APO now meant the US Armed Forces Postal Service, a glorious perk to which we had full access in Manila for the first time because of the US bases nearby. The APO system did not automatically serve embassies; the smaller ones without nearby bases, including several where we later served, had to rely on the inferior diplomatic pouch; in Jakarta we had been able to receive only packages via APO.

have to be shut down, 'but there's absolutely nothing to worry about, these things fly like a dream on one engine.' Unhuh. At the time we were right over the middle of Mindanao, which is a very large and jungley island. The engine didn't quite quit, but they had to leave it [the plane] in Davao pending arrival of spare parts, and everyone came home commercial . . . . [9]

At the time the engine began sounding weird, we were flying in big circles over the forest. Knowing something about what military attachés do for a living, I figured we were probably taking pictures of something of interest below. However, once the engine acted up that mission was quickly abandoned and we headed in a straight line to our destination.

In Davao, we learned that it would take six days to get spare parts and fix the plane, which didn't bother us because we had already planned to continue on to Cagayan d'Oro by a commercial flight, but it meant that the majority of our fellow passengers, other embassy and military personnel hoping for a free round-trip to Davao's excellent hotel and nice beaches, had to pay their own way back to Manila.

For us, it was back to work in situ, one of the pleasant things about the Foreign Service being that practically anything interesting you do beyond the capital city can legitimately be considered "work." Barbara wrote home on Davao Insular Hotel stationery:

Davao . . . is a boom town, getting rich on lumber and bananas. Del Monte, Dole and United Fruit all export bananas, all fresh, and all to Japan. Among them, slightly over one banana boat a day leaves Davao. I don't know the figure for lumber, but one certainly passes a lot of flatbed trucks loaded with logs on the road. The coral reefs in the area are [still] lovely. I hired a fishing boat and went exploring while Bob interviewed the mayor, an activist Catholic priest, etc. The next day he [Bob] played hooky and we plus one of the Marine guards who had hitched a ride with the plane went to visit the cultured pearl farm and do some snorkeling. We had a lovely day, but a wild ride home. The boat driver (boat was an outrigger with a 16hp Briggs and Stratton

---
[9] Bob letter to Dear Folks, September 8, 1974.

*motor) was an expert, the way he avoided burying the nose of
the boat in the waves (huge following swells) was a pleasure to
watch. [We must have been too poor for Barbara to consider
buying some of those cultured pearls.]*

   *That evening, Bob had an interview with the scion of an old
established business family, but they invited us to dinner instead
of just an interview and we met two of the most interesting
people we've yet met in the Philippines. They have set up a
family foundation which runs a medical and birth control clinic
that ministers to squatters. In addition, she runs a handicraft
workshop to employ squatter women and they are beginning
projects to employ the men. All cities in the Philippines seem
to have huge squatter problems, just as Indonesia does . . . . We
also met a Canadian with the UNDP, busy drawing up a long-
range development plan for Mindanao, which, however, has
not been coordinated with the plan of the Philippine National
Development Council. I should think he would have a feeling of
irrelevance . . . .* [10]

   We noticed during our tour of a Davao plantation that many
huge stalks of bananas were being dumped in ditches along the
road. They had "green rot" and could not be exported because
they would ripen on the boat and spoil the whole cargo. We
cut off as many as we could carry and took them home. These
were international standard "Cavendish" bananas, not one of
the scrawny but even better tasting Southeast Asian varieties.

   The letter continues with a description of our next destination:

*Cagayan depends economically on its port and has historically
exported the products of the high fertile plain behind it, plus
coconuts from the coast. Today the most important products are
the pineapples and tomatoes from Del Monte. Besides exporting
a certain amount of fresh pineapple direct to Japan, Del Monte's
huge cannery here (it even makes the cans) produces catsup,
stewed tomatoes; crushed, sliced, juiced and every other kind of
canned pineapple; tropical fruit cocktail, vinegar, and pickles.*

   *The plantation is 20,000 acres, mostly of whitish-green
pineapple prickles. The plantation managers' housing has*

[10] Barbara letter to Dear Mother and Daddy, September 1, 1974.

a gorgeous setting around a manicured golf course with a veritable botanical garden of flowers and trees on the premises. Even the workers' camps have lovely lawns and about every second house raises orchids. It's quite an operation.

We sent brother-in-law Ron Theobald, a food broker in Cincinnati, a set of photos of the Del Monte operation so he could see how pineapples are produced.

Barbara's letter captures the essence of what our excursions away from the capital city were like. They were official yet informal. After most trips, I wrote reports trying to summarize the political and economic character of the region in question. In both Indonesia and the Philippines, such reporting almost always included a snapshot of economic development. We talked to anyone who could help us understand what was going on, but protocol (or just plain good manners) also required a call on a local official or two.

We frequently made calls together partly because, as we had discovered in Sarawak, people were often more interested in a pretty wife than in a solo male official. Of course Barbara had much easier access to women than I did, and saw and remembered things that I missed. We usually found time to go sightseeing or snorkeling together—you never knew where you might discover something of more than recreational interest. (And, as noted elsewhere, we sometimes did things, even with the children along, that seem a bit foolhardy in retrospect.)

Every location was different. As Barbara's reference to calling on an "activist" Catholic priest suggests, one thing that was very different in the Philippines as compared to Indonesia was the importance of the Roman Catholic Church. In 1974 it was in many ways the most interesting political force in the country. In Manila, Bishop Jaime Sin, later to become Cardinal Sin,[11] was well into his long career as a vocal critic of Martial Law. In rural areas the Church was, thanks to the Spanish heritage, a ubiquitous presence, and there were still many Americans both serving as parish priests and running Catholic schools.

---

[11] Not a joke.

Few if any of them were radicals, but many were astute observers of local politics, especially when peoples subject to their ministry were vulnerable to abuse by the authorities. I did not write about the Catholic Church in national politics because that was the territory of my immediate supervisor, Charlie Salmon. He was a devout Catholic himself and he handled this job with a degree of disarming humor and understanding that I never could have matched.

However, talking with priests often helped me to understand an area. Political Counselor Frazier Meade, himself a stalwart Episcopalian, told me I should not take Barbara along on rectory calls because "all those crotty old priests" were accustomed to running around in their underwear, were not strong on housekeeping, and might be upset by the presence of a woman. We found that to be rarely, if ever, the case, as long as one didn't wander in on them unannounced.

Even under Martial Law, the Philippines still had the trappings of American-style democracy, but little of the nominal machinery of government had any real meaning. What did matter (and still does) was the entrenched economic elite, many with roots into the Spanish era—indeed some members of the older generation still spoke Spanish. A few members of this oligarchy had long since become American citizens and internationalized both their businesses and their families, the Cojuangco family which owned our house in Manila being a prime example.

The Marcos dictatorship was personal, in contrast to the army-based regime of Suharto in Indonesia. The oligarchy gave the impression that distribution of wealth in the Philippines was vastly more uneven than in Indonesia, but when I wrote a book comparing the two countries I found that the Indonesians were apparently more unequal—the rich just didn't, at this time, flaunt their money quite as much.[12]

There were other differences between the two countries that really mattered. Partly because the Filipinos had never had a real national revolution—they had, as noted earlier, been as much seduced as conquered by the Americans—the

[12] See the figures in the table in Robert Pringle, *Indonesia and the Philippines: American Interests in Island Southeast Asia*, Columbia University Press, 1980, p.16. It still seems a bit hard to believe.

country was not as well integrated politically as Indonesia. Tagalog was relabeled "Pilipino" in an attempt to make it a national language like Indonesian. But Tagalog is a more difficult language than Malay/Indonesian and had no prior history of use as a *lingua franca*. Those two factors plus the powerful prevalence of English made Tagalog much more difficult to "nationalize."

Finally, and very important politically, the Spanish heritage included much cultural blending, whereas the Dutch-Indonesian equivalent encouraged elaborate ethnic and legal distinctions. In the Philippines, for example, it was often difficult to tell who was "Chinese" and who was not. Ferdinand Marcos, to cite the most famous example, came from a province, Illocos Norte, where just about every educated person was a Chinese *mestizo*, and so, almost certainly, was he. Not surprisingly we see something similar in Mexico, where the distinction between "Indian" and European has remained far more blurred than in the United States.

As noted earlier, the most famous and popular aspect of American rule in the Philippines was English language education, built on a respectable foundation laid down by Spanish friars. That it was in English probably mattered more than that it was widespread, because it created a labor force willing and able to work anywhere in the world, and millions of Filipinos are still doing just that. The result, not surprisingly, is a society that is focused to an unhealthy degree on foreign opportunities, including emigration, rather than on fixing the Philippines.

Not Learning Tagalog

We learned first hand about the impoverished, English-speaking middle class when we decided to study Tagalog. Our teacher, Aida Flestado Erestain, had come to Manila because her husband found a supervisory job in a Levi Straus blue jeans factory there. They lived in penury not far from us; it was the first, and perhaps the only, time we have had friends who lived in a dwelling partially constructed of old cardboard boxes. When we visited Aida's home village in southern Luzon—near the spectacularly symmetrical and highly active

Mayon volcano—we were shocked by its poverty, although it was certainly no worse than a bad Manila slum.

We struggled with Tagalog for about two years. We had enjoyed speaking Indonesian in Indonesia and hoped to repeat the experience in the Philippines. Our attempts to attain even minimal fluency didn't work, partly because Filipinos saw no reason to use Tagalog with Americans in everyday situations, since they prided themselves on speaking our language far better than we spoke theirs.

Tagalog is, moreover, a very difficult language, with a complex grammar totally different from that of the almost grammarless Indonesian language, despite being in the same linguistic family. For example, if you change the focus of a sentence in Tagalog—"focus" being something expressed in English mainly through audible stress—tenses and cases in the rest of the sentence change along with it. To illustrate, if you say "he *hit* the ball" (he didn't drop it) instead of "he hit the *ball*" (not the policeman), the noun and verb endings change accordingly. It is as bad as Latin, but no one is expected to speak Latin these days, and who knows if most ancient Romans actually used the complex grammar we know and love.

Visiting some Real Headhunters

In October, a month after our Mindanao trip, Barbara, Jamie, and I headed north to visit the Ilongot people, at the invitation of Stanford University anthropologist friends, Shelley (Michelle) and Renato Rosaldo, who were doing research there.[13] The Ilongots were former headhunters who had retreated into a remote, mountainous area as settlers from the lowlands swarmed into every corner of Luzon. Most other mountain people had already abandoned much of their traditional lifestyle and become Christians. There were fewer than 5,000 Ilongots, living in "villages" of single houses, half a mile to a mile apart, scattered across a mountainside and quite unlike anything we had seen before.

[13] The Rosaldos' research on the Ilongots was published as Renato Rosaldo, *Ilongot Headhunting: A Study in Society and History*, Stanford University Press, 1980. Shelley died tragically in 1981 when she fell from a precipitous mountain trail in northern Luzon.

The Rosaldos were living with them in classic anthropological style. At first they had been determined to have nothing to do with the missionaries, American fundamentalists belonging to the New Tribes Mission who were specialists in converting remote ethnic groups. But when the Rosaldos discovered how long it took them to walk to their field site at Kakidugan, they relented so they could travel and get supplies by missionary aircraft. This involved getting the Ilongots to build them an "airstrip" which was duly included as a line item in their grant application to the National Institutes of Mental Health: "One Airstrip: $100." The aircraft were single-engine Piper Cubs and when we flew in we were allowed Jamie plus 24 pounds of baggage—Annie had to stay home with the cook again.

It was typhoon season and at first, due to bad weather, the missionary pilot couldn't get out of his base to come fetch us in Manila, so we left a week late. Barbara wrote:

We had a marvelous flight north—flying about a thousand feet up is very entertaining. But when we got to the mountains there was a solid layer of fluffy white clouds above them, and when the pilot finally found a hole, he discovered that our friends' airstrip was weathered in. So we had to land at the mission base about 1500 ft lower. The weather got worse and worse, and sure enough, another typhoon. So we spent 2 ½ days with the missionaries . . . nice people, good cooks, but a lot of subjects are difficult to talk about. . . . On Friday, we finally got to Kakidugan—what an airstrip! It is 400 ft long, undulating, and the grass is mowed by grazing cows.[14]

The Ilongots were marvelous hosts and Jamie, who was blonder then than our grandson Alexander was at the same age, was a major hit. They showed him how Ilongot children play: a yam is rolled down a slope and the kids shoot at it with miniature bows and arrows. Jamie was not skilled enough to hit a rolling target, so the father of the household put legs on a big yam, one that could stand still and Jamie could get right on top of it. Then he fashioned a tiny bow with five different kinds of specialized arrows, for fishing (three-pronged), large animal

---

[14] Barbara letter to Dear Mother and Daddy, October 25, 1974.

*Ilongot ceremonial fencing demonstration for us at Kakidugan, the Ilongot
settlement which was the research site of Shelley and Renato Rosaldo.*

hunting (big blade), birds (small pointy blade), etc. Carving all
this with a small knife took him about fifteen minutes. After we
left, we didn't allow Jamie to play with it, and, framed as a wall
hanging, it remains one of our prized possessions.

Jamie repaid their hospitality in kind. He shared one of
his "toys," the Richard Scarry picture book *What Do People
Do All Day*, which he "read" to his playmates. As this visit
occurred in his pre-reading days, what he was doing was
naming the objects pictured, but it didn't matter because the
colored drawings were enticing to the local children who had
no access at all to colorful illustrated books—and who might
never have even heard of reading or school.

Then the Rosaldos and a contingent of Ilongots paid us a
return visit at Thanksgiving. Renato came first, but before
the rest of the delegation could get to our house, the worst
typhoon of the season arrived on Thanksgiving Day. One
hundred and twenty mph winds blew over our orchid stand
and our TV antenna, but the electricity came back on just in
time to cook the turkey, and the house suffered no serious
damage. Shelley and the Ilongots were delayed, however, and

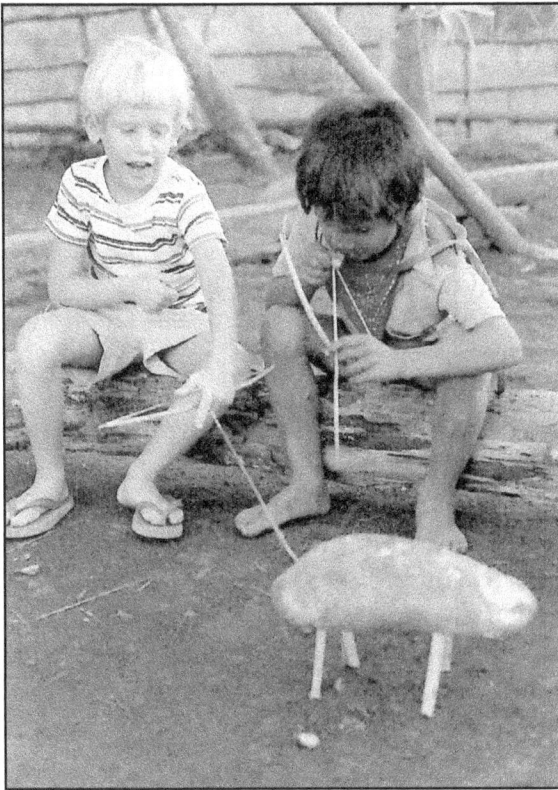

Jamie practices his aim on a sweet potato pig at Kakidugan.

missed Thanksgiving dinner. In those pre-cell phone days, we were out exploring Chinatown with some Chinese friends when they finally arrived.

At first the Ilongots were somewhat abashed by our large house, especially the high ceilings, but, Barbara wrote,

By now, three days later, people have gotten used to the house— we spend most of our time, and eat meals on, the large stone porch. As I write this, the Ilongots are busy catching goldfish with their hands to put them in a bucket while we drain and clean our pond; the whole operation is causing great hilarity. We have been to the museum of tribal cultures, the airport, the TB clinic (nobody here has it although it is rampant among the Ilongot population as a whole) and Shelley took everyone shopping for cloth, pans and shovels yesterday.[15]

The visit took on a bit the air of a grade-school field trip, because our visitors were total innocents about traffic, and someone used to the big city had to act as a crossing guard whenever we came to a street. The Ilongots enjoyed sleeping on the porch, but the biggest hit of the visit for them was a tour of a big Philippine Airlines jetliner, arranged by our military attachés. They knew a lot about small airplanes but were amazed by features like tray tables, reclining seats, and ashtrays in the big one.

My interest in the Ilongots went beyond the fun of getting to know them. Although an extreme case, they were in many ways typical of the northern minorities, marginalized from mainstream Philippine society, threatened by settler encroachment (including both lowlanders and more numerous tribal groups), unserviced by and generally ignorant of the Philippine government, and vulnerable to recruitment into a growing communist insurgency in the region, and I wrote an official report on our visit.[16]

More Official Travel, and Weekend Diving with the Wealthy

In December, 1975, I visited the city of Zamboanga in southern Mindanao. A charming but perennially violent town, it had once been the capital of "Moro Province," under the command of General John J. ("Black Jack") Pershing from 1909 to 1914 before he became famous as the commander of US forces in France during World War I. The Colt 45 pistol, designed to stop a charging Moro in his tracks, was introduced for use here. It was my first visit to the Muslim area of Mindanao, and, because my superiors were so nervous about allowing American officials to go there, it was to be my last for quite a while. Barbara and the kids stayed in Manila. I wrote that . . .

Zamboanga (visited December 13-16) is a piquant blend of flowers, tourists, refugees and bored soldiers and sailors

---

[15] Barbara letter to Dear Mother and Daddy, December 4, 1974.
[16] "The Ilongots, Tribal Tribulations in Northern Luzon," airgram, n.d.

*engaging in sporadic shootouts with each other. Although the
city center is normally peaceful, rebel activity remains high in
the hinterland and is particularly intense on Basilan Island,
which has been the scene of recent large-scale operations by
the [Philippine] armed forces.*[17]

The Muslim Philippines is the ultimate *plus-ça-change*
land; as this is written US Special Forces have been back in
the area for some years, and Basilan is not yet "pacified."

By the end of 1974 our life had settled into a pleasant if

*Dad has just finished a scuba dive, and now
it is time for Jamie's snorkeling lesson.*

---

[17] "Zamboanga and Vicinity: Refugees and Recession," Manila A-12,
January 15, 1975.

*Barbara underwater with a live Murex ramosus in one hand, and fresh
and used flashbulbs in the other. Below about 30 feet, divers (and cameras)
perceive little color in coral or fish, so flash is a necessity—but early in our
diving career, sport divers did not yet have flashguns.*

sometimes frenetic routine of work, including travel, official
entertaining (Manila had a larger and more active diplomatic
community than Jakarta) and scuba diving plus shell collecting
expeditions on weekends. I bought a Nikonos camera and
slowly learned to photograph the colorful fish, coral and shells
we could see underwater. Indeed, I switched principally to
color film for my photography and stopped doing my own black
and white processing, as I had done in Jakarta. I was unaware
that early color prints would fade badly after only a few years,
although Kodachrome color slides have lasted very well.

The diving and snorkeling was excellent exercise, a matter
of some importance since I got little other exercise, although
we played some tennis at the Army-Navy Club (another
colonial relic) next door to the embassy. I discovered on our
trip home from Manila in 1977 that I could hold my breath
for almost three minutes and free dive to a depth of 100 feet.
It was quite safe, because when you free dive, just holding
your breath without air tanks, there is no decompression risk
from rapid ascent, as there is with scuba, because you are not

breathing air under pressure. This constant exercise of lungs and legs almost certainly redounded to my benefit when I had to have heart surgery two decades later.

We became expert at finding pristine reefs, most of those near Manila having been destroyed by pollution and fishing with dynamite or concentrated pesticides which kill coral as well as fish. We would hire an outboard-powered outrigger canoe (*banca*) and the owner would drop us off on a nice reef-fringing beach on some uninhabited island where we could camp and go diving. Then he would come back to pick us up the next day. We did this a number of times with the kids in tow, instructing them to stay on the beach while we disappeared underwater, usually for at least forty-five minutes. They always did, but it makes us quake in retrospect.[18] We were careful not to get into strong currents, which are by far the most dangerous aspect of this kind of diving, as you can easily be swept out to sea, which, without a boat nearby, can be fatal.

Diving also gave us a pleasant entrée into the Philippine wealthy class. They had discovered the pleasures of coral reef gazing and it became a fad, all the more so since the Marcos regime was restricting the amount of money that the rich could take abroad, encouraging them to live it up at home. Our friends the Taylors, who owned a marble quarry at Puerto Galera on the island of Mindoro, sometimes invited us to visit them. We had met them on our first trip to that island when they hired the only ferry returning to Luzon at the end of one weekend for their family's exclusive use. Needing to return to Manila for work and school, we had begged our way, scuba tanks and all, onto the ferry with them.

The Spanish once built some of the famous Manila Galleons on Mindoro, utilizing its rich stands of tropical hardwoods. It was close to Manila, yet relatively unspoiled, and still had tribal people living in its mountainous interior. We divided our time between the Taylors' comfortable hillside house and camping on the beach to go diving. A nearby Catholic mission allowed us to use their washrooms.

No place in the Philippines was more famous for extravagant

---

[18] Or at least we thought they did; Annie contradicts us when we mention this now. At least they must not have gone far into the water.

displays of wealth than the island of Negros with its sugar plantations. The owners were very rich because they paid their workers very little, and because, under our sugar quota system, they exported sugar to the US and were paid the US price, much higher than the world market price. We were invited to attend a scuba training course for an assemblage of these "sugar barons" being given by the same Colonel Gilleland who had taught us how to dive soon after our arrival. Bob wrote:

Although the [Philippine] government is skimming off four-fifths of the current fabulous sugar profits for which you folks are paying [by US subsidization of the import price] . . . there is enough gravy (or syrup) left over to maintain the sugar types in affluence plus . . . . The crowd we were with included the governor of the province, who sponsors the diving [Alfredo "Junior" Montelibano] and has purchased a small island, to which he commutes by helicopter with his blonde Australian "companion" and her two blonde friends . . . . The governor, a sugar baron in his own right, is estranged from his wife, a leading member of the Lopez family (also founded on sugar) whose assets Marcos has confiscated and whose heir is in the clink. FM [Ferdinand Marcos] has made much out of how he has cracked down on the oligarchs. In fact it has been a very selective process involving his unfriends. In the meantime a lot of his friends have become new oligarchs.[19]

Another guest pointed out to me that the wealthiest diver present, Isidro "Ding" Lopez, managed forty-seven sugar plantations owned by him or other members of the Lopez family, which produced enough sugar to yield a profit of over $2 million even after the government's four-fifths share was subtracted. We noted that the sugarocracy seemed to socialize well together even when those present included political rivals.

The kids were doing fine. Although Jamie wasn't learning much, he enjoyed his Cub Scout camp-outs in the schoolyard. There was a dog show, in which he entered Boots. Then in January he discovered (and "rescued") a drowning bat in our pond—the one that the goldfish routinely floated out

---

[19] Bob letter to Dear Folks, January 25, 1975.

of during typhoon rains. We didn't capture the bat, so Jamie had to have a course of rabies shots, all fourteen of them, The shots were still sub-cutaneous, which meant they stung severely, but they were given in the back not in the stomach as they once had been, which reduced the pain somewhat.

We were glad it wasn't Annie, who always screamed like a banshee when she had shots. But Jamie endured them without complaining, [20] and his sister noticed this. The next time she went to the doctor for an inoculation, probably for cholera which we were still getting every six months, she announced that she was going to be like Jamie and not cry, and she did not, from then on out. At about this time Barbara wrote home, "Jamie is in a paper airplane stage (Jane sent the perfect present for Christmas) and the house is littered with fallen aircraft. Annie is her usual carefree self, always singing away. She is the only musical one in the family."[21] Before long she was studying ballet in the children's program of the Manila Cultural Center,[22] resulting in a memorable photo of her pointing her toes out of sync with every other little ballerina.

The Cebu Interlude: Jamie Learns to Read

At about this time, in April 1975, we went to Cebu, capital of the island of the same name, to fill a gap between US consuls.[23] Cebu is an important place, the metropolis of a wide area where Cebuano is spoken. Indeed, it is spoken by more people as a native tongue than any other language in the Philippines—and is reportedly a lot easier to learn than Tagalog.

We happened to arrive in Cebu just in time for the end of the Vietnam War and the evacuation of Saigon. Many of the evacuees came out via our big Philippine bases. But while our colleagues in Manila were working day and night to help with the evacuation, we were blithely exploring beaches up and down Cebu Island and its neighbors. The consulate was mainly a visa-issuing operation, so I did very little real work

---

[20] Ibid.

[21] Barbara letter to Dear Mother and Daddy, February 28, 1975.

[22] Barbara letter to Dear Mother and Daddy, June 25, 1975.

[23] We had visited Cebu previously in 1973 on R&R from Indonesia; see Chapter 6.

aside from a couple of papers on land reform and the local Chinese community. We had plenty of time to explore the local churches, many of them battered by earthquakes and poverty, often bereft of their old wooden statues and carved pews, mostly with tin roofs, but some still with their original painted, barrel-vaulted ceilings.

We stayed in the consul's residence, a marvelous old wooden house on stilts which we knew from our previous visit, with a large back yard flanked by wealthy, friendly neighbors, so the children had no lack of little friends to play with. Soon after our stay, the embassy, in an all too typical fit of insensitivity to charm, sold it and bought a more modern, much less appealing house in the suburbs.

The travel was spectacular. Barbara wrote of one visit to see Filipino friends of her parents' neighbors, the Garvers:

Bob took leave and we drove south and crossed on the ferry to Dumaguete City in Negros. That's where Silliman University is, and we met the Garvers' friends, Quintin Doromal [who is now the President of Silliman] and his wife. He remembers you both from a party the Garvers gave. The road south is terrible, not impassable, but so full of potholes that it took us over four hours to go 134 km. in a jeep wagoneer. (The road up the west coast coming back was even worse.) Then some of the ferries were broken, so we had to wait five hours to cross. We put the time to good use by going diving—the Cebu coast is one big coral shelf; however we arrived in Dumaguete at 6 to find a formal dinner invitation from the Doromals for 7, and all of us salty and with wet hair. We made it; air conditioners make good hair driers. Furthermore, the children's company manners were impeccable—for once. They seem to understand when they ought to behave.

The second day we were there we rented the university's outrigger and went off to dive at their new marine preserve. It was the clearest water we have seen anywhere because the small island is solid coral and has no water . . . [flowing from silted rivers into the ocean off its shores], its reef has not been exploited, and it teems with coral, fish and shells.[24]

The Cebu assignment took place during a school vacation, or at least most of it did, and that was the time that Barbara used the books she had ordered to teach Jamie to read. The series she had selected was from Open Court publishers and, not understood by her at the time, it was heavily based on phonetics, not the whole-word approach to learning to read. That was fortunate, because we would ultimately find out that visual perception and visual memory were Jamie's weak spots, and recognizing word patterns by sight would not have worked for him.

Every morning he had a lesson, and after learning a new sound that accompanied a new story, attempted to fill in the workbook. In a very short time, he was reading at first-grade level. But his difficulty in writing persisted, and even fill-in-the-blanks written exercises and workbooks were difficult for him. Barbara had this to say when he was seven and a few months: "Jamie has really learned to read now and is enjoying such delights as reading under the covers after going to bed; he can also read to Annie . . . but his fingers and pencil still do not coordinate very well."[25]

We had long wondered why his omnivorous mind, evidenced in conversations about topics as widely varied as the growing habits of plants and the guns of Corregidor, as well as why bats should not be rescued, and on and on, could not cope with reading and writing. Now that the reading had been solved, his inability to write down words that he could read brought this issue to the fore. His Grandmother Cade suggested the answer when she sent us a newspaper article about this phenomenon, which was just being recognized by educators. They called it simply "learning disabilities" and described it, more or less, as a neurological dysfunction in the brain that prevented bright children from mastering certain, but varying, routine tasks. Special teaching methods, it was said, would reach such children.

This information, plus the subsequent discovery that

---

[24] Barbara letter to Dear Mother and Daddy, May 16-19, 1975. Saigon had fallen to North Vietnamese forces at the end of April.

[25] Barbara letters to family, August 3 and August 30, 1975.

a teacher trained in an early method of teaching learning disabled children (the Slingerland method) was on the staff of Faith Academy, a missionary school on the outskirts of Manila, resulted in Jamie's transfer to that school in September, 1976. (Faith Academy operated on a US school calendar.) So that is where he attended third grade. [26]

Later, back in Washington, Barbara would take courses in learning disabilities—theory, and how to cope with them. She learned that certain perceptual functions, in Jamie's case processing and reproducing information presented in written form, in particular, producing it in handwritten form, was what came to be called a "*specific* learning disability." She also recognized our good luck in having found at Faith Academy a teacher trained in a method that focused on that kind of difficulty. Had he, for example, had trouble with processing auditory information, all Faith's special teaching would not have helped as much. As it was, he made some slight progress in writing and spelling; he also got a good grounding in phonetics, which even in the age of spell-check still stands him in good stead.

The classroom became a more positive place—in terms of Jamie's own perception of his progress—than it had been at the Montessori school, although I still credit his teachers there with never having been unkind or discouraging to their student who couldn't keep up. However, September 1977 was going to begin the first year of implementation of the recently passed "Education of All Handicapped Children" Act (PL 94-142) in the United States, and therefore we decided to limit our posting in Manila to three years and get Jamie back in a US school in time to be one of the first children who would benefit from the new law.

Barbara and the Jesuits

By early June, 1975, we were both teaching at the Ateneo de Manila, a Jesuit University and one of the most prestigious in the Philippines. Bob's involvement was not much work, a seminar in Southeast Asian History. He met a number of bright

---

[26] Barbara letter to Dear Mother and Daddy, November 6, 1976.

young Filipinos and persuaded one of them, Ray Ileto, to go to Cornell for a PhD; Ray has since had a distinguished career teaching Southeast Asian history in the US, the Philippines and Australia.

Barbara was hired to teach Medieval European History, because the Middle Ages were the formative period of the modern Catholic Church, as well as Modern European History, and both were required of freshman students. This first, and only, venture into university teaching turned out to be fun, though demanding, as a job (compensated more-or-less at the honorarium level), but also, and equally, as a window into Philippine society.

In the classroom, I encountered freshman students who were young, having spent only six years in elementary school (no compulsory kindergarten) and five in high school, for a total of eleven years formal education, and much of it must have been of the memorize and regurgitate type. Yet the good fathers who ran the Ateneo had mapped out for them a curriculum at European level, and plunked them in large lecture classes, with no small sections or graduate assistants to the professors. Two exams and a paper were the norm for these introductory courses. My initial lectures went way over their heads, but my high-school teacher reaction to the testing/grading situation worked: give them weekly quizzes. Here is my summary of weeks one and two:

In the medieval history class, I reviewed classical and early imperial Rome in one hour (!) and then asked them the next time "If you had been a patrician [which most were in twentieth century Philippine terms] at the height of the Empire, what would your life have been like?" About 2/3 of the students answered, "Beautiful. I would have loved it. Slaves to wait on me and banquets every night (a banquet menu I read made a great impression), etc., etc." One girl said she would have studied literature and philosophy with her Greek tutor and no science, and she would have liked that because "I hate science." We needed some practice before the exam in that class . . . .

Still, it's going better in terms of content than the Modern History class. I tried to start with an overview of the waning Middle Ages—trends like the revival of international commerce and the consolidation of territorially-based monarchies. I lost them completely, had to go back and start again in simpler terms. Medieval history is sufficiently concrete—Romans, barbarians, manors, knights, kings—to be not too hard to present or to follow. But national states and absolute monarchy and so on are not only harder to put your finger on; they're rather far from the Philippine experience . . . . Plus, most of the students in that class are budding doctors and this term they are panicked about anatomy, so history has a low priority. Still, it's fun; the other faculty members are very nice and it's a better way to get to know Filipinos than cocktail parties.[27]

I did, however, also remark more than once in my letters that preparing for university lectures took longer than getting ready for high-school classes, with their student-participation activities like maps, play-acting historical scenes and so on. That was before I encountered Madeira and advanced placement courses.

After a few bumps, it must all have clicked, because I taught one-and-a-half years until we left in 1977. I discovered at some point when I had to pick up my paycheck, such as it was, that I, along with many other teachers, was being paid "off the books," presumably another trick to foil the Philippine tax collection system. But my students were learning, and I received two memorable term papers in reaction to an assignment made up of several quotations from medieval sources.

The first, from Machiavelli's *The Prince*, elicited the response: "I know that Machiavelli was right from personal experience." Indeed! It turned out that this young man's family ran the province of Ilocos Sur as a personal fief. His grandfather, the congressman from that district, was murdered by his political enemies in the Vigan Cathedral in October, 1970. Shades of Thomas à Becket, but Grandfather was no cleric. My young student reminisced, "I used to watch my father and grandfather take out our private army during political campaigns."

The second paper was simply amusing. Responding to a quotation from *Beowulf* in which the hero was seeking

---

[27] Barbara letter to family, date missing.

Grendel, "gruesome prowler of the border land, ranger of the moors, the fens, and the fastness," the student wrote: "I know that this quotation is from a medieval story because the Moors [the word, in Pilipino *Moros*, for the Muslims in the southern Philippines] lived there." My marginal comment was "And who were the Fens?" I can't remember whether the rest of the paper showed any comprehension of the text at all.[28]

Family Activities in Manila

Life was full. Jamie had a new friend, Peter Sienkiewicz, a Polish neighbor whose Dad worked for the UN's International Labor Organization (ILO). There is a funny letter from Barbara about the two of them decorating each other with finger paint and flooding both bathrooms trying to clean up the evidence. "Jamie's really getting into the Tom Sawyer phase now."[29] Peter is today a successful businessman in Poland. A large Filipino family who lived nearby, the DiChupas, also provided playmates and became good friends of all the Pringles.

In mid-June we co-hosted a big catered farewell party for Bob's boss, Political Counselor Frazier Meade and his wife Susie. The setting was the embassy lawn looking out over Manila Bay, certainly one of the grandest settings of our Foreign Service entertaining career.[30] We were sorry to see the Meades leave, but Frazier's replacement, Bob Wenzel, turned out to be a fine boss, and equally tolerant of my sometimes less-than-mainstream reporting interests. His wife, Renee, was just as good a friend of Barbara as Susie Meade had been.

At about the same time we joined a group of embassy families in a hike up the dormant (for the moment) Taal Volcano, a couple of hours by car south of Manila. Taal has erupted over thirty times since the Spanish conquest, and is big enough to threaten Manila when it goes on a rampage. It has a large crater lake with an island on which sits a smaller crater in the middle. It was a very hot day, and we all decided somewhat foolishly to hire canoes and cross to the island,

---

[28] The quotations were taken from the papers themselves, somewhere in Barbara's teaching files, which may or may not still exist.

[29] Barbara letter to Mother and Daddy, June 25, 1975.

[30] Ibid.

logically named Volcano Island.

Scrambling up the ashy slope of the island was easy, but coming back to the lake was a lot harder because we had no guides, there was no path, and rain had cut deep ravines through the slope. It kept getting hotter and hotter, and if you didn't guess correctly which ravine to follow on the way down you had to go back up and start over when your false-start ravine intersected with another, because the ravine slopes were too steep to cross. We had absolutely no warning of this risk.

Whew indeed! The wife of one of my Political Section colleagues nearly passed out and had to be carried down, with three gents attending her. Meanwhile, the two moms and four children went ahead, trying to find the correct route by exploring one false spur after another. All the kids including ours were tired but heroic. Barbara wrote, "Annie, tough little specimen that she is, was never really physically tired; she just got tired of the idea of walking more. Jamie did begin to flag seriously, but he is persistent and he made it."[31] Finally reaching the bottom, and the boat, Jamie and Anne peeled to their underwear and jumped in; the other, more proper, boys held back for a while, but finally decided they were too hot to stand on ceremony.

On July 24, 1975, Barbara wrote "We have a Peace Corps friend from Iloilo [pronounced ee-low ee-low] visiting for a few days while he puts regional planning data through a computer."[32] This may have been our first glimpse of the Information Age.

By late 1975 we were getting a bit tired of maintaining our sooty Agno Street mansion with its ornamental pond. As the summer rainy/typhoon season began, Barbara wrote that we were digging a drainage ditch for it:

Our ornamental pond elicits oohs and ahs whenever we have guests, but I'd just as soon have grass. The children could play on it and it wouldn't leak, flood, need to be cleaned, etc.—every time we drain the pond we have to catch and attempt to keep alive the ornamental fish (100+, the big ones had babies) that are supposed to eat mosquito eggs.[33]

[31] Barbara letter to Dear Mother and Daddy, July 30, 1975.
[32] Barbara letter to Dear Mother and Daddy, July 24, 1975.
[33] Barbara letter to Dear Mother and Daddy, July 10, 1975.

Despite the mosquito egg- (or larvae-) eating fish, we still had to take malaria medication the whole time we were in the Philippines, partly because of frequent travel to rural areas. The pond and its contents nonetheless had their moments, and we have memorable photos of Clay and Char sitting on the bridge spanning it when they came to visit for Christmas later that year.

Near Miss in Zamboanga

In August Bob went back to Mindanao and Barbara was able to join him in Zamboanga for a three-day conference on ethnic minorities in the southern Philippines. We had a splendid time exploring the local markets and Barbara was able to visit Isabella, the capital of Basilan, as well as a Yakan refugee camp, the Yakans being a Muslim group from Basilan who do beautiful weaving. The conference was held at Zamboanga's famous old hotel, the Lantaka, which looks over a pretty strait with some nice sandy islands, and we also stayed there. We had a little time every morning before the conference started, and the islands were just too tempting, so at least three times we hired an outrigger to scoot across to them and do a little pre-breakfast shell collecting.

We found some gorgeous green, brown and white olive shells, *Oliva tricolor*, quite scarce, and enjoyed ourselves thoroughly. A week or two later a young Japanese airline stewardess was kidnapped, apparently by Moro rebels, while sunbathing on the exact same little islands. Shudder! Imagine if it had been us! We could see the headline: "US Embassy Muslim Expert and Wife captured by Moros while Collecting Shells in Zamboanga"!!! This was the place where the Monkeys had no Tails, according to a racist US Army ditty of the Pershing era.[34] However, we still have some of those olive shells, which we never found anywhere else.

Meanwhile, Annie was having a banner summer. She celebrated her fifth birthday thus:

---

[34] According to Wikipedia it was set to the tune of the official Philippine Constabulary Band march and became the regimental march of the 127th US Infantry Regiment.

Her heart's desire was a decorated birthday cake of the sort that are a specialty here. So on Monday I took her to the bakery and we ordered a splendid confection with Snow White and the seven dwarfs on top. This creation we took to school on Tuesday to share with all her classmates. Annie was in seventh heaven; it never even occurred to her to ask whether she was getting any other presents.[35]

But she did, and the principal one was that pink-checked gingham long dress, which both Zoe and Penelope enjoyed wearing more recently, that she picked out herself at a small shop selling hand-sewn children's clothes.

Then, at the end of September, she broke her arm at Seafront, the embassy recreation club, apparently by spinning on wet grass while Barbara took a visiting pooh bah's wife shopping at the commissary. Barbara doesn't remember all the details, but our dog was with them because he needed a shot, and she was really exasperated when the important guest a) balked at taking a taxi home and b) refused to take the dog with her when she realized the taxi was her only option. So somewhere in our scrapbooks is a note to Bob from his secretary, delivered in the middle of a meeting, to the effect of "Annie has broken her arm; Barbara is with her in the medical clinic [which was in the embassy compound], but the dog escaped and is loose in the compound and Jamie is chasing him." The break was severe; Annie wound up with a plaster cast from wrist to shoulder, and Barbara made her a red polka-dot sling to hold the casted arm.

Indonesian Holiday

In October we went back to Indonesia, using the same Merpati Airlines charter to Bali that we had had taken seven months earlier, but this time we took the kids along. Annie was sporting the red polka-dot sling around her broken arm. We have a photo of all of us in a small sailing *perahu*, and there is a plastic bag over Annie's whole arm and cast. It turned out to be more

---

[35] Barbara letter to Dear Family, August 30, 1975. This letter also tells the story of the Japanese air hostess's kidnapping—and release.

of a trip than we had anticipated because the Merpati charter operation went out of business shortly after we left.

Everything began well. We spent three days in Bali, where the children enjoyed the dances. Annie was no longer spooked by the fearsome witch Rangda, as she had been as a younger child. Then we flew to Jakarta, arriving during the big Muslim holiday of Lebaran, when it is customary to call on friends, and of course we did, in addition to going to lots of parties. The kids even went to school with old friends for several days.

We stayed with Phil and Cindy Wilcox; when Cindy's parents arrived for a visit, we moved to John and Sirkka Monjo's house (except for Jamie, who had an allergic reaction to something growing in their garden and got to stay with his friend John Clinton). The Wilcoxes gave a big party for us, for which Barbara sent Cindy a suggested guest list including a who's who of our Indonesian friends.[36] We also went diving in the Thousand Islands (Pulau Seribu) north of Jakarta. We had snorkeled there a lot, but had never before seen its underwater scenery with scuba.

From Jakarta we flew to Jogjakarta in Central Java—more sightseeing, batik-buying, etc. Then we took the train, third class, to Surabaya in East Java, because there was no air connection. The train broke down about halfway there, miles from the nearest town, and we spent a couple of hours sitting on the tracks (the unair-conditioned cars were too hot) waiting

---

[36] The listed included Mr. and Mrs. (Danny) Harun al-Rashid (Embassy employee); Mr. and Mrs. Ismid Hadad, LPPPES; Mr. and Mrs. Kusnaka Adimihardja (member of Parliament); Major and Mrs. Harjono Guritno; Mr. and Mrs. Suharsono Kramadibrata (Georgia Pacific); Mr. and Mrs. Hamid al-Gadrie; Mrs. Dorodjatun Kuntjoro Jakti [apparently Djatun was still in jail]; Mr. and Mrs. Fikri Djufri, *Tempo*; Mr. and Mrs. Goenawan Mohamad, *Tempo*; Mr. Ekki Sjahruddin, Mr. Ridwan Saidi, HMI; Dr. and Mrs. Taufiq Abdullah, LEKNAS; Drs. and Mrs. Mar'ie Muhhamad; Ambassador and Mrs. Nugroho; Professor and Mrs. Fuad Hassan; Mr. and Mrs. Pandam Guritno (the *wayang* expert); Mr. and Mrs. Fachrur Rosi; Mr. and Mrs. Hassan Shadili; Tapi Omas Ihromi and her husband; Mr. Herman Lantang; Mr. and Mrs. Lim Bian Kie; Mr. and Mrs. Sabam Siagian; Mr. and Mrs. Harry Tjan; Mrs. Pudji and Abdul Azis. Closer, or more elderly, friends that we preferred to see at a smaller gathering included General and Mrs. Jusuf Singadekane, Dr. and Mrs. Sjafruddin Prawiranegara, Mr. and Mrs. Zainal Abidin, Ms. Jo Abdurrachman, and Filino and Mary Harahap . . . not counting more Embassy and other foreign friends.

for the brakeman to fix the locomotive ("*Lokonya rusak, Pak,*" they told Bob). He did, but it broke down again at the next station stop, and we finally arrived in Surabaya by taxi in the middle of the night. Bob's observation in a letter thanking the Monjos was "Java is as dream-like as ever, especially by moonlight." Barbara's was "The moon was full and the whole thing reminded me of *Dr. Zhivago*, except for the temperature."

We stayed in Surabaya with David and Sarah Barnett. David was a former consular officer who was ostensibly in business, managing a shrimp processing plant and collecting antique hanging lamps for sale—we bought some of ours from him. The only trouble was that, apparently to make ends meet, he was also spying for the Soviets, and after returning to the US was eventually caught. That drama was still in the future; all that mattered to us was that the Barnetts, who had a big house with a garden and children the age of our kids, were hospitable friends. We have a photo of us with them around their swimming pool.

Having recuperated from the Great Train Fiasco, we caught a commercial flight from Surabaya back to Bali on October 21, as planned, only to find that that the Merpati charter company had, in our absence, gone definitively belly up. However, their agent in Bali told us that Merpati would honor its commitment to fly us back to Manila and would pay for our additional stay at the Bali Beach Hotel until that could be arranged.

Horrors—stranded on Bali in a really nice hotel that we knew and loved! An appropriately distressed call to superiors in Manila ensued. What could they do but say "Well, OK . . . ." So we snorkeled, enjoyed the scenery, linked up with the Wilcox parents, who by this time were also visiting Bali, did more Christmas shopping, and saw a great cremation ceremony with the funeral tower being carried through brilliant rice paddies:

It was a small ceremony but very colorful, and lots of racing around with the tower to baffle the demons. Jamie and Anne were both fascinated with the theology of cremation, and who knows how they finally figured it out for themselves; we answered endless questions both coming and going.[37]

---

[37] Barbara letter to Dear Mr. and Mrs. Santa Claus Cade, November 4, 1975.

Finally after several days the long-suffering Merpati agent got us on a Cathay Pacific flight to Manila. But—another shock!—we would have to go via Hong Kong on Cathay Pacific, which at this time was famous for its classy service, and overnight there to connect with another Cathay Pacific flight to Manila. This routing was not quite as great as it sounds, because we arrived in Hong Kong at eight in the evening. We had time only for a ferry ride to Kowloon and a double-decker sightseeing bus ride to enjoy all the lights of the city at night, plus dinner, before bedtime at midnight and an early morning departure. Annie loved the bus, but was so tired we doubted if she remembered any of it. We had only thirty dollars left so, in the days before we had a credit card, we could not have stayed longer even if we had wanted to. [38]

The Parents Do the Philippines

Our next major event was a Christmas visit from Clay and Charlotte. We gave a big party for them and had a smashingly successful family celebration. Bob wrote,

The kids are fine, having had a glorious Christmas what with a combination of grandparents and some very successful presents. (Anne's was a Barbie doll with elaborate wardrobe—!—and Jamie's was, well, a lot of things but especially a great addition to his Lego armory and a microscope. They are both doing well in their very different styles. J has become something of a reading fiend and has a great vocabulary in subjects that interest him— mainly science. (He never stopped plaguing grandfather with questions for a solid month.) On the other hand he is slow at math and generally uninterested in mechanical mental chores that strike him as dull. Heredity may have something to do with all this. Annie just zips around like a supercharged sunbeam. She is a natural hellion but eventually responds to discipline if she knows she can't push her luck any further. She is going to be

---

[38] The trip is covered in Barbara letter to Dear Family, on Bali Beach Hotel stationary, October 21, 1975, and the letter cited above. Merpati Nusantara Airlines was founded in 1961 by the Indonesian Air Force and is still a major airline at this writing.

a classic American headache teenager. However she has been very good in school and perhaps because she is the oldest in her group has been very helpful for her teacher, so maybe there is hope. She learns anything she feels like learning, and fast.[39]

We then headed north to Baguio in northern Luzon, established by William Howard Taft, our first governor-general of the Philippines, as a summer capital for American administrators. Taft, who weighed 300 pounds, suffered a lot from the tropical heat, and he thought that his American staff would perform better if they had a "hill station" to which they could retreat in the hottest months of the year, the way European diplomats did in pre-air-conditioning Washington, DC. So off he went to Baguio, which is 5,000 feet higher in elevation than Manila, and at the end of his journey he sent a cable to Secretary of War Elihu Root, "Stood trip well. Rode horse to elevation of 5,000 feet." Root replied, "Referring to your telegram . . . , how is the horse?"[40] Taft, whose sense of humor was as ample as his girth, was so amused by Root's cable that he released the exchange to the local press, meanwhile reassuring Root that the horse, a very large specimen, selected by the US Army just for him, was fine.

The old governor-general's house in Baguio, which became the US ambassador's summer retreat, is balanced on a ridge overlooking pine-clad slopes and must be haunted; it was the site of the final surrender of Japanese forces in the Philippines at the end of World War II. The Japanese commander, Yamashita Tomoyuki, the "Tiger of Malaya," who had conquered the British forces in Singapore at the beginning of the war, was executed for war crimes in the Philippines in 1946 after a controversial military trial.

Successive US ambassadors have allowed other embassy employees to use their cool Baguio retreat (as we did) when they weren't there. In winter it occasionally snows, a fantastic rarity in the Philippines. During our visit, there was only a heavy frost, but we awoke to find Annie and Jamie, never yet

[39] Bob letter to Dear Folks, January 19, 1976.
[40] Out of family loyalty I have to cite Henry Pringle, *The Life and Times of William Howard Taft*, New York, 1939, I, pp. 235-236, but there are other sources.

having seen snow (in Jamie's case, that he could remember), gleefully making footprints in it.

Nearby was Camp John Hay, a US "air base" with no airplanes, but a famous, very well maintained golf course. It was enormously popular with Filipinos, so much so that during later acrimonious negotiations over the return of our more serious bases, Clark and Subic, they wanted us to retain Camp John Hay, because, it was rumored, they thought golfing there was like going to the United States and were worried that it wouldn't be properly maintained if was turned over to Philippine management. It was one of the reasons why 200,000 thousand Filipino tourists and golfers visited Baguio every year during Holy Week, the hottest time of year, and it was not returned to Philippine control until 1991, more than a decade after Clark and Subic.[41] It is now a private resort.

From Baguio we headed further north by rental car to see the famous terraced rice fields of the Ifugao people, one of the most numerous of the northern minorities. Midway through an all-day drive on mostly unpaved roads we pulled over to gaze at the mountain scenery. There had recently been a lot of rain, and Charlotte, much to her annoyance, had another third-world adventure (comparable to the bathroom drainage adventure in Indonesia) when one of her shoes got stuck and came off in the viscous mud of the roadside. We rescued the shoe and helped her hobble back to the car.

There was, thankfully, a nice government hotel at Banaue, our destination, tastefully set among the spectacular terraces. The next morning we walked to a village on a typically precipitous mountain path. We crossed a ridge from which we could see our destination, still a long way down. The parents decided to wait for us at the top of the ridge, where a bench had been strategically placed, while we continued. As a result they got to see something we missed—an Ifugao family, dressed in full tribal regalia, the man carrying a spear, on their way to a celebration.

The parents left soon after, having decided to visit Taipei and see its great collection of imperial Chinese porcelain

---

[41] On the Baguio and Ifugao trip, see Bob letter to Dear Folks, January 19, 1976.

and other art on their way home. They were sorely missed
by the kids, especially Jamie, who announced that that we
should return to the US in two days to catch up with them.
When Barbara pointed out that Washington was not the same
as Cincinnati, he replied, "Yes, but there are more roads to
Grandmother's from there." [42]

So the parents missed our long overdue trip to Corregidor,
the fortress at the mouth of Manila Bay from which MacArthur
had departed by submarine, most of his troops having already
been captured by the invading Japanese, pledging "I shall
return." We went in a group organized by the US Embassy
ladies on a Philippine Navy minesweeper, complete with lots
of guns, which kept the kids enraptured. Bob wrote:

*Corregidor was blasted six ways to Sunday by both incoming
(Japanese) and retaking (US) forces and there is nothing much
left of the elaborate prewar fortifications, buildings, etc., which
cost the US taxpayer $150 million in depression dollars. But
what there is impresses and has the romance of other ruins, like
Angkor Wat, of the kind that the Philippines lacks [except for some
old Spanish cathedrals]. You can clamber around on the 12-inch
coastal defense guns, which like their more famous counterparts
in Singapore were pointed rigidly out to sea and hence never fired
a shot, because the dastardly Japanese landed on the Bataan
Peninsula to the north instead of coming straight in [through
Manila Bay into the teeth of the American fortress] as they were
supposed to do. These [guns] should be labeled as international
monuments to the Military Mind, which is still with us. [43]*

There were some tourists, mostly Americans and Japanese,
and nice beaches in sheltered coves, and we thought
Corregidor would be a great place for a hotel, which had been
planned but never completed.

Early in 1976 we made additional trips into northern Luzon
for several reasons. The Maoist NPA (New People's Army)
insurgency was exploiting disaffection with government
policies, especially the Chico Dam project which would flood

---

[42] Barbara letter to Dear Mother and Daddy, January 20, 1976.
[43] Bob letter to Dear Folks, January 19, 1976.

many rice terraces, and that was still one of my reporting beats. In addition, we wanted to visit Sagada, the principal place of the Bontoc people; a good friend, Albert Bacdayan, who got his PhD at Cornell (in anthropology) at the same time as I did, came from that area. Finally, the Bontocs along with many other Luzon uplanders, formerly referred to as "Igorots," are staunch Episcopalians, and since we attended Holy Trinity Church in Manila, and Barbara, as noted earlier, was head of Holy Trinity's chapter of Episcopal Church Women, she got directly involved with lady Episcopalians from all over the Luzon highlands.

We went to see the Bontocs of Sagada at the end of March. They had been converted to very high church Anglicanism by a redoubtable American missionary, Father John Staunton. He had arrived in Sagada in 1904 and built an extraordinary mini-empire (he was also an engineer), which included schools, a church, a hospital, a sawmill, a machine shop and more. He employed hundreds of Bontocs to haul machinery over mountain footpaths from Manila. Staunton thought the Episcopalians should merge back into the Roman Catholic Church, and he converted to Roman Catholicism himself after leaving the Philippines in 1924. Barbara wrote:

Even today, the churches in Sagada and Bangaan [Albert Bacdayan's home village] chant half the service (including the Lord's Prayer), ring bells—both handbells and the church bell, throughout, and in general exalt pomp and circumstance. The Sagada Church is a masterpiece of stone architecture; it even has a stained glass rose window above the altar. The church at Bangaan, which three quarters of the congregation attends in traditional dress, is a huge pine edifice with a view for miles around. After church we walked on to see the terraces, all stone, and quite as impressive as the Ifugao ones at Banaue. Then we had lunch with Albert's mother and the children played with some of her grandchildren who were up from Manila.[44]

Barbara and the kids also explored some caves where the pagan Bontocs had buried their dead in stacks of coffins,

[44] Barbara letter to Dear Family from Baguio, April 1, 1976, with sketch map.

in a complex which reputedly continued through an entire mountain. They came back to Baguio on a Dangwa bus. These were a famous Mountain Province institution, with one open side, no aisle, and seats all across, making for a knuckle-biting experience if you were seated on the open side going around a corner next to a drop-off.

Minority Issues in the North and South

Meanwhile Bob was off trying to take the political temperature of the minorities living along Luzon's mile-high-plus mountain spine. There were three main groups: the Bontocs, the Ifugao (whom we had visited with Clay and Charlotte) and the Kalinga. Their traditional lifestyles had much in common: headhunting, terraced rice fields, and no conversion to any world religion until European and American missionaries arrived. We were right at home with them because they are part of a larger family of highland peoples spread across the Malay Archipelago (writ large), including the Ibans with whom we had worked in Sarawak, the Toradja of Sulawesi (Indonesia) and the Batak of North Sumatra (also Indonesia) and many more. We recognized familiar traditional artistic traits, including old trade beads, cave burials, wonderful weaving and (sometimes) basket-making. Bontoc baskets had a special panache because they aged to a shiny black from the pervasive smoke of the house lofts where they were stored.

All these groups were internally diverse and there were others, like the Ilongots already mentioned. As we might have guessed from meeting Albert Bacdayan, the Bontocs were famous for being the most outwardly mobile of the mountain people, and at the time of our visits there were reputedly 600 Bontoc nurses working in Chicago alone. The Kalinga were the northernmost of the Igorots and the most impacted by the new dams and other less salubrious aspects of "civilization."

Bob's conclusion, not exactly startling, was that growing political tension in the area resulted from the government's assumption that the economic wealth of the mountains was a national, not local, asset; that the authorities been had been maladroit in managing the resentment that ensued, but that the possibility of a generalized mountain insurgency linked with the communist NPA was remote. This was partly because the mountain minorities, unlike the Muslim rebels in the south, had no unifying element similar to Islam, no foreign source of arms similar to Libya's Qadafi (already by this time a global nuisance), and no offshore sanctuary comparable to the Muslim areas of Malaysian North Borneo.[45]

Indeed the Muslims of the south and the former headhunters of the north were the only Philippine minorities that most people had ever heard of. However, there were also significant numbers of "tribal people" on Mindanao, who were not Muslim, not warlike, culturally intriguing, yet easily displaced by aggressive lowlanders. In December we visited one such group, the T'boli people, numbering over 100,000. The T'boli lived around Lake Sebu on a large plateau in South Cotabato Province, one of the most remote areas of the Philippines. Formerly empty valleys below them were filling up with Christian settlers, and loggers were stripping the hillsides.

The region became famous when a flamboyant Harvard classmate of Bob's, Emanuel "Manda" Elizalde, set himself up as the protector of all Philippine minorities, with the support of President Marcos. Manda was the playboy son of a wealthy, polo-playing Spaniard resident in the Philippines and his American wife. In 1971 he attracted worldwide publicity when he claimed to have discovered a "lost tribe" of about thirty people, the Tasaday, living in a cave in deep forest. An American friend and neighbor of ours, John Nance, had written a book about them.[46] The T'boli area was the jumping-off place for Manda's helicopter-borne VIP visits to see the Tasaday. At the time we were there, the most recent had been Gina Lollobrigida, in her role as a photographer. Controversy raged around the Tasaday, as to whether they were an ancient never "civilized" group of hunter-gatherers, a hoax, or simply

---

[45] Based partly on interviews with William Henry Scott, a veteran Episcopalian missionary-historian and prolific writer on the mountain minorities of Luzon.

[46] John Nance, *The Gentle Tasaday: a Stone Age People in the Philippine Rain Forest,* New York, 1975, with a forward by Charles A. Lindbergh, one of Manda's VIP friends. We knew Nance through his children, who attended the same Montessori school as ours, and he was probably the one who called our attention to what became our house on Fresno Street.

a breakaway fragment from some other nearby minority who had decided to reject modernity and live in the forest.

In his role as state protector of minorities, Elizalde wanted to control the T'boli as well, and his organization, PANAMIN,[47] was at loggerheads with a strong-willed American Catholic priest, Father Rex Mansmann, who was running a mission to the T'boli. We liked Mansmann; he was not trying to convert the T'boli to Catholicism, at least not too fast. His clash with PANAMIN seemed like classic turf war, with Elizalde reveling in his role as King of All the Tribes, and Mansmann suspicious of his high-profile, self-glorifying wheeling and dealing, as most observers were. PANAMIN was building houses for the T'boli that imitated the famous horned-roof style of the Indonesian Minangkabau people and looked nothing like genuine T'boli houses. Barbara thinks we met my famous/ notorious classmate; I do not remember it and we were not nearly prominent enough to have been invited to visit the Tasaday.

As for the T'boli, they were quite spectacular:

Like the Balinese of Indonesia they are a people extraordinarily gifted in art and music. T'boli tie-dye weaving in abaca, and T'boli beadwork, basketry and brass-casting are now (thanks to the efforts of one Peace Corps volunteer, Dorothy Anderson) the basis of a rapidly expanding handicraft industry which already grosses more than 500,000 pesos annually. T'boli music and dance is exceedingly rich. They love horses and even practice a form of horse fighting for sport. Perhaps most striking to the first time observer is the T'boli preoccupation with high feminine adornment. T'boli women bead, coif and paint themselves for any occasion (even before going to bed) and thanks to bell-bedecked girdles and brass bangles they jingle when they walk.[48]

Yet, as I discovered, virtually nothing had been written about the T'boli compared to other pagan minorities in Mindanao. For years we contributed to Father Rex's Santa Cruz Mission, but lost touch after he retired. In recent years the T'boli have

---

[47] Short for Presidential Assistant on Minorities.

[48] Diary entry, December, 1976. Barbara bought a T'boli necklace made of plastic beads, created by melting toothbrushes, and little brass bells.

become a major tourist attraction and the Lake Sebu area is now overcrowded with resort development, something they have in common with the Balinese.

Barbara's letter describing our preparations for the T'boli trip is a classic snapshot of our Foreign Service lifestyle:

Packing for this junket—we leave on Monday—is a bear, because we are doing so many different things. On Monday, Bob must be neat and official to make calls. On Tuesday we fly to a valley near the T'boli mission, then go by jeep and a two- or three-hour walk to the mission. I have two backpacks, full of jeans and sleeping bags for that part of the expedition. But next Friday we walk back out, and take two busses to an American banana plantation where we will stay overnight. Presentable clothes required. And if everything is on schedule, always doubtful, we plan to dive in Davao on Sunday—diving equipment required. On the way home on Monday, we shall stop in Cebu and tell the Consul there about the trip, presentable clothes required again. I have our clothes for the banana plantation packed in plastic bags in the backpacks; hopefully they won't get all smoky, but I have spent the whole morning figuring this out.[49]

By this time Bob had picked up a new job at work, compiling a time line of the squabble over the contested reefs and islands in the South China Sea. He wrote home:

We are having a rather interesting flap over the Spratly Islands which are claimed by China, Vietnam and the Philippines [and Malaysia, and Brunei, and . . . (?)] The claims have been traded back and forth for years but what set off and sharpened the last round was offshore drilling by the Philippines. It is really an incredible situation, with Vietnamese, Nationalist Chinese and (of course) Filipinos all sitting on various of these godforsaken sandbars in the middle of the South China Sea, the Soviets making loud noises in support of the Vietnamese, and the (Peking) Chinese making it clear they won't be left out. If anyone strikes oil it really could get messy. My solution is to turn the whole area into an international scuba diving preserve, which

[49] Barbara letter to Dear Mother and Daddy, November 6, 1976.

(barring oil) is really all it's good for.[50]

No one listened to the proposal for an international scuba park and no one has struck oil, but thirty-six years later squabbling over the disputed South China Sea islands continues, and, thanks to China's rise, it has become a major geopolitical issue.[51]

Work at the embassy included the usual shepherding of VIP visitors. One always expected the worst from the biggest names, but sometimes we were surprised. An especially nice surprise was Claire Booth Luce, moneyed socialite, widow of *Time Magazine* founder Henry Luce, and prominent Republican congresswoman, who turned out to be an ideal official guest:

It was worth the price of admission to see her stand up to Imelda Marcos, who was all set to keep her going on an all-night tour of Manila when she was due for dinner at the Ambassador's. We reached such a pitch of conviviality that she encouraged me to apply to the Luce Foundation for my sabbatical project.[52]

In late May we went back to Cebu on vacation, swapping houses with the new Consul, Don Ellson, and his Turkish wife, Aisa, who came to Manila while we were in Cebu. We had hoped to spend a lot of time diving and visiting areas that we had missed on previous visits, but our visit coincided with an enormous and very early typhoon named Didang, which rampaged across central Luzon. Even in Cebu the weather was stormy and the seas rough. "As for our vacation, it's a good thing diving is practiced *under* the ocean," Barbara wrote.

For a change we had decided to travel to Cebu and back by boat. On the way down, we were on a once stylish Japanese Inland Sea steamer, now with broken air-conditioning and

---

[50] Bob letter to Dear Folks, June 20, 1976.
[51] Four decades later the ruckus had become sufficiently serious to motivate the Philippines to invite the US to renew a military presence at five locations, including Subic Bay.
[52] Bob letter to Dear Mark and Kate, September 12, 1976. It isn't clear whether I ever took her up on her offer; I eventually got the needed grant from Rockefeller.

windows that had to be pried open with a crowbar.[53] Coming home on the M.V. Cebu was better, running through huge brown swells colored by Didang's trash-laden runoff, visible far out to sea.

Despite the weather, we were able to rendezvous with members of the Haribon Society, the Philippine equivalent of our Audubon Society, named after the huge and highly endangered Monkey-eating Eagle found only in the country's disappearing old-growth forests. After various adventures with small boats, cancelled ferries, high waves and sleeping in the municipal building of the small town of Oslob in the south of Cebu island, we did do some diving with the Haribon group. Finally the weather cleared and we flew to Bohol, another island near Cebu, famous for its Chocolate Hills. This scenic wonder consists of over a thousand symmetrical, conical grass-covered karst hills that turn brown (hence "chocolate") in the dry season.

But Bohol also has beaches, and although the one we visited was rocky, with waves crashing in, we found, to our amazement, live specimens of *Conus generalis*, the General Cone, a pretty and scarce brown-and-white banded shell with a tapering spire on top. Why should a delicate snail be so happy in a rocky, weedy, habitat, tumbling around in the surf, as these were? Most cones prefer quiet sand where they can burrow peacefully.

Malacological Paradise

As the reader will be aware by now, we had continued our shell collecting in the Philippines. There, for the first time, we encountered massive commercial shelling, along with mountains of ill-cleaned, rotting shells in warehouses. The shell dealers who owned them grubstaked collectors who traveled to the furthest corners of the Philippines in outrigger canoes to find the best supplies, often using crowbars to harvest them by tearing up (and heavily damaging) coral reefs. The dealers then exported them to tourist outlets around the world, especially in countries which had banned

---

[53] Barbara letter to Dear Family from the MV Cebu, May 29, 1976.

shell collecting or simply didn't have many colorful shells of the kinds common in tropical seas. Today, many, if not most, of the reefs we enjoyed are grey and dead, no longer home to interesting mollusks and pretty tropical fish.

We learned that, as with most kinds of animals, habitat is everything. Some shells live in sand. Those that burrow through it, like the brightly-colored olives and augers, usually leave trails; just stick your hand in at the fresh end of the trail and—presto!—you usually get the shell. Often the animal of a sand shell envelops the shell most of the time and deposits shiny material on it (pure calcium carbonate, which is why it is so sensitive to acid). Sand shells, and cowries, can withdraw into their hard, shiny "houses" when threatened.

Cones, named for their conical shape, often live in sand or mud, but most are usually covered by a thick, dirty-looking skin. To see the often beautiful pattern on the shell, you have to scrape the skin off, in addition to getting the animal decomposed and extracted. You have to be careful when handling live cones because they are predators, and live by killing other shells and fish with little poisoned darts which they can shoot for considerable distances under water. Never put cones in your bathing suit pocket! A sting from a Geography Cone can be fatal. Today cone shell toxins are being studied for their remarkable, multi-lethal venoms, which may have valuable medicinal properties.

All seashells lose their exterior colors and pattern once the animal inside dies and they are exposed to salt water. Bivalves like clams and oysters can simply be pried apart, and the animal removed. But to get good specimens of the spiraling, snail-like ones, you have to let the animal die inside its shell. (Boiling is not recommended.) Then you must get the decomposing animal out of the spiraling interior before the corpse rots and generates acid, which will etch and ruin the shiny finish of the shell.[54] To do this cleaning easily you need a good beach (or a swimming pool with a tolerant owner). Once the shell starts to rot, you bang it up and down in the

---

[54] One famous big Indo-Pacific helmet shell lives on spiny sea urchins, digesting them with powerful, purple-colored acids in its stomach. If in cleaning them you puncture the stomach and get this purple stuff on the gorgeous, shiny orange underside of the shell, that will also ruin its finish.

surf repeatedly. If it still smells the next morning, or two or three mornings later, repeat the process. Even in the days before security concerns, this hobby did not coexist well with air travel or with really snooty hotels, because nothing smells quite as rotten as a bag of rotting seashells.

By now you have probably deduced why we stopped shelling a long time ago—but not until after serving in Papua New Guinea, where a few were just too good to resist—in favor of watching and photographing birds. In fact, we were always careful never to destroy habitat such as live coral and always to replace slabs of dead coral that we turned over looking for shells. The old rule was that, since most shells are nocturnal and only come out at night, it would be hard to deplete the population as long as you didn't destroy habitat to get at them. However this rule doesn't work when there are just too many people picking up live shells, much less walking on or bumping into fragile coral as they search for them.

Many shells are "rare" mainly because their habitats are relatively inaccessible. The classic example is the Golden Cowrie, which likes crevices in rocky cliffs with surf smashing against them. This is hazardous terrain for collectors; also, few shells can survive the turbulent, rocky habitat without being broken, resulting in unsightly "growth scars" on the shell. So perfect specimens are expensive.

Like everything else in the Philippines, it seemed, shell collecting came with an inevitable visa moment. This was the case with our friend Fernando Dayrit, a high-end shell dealer but also a serious amateur malacologist (scholar of shells), so much so that a small cowrie he discovered is named after him, *Cypraea dayritiana* (Dayrit's Cowrie). His wife taught chemistry at the University of the Philippines, and he had several daughters educated to the PhD level in the US. We got to know him and bought some shells from him, but mostly he insisted on giving them to us. This continued well after we returned to the US; we would get a package of shells around Christmas, often extremely interesting and sometimes valuable; we have both a Golden Cowrie and an even more valuable Leucadon Cowrie from him.

I should have known what was coming. I had already helped him with one family visa problem that was an easy fix.

Indeed, such "problems" were generally not really problems at all, but most Filipinos believed devoutly that all of them required an American *deus ex machina*. Finally, long after we left Manila, he sent me another visa problem that was clearly impossible for me to fix, and I had to tell him "I'm sorry but . . . ." It was a classic Fil-Am misunderstanding. After that he did not reply for a long while to our Christmas cards and, a relief, the shells stopped coming, although we still have a few, unwrapped and labeled in their neat cellophane packaging. Happily, in the years just before he died, we received several Christmas letters and one more unrequited shell gift. He was, despite this problem, a charming and talented person.

While in Jakarta we had acquired a custom-built, glass-topped coffee table to display some of our shells and it, much altered, has been the centerpiece of our living rooms ever since. We had trouble with the cat getting in under the glass to play with the shells, so while visiting in Manila, Clay designed four glass strips, one for each side, to solve this problem. The strips also served admirably to reduce dust on the shells and the blue velvet cloth under them, especially in the dry Sahelian countries of West Africa. En route to Burkina Faso in 1984, the table was mistakenly left in storage in Washington (although the glass top and side strips arrived), so we had a new, and more attractive, table made there. The glass top has been broken at least twice, once in shipping and once when Bob was cleaning the living room chandelier at 216 Wolfe Street and a glass pendant fell on it. We could never take our shell table on Antiques Road Show; it would take too long to explain.

In April, 1976, we learned that our landlord was selling our house on Agno Street. We thought it was going to be torn down for some kind of new development, but at this writing it is still apparently there.[55] We had not lost our aversion to Manila's "villages" (gated communities) and wanted to stay in the old downtown area. The new administrative officer in charge of housing told us that, if we found a house we liked, the embassy would rent it, a decision he no doubt came keenly to regret. The house itself, located at 220 Fresno Street in Pasay City, only six blocks from Agno Street, was nice enough,

[55] From Nita Churchill, February, 2012.

owned by a bowling magnate named Torres who had moved
to the suburbs. Barbara wrote:

*It too is an old American-era number, not as big as [Agno
Street] though, with fifteen-foot high ceilings, big windows,
quaint plumbing, etc. In style it is, I guess you'd say, Victorian,
[Queen Anne actually] with three bay windows in the living
room. It has a nice front porch, a nicely planted front yard
with two big trees, much less space than we have now, but in a
quiet residential street, and a concrete back yard for bicycles,
wagons, etc . . . . [It is] basically one storey, with two original
bedrooms beside the living area and a new addition in exactly
the same style on the other side of the house. Above the kitchen,
however, is the master bedroom with windows on three sides, in
a sort of cupola arrangement. . . . There is a separate little house
with two bedrooms and a washing area for Lita and Tessie. The
house is in a bad flooding area, but it is up about six feet, and
the maid's quarters and garage are also both raised, so we can
always be high and dry and row out in our rubber boat.*[56]

More importantly, the former tenants had been running a
business out of our house, and they had jury-rigged the wiring
to steal electricity, leaving a mess of different voltages, which the
embassy plus the Manila power company tried to get working
properly the whole time we lived there, without success. Our
new neighborhood was, to put it mildly, a happening:

*We have a couple of well-maintained old houses across the street,
one of which is occupied by a mysterious Catholic "community"
(females, not exactly nuns, they say, but "living the gospel") and
the other by rich Chinese with a swimming pool. The lower end
of the street, which is only a block long, is the* barangay *(ward)
basketball court and is in use about eighteen hours a day.
One of Annie's schoolmates is in the house next door, which is
unfortunately one of the really run-down numbers on the block.
Leveriza, the street which crosses ours, at the end of the basketball
court, is lined with squatter shacks and is a major jeepney*

---

[56] Barbara letter to Dear Mother and Daddy, May 6, 1976. Ah, the
optimism of youth!

route, although very narrow. Within walking distance we also have the Cultural Center of the Philippines (Madame [Marcos's] grand display on Manila Bay), several luxe new hotels under construction, a huge new shopping center complex, the old Rizal Memorial Stadium (sports), at least one hospital, any number of small factories, lumber yards, warehousing operations, and last but not least, "motels" which in the Philippines means a place where you take the girl you have picked up somewhere else (these also cater to Japanese tours where sex is part of the package and have become bigger business than ever.)[57]

We moved on June 9, 1976, with the typhoon season coming on, and soon discovered that our new home was even more flood-prone than Agno Street had been. The house had a septic tank, but storm water throughout Pasay City exited through open channels along the sides of the streets, which plugged up whenever it rained hard, leaving our yard under three feet or more of water full of garbage and trash. Coming home from work, I waded through the flood wearing Bermuda shirts and carrying my office clothes in a bag. At about the same time there was a bad earthquake and tsunami in Mindanao, which killed 3,000 people. Barbara wrote her parents in North Carolina not to get too excited about a near miss from a hurricane.[58]

Our only real experience of the tragedy unfolding in Vietnam after the American withdrawal came at about this time:

. . . Bob spent all Saturday working on and greeting a group of Vietnamese refugees, all professional people and their families, including one Harvard-trained dentist, who had fled in some leaky old tub and had been picked up by a US Defense Department contract oil tanker; it was on its way to Bahrain, but diverted to Subic [our big Philippine navy base]. The Filipinos would not accept the refugees, and our official policy is that we won't, though Bob says we ultimately will, for this group anyway, and there were many negotiations to allow them to land temporarily here. It was costing thousands a day to tie up the tanker; the crew however, was so impressed with the group

[57] Bob letter to Dear Folks, June 20, 1976.
[58] Barbara letter to Dear Mother and Daddy, August 9, 1976.

that they wept when they left, and the captain has already arranged a US sponsor in his hometown for one family.[59]

But the same letter revealed that family life in the Pringle household was proceeding normally. It contained a request to Grandfather for some model paint for Jamie (grey, blue, red, black and green, please) and a note to Grandmother that Annie was now wearing size 7 dresses, even though her sixth birthday had just passed. The party was "a celebration to end all." There had never been such a looked forward-to birthday party. And when it was all over, Anne sat, somewhat wiped out, in the rocker and mused, "I wish my birthday was still going to be tomorrow." We didn't go diving on the weekend because of an algae bloom, but we did have an interesting evening meal during the fasting month with Islamic friends from the Egyptian Embassy: "When Bob's secretary received the invitation for 'breakfast' at 6 p.m., she really thought we had nutty friends."

Christmas in 1976, despite the absence of grandparents, again proved that tropical Christmases can be loads of fun. Annie and Bing-Bing (more correctly Bheng) played all day with their new Barbie dolls and accoutrements for them; Jamie was totally happy with his electronics kit and model electric motor, which was "supposed to drive a boat, which it does not, because the boat swamps and the motor gets wet." Afternoon was devoted to a swim, and the turkey came in the evening, when it got cooler.

A few days later, we left to travel north through Luzon again, this time west of the central mountain chain, around the top of the island, then back south on the east side of the island, a total distance of about 1,100 miles. We were on vacation, so we took our own small station wagon rather than an embassy 4-wheel drive, and were almost stopped by one hideous stretch of road under construction around the northernmost coast. At the time we were driving over it, the roadbed was nothing but machines and axle-deep mud, "earth with no foundation made wet by mountain springs which had been bulldozed open." Those machines, however, twice flattened a track through the earth in front of us so that we could drive

---

[59] Barbara letter to Dear Mother and Daddy, August 31, 1976.

over it, and the second time the truck behind us had to push the car. All this on a roadbed being created "about 500 feet straight above the Pacific Ocean."

On the way north, before that adventure, we visited Ilocos, the home of the Marcoses, and saw the famous cathedral in Vigan in which Congressman Floro Crisologo had been gunned down in the by his political rivals, as described by his grandson in Barbara's class at the Ateneo (see above). Vigan was clearly still proud of its mafia (or warlord) tradition, and even though actual violence had apparently waned in Ilocos as elsewhere, most churches in the Philippines still had large wooden boxes by the door where worshippers were supposed to deposit their guns before entering. We always wondered whether this gun mania could be laid at the feet of American uncivilizing influence. Vigan was full of big old houses built by the Chinese-mestizo upper crust, who had become rich in the Spanish era by trading Chinese porcelain for Igorot gold. There was also a VOA broadcasting station with a wonderful beach, much appreciated by the younger set.

The best thing we saw in Ilocos was the wonderful "earthquake baroque" San Augustin Church at Paoay, built in 1710, at a time when conventional churches in this area were routinely reduced to ruins by earthquakes. The solution was to lower the height of the building and enlarge the buttresses, resulting in a style that looked like a normal Spanish baroque cathedral reflected in one of those funny mirrors at the county fair that make you look fat. It seems to have worked, and although this marvelous building was very run down when we visited, more recent photos suggest that it is being better taken care of now.

After the muddy drive around the north coast, we had to cross the Cagayan River and drive a further fifty miles before we reached a town large enough to have a hotel. The ferry crossing occurred just at sunset, and we remember a lovely ride sitting on the deck watching the day fade away. The town, the provincial capital Tuguegarao, and its "best" hotel, the Olympia, which Bob described as a "grease impregnated disaster," were another story entirely. The hotel did, however, find us a room hours after dark, in which the kids slept on a mattress on the floor.

When Barbara investigated why Annie was balking after

having been told to brush her teeth, she discovered an enormous, hairy spider hanging from the ceiling of the filthy bathroom, in which the shower had to be turned on and off with pliers. All of us were exhausted, but Annie, lying on her mattress, could see the spider through the transom above the door. Barbara said, "Don't worry; it can't get out," and shut both door and transom. It was still there in the morning, and did no one any harm, but it was quite alive, moving slowly across the wall.

The next day, we headed south back through the Cagayan Valley, famous for its cigar tobacco. Bob was smoking Filipino cigars at this point and today we still have quite a few Tabacalera cigar boxes, made of wood, around the house. He wrote, perhaps partly reflecting our grimy hotel experience of the night before:

Driving through the Cagayan Valley is, from the scenic point of view, an un-Asian experience. The valley is enormous; there is an obvious abundance of un- or under-cultivated land, and evidence of the beginnings of commercial, mechanized agriculture. (It is widely rumored that the Marcos family has extensive holdings in the valley.) But the small farmers have obviously not profited appreciably from the relatively favorable man-land ratio. As it tends to do throughout the southern hemisphere, poverty is probably re-creating itself even in this resource-rich area.[60]

Early 1977 was then filled with many weekend diving trips, especially to Verde Island in Batangas Bay. We had a favorite small resort on the mainland, and hired bancas or a ferry, depending on the number, to go out for the day. Some of the trips to islands with nice beaches were with the Haribon Society mentioned earlier.

In March, Barbara, with her friend Mary Ng, a talented American weaver married to a Filipino, arranged a trip for twelve women to visit Mountain Province, concentrating on crafts and weaving. In a coup, we persuaded Mrs. Sullivan, the ambassador's wife, who had never traveled without him, to

---

[60] Bob Diary entry, January 10, 1977; other details of the trip are in Barbara letter to Dear Family, January 5, 1977, the first page of which also describes Christmas Day, before we left on the trip.

go along. She enjoyed the trip, was a good sport about delays caused by a landslide and a clogged fuel line on the bus, and also put us all up at the ambassador's residence in Baguio the first night. It was very dry, so the roads were in much better shape than during the grandparents' visit, but the rice terraces were not nearly as lovely.

There were lots of old baskets for sale (but no beads, I observed), so you can imagine what the bus looked like on the way home. I bought two, but which of the ones we still have, I don't know. I observed that, thenceforth, I was in charge of loading the bus every day, because I was the only one who could fit everything in. (Mary's book about an Ifugao basket weaver is stored in one of our Philippine baskets.) Bob brought the children up to Baguio for a long family weekend at the end of the trip; we were guests of Fr. Gaby Dimanche and his wife Clenia, usually the pastor of Holy Trinity Church in Manila, but temporarily seconded to be headmaster of Brent School in Baguio. His son Jacques was a pal of Jamie's. This was again strawberry season, so we went home with lots of them, plus mushrooms, to enjoy in hotter Manila.

More Adventures in Moroland

In May, 1977, a month before our departure from the Philippines, Bob's nervous superiors finally allowed him to make a ten-day trip to some of the more restive areas of Mindanao, where the Muslim rebellion had been most active. Interest in the area was high because of Qadafi's continuing support for the rebel Moro National Liberation Front (MNLF), leading Imelda Marcos to attempt negotiating with him personally.

A lull in the fighting continued following a ceasefire agreed upon about six months previously. The government still relied on a two-pronged approach, lavish expenditure on showpiece development projects, and cooperation with traditional Muslim aristocracies, who were themselves a prime target of the rebels. It seemed clear that the possibility of armed conflict would remain high as long as heavily armed and ill-disciplined adversaries faced each other.[61] But for the moment it was a good time to visit the Muslim areas.

Bob has no recollection of visiting Cotabato City, sometimes a center of unrest,[62] at this time, and Barbara was not accompanying him because packout was imminent. However, during one of our earlier trips to Mindanao, she had gone to visit her good friend Lourdes Mastura there. Lourdes' husband Michael was a graduate of Notre Dame, the descendent of a Sultan (and also of Chinese ancestry) and a prominent Muslim leader. On that visit Barbara had acquired two beautiful examples of Muslim (in this case, Maranao)[63] art: the tall rooster (*Sarimanok*), and a robust wooden game set, human-headed but with a bird's tail, both covered with inlaid mother-of-pearl decoration and among our most prized possessions. The latter she managed to hide for several months, when it became a surprise Christmas present. (See photo earlier in this chapter.)

Travelling alone, Bob went to Jolo, once the capital of the Sulu Sultanate and home of the pugnacious Tausug ("People of the Current"), who fought pitched battles against General Pershing as late as 1913. He managed to procure some samples of their beautiful weaving. They were engaged in farming a new cash crop on coral reef flats, a kind of seaweed used in making brake fluid for jumbo jetliners.

But the big adventure was going to Tawi-Tawi, at the tail end of the Sulu Archipelago. The local population consisted of Samals, who were Muslim, and Badjao sea gypsies, pagans who lived on their decorated boats. Sea gypsies were famous in Southeast Asian history as pirates, unpaid militias and occasional state-makers, like the ones who helped the first ruler of Malacca, the ancestor of modern Singapore, to establish

---

[61] Bob Diary entry, June, 1977.

[62] Cotabato = Kota Batu, meaning stone (fortified) city in Malay (Indonesian).

[63] "Maranao" is a geo-ethnic term meaning people of Lake Lanao, just inland from Cotabato City. The Muslim inhabitants, the Iranao, or *Illanun*, were once much feared pirates whose big war boats went on raiding expeditions around Borneo and into the Straits of Malacca, sometimes with the participation of Ibans, a phenomenon I had learned about while exploring Iban history in Sarawak; see *Rajahs and Rebels,* pp. 50-51. Marawi City, the metropolis of this area, was heavily damaged by government troops in 2017.

himself as a maritime hegemon in the fifteenth century. In Tawi-Tawi, a Badjao who converted to Islam automatically changed ethnicity and became a Samal, a social process we recognized from Sarawak. From most of Tawi-Tawi it was possible to see Sabah, part of Malaysia, from the beach.

As usual getting there was indeed half the fun, especially on the local airline, Swiftair. Bob wrote:

Truly confidence inspiring, Swiftair . . . has three DC-3s. At the moment one is [grounded] for a lack of spare parts, and the second is out of commission following an unfortunate incident on March 31, when its pilot ran amuck, spraying the passenger compartment with bullets and killing seven passengers. This plane still flies but the bullet holes are deemed unaesthetic and haven't yet been patched, so the plane is kept out if service. The third plane, in addition to making the Tawi-Tawi run via Jolo, services a scheduled flight to Tarakan in Indonesian Borneo every Tuesday. Due to the loss of his other pilot, who is now in Zamboanga City jail, Swiftair's owner, a former PAL [Philippine Air Lines] pilot named Captain Lim, now pilots all flights himself wearing a powder blue uniform with silver epaulets. Swiftair's motto is "Rise with the sun, fly Swiftair" and it certainly provides one of the more sensational aviation experiences in Southeast Asia.[64]

Swiftair may still be alive. At any rate, when we visited Cuba in November, 2016, there was a "Swiftair" plane on the runway in Havana, along with one from Eastern Airlines, long since defunct in the US.

Some months before this trip we had decided to reduce our tour in the Philippines from four to three years, for several reasons, the first being Jamie's need for appropriate schooling. In addition, Bob was definitely having a twinge of mid-career malaise. He didn't like "the superficial emotionality that surrounded our 'love-hate' relationship" with the Philippines.[65] His job was going a bit stale:

[64] Bob Diary entry, June, 1977.
[65] Bob letter to Dear Folks, April 11, 1976.

Work has been less than 100% fun. It's partly that I have been doing the same thing for six years now and am tired of writing reports which disappear into the maw of the State Dept., rarely with any visible effect. It's hard to see what the function of this ritual activity may be, beyond self-education. [I later changed my mind about the utility of reporting—see closing chapter.] The life is still entertaining and varied and I am still not sure that I would rather do anything else, other than be rich and write occasional books about whatever seems interesting.[66]

He thought it might be useful to take a year of leave without pay from the State Department and write about his experience in Indonesia and the Philippines. Another book would allow him to convey his opinions to a wider audience, and also recharge his academic credentials, which were getting a bit stale. He began to write grant applications, with important support from Professor George Kahin at Cornell and Bill Sullivan, his ambassador in Manila. In February, 1977, he received word of a $25,000 grant from the Rockefeller Foundation for a one-year project to write about Indonesia and the Philippines.[67]

Packing out was easier the second time around. Barbara wrote, "We pack out on May 8. We leave Manila on June 18 . . . I am looking forward to having a last month to do last minute things I had always intended to do, as well as farewell functions, without the hassle of packing thrown in."[68] We had learned from the chaos of leaving Jakarta. Besides, as she also noted, on this move it would be highly desirable to have moved into our new home at 103 Prince Street before the kids started school—if she found a job, which was looking less and less likely.

But we weren't going to suffer in Manila. The weekend before packout, we went on a final diving trip to Apo Reef, far out in the ocean from Mindoro and therefore pristine, a destination we had always hoped to reach. Eight friends went with us, including Charlie Salmon, who distinguished himself by wandering off the side of the boat, fortunately while some of us were still awake, after a rather boozy party one evening. And, after that, Bob fitted in the trip to Cotabato and Jolo

---

[66] Bob letter to Dear Folks, January 19, 1976.
[67] Barbara letter to Dear Mother and Daddy, February 25, 1977.
[68] Barbara letter to Dear Mother and Daddy, May 5, 1977.

mentioned earlier.

We had discovered that we could travel back to the US via Air Micronesia and stop at some of the best diving areas in the Pacific. Our route took us from Manila via Guam to Palau, the most populous not-yet-country in Micronesia and the site of famous underwater terrain, from semi-stagnant brackish water ponds full of unique creatures to fringing reefs dropping off to profound depths patrolled by giant sharks—and a blue hole to boot. One day, we rode currents past turtles and other shallow water creatures; even Jamie and Anne could share that. We went on to the island of Yap, where we saw its famous, gigantic stone money and went diving with some missionaries in a sandy area covered with dozing polka-dotted nurse sharks.

We did some diving in the Truk Lagoon, littered with sunken Japanese warships and freighters. We dived, but the children snorkeled over the bullet-ridden wrecks of Japanese Zero fighters. There is a slide of Jamie, in his snorkeling gear, sitting in one of them as if piloting it. It was in shallow water, but he was obviously good, like his dad, at holding his breath under water. Above water, Truk, like too many other islands in the Pacific (Palau was an exception), resembled nothing so much as a depressed American Indian reservation, hardly a great advertisement for four decades of US trusteeship. We finally reached Hawaii via Ponape to catch a flight bound for the continental US. We would spend the next six years in Alexandria.

8

Washington, 1977-1983

The next six years of our lives were to be less glamorous than the previous seven, but no less important. Barbara embarked on a new chapter of her teaching career first at Alexandria's T.C. Williams High School and then at the Madeira School. Bob took a kind of sabbatical year to write a book and switched his Foreign Service specialization from Southeast Asia (politics) to Sub-Saharan Africa (political economics).

Readjusting to Home

The kids, ages seven and nine, began to put down American roots. At the time, the conventional Foreign Service wisdom was that it was better to be abroad with children when they were babies through their grade-school years, a period when activity with and within the family is the locus of a child's life. Dangerous posts, especially in countries involved in war or plagued by civil unrest, as well as very small ones with inadequate local medical facilities and no resident embassy doctor were obvious exceptions. However, most small posts had some sort of embassy supported "American" or "international" English language school and a resident nurse, if not a doctor, as well as some sort of American or diplomatic community center to educate, care for, and entertain expatriate children. Moreover, small children generally adjust painlessly to foreign circumstances, especially where affordable childcare (i.e., servants) is available.

So far, so good. But as children reach adolescence things change fast. They look for emotional support outside the family and seek to find several "special" close friends. Fitting into the crowd becomes paramount. Children reared abroad find it increasingly difficult to reinsert themselves in a US school at the secondary school level because of angst about losing friends and making new ones and because of lack of familiarity with teen-age mores at home. Looking back, we think we did the right thing with our children when we brought them back for a long stay in the US in middle grade

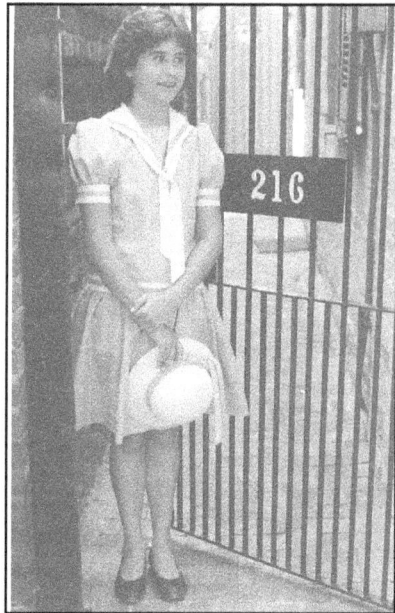

(Left) Home in the US: Jamie caught a shad and a small striped bass on a successful fishing expedition in the Potomac. (Right) Annie poses in what is probably an Easter outfit, in front of our second Alexandria house.

school, although we did not realize it at the time.

They both considered Alexandria to be "home" and though the separation from family for boarding school was not always easy, neither had an especially difficult adjustment to that phase of their schooling. At both Madeira and Potomac, Barbara encountered Foreign Service children who, having lived abroad most of their young lives, struggled to cope in their new American schools when they came "home" as teen-agers.

Just before our departure for Indonesia we had decided to rent out 103 Prince Street and move Helena into a more manageable and less physically challenging apartment not far away, at 500 Bashford Lane. By the time we returned, it was clear that with two growing children we would need a bigger house, but we could not sell the old one until we lived in it first without losing the tax advantage of ownership. So live in it we did, for two years. In the late summer of 1977, after several weeks of boarding with David and Helen Kenney at their splendid house in Georgetown until our tenants moved out, we moved in.

Moving day would have made a hilarious You-Tube video today: when the crates from Indonesia and the Philippines arrived, a large work crew from a street repair company was amazed at the furniture, carvings, paintings, and baskets coming out of them. Of course, given the tiny size of 103 Prince Street, most boxes were opened and the contents unwrapped right there on the sidewalk (luckily the weather was fine). The workmen did not earn their wages that day; they were too fascinated by our exotic acquisitions.

Of course we had to put much of our bulky Indonesian furniture in storage, including the Chinese bed-bookcase, but in general the old house on Captain's Row was a pleasant experience. Jamie enjoyed the attic bedroom (formerly Robert's Roost). Annie did not have a room of her own. Instead our neighborhood carpenter, Manuel, made a purpose-built bed, painted yellow, for her in the second-floor passageway between what had been Bob's mother's study and the miniscule bathroom. It had shelves along the wall, and drawers underneath; she liked it so much that there was a crisis when we had to leave it behind in 1979.

Barbara and Bob got the best room in the house, the master bedroom with its gorgeous early 1800s mantel and a bright southern exposure looking out over the cobblestone street. By the time we arrived in 1977, the long coal trains running down the middle of South Union Street, which had so aggravated HHS, were no more. The house, elegantly refurbished but no bigger, recently went on the market with an asking price of just under a million dollars. It sold, although at exactly what price we don't know.

As explained earlier, one of the main purposes of curtailing our tour in the Philippines had been to take advantage of new federally financed services for children with learning disabilities. We knew that our nearby primary school, Lyles Crouch, was participating in the program, and Barbara had corresponded with the school to make sure they reserved a place for Jamie, now a fourth-grader. But when we arrived the principal said that, since Jamie was a new student, he would have to wait until the second semester to be tested and placed appropriately. Barbara replied that she would show up at Lyles Crouch every day until the promised place materialized, and as a result, Jamie was the first LD student in Alexandria to be tested and given special education services. A talented and well-trained young teacher taught him spelling, writing, and math skills (the latter including how to show his work, rather than doing it in his head) for half the day, and the school placed him in honors science and social studies classes. Over the next three years, Lyles Crouch did very well by him, teaching him to type in order to deal with his deficiencies in producing the written word, while giving him full opportunity to bloom in the content subjects.

Most importantly, the teachers succeeded in maintaining his sunny outlook toward school, which had existed ever since he was learning very little at Manila's Montessori school. Barbara remembers in particular one marionette show that he and other students in the new special education program produced to inform the rest of the pupils at Lyles Crouch what their special classes were all about. Of course they were special! Not disabled or handicapped!

Annie began at another school, Maury, a bus ride away in Rosemont. The reason for this division of the primary schools was that the Virginia schools had just been desegregated, after years of "massive resistance." Under the new regime Lyles Crouch, which had been the black school in our part of Alexandria, became the integrated school for grades 4-6, while Maury, the old white school, was now for grades 1-3. One of Annie's first neighborhood friends, Latney Montague, whose parents lived at 207 Prince Street in one of the most elegant old houses in the city, was also attending Maury.

After Barbara got a job teaching at T. C. Williams High School, which started at least an hour-and-a-half earlier than the grade schools, his mother kindly agreed to let Annie stay with them each morning until the bus came. Four decades later, Latney told us that what he remembered about Annie was that she talked all the way as they walked to catch the bus each morning.

The distant school, however, did complicate Annie's making friends with neighborhood girls, many of whom attended schools other than Maury—St. Mary's Catholic School, St. Agnes (Episcopal) and Burgundy Farms, a small independent school in the countryside south of Alexandria. (Perhaps their parents, in Alexandria when desegregation was implemented, had been leery of the public schools then.) That is the reason I started the Brownie troop, which became a Girl Scout troop, and lasted until we were transferred abroad again; it fulfilled the reason for its founding admirably. Though all local children grades K-5 attend Lyles Crouch now, and many parents in Old Town send their children there, many children also attend local private or parochial schools. I find it unfortunate that no neighborhood Brownie/Girl Scout troop exists any more.

Both Annie and Jamie did well in their new schools. Teachers in the Alexandria system, as well as students, had of course been integrated. We were curious about which system our kids' teachers had come from. When we asked Annie whether her teacher was black or white, she responded after thinking about it, "white." As the famous song from South Pacific says, "They've Got to be Carefully Taught," and she had not been; when we finally met the teacher, she was unmistakably black. In fact, both children flourished under teachers from both races over our six years at home.

Outside school, Old Town Alexandria was the kind of neighborhood in which children could walk over to their friends' homes after school on their own, as it still is. In fact, Annie and Jamie were latchkey kids, though only for an hour or two, once Barbara started teaching. With the exception of orthodontist appointments (later, and only for Annie) and weekend away soccer games, they walked to their various activities, like soccer practice, drama (for Annie), and Cub Scouts and Brownies.

Jamie had a buddy on King Street, an elderly gentleman with a little store that sold radio tubes and other becoming-outdated electrical parts, with which our son constructed various clocks and radios and, finally, our first computer. Jamie also wanted to become an amateur archaeologist by helping at the excavation site which is now the city courthouse, but the adults working there were afraid he might fall down a well, and wanted one of his parents to accompany him each Saturday morning, impossible when Barbara began teaching. We still shake our heads when we observe how much chauffeuring parents now have to do for their children.

Not long after moving into 103, we yielded to Annie's persistent pleas for a dog. Enter our small, fluffy white canine. Barbara decided to choose him herself at the animal shelter, because she believed that if she took the kids along they would inevitably fall in love with a Great Dane. Annie wanted to name our new family member, possibly a Peke/Pomeranian mix, "Peace in the Middle East," but we persuaded her that was too long, and he became Pax. He had obviously been traumatized, and so almost immediately he ran away. Jamie

Prince Street during a winter snow. 103 Prince Street is the last house on the left before the big warehouse.

Price 20¢
March 15-21, 1978

REMEMBER WHEN? — Just last week this little girl with the big shovel was pushing white stuff off the sidewalk in the 100 block of South Union Street. Happily, it seems long ago. Staff photo by Ross Stansfield

Annie liked to help by shoveling—
and got her picture in the paper because of it.

and a friend found him in a neighbor's yard; this would not be the last time our disoriented dog ran out of a familiar garden and got lost, including one memorable episode much later in Ouagadougou when we were packing out. However, we loved him, and our first photo shows him with Annie in front of a toasty fire in the dining room at 103 Prince Street.

Another vivid early memory of Pax comes from the great snowstorm at the end of February, 1979. We parents had been out late, at a film about Indonesia (*Max Havelaar*) and, waking up semi-conscious, Bob asked Jamie to take Pax for a walk. Jamie came back and announced that he couldn't; there was too much snow. "What kind of story was that?" thought Bob, stumbling downstairs to check. But it was true, it was almost impossible to open our big, elevated front door. Barbara was happy because the George Washington's Birthday Parade (a big deal in Alexandria, his hometown) had to be cancelled, and she did not have to march in it with her Brownie Troop.

Pax would in time accompany us on two African assignments, to Upper Volta and Mali. He couldn't go to Papua New Guinea because of its Australian-style, one-year quarantine requirement, so he spent two years with sister Jane, whose unfenced yard in Cincinnati provided no limits that Pax recognized. She finally hung a little note on his collar with the Theobald address and phone number on it, in case he wandered: it was useful several times. He died at a ripe old age, nearly twenty years, and his ashes were buried in the garden at 216 Wolfe Street. We thought that was the end of his life, but in 2011 we found him at a filling station in China, on the way to Luoyang, and we have a photo to prove it. We remembered how he loved to dig holes in the beach at Pine Knoll Shores, chasing imaginary creatures. He had obviously dug his way down from our garden and emerged in his ancestral home, at the least the Peke side of it.

Bob's Year at the Carnegie Endowment

My "sabbatical" year of leave-without-pay began in September, 1977. The Rockefeller fellowship of $25,000 was approximately the equivalent of my Foreign Service salary. Like most such grants, mine required that I find an institution of some kind to administer it, presumably to make sure that I did not decamp to Bali (or wherever) with the cash. Tom Hughes, my former boss at INR, offered me a place as a "Project Director" at the Carnegie Endowment for International Peace, and research for my book-to-be became its "Indonesia-Philippines Project."

The Endowment was far more than a grant administrator; it shouldered most of my research costs. It provided me with free office space, secretarial service, even a student intern, David Yang. Most important, it gave me the congenial, stimulating surroundings of a major foreign policy think tank with many interesting programs and a first-rate journal, *Foreign Policy*, which appeared in a jaunty narrow format.

According to the terms of my grant, I was supposed to write about "American interests in island Southeast Asia," which became the subtitle of the eventual book, applying a broad definition of "interests" to one geographic region. I soon discovered that "national interests" are irreparably in the eye of the beholder—vague and subjective. So I decided to draw on my experience in Indonesia and the Philippines to present my own opinion of what such interests were or should be, based on my experience in two countries that were quite different, but close enough for comparison.

I argued that US policy was preoccupied with short-term crises, and that our real interests involved long term issues, including economic development and the environment. At a time when democratization and human rights were only beginning to be recognized as policy concerns, I took issue with our traditional focus on the political stability of anti-communist allies, regardless of how inevitable revolution might be. Perhaps the best chapter of the book, and certainly the most prescient, was the one on environmental problems looming over the fragile tropical forests and coral reefs of both countries. Of course, this thinking was more than slightly utopian, but I felt good getting it off my chest.

I was lucky that, at this time, the State Department was actually encouraging writing and publication by Foreign Service Officers. I knew that much of what I wrote would be influenced by my prior access to classified information, given that virtually all candid official political analysis, including that which I had written, is sensitive, hence classified, because it requires criticism even of friendly countries. My introduction argued that "in only a few cases have I been aware, on the basis of previous official access, of key facts or arguments which are concealed by official secrecy. In no instance was this information of critical importance for purpose of analysis or judgment."[1] This was not wholly accurate. I was nervous when I submitted the book for State Department review, as required, fearing that there would be objections, especially to opinions which were contrary to US policy. In the event, there were none. That might not have been the case a few years later.

The resulting book, *Indonesia and the Philippines: American*

---

[1] Robert Pringle, *Indonesia and the Philippines: American Interests in Island Southeast Asia*, New York, Columbia University Press, 1980, Preface, p. x.

Interests in Island Southeast Asia, was published in 1980. It was dedicated to Jamie and Anne, "who enjoyed the Island World from their own perspective."

I found time at Carnegie to write an article on the ailments of the Foreign Service, entitled "Creeping Irrelevance at Foggy Bottom." The thesis was that the State Department had, since World War II, progressively handed over many of the essential tools of foreign policy to new agencies: intelligence to the CIA, public affairs to the US Information Agency and foreign assistance to AID, to name the main losses. These changes had left many of its officers undereducated on the most important tools of diplomacy, and its ambassadors at risk of becoming little more than housekeepers for other players over whom they had no real control, despite the Chief of Mission's vaunted presidential authority.[2]

I enjoyed the senior scholars who frequented the Carnegie Endowment, especially Selig ("Sig") Harrison and the Editor of *Foreign Policy*, Sanford Ungar (later President of Goucher College, among many other accomplishments). The Endowment still had its original office in New York, and in 1978 we all got to go to New York for the annual meeting of its trustees, held on the top floor of one of the World Trade Center towers. I remember looking straight down from the overhanging reception area at the ant-like cars and people on the street a hundred floors below, a view which came back to me vividly at the time of the building's devastation in 2001.

Barbara at Madeira and the Saga of Jean Harris

I began to teach soon after our return from the Philippines. Finding new employment every two to four years is one of the crosses Foreign Service spouses must bear. On the other hand, one never gets bored with one's job; I do not think I would have been a teacher for my whole life if I hadn't had the challenges of new courses and different sorts of students every so often. For a brief period after our return, I substituted in the Alexandria public school system, where, because of

---

[2] "Creeping Irrelevance at Foggy Bottom," *Foreign Policy* (Winter 1977-78), pp. 128-39.

Jamie's trials, I was particularly successful with "problem" students. Thus, when a teacher of the five special classes in American History aimed especially at vocational students at T.C. Williams High School walked off the job, I was once again employed.

I enjoyed the work and succeeded with these non-academically inclined students by using (with permission) a specially prepared syllabus developed by New York City schools. I awarded students as much credit for diligent work and good behavior as for actual mastery of the historical content of the course. I liked being near home and would have stayed for another year or more. However, in what I have always considered as cowardly cover-my-ass behavior, the school system administrators refused to re-hire first-year teachers—regardless of their performance or specific need for their skills—before they were certain the system wouldn't have too many teachers the next fall.

Fortunately, Ann Scott, whose son I had taught in Jakarta, wanted to hire me for a job at Madeira, and since we needed two incomes in the expensive US capital area, I accepted that job, along with a much longer commute. I remained at Madeira for five school years, until the spring of 1983, and in retrospect consider the change a very good one, for both personal and professional reasons.

I had never taught in a situation like Madeira before. My colleagues there formed the most thoughtful and interesting faculty I was ever a part of. From Dr. William A. Brown, whose AP Modern European and Twentieth Century History courses I took over, to the riding instructors who gave lessons to faculty members on Wednesday afternoons, each was highly accomplished in his or her field. (No tenure here—just annual contracts based on excellent performance.)

Dr. Brown had a doctorate in European history and had written his thesis on Dante's *Divine Comedy*; he also had an almost operatic level voice, and starred in both musical and theatrical performances; he returned to Madeira two years into my stay to become Academic Dean. (Much later, he would be Captain Hook to Annie's Mr. Smee in *Peter Pan*.) Dr. Margaret McBride, a French woman who taught AP French Literature, allowed me to audit her classes. And Ann Scott, chairperson of the History Department, guided me in course preparation and teaching methods for highly structured courses given by several teachers to all girls at one level—Twentieth Century History for freshmen and American History for juniors.

The math teachers won high praise for their ability to make that usually terrifying subject comprehensible, and the English Department was staffed by men and women of a variety of life styles and backgrounds, the perfect mix to give students a whole range of perspectives on the literature they were studying. I co-advised one class, from freshman to senior year, with Katherine Nevius, the young choral music teacher who raised champion boxer dogs on the side. Finally, in my second year, Dr. Stuart Davis, highly trained in American History, and his wife Pam, who became lifelong friends, arrived as on-campus residents.

The Madeira girls had classes four days a week. Wednesdays, however, were given over to real-life experiences. Upperclass girls had off-campus experiences. Sophomores worked in groups at various NGOs in the region, and upperclassmen had "Wednesday jobs," juniors at the offices of various Senators or Representatives on Capitol Hill and seniors at a business, NGO, or government office of their choice. Senior year, the girls had to apply for and get their own jobs.

Freshmen began their Wednesday experiences on campus with a series of weekly orientations in such vital topics as study skills, personal health and sexuality, money management and the natural history of the Madeira campus. In the spring they visited various Washington institutions and monuments, basically learning about the city in which they would later have to operate semi-independently. For several years, I ran the freshman program.

Faculty members were sometimes involved in various ways, but usually their Wednesdays were reserved for lesson planning and grading (Imagine that!), faculty meetings—and for those who wanted, riding! I learned how to ride a trotting horse, but never did get the hang of cantering. I fell off once trying to learn, but just suffered some bad bruises in that episode.

Real-world drama intruded on the campus once during my tenure there, in March, 1980. The headmistress, a well-known educator from the high society suburbs of Detroit, Jean Harris, murdered her ex-lover, Dr. Herman Tarnower, a famous cardiologist and author of the Scarsdale Diet book. As a young and harried mother, as well as commuting teacher, I had listened with some mystification to Jean pontificating about a woman's ability to do it all if only she could "be just as strong as a man." I found myself wondering if there was something wrong that I, a college graduate with an advanced degree, couldn't manage a stratospheric, highly remunerative career.

However, Jean, who had two grown sons, had failed in her marriage and been alone to concentrate on career goals for years. Far younger than she, I was not a close friend, and knew nothing about her personal life, certainly not her love life. So it was with astonishment that early one gloomy Saturday morning, driving Jamie to take his SSAT exams at Potomac School, I heard that someone named Harris, who lived in Greenway, Virginia (then a postal address solely for Madeira), had murdered the famous diet doctor. At first I thought it must be one of her sons, but the next brief news broadcast, as I was driving home, set me straight. Apparently, even a high-powered career woman needs emotional support one way or another to weather the stresses of a demanding job.

Jean had snapped after having dealt with fallout from a senior prank in which several senior students, who felt no one would sanction them so close to graduation, had sneaked bottles of wine into the dorms and there consumed it. Further overwrought because she had run out of a sedative that Tarnower had prescribed for her, she got into her car after the girls had left for spring vacation and headed north through the darkness of night straight to his home, with a handgun she had recently purchased. She later said she intended to shoot herself, but somehow ended up killing him instead. The end of this sad story is public knowledge.

Helena's Story

We continued to be preoccupied with Grandmother Helena. She had published her last major book, *The War on Powder River*, in 1966. It was one of her best, a history of the 1892 Johnson County War in Wyoming, which had survived in the mythology of the West as a classic dust-up between cowboys (the villains) and small farmers (the oppressed heroes). In fact the conflict was about wealthy, non-resident, would-be cattle barons, including minor European nobility, hoping to get rich by running cattle on public land, and small ranchers (not farmers) who sometimes stole their cattle. The wealthy owners finally sent a train full of hired guns north from Cheyenne to punish the "rustlers," one of whom, the hero of the tale, was killed resisting them. The countryside rose against the well-heeled invaders and they were in mortal peril until one of them managed to get word to a family friend, President Benjamin Harrison, who ordered the US cavalry to ride to their rescue.

Helena's book got the story straight and made her something of a heroine in Johnson County, just south of Sheridan, home of Bob's sister Margot today, where the "rustlers" had always been seen correctly as the good guys. There has never been a remotely accurate movie about this quirky episode, although it could be a great one. *The War on Powder River,* along with *We Pointed them North* (published in 1939) and *A Bride Goes West* (1942), remains in print today.

The problem was that Helena did not have the means to live in the fashion to which she would have liked to become accustomed: perhaps a cabin by a clear stream on someone's ranch in the West she adored. We could not help her sufficiently without gravely compromising our own financial well-being, and matters got worse as her own professional capacity faded. She was no longer able to sell occasional magazine articles as she once had; indeed it became increasingly difficult for anyone to make a living by freelance writing. My father, Henry Pringle, had discovered this by the time he died in 1958, and he always advised me not to attempt professional journalism.

After his alimony payments stopped, Helena borrowed against shares of stock she had inherited from her prudent, Latin teacher father as long as she could. Then she discovered to her chagrin that she had to sell what was left, and—even more annoying—that she owed substantial capital gains taxes on money already spent! That was when she turned to us for help with her mortgage payments (as related in Chapter 5), and with Clay's help, we bought the house from her for a promissory note and the obligation to support her for life.

When we took over ownership of 103 Prince Street, the house was valued at about $35,000. We acquired it just as the Old Town Alexandria real estate market was taking off, and by the time we sold it a decade later in 1979 its value had more than quadrupled.[3] Had we not acquired it or some other house when we did, it is very unlikely that our purchasing power would have kept up with the real estate boom. After living in the house for two years following our return, in order to avoid capital gains taxes, we were able to sell it for $137,500 and buy 216 Wolfe Street, where we still live, for $207,500.[4] We were able to do this with the money received from 103 plus a $70,000 mortgage. 216 Wolfe was a larger and more practical house, which actually had a bedroom for each child, as well as a small walled garden in which flowers and trees could be grown.

None of this made for a pleasant relationship with Helena. She was grateful for what we were doing, but her gratitude was overwhelmed by her ongoing need for more money. During our seven years in Indonesia and the Philippines she had continually bombarded us with requests for money to cover her miscellaneous medical and other bills. She didn't enjoy doing it, but could see no alternative. At the same time her letters were often full of interesting observations, especially on US politics, and after one in 1976, about why she liked Jimmy Carter, just becoming well known, she added, "Darling, I try to earn a fractional percentage of what I cost you, by keeping you amused."[5] She never seriously considered seeking more orthodox employment—the one time we persuaded her to do so, at a bookstore, it was a miserable failure. By the time we returned from the Philippines she was seventy-eight years old and no longer physically or emotionally employable, especially in a menial job, the very idea of which she detested.

---

[3] Details for this paragraph are primarily from Bob letter to Margot, October 19, 1968, which states that 103 would probably sell at the time for 30,000 or 35,000 dollars.

[4] Sale and purchase prices for 103 Prince and 216 Wolfe are from the *Alexandria Port Surveyor*, January 16-22, 1980, part of the *Gazette*, as it then was.

[5] Helena letter to Bob and Barbara, November 13, 1976.

During the course of 1977 it also became clear that she could no longer care for herself. She had to be hospitalized several times for fainting spells resulting from too much drink and too little food—it was never clear which of these was the more important factor. Her doctor, a crotchety character, was totally unsympathetic, and concluded that a nursing home was the only way to restore her physical health. Since she had no significant assets or income other than Social Security, we were able to get her a Medicaid-funded bed in Woodbine Nursing Home, not far from us. She would live there for the rest of her life.

She detested "the slammer," as she called it, especially at first, and she let the Woodbine staff know it in no uncertain terms. They were unused to cantankerous authors as patients, and for a while they took her seriously when she threatened to expose their shortcomings in the *Washington Post*. She did not like residents with dementia wandering into her room, and once she smacked one of them with her cane, precipitating a minor crisis.

She had become an enthusiastic Episcopalian years previously when she could no longer afford psychotherapy, and we took her regularly to Christ Church, the church of George Washington and Robert E. Lee, which we had joined partly because it was her church. We ferried her to church, had her over to dinner, smuggled cocktails to her, and bought fancy goodies for her at Sutton Place Gourmet. We got her typewriter installed in her room, although she rarely used it. Her bank account at Burke and Herbert, into which occasional royalty income from her books was deposited, could not rise above a certain level—I think I was $700—or she had to forfeit the balance to Medicaid, but we were able to buy treats for her with the surplus. When we went abroad, a nice lady at Christ Church, Joan Woodbury, took her to Church occasionally, and our beloved Burke and Herbert, an Alexandria institution, kept a familial eye on her bank account.

Her physical health improved greatly, and although she would never admit it, she began to tolerate Woodbine, if never quite to like it. The nursing home itself improved greatly over the years, especially in the quality and frequency of lectures, informal concerts, social features, and more humane ambience—they even instituted cocktail hours, although she became increasingly less interested in alcohol until she did not drink at all.

She stayed at Woodbine until the spring of 1999, when she died just short of her one-hundredth birthday. I came back to visit her from South Africa about a week before her death, and could tell that she was slipping away. Margot arranged a service for her in Sheridan, Wyoming, perhaps as close to a spiritual home as anything she ever knew, and took charge of her ashes, to be scattered in Powder River, although at last word a portion of them are still on a shelf somewhere in the depths of Margot's Sheridan home.

We Move to Wolfe Street

The move from Prince Street to Wolfe Street was no less chaotic than moves from country to country had been, especially since we did much of it ourselves, with help from friends. The never-to-be forgotten episode in the process was the installation of the Chinese-bed bookshelf, made from extremely heavy tropical wood, in the living room. The top panel acts as a keystone, sort of, and holds the entire bookshelf together. Until it is placed firmly on top of the side panels, with all shelves and the back lattice work in place, nothing can stand alone. So enough pressure must be applied on both sides to prevent already placed lower shelves from falling, while allowing the insertion of the middle and top ones. Charlie Salmon, my friend and former boss in Manila, will never forget the afternoon we put it up.

The house, built in about 1810, had a few unexpected kinks, pre-purchase inspection notwithstanding. The most serious, and as yet incompletely remedied, is the fact that the old brick foundation was never meant to keep out all water flowing ever so slightly downhill toward us from the houses on our east, Lee Street, side. We fixed additional flow from the direction of the alley by creating two levels in the rear brick patio, and putting in a French drain halfway back. A young bricklayer from far western Virginia, Otis Light, willing to work for a price we could afford, installed a proper foundation for the back addition, excavating no more than a few feet at a time so the whole structure wouldn't fall in. It had previously,

Moving into our "new," but still historic home at 216 Wolfe Street—a scene that, with variations, is one of the defining motifs of Foreign Service life.

we discovered, been supported by brick pilings, between which someone had banked earth, presumably to keep out a draft underneath the kitchen floor. His work was so good that when we added a third storey to the addition in 1995, it needed no extra support.

Our beloved former Indonesian servant, Pak Sujadi, then working at the Kenneys' Georgetown house, came over one day and helped lay the patio bricks. Barbara built the brick wall along the lower level, as indicated by a small brass plaque: "*Hunc Murum Barbara Cade Pringle Aedificavit AD 1979.*" Bob, and perhaps Jamie, helped with digging holes for the foundation, but having a surer eye for spatial relations, Barbara laid all the wall bricks.

Water control aside, the house has provided a comfortable living space for the years we have been home, and an easy and profitable rental when we were abroad. In the days when every teenager needed a boom box and wanted to run it full blast, we were abroad. But earlier, when Jamie and Annie were in grade school and junior high, their own tiny rooms were enough to keep them happy, though Jamie had loved

Barbara the bricklayer, building a new garden wall in the process of coping with an ancient backyard drainage problem.

his attic aerie and Annie her yellow bed at Prince Street. The small attic "family room" with our TV was enough for viewing at reasonable hours; we even watched the famous Redskins 1983 Super Bowl victory ("The game isn't over 'til the Fat Lady sings.") up there, with Pax racing around in circles every time we cheered.

Later, when we returned from Mali in 1990, the young birds had flown the nest, and we extended the attic level to create marvelous new storage and library space running the length of the house. Thus altered, the house has since been a comfortable size for only two of us, though we have sometimes wished that it had just a little more space as a daughter-in-law and son-in-law, plus three grandchildren, have joined the family. Old Town Alexandria remains one of the more convenient and pleasant neighborhoods in the whole metropolitan area, despite accelerating over-development along the Potomac waterfront.

By the time we returned from the Philippines, Barbara's sister Kathy, who had previously worked on the Carter campaign, had a high-flying job at the White House as Rosalyn Carter's Director of Projects. She bought a small house in Southeast Washington, which we visited often. On at least one occasion, Jamie and Annie, along with Heather and Heidi, got to visit Amy Carter and go swimming in the White House pool, and be photographed by a White House photographer as the President boarded his helicopter on the South Lawn.

Though we were not yet home for Carter's inauguration in 1976, to which Kathy obtained tickets for other family visitors, Barbara did later get to attend the entertainment after a state dinner for the President of Kenya, to which Mother and Daddy, to their great delight, had been invited. This occasion

Cincinnati-on-the-Potomac

KATHRYN CADE

One of the most demanding jobs in town belongs to Kathryn E. Cade, 30, who grew up in Mariemont and now works in the East Wing of the White House as director of projects, issues and research for Rosalynn Carter, wife of the President.

The job reflects Mrs. Carter's departure from the traditional sort of first-lady type work. Rosalynn Carter is not your typical first lady; after a year and half in the White House, she is already thought by some to have greater influence in political affairs than even Eleanor Roosevelt had. In 1976 she not only campaigned for her candidate-husband but also spoke her own mind about mental health, problems of the aging, and the problems of cities. Now, as she pursues these interests, her assistant is Kathryn Cade. She organizes Mrs. Carter's travels and usually travels with her.

Cade, who describes herself as "30 and aging fast," is the daughter of Mr. and Mrs. Clarence Cade, who live on Park Lane in Mariemont. She was graduated from Mariemont High and Radcliffe College.

She says the East Wing staff of which she is

By Warren D. Wheat

a vital part does not think in terms of "working for" Mrs. Carter because she "is so perfectly willing to entertain your ideas, she creates a sense that you are really working together, that you share a common purpose."

Cade works in a tiny — but bright and airy — office near the Presidential family quarters and the state dining room.

Cade says Mrs. Carter fits no mold. "She has a job to do and she is going to do it, and whether some outside observer thinks she is being effective is really not terribly important to her."

Although her long days of seemingly endless work tend to obscure the fact, Cade does realize she sits near the seat of great power. But, she said, "I look upon this as just a unique experience in my life, and I am sure that whatever else I do, I'll never do anything quite like this again. You have to keep reminding yourself, in the midst of a really horrendous day when everything is falling apart, that it really is something very special — you should take time to enjoy it."

But, she says, "It's like living in a fish bowl." When off the job, she explains, "You can't really talk about what you do."

Continued

Barbara's sister Kathy was so effective working for the Jimmy Carter campaign that she was hired to work for Mrs. Carter in the White House.

was memorable in the family for several reasons, among them Char's fashion statement, as remembered by Kathy:

The dinner was for Kenyan president Daniel arap Moi. Mrs. Carter remembered that Daddy and I had been on safari there so decided to invite the parents. They were in North Carolina when the dinner was planned. When the social secretary asked if I wanted to call Mother to tell her about the invitation, I told her no, that I wanted Mother to be surprised when the invitation arrived in the mail. I then said that I was sure that Mother would call me immediately, and her first words would be "I have nothing to wear. All my nice clothes are in Cincinnati." Sure enough, that is exactly what happened. When she called and said same, I asked her if she had something in Cincy she would like to wear. She said yes, so I suggested she have Jane go to the house and send the dress via FedEx, something that was at the time for Mother quite an extravagant idea. But that is what happened. In addition, she borrowed the mink stole of my assistant, Barbara Langhoff, and looked quite elegant that evening. Daddy rented a tux from a company in New Bern![6]

[6] Kathy Cade e-mail to Barbara, June 2, 2015.

One day in the summer, Amy Carter had no playmates and her parents were both leaving on official business. Kathy knew just the last-minute solution: invite her nieces and nephew over to play and swim in the White House pool with Amy. Here is the ragtag bunch waving good-by as President and Mrs. Carter walk toward the helicopter to leave.

Barbara remembers something about Daddy's nearly forgetting the tux, which was hanging on a shower rod in Pine Knoll Shores—or maybe he did forget it, and we rented another for him in DC. Both parents had a wonderful time at the great event.

Joining the Africa Bureau (AF/EPS)

As my time at the Carnegie Endowment for International Peace drew to a close, I had no idea what my next assignment in Washington would be. Leave without pay was not a real assignment for career purposes; almost anything that took you away from the Foreign Service "mainstream" (i.e., the regional bureaus) was regarded as an impediment to promotion. But, having been away for a year, I decided I might as well continue my absence for a bit longer, first by proposing and organizing, with old friend Erland Heginbotham, a State Department-funded seminar on Indonesian Rural Development.[7]

More than thirty scholars and officials attended, including experts like Jamie Mackie, Peter Timmer and Donald K. Emmerson. It turned out to be an underwhelming discussion of how to focus foreign aid on poor, rural Indonesians, with no clear solutions proposed. As noted earlier, none of the experts had yet realized that Suharto's program of using oil profits for rural development on Java would work as well as it did. But the experience persuaded me that I needed some formal training in economics, a subject I had studiously avoided at both Harvard and Cornell.

The State Department had just the thing: a six-month course for the uninitiated, which claimed to be the equivalent of an undergraduate degree, in economics. I was now out of synch with the assignment cycle, so I enrolled in it from January to June, 1979. The course included such oddities, in retrospect, as studying some early programming language, though not long enough to do much good. In addition, the State Department had a mainframe computer, which we got to play with.

My evaluation said, very generously indeed, that my grades in mathematics, statistics and econometrics had been "quite acceptable," given that I had studied no math since high school. My grades in other subjects were good. The evaluation concluded that I should be able to use my training to integrate economic and political analysis into a "comprehensive approach to Third World policy issues,"[8] which was certainly what I was hoping for. The course was about all one could expect from a six-month investment, but it made me feel like a *foie gras* goose—too much stuffed in too fast: the things you were already good at were what you remembered, but you didn't have time enough to vanquish your old biases, much less master subjects you had never learned at all.

Just before beginning my leave without pay, I had called on Richard Holbrooke, then Assistant Secretary for East Asian and Pacific Affairs, best known for his much later work on the Balkan peace agreement. Holbrooke was already famous as one of a coterie of bright, liberal former FSOs (Tony Lake was another, as was Dick Moose) who left the career Foreign Service after Vietnam to play the riskier game of working for the campaigns of presidential aspirants and then, if your man won, seeking higher-ranking political appointments.

With a new Democratic administration in power for the first time since 1969, Holbrooke was on a fast track in the Carter State Department. I thought that despite his Democratic connections, he was way too conservative, but also a wheeler-dealer, an opportunist, not the kind of expertise-based policy maker I admired. He was, moreover, five years younger than I was, and I was no doubt jealous of him and all his tribe of "inner-outers." When I interviewed him about another job in Asia, I told him I wanted to dissociate myself from certain aspects of US policy, such as our preoccupation with the Philippine bases, and that I was thinking about an assignment not associated with *Southeast* Asia.[9] Needless to say Holbrooke did not call me back begging me to reconsider.

So I was ready to listen when Carl Cundiff showed up at the end of the six-month economics course hoping to recruit some of its graduates to work on Africa as part of his Economic Policy Staff in the Bureau of African Affairs (AF/EPS). While I did not intend to abandon my Southeast Asian specialization, I was beginning to realize that it was not enough; it was important to have some expertise in more than one geographic area, to gain perspective on issues that were both local and global. I knew nothing about Sub-Saharan Africa, but what better time to begin learning? State's Africa Bureau did not cover Africa north of the Sahara, from Egypt to Morocco, because that area was correctly viewed as essentially part of the Middle East, colored by its history as part of the Roman Empire and the Arab conquest. The great desert, not the Mediterranean, has always been the real border and barrier between cultural and political zones.

Transferring to AF (the Bureau of African Affairs) for three years was a momentous move. For reasons that will become clear, I would almost certainly never have been promoted fast

---

[9] Bob note on conversation with Richard Holbrooke, August 22, 1977.

enough to be considered for an ambassadorship without this change. We would not have been assigned to Ougadougou, Bamako or Pretoria. The experiences of our children in their formative years would have been very different. My career track over the next decade would further illustrate the crap-shoot aspects of a Foreign Service career. Its motto might well be "Gain hope all ye who enter here, because you never know what will happen next." It also helps to explain why FSOs spend an inordinate amount of time concentrating not on their jobs, but on trying to game their next jobs. I suppose this is also somewhat true of the military, which, like the Foreign Service, has a personnel system where rank is vested in the individual, not in the job.

AF/EPS was composed of an Office Director, a Deputy Director, three lower ranking FSOs and two secretaries (later to be renamed OMSs, for Office Management Specialists). There were as yet no computers. The better secretaries could type like the wind on their IBM Selectrics, and they could also manage schedules and appointments and handle visitors—all jobs which today are done by the diplomats themselves, except for the most senior. The best were extraordinarily capable and still are, but there are far fewer of them left. It's one reason why today's diplomats have less time to think or get out of the office. To put it another way, the replacement of clerical help with computers has arguably *reduced* productivity.

In theory, the mission of AF/EPS was to advise the Assistant Secretary for Africa, and through him the Secretary of State, on economic policy issues, bringing to bear economic skills such as those I had just supposedly learned in my six-month course. Although the US remained preoccupied with stopping the spread of communism everywhere, the relevance of economic factors to this goal was recognized somewhat earlier in Sub-Saharan Africa than elsewhere because of the continent's massive poverty. Huge amounts of foreign aid, relative to population, were already flowing to Africa, and in the absence of significant military or political cooperation, it was by far the most effective tool we had. (Achieving democracy would not be a US policy goal for years to come.)

In fact, when I joined AF/EPS an officer didn't need much economic training to work there. The most important real goal of the office was to capture a sufficient share of our foreign aid budget for what we deemed to be the most deserving African countries, either because they were on our side in the Cold War, or because they possessed raw materials we needed. An FSO working there needed only to be able to add up a column of numbers and perceive which country was which. It was also very important to understand what the US Agency for International Development (USAID, or just AID), then a semi-independent agency, was doing. That meant believing in the value of economic development, as opposed to just handing out money to countries and dictators deemed to be on "our" (read anti-communist) side. Mobutu Sese Seku of Zaire, the former Belgian Congo, was the classic example of the latter.

Most AID professionals saw themselves as engaged in a constant struggle with State Department counterparts who were blind to everything except crude political factors. Indeed, we in EPS found ourselves not infrequently opposed to State colleagues on the country desks as we struggled to slice up the AID and PL (Public Law) 480 food aid pies.

As a newcomer, I went to the bottom of the small heap in EPS. I was responsible for two things: allocation of food aid under PL 480 and the administration of the Special Self-Help Program, a program unique to AF which enabled US ambassadors to distribute small grants at their own discretion. Many ambassadors were convinced that these small, no-strings-attached grants were the best conceivable use of AID funds, as opposed to huge, multi-year projects with big American staffs increasingly managed by contractors, which the ambassador sometimes had trouble understanding, much less controlling.

AID regulations did have to be followed even for Self-Help (the money after all came from the AID budget). Of these, the most contentious was an unimaginative ban on sports equipment. Some of our old-school ambassadors, imbued with prep-school values, believed fervently that soccer balls and other sports paraphernalia were by far the most effective way to promote US values at the village level, and they never ceased to fight the ban on them. For me, managing "Self-Help" was a great way to get to know Africa. On trips to Africa it gave me an excuse to go into rural areas. It was a valuable tool, especially in countries which, because of small size or bad behavior, received no other US foreign aid.

But first, still in Washington, I had to learn where each country was, and which one went with which cable address, an ongoing geo-quiz. There were those Z's we had never heard of: Zambia, Zaire and Zimbabwe. A cable from Embassy Bamako meant Mali. Malawi, not be confused with Mauritania or Mozambique, went with Embassy Lilongwe. Then the Guineas: ex-French Guinea (Embassy Conakry), ex-Portuguese Guinea Bissau (Embassy Bissau), ex-Spanish Equatorial Guinea (no embassy yet) . . . . Who knew the Spanish had ever had a colony in Africa . . . ? No, not Papua New Guinea, that's in the South China Sea . . . . Arrgh!

Years later when we were actually serving in Papua New Guinea, at Embassy Port Moresby, a piece of our mail was misdirected to Embassy Conakry. A communicator there forwarded it to us with a scrawl on the envelope, "Not even close!" It was enough to reinforce loathing for the Congress of Berlin, the finale of the colonial "scramble for Africa," and everything it stood for.

PL 480 food aid was a far more complex issue. The program was conceived and driven by US farm interests and by the need to do something with our supplies of surplus agricultural products. The key problem was how to unload our extraneous food on needy Africans, thereby helping our own farmers, without destroying the livelihood of the African peasant farmers whom we were trying to help. Floods of ink flowed over this dilemma, without ever solving it.

Then there was the issue of "counterpart funds," the local currency, often of dubious value, generated by the sale of food under Title I of PL 480. Such funds could be used to pay the local expenses of AID projects, but often accumulated relentlessly.[10] The least controversial PL 480 category was Title II, under which food could be given directly to charitable organizations. One of the biggest Title II programs in Africa at that time was in Upper Volta (now Burkina Faso), our next

---

[10] See Chapter 6 about our 1970 visit to Burma, where we changed $100 at the U.S. Embassy for enough Burmese *kyat*, from accumulated PL 480 counterpart funds, to pay all our internal expenses for a week of travel, including internal air fare and as many souvenirs as we could carry, making this one of our all-time cheap as well as fascinating vacations.

country of assignment, where about \$6 million yearly went to the Catholic Church to feed the students in its school system in this heavily Catholic country. (I had seen an even bigger one in Vietnam in 1961.)

One of the more annoying requirements for any junior officer in a regional bureau was serving as duty officer in the Assistant Secretary's office on Saturday mornings, done on a rotational basis. It normally involved a dull routine of making sure that appropriate recipients were notified about the arrival of important messages, and with luck one could resume one's normal weekend activities by early afternoon.

Saturday, September 22, 1979, one of my earliest stints, was different. Suddenly it became apparent that some kind of crisis or other alarming event was going on somewhere in Africa. At one point, a trio of officers from INR, the Bureau of Intelligence and Research, where I had once worked, filed into the Assistant Secretary's office like some kind of pagan procession, one of them carrying a globe. Before long it was rumored that one of our satellites had detected what looked like (and indeed was) a nuclear test in the southern Indian Ocean, a cooperative venture between our friends the Israelis and the pariah South Africans. The event and our knowledge of it was classified beyond Top Secret for decades.[11]

The Assistant Secretary in question, Richard Moose, was one of the "in-and-out" (of government) ex-FSOs of whom I disapproved, mainly on the basis of my earlier reaction to Richard Holbrooke. But Moose turned out to be a competent and convivial boss. Armed with an Arkansas accent and a disarming stutter, he was seriously interested in the economic issues that were of primary interest to my office. He had his own story about the boredom and peril of being a duty officer, in his case as a watch officer for the entire Department, when he was still a junior FSO. The Watch was a 24/7 team that looked out for incipient crises and other after-hours emergencies, making sure that appropriate actions were taken. On the occasion in question, Moose was finishing a graveyard shift at the end of an apparently eventless night.

[11] This was the Vela Incident of Saturday, September 22, 1979. See http://www.globalsecurity.org/wmd/world/israel/nuke-test.htm4:22 PM.

As the sun was coming up, he scribbled in the Watch Office log: "Rosy fingered dawn observed," a reference to a famous passage in Homer's *Odyssey.*

However, apparently at about the same time there had been a near accident involving a nuclear weapon on a US military aircraft in Turkey. There was recrimination about why Highest Authority had not been notified sooner. Mr. Moose's cryptic note suggested to the less-than-literary investigators that the Watch had picked up some pertinent information and failed to follow through, and all manner of uproar ensued. The moral, one I always had trouble learning, was that humor and bureaucracy are a dangerous mixture.

I traveled to Africa for the first time in October, 1979, to consult with embassies and local officials about economic issues and programs, especially PL 480 and Self-Help. The first stop was Zambia, once Northern Rhodesia. I was hosted by a famous US ambassador, Frank Wisner, and his lovely French-born wife. The capital, Lusaka, was threadbare, but quaintly charming, its stores filled mostly with long, empty shelves. It was also expensive; a flimsy notebook for a diary cost me US $4.75 in overvalued local currency. I did not get to Zambia's fabled copper belt, a mineral-rich region straddling the Zambia-Zaire border. Nor did I have time to visit Zambia's well-reputed game parks, none of them near Lusaka.

Like several newly independent countries in southern Africa, Zambia was being crippled by conflict with a powerful neighbor still under white rule, usually South Africa but in this case Southern Rhodesia. The Rhodesian leader, Ian Smith, had unilaterally declared independence in 1965. Zambia gave sanctuary to black guerillas struggling to liberate what they called Zimbabwe, and Smith's tough white commandos struck back. I wrote in my new diary:

Defense capability [in Zambia] must be awful—a few months back the Rhodesians just drove across the border, all the way to Lusaka, blew up [Zimbabwean guerilla leader] Nkomo's house... had a few beers and drove back. It took the [Zambian] military two hours to get to the scene.[12]

Tanzania was my second stop. Dar-es-Salaam, the capital, had nice beaches, even downtown. It was familiarly polyglot, its large Muslim minority reflecting centuries of Arab dominance. It had at least one gigantic, lit-up mosque, as well as big Lutheran and Catholic churches.

Tanzania's economy was struggling under the leadership of its famous founding President, Julius Nyerere, a fervent exponent of African socialism. Everything was still run by state corporations, and although not all were bad, enough were to make a difference. Tanzania's balance of payments problem reflected failure to develop an export sector, potentially including agricultural products like pyrethrum, used in insecticides. Promising tourism possibilities were as yet unexploited. Finally, Nyerere's war to unseat the tyrannous Idi Amin in neighboring Uganda was costing far more than his country could afford.

One result was that Tanzania couldn't pay for the imported food it needed, especially rice. We were eager to fill the gap with our subsidized rice exports, but so were the Japanese, who paid their farmers extravagant prices, resulting in huge surpluses. In 1979 they were beating us hands down, sending 60,000 tons of their rice to Tanzania annually versus only 6,000 tons of ours. This was causing distress in our Department of Agriculture and among its rice-growing clients in Texas and California, who pushed their congressmen hard for more government subsidies to help them catch up with the Japanese.

A new influx of Peace Corps volunteers was increasing demand for Self-Help small project funds, which they often administered:

Self-Help: will have to tackle this urgently on return. Tanzania wants $20,000 [yearly] which seems reasonable—they have Peace Corps Volunteers here again now after a long hiatus— Nyerere threw them out in the late 60's when US-Tanzania

---

[12] "Diary of trip to Zambia, Tanzania, Zaire, and Congo (Brazzaville)," October, 1979.

relations were at rock bottom—part of the problem was PCV obstreperousness, hippy-style, tangling with serious Brits and Tanzanians who thought education should just teach you how to pass courses! The problem will not recur, because the Tanzanians are off their ideological anti-US high, and because today's American youth have come full circle back to sober achievement-oriented-ness.[13]

I enjoyed being back in a tropical world which included coral reefs. Having prudently brought along a mask and snorkel, I discovered a hotel half an hour out of town (the Kunduchi, still in business at this writing) with offshore islands and snorkeling tours, vaguely Moorish décor, but no air conditioning.

The last two stops on this maiden trip to Africa were Kinshasa, capital of Zaire, the former Belgian Congo, now the Democratic Republic of the Congo, and Brazzaville, capital of the Republic of the Congo, also known as "Congo-B," famous for being a Free French stronghold during World War II—it's where Humphrey Bogart went after leaving Casablanca. My flight followed a wandering route past Mt. Kilimanjaro, which obligingly poked up through the clouds as we went by, then (after a change at Addis Ababa) via Nairobi to Kinshasa—all on Air Ethiopia, one of the best airlines in Africa.

Kinshasa and Brazzaville lie within sight of each other at an elevation of over 1,000 feet, separated by the Stanley Pool, where the Congo River is blocked by a ledge. Downstream, many miles of rapids and falls make the Congo a potentially huge source of hydroelectric power, with an estimated 13% of world capacity. This would become a huge opportunity and headache for us, described at greater length in Chapter 13.

Historically, the Congo rapids blocked access to the interior until late in the colonial era, which is why Henry Morton Stanley, after whom the Stanley Pool is named, was able to gain fame exploring the upper reaches of the river as late as the 1870s. Almost three thousand miles in length, the Congo flows in a great loop through Zaire, a country bigger than the US east of the Mississippi. In 1979 it was still suffering under the dictatorship of Mobutu Sese Seko, who had an unrivaled

---

[13] Ibid.

ability to play on the post-World War II US preoccupation with anti-Communism, to the detriment of his people.

The Belgians had created an economic powerhouse in what was to become Zaire, fuelled first by rubber, later by cobalt, copper, gold, uranium and other minerals. They deemed democracy to be totally out of the question, until it was too late to begin preparing for it. But they needed infrastructure, especially railroads and riverboats, and blue-collar Congolese labor to run it. The result was a profoundly unbalanced educational system: perhaps the best in Africa through primary school, but virtually nothing beyond that.[14]

All this fell apart under Mobutu. One of the spectacles of Kinshasa in 1979 was miles of inoperable river steamers, many of them huge, rotting along the banks of the Stanley Pool. Only a handful were still serving the roadless interior. Mobutu did keep the mining economy productive enough for his own survival. Most of it was located in Katanga, around Lubumbashi (ex-Elizabethville), far away from Kinshasa. I would not go there until I became the Central Africa (AF/C) Office Director a decade later.

In Kinshasa I stayed with John and Judy Heimann in a well-maintained high-rise apartment building constructed for expatriates. John was Economic Counselor at our embassy. He was an ideal host for me because the purpose of my visit was, as always, to gain a better understanding of the parlous economic situation, and to talk about our large PL 480 food aid program.

I found lots of parallels with Indonesia:

There is the same physical and economic deterioration [as in Sukarno-era Indonesia]. The colonial architecture of Leopoldville [Kinshasa] is strikingly reminiscent of Batavia [Jakarta], and in the same kind of decay. There is the same superfluity of charm/sophistication at high levels of government (and the same absence of middle-level skills). What is lacking is the kind of fierce, reactive nationalism that characterized Indonesia. Herein lies hope, at least in the eyes of some: those who believe that Zaire has "bottomed out" think that, as corrupt

---

[14] John Gunther, *Inside Africa,* London, 1955, especially p. 647.

*as the present rulers may be, they realize that things cannot go
on at the current rate of deterioration without (even to them)
unacceptable damage to the economic superstructure.*

*So they have been willing to accept a classic IMF package:
ceilings on expenditures, borrowing, salary limits, money
supply limit and a watchdog team headed by a tough German
ex-central banker. They have swallowed all this, more or less,
and the question is now whether it will stay swallowed . . . .*[15]

Of course the medicine did not stay swallowed, but in
situations like this the IMF, goaded by politically-motivated
backers like the United States, then as now usually has no
choice but to keep trying. It is worth noting that all this was
happening well before the HIV epidemic, which was to hit
Zaire hard, or the civil war which followed Mobutu's demise.

Brazzaville was my next stop. John Heimann told me that I
was going to a country where the two great economic theorists
of modern times, Marx and Milton Friedman, reigned together.
He was referring to the Marxist theory espoused by the long-
time strong man of Congo-B, Sassou Ngesso, and the real-
world ethos of a small country with a hard currency, centrally
banked in Paris. Congo-B nestled tick-like on the flank of a
huge, resource-rich state with its economy in tatters and
much in need of a neighbor where business could be done. It
also mattered that Brazzaville had been the capital of French
Equatorial Africa, and it had relatively strong intellectual
infrastructure.

To get there from Kinshasa one took a ferry three miles
across the great brown Stanley Pool, dotted with clumps
of floating hyacinth. It still reputedly had a few resident
crocodiles, but some expatriates went sailing there anyway.
The ferry was a mad scene crowded with lady smugglers, with
a near-riot at either end as they fought to get on and off. The
two Congos were never on the best of terms, so immigration
requirements were complex. Fortunately there were excellent
embassy "expediters" to guide visitors through it all.

The ambassador, Bill Swing, another friend, greeted me at
the "beach" in Brazzaville, with his econ-commercial officer,
Cindy Hanson. The rest of the embassy's American staff

---

[15] "Diary of trip to Zambia, Tanzania, Zaire, and Congo (Brazzaville),"
October, 1979.

consisted of an administrative officer and six marines. Bill most unusually did not have a DCM, reflecting our historically poor relations with communist-leaning Congo-B. Cindy was an attractive divorcee; Bill was also divorced. She acted as a kind of unofficial hostess at the lunch he gave for us, and there was much kidding about that. From his Residence you could look across the Pool to the ambassador's Residence in Kinshasa. This was important because both embassies had emergency evacuation plans that required boating across to the other side. No one had figured out what to do if both Congos had a crisis at the same time or went to war with each other, not an impossible nightmare.

I noted in my diary that the two Pool capitals would make a great high school economics field trip, Karl and Milton on one side, smugglers, hyacinths and crocodiles in the middle, and Capitalist Paradise Lost on the other.

During my time in AF/EPS, I averaged at least one trip to Africa a year. In 1980 I went back for two conferences, first of the newly created Southern African Development Coordination Conference (SADCC) in Mozambique; the second of USAID agricultural officers at a small game park near Nairobi, Kenya. In addition, I visited Madagascar and Malawi.

SADCC had been created the year before as an alliance of black-ruled "front-line states," including Mozambique, which felt threatened by South Africa. I got to shake hands with its President, Samora Machel, whose widow Graca was later to become Mrs. Nelson Mandela. The capital, Maputo (formerly Lorenzo Marques), had once been a favorite watering hole for white South Africans as well as one end of their most direct railroad route to the Indian Ocean. The country had subsequently been impoverished by the departure of its Portuguese colonial masters and South African tourists and businessmen, while the new Marxist Mozambican government served (as in Zambia) as a base for anti-apartheid guerillas. Machel was still on our "blacklist" for his revolutionary ties to East Germany and other communist countries, but our relations were on the mend.

I wrote at the time, "One senses that the Mozambicans are essentially conservative in the sense that they will not easily abandon the old revolutionary faith. One also senses the dogged desire to make things better, and this is pushing them inexorably toward regional cooperation and economic pragmatism." [16] This trend would continue, all the more so as everyone began to realize that this California-size state was loaded with minerals, transportation corridors, good agricultural land and other economic assets.

The USAID conference in Kenya pondered how to deal with declining per-capita food production in Sub-Saharan Africa, a growing concern. The policy pendulum was already swinging toward using foreign aid to push sometimes reluctant Third World countries toward policy reforms, such as not fixing prices so that farmers were effectively taxed and consumers subsidized, a change discussed at greater length below. As for having the conference at a game park, albeit a small one, it was more logical than it sounds. "You can't just wander off in the middle of a game park; it's a case of seat or be eaten."

On to Madagascar, the incredibly exotic, Texas-sized island off Africa's east coast, with a language and culture related to Indonesia and certainly "*not* part of Africa," I wrote. We were worried that Madagascar's radical ruler, Didier Ratsiraka, would give the Soviets a naval base at its northern tip, but we had little to offer by way of persuading him not to, since we had no aid program. Following years of trying to isolate Ratsiraka, we had only recently appointed an ambassador. Madagascar proved the importance of having an aid program in countries where political crisis is the result of agricultural problems, in this case flagging rice production. We didn't have one, so we were reduced to irrelevancy.

I bought some cheap vanilla beans, for which Madagascar is famous, to take home (no idea how I got them through customs) and saw the phenomenal, Polynesian-style royal palace in Antananarivo, which was gutted by fire before my next visit, with Barbara, more than fifteen years later.

In Zimbabwe I spent most of my time visiting Self-Help projects operated by our new embassy, which we had opened only after the end of Ian Smith's white-minority government the year previously. With its prosperous, white farmer minority on sophisticated farms reminiscent of Iowa,

---

[16] "Report on a Trip to Mozambique, Kenya, Madagascar, Zimbabwe and Malawi, November 24-December 17, 1980." All subsequent notations from this trip are from the same report.

Zimbabwe's perilous division was clear. It looked to me not unlike the racial divide between rich Chinese and rural Malays in Malaysia. I opined, not very originally, that Zimbabwe would have to work out a similar multi-racial compromise. Even if it did, there would, as in Malaysia,

. . . probably be a constant series of new frictions as the black masses levy new pressures . . . with some outer limit of systemic tolerance. Like a nuclear reaction, the result could be highly productive if it doesn't get out of control.

But of course it did get out of control, under Mugabe; the white farmers fled, the economy crumbled and the mess has endured up to this writing.

Our last stop was Malawi, still under its Life President, Hastings Banda, a former medical doctor and graduate of Central State College in Wilberforce, Ohio. I spent a day in his beautiful country touring Self-Help projects in a rural area, mile after mile of villages and mango trees obviously producing so much fruit that no one could eat it, much less clean up the resulting rotten mess. Banda was famous for enforcing morality and formality, and the two officers assigned to accompany me both wore suits and ties in the sweltering heat. I was treated to dinner at an equally formal, terribly British Malawian Army officers mess.

Despite Banda's squeaky-clean autocracy, Malawi had lurched from respectable (6%) annual growth to soaring debt as prices for exports (tobacco, tea and sugar) stagnated, oil prices went up, and drought arrived. Still it looked a lot better than most African countries:

If this one can't make it, is there hope for any among the less endowed? At the very least this spike-shaped country buried in [surrounded by] Zambia, Zimbabawe and above all Mozambique proves that regional economic cooperation will be a necessary part of any therapy. The alternative will be to leave the continent in 2000 as we find it in 1980, littered with cripples.[17]

---

[17] Actually, Zimbabwe does not border Malawi, but across a lake, Tanzania does.

Policy Reform

As I learned more about Africa, my work increasingly shifted toward policy reform issues and occasional speech writing. On policy reform we worked closely with AID and the international financial institutions or "IFIs," the World Bank and the IMF. It had become clear that there was no point in pouring money into Africa to improve farming technology, if the policies in place nullified the results.

Exchange rates, for example, were typically set so that local currencies were overvalued. A hypothetical example: the Lower Guinea *makumba* would be fixed at five *makumbas* to the dollar, whereas its real value, measured by its comparative purchasing power, was ten to one. When a farmer's coffee was exported, the foreign buyer paid in dollars or some other internationally acceptable currency. But the Lower Guinean government captured all such foreign exchange income, and converted it to *makumbas,* which the farmer received at the official rate. The result was a 50% tax on coffee exports and a severe disincentive to coffee farmers, while government, holding the dollars, reaped a windfall profit. One inevitable indicator of such a policy would be the existence of a black market in Lower Guinea for exchanging dollars into local currency at a fair (market) rate. And one inevitable result over time would be a negative effect on Lower Guinea's economy.

Other destructive policies besides phony exchange rates included excessive printing of money, or extreme deficit spending leading to rampant inflation; internal price controls which made food cheap for politically influential urban consumers but pauperized farmers; overemphasis on investment in uneconomic industry; high tariff walls to protect such investments, and more. The beneficiaries were almost always the ruling political class, which portrayed the necessary reforms as imposed by a cabal of foreigners. Such reforms, they argued, were no more than an effort to strangle national development, and were a threat to needed social services like education and health care, which in truth were all too often non-existent outside of capital cities.

"Conditionality," the word that critics used, became an epithet. Their argument in its most extreme form was that

African governments knew best, and that foreign aid should be without strings of any kind attached. I would later have a good look at the results of relatively well-crafted economic policy reform measures in Mali. But economic reform could not attack the greatest of all impediments to development, endemic political instability and outright warfare, sometimes (as in Zaire) linked with decades of US support for anti-communist dictators. This plague is still raging in Africa as this is written.

Proponents of economic reform were riding a wave that emanated mainly from the World Bank and the IMF. Our bible was a World Bank publication, *Accelerating Development in Sub-Saharan Africa*,[18] better known as the Berg Report. Our guru was the report's principal author, Elliot Berg, an economist with a rare ability to discuss economic issues in terms comprehensible to generalists. He and his wife were neighbors in Alexandria and became good friends.

By this time AF had a new Deputy Assistant Secretary in charge of economic issues, Princeton Lyman, an AID officer appointed to a State Department position. He came from a Jewish family of modest means, one of several brothers; two others were named Harvard and Yale. He was soft-spoken, unassuming and much smarter than he seemed at first glance. It was a joy to watch him negotiate, because opponents often mistook his mild manner for weakness, until they found themselves outmaneuvered in a kind of intellectual ju-jitsu. Lyman's record proves that nice guys, if they are smart, can finish first sometimes.

He later served in many senior positions, most notably as ambassador to South Africa from 1992 to 1995, during the critical period just before the election of Nelson Mandela. During this time Lyman persuaded the apartheid regime to allow USAID to support South African non-governmental organizations in preparing for multi-racial democracy.[19]

By this time President Jimmy Carter had been defeated and Ronald Reagan was assuming power, in the usual snail's pace

---

[18] The World Bank, *Accelerating Development in Sub-Saharan Africa: An Agenda for Action,* Washington, 1981.

[19] Lyman's account of this period is in his book *Partner to History: The U.S. Role in South Africa's Transition to Democracy,* Washington, U.S. Institute of Peace Press, 2002.

manner of presidential transitions in Washington. Barbara had written on January 11:

Things have been somewhat tense at the State Department ... at that stage where the sky has turned yellow and you know a big wind is about to come. In AF, the question is how much of a shift [there will be] toward hard line anti-"Marxist" policy in places like Angola and Mozambique, and above all, how much warming up toward South Africa? A lot of freight is riding on the latter and there is a great possibility that the new boys will only learn the hard way that the 'idealistic' policies now more or less in place are in fact the only practical approach. Bob may become Office Director [in AF/EPS] where he is now working, or he might be doing something totally different in four months, depending on how things go.[20]

However within a short time it appeared that the barbarians had not descended after all, at least not on the Africa Bureau. Our new Assistant Secretary, Chester A. Crocker, a Professor at Georgetown University, was a conservative, but a serious Africa hand and no right-wing radical. He was married to a white Zimbabwean, and this alone was, unfairly enough, sufficient to arouse suspicion among many liberals. He believed that it was possible to negotiate with the White South African regime and he turned out to be correct. Knowing almost nothing about the region, I was, like virtually all liberals, doubtful about his new policy of "Constructive Engagement" with the Boers, but I got along well with Chet Crocker from the start.

At the other end of our building where USAID was located things were not as rosy, at least not at first. No doubt the Republicans were ideologically opposed to foreign aid generally. Many did believe that Africa's economic salvation would have to come via the private sector, until they realized how limited it was. More importantly the Reagan transition team seemed to have decided that AID was a hot bed of liberalism or worse. Some of its early senior appointments to AID acted a bit like commissars in the Soviet Union, clearly thinking about purges.

---

[20] Barbara letter to Mother and Daddy, Kate and Mark, January 11, 1981.

Eventually suspicions cooled on both sides and not that much changed, but not before a good friend, John Mullen, had been badly startled because of me and my little blue Datsun.

Mullen was the Deputy Director of the legal staff of AID and lived (still does) around the corner from us in Old Town, Alexandria. We carpooled together, and it was another of those great carpools where all the outstanding problems of the world are solved every morning on the way to work, leaving everyone feeling encouraged and ready to face grim reality. We normally used John's car, an elderly Volvo wagon. One day when it was undergoing repairs we came in my blue Datsun, which was still sporting a Carter-Mondale bumper sticker. John borrowed my car for a luncheon errand, pulled out of the State Department basement where we parked, and stopped at the first traffic light.

Who should pull up beside him but the most feared of the new AID quasi-commissars? He leaned from his window and yelled "John, that certainly is an *interesting* bumper sticker you have!" John had not looked at the back of my car and could only sputter back that he had no idea what the man was talking about, and anyway it wasn't his car. It made a good story, and happily there were no serious repercussions; Mullen went on to be AID's senior legal officer.

My last two years in AF/EPS were about as good as a Washington assignment can be. Princeton Lyman and Chet Crocker turned out to be a great supervisory team. I was by this time the Deputy Office Director, a relatively low-ranking position for someone of my age. But now my work—and indeed the work of the whole office—changed from piecemeal advocacy of more resources for Africa toward policy work centered on the need to do something about Africa's declining economic performance, following the principles laid out in the Berg Report. It was not what anyone would have predicted for the new Reagan Administration. But these were still the days—may they return again!— when "conservative" Republicans could be more effective at realizing liberal goals than "liberal" Democrats, a paradox already epitomized by the Nixon-Kissinger opening to China in 1973.

The year that Crocker arrived, I became the AF/EPS Office Director, through no fault of mine or his. It happened because the Office Director, Don Born, was absent-minded. Born, bright and liked by everyone, was doing an excellent job. The problem was that he was facing a promotion threshold—he had to advance in grade or retire—but he forgot to make this clear to Crocker or Lyman until it was too late for them to make the necessary high-level effort on his behalf. Without going into bureaucratic detail, his problem resulted from a "bad year or two," as he put it, at the beginning of his career, resulting in slow promotions, combined with a requirement to reach a senior position within a certain number of years. The net result was that he retired and I took his place. I was suddenly in line for promotion to a senior position, which six years later would put me within range of an ambassadorship.

As an Office Director I was for the first time actually managing an entire office—the key to advancement—rather than partially supervising one secretary. That, combined with our change in direction toward policy issues, opened up opportunities for creativity as well as increased exposure to senior officialdom.

Previously, State desk officers working on African countries had had little need for economic expertise. Now they were dealing constantly with issues like debt rescheduling, multilateral aid and the mysteries of food aid (PL 480). Few of these programs were a direct responsibility of the State Department, yet they vitally affected the political progress of African countries, which was the chief concern of State Department desk officers. Some officers did not need help, but many had no economic training or aptitude, and equally little knowledge of the other agencies involved.

One of EPS's most valued roles became counseling them about what was going on and how to cope with it. We took to giving mini-seminars on the thorniest economic policy challenges, debt rescheduling being at the head of the list, and—this being before the age of e-mail—we sent cables to embassies to help demystify such topics. They were captioned "Official Informal," meaning they did not have to be cleared with other interested parties and we could be frank about subjects on which not all of the relevant US agencies agreed.

I also did quite a bit of speech writing for Crocker, on subjects like business opportunities in Africa and the importance of economic policy dialogue with the Africans. And I helped draft a memo to the Secretary of State, George Schultz, on "Africa's Economic Crisis." Schultz acted on it and the result was much greater attention to the problem, if far from enough to solve it. I received a Superior Honor Award for the Crisis memo.

Reviewing my annual performance evaluation in June, 1982, Crocker wrote:

> As a newly appointed Assistant Secretary, I was faced early in the new Administration with a number of tough personnel decisions for which previous experience had only imperfectly prepared me. My decision to promote Mr. Pringle from deputy to office director in EPS is one of the smartest personnel decisions I have made here, or anywhere else. He has blossomed gracefully into one of this Bureau's heavy hitters. His skills and force of persuasion have been particularly noteworthy in frequent interactions with the management components of AID, at a time when that organization was undergoing considerable internal realignment and when State-AID working relations had many opportunities for lapsing into negative bureaucratic contests.[21]

Even accounting for the hype required for such "efficiency reports," this one makes clear that my job in AF/EPS had turned out to be far more productive and interesting than I had anticipated.

Traveling in Style

I continued to travel. In January, 1982, I represented the State Department on a high-level trade and investment mission to four countries (Morocco, Ivory Coast, Nigeria and Cameroon).

---

[21] Chester A. Crocker, U.S. Foreign Service Evaluation Report on Robert M. Pringle for 1981-82, June 5, 1982.

Secretary of Commerce Malcolm Baldridge, the son of a Nebraska congressman and an active and respected advocate of widening trade relations with developing countries, headed the mission. A Yale graduate and industrialist, he was proud of his avocation as a professional rodeo calf roper. He often wore his trophy belt buckle on the trip, and he died five years later in a rodeo accident at the age of sixty-four.

The delegation had a dedicated US Air Force VIP airplane. It was luxury unimaginable: excellent food, drink, assigned seats which never changed during our two weeks on the road, plenty of storage space for souvenirs, and embassy staff to get us through the formalities at every stop; in other words the kind of travel normally enjoyed only by the President, Vice President and junketing congressmen. I was struck by the fact that the quality of our hotels was inversely proportional to what they charged, with the cheapest and best in Rabat (Morocco) and the most expensive and worst in Lagos (Nigeria). If I wrote anything about this five-star boondoggle, it has not survived.

My trip to warm, sunny Africa coincided with a ferocious spell of winter weather in Washington. On January 13, about a week after I departed, an Air Florida jet taking off from National Airport in snowy weather iced up and could not gain altitude. It hit the north span of the Fourteenth Street Bridge and went into the river, killing seventy-eight passengers and several motorists. Barbara and Mary Beth Stoddard, a fellow teacher at Madeira, were driving home on the George Washington Parkway at the end of the school day and were going past the bridge when it happened. It was it clear that something was going on but they had no idea what, so they just kept going. Meanwhile a Madeira bus loaded with students coming back from their Wednesday jobs on Capitol Hill had a narrow escape; they were on the other side of the river, about to cross the southbound span of the bridge, when the plane hit the northbound span and plunged nose first into the river.

Two days later, the coldest weather in almost fifty years arrived. Five-degree below zero temperatures[22] caused the external drainpipe from the kitchen sink to freeze solid. The

---

[22] In our files is a clipping confirming this extreme cold.

water company was swamped with service calls. Of course, school was called off. Barbara finally found a plumber working on a house across the street and gave him twenty-five dollars to use his blowtorch on our pipes. When I returned a week later, I got a slightly sardonic welcome home card from the family, adorned with a large snowflake, to remind me of what I had escaped jetting around the tropics and lolling on the beaches of Abidjan.

Six months later I went to another meeting of SADCC in Maseru, the capital of Lesotho, a small, mountainous country entirely surrounded by South Africa. Lesotho is one of two such enclave states, the other being Swaziland. Lesotho was created due to the influence of a famous African leader, King Moshoeshoe, and Christian missionaries, who successfully lobbied the British to protect him and his people from being swallowed up by the South Africans. As noted earlier, SADCC itself was created in 1980 to help South Africa's black neighbors, the "front line states," especially those engaged in guerilla warfare against the apartheid regime.[23]

It was certainly no accident that just before the Maseru conference there had been a particularly brazen South African raid on a guerilla camp inside Lesotho itself. As a result, most of the conference was spent delivering speeches denouncing this act, and despite Chet Crocker's efforts to attempt "Constructive Engagement" with South Africa, we felt it necessary to pronounce a vigorous denunciation of our own.

W. Haven North, the deputy director of AID's Africa Bureau, headed our delegation. We had decided to return by driving from Maseru through South Africa to Johannesburg and getting a flight to the US from there. Because of our remarks at the conference, we expected the South Africans to give us a hard time when we crossed their border with Lesotho, but we decided to proceed as planned. The border crossing is at a bridge, later made famous by the 1987 David Attenborough film, *Cry Freedom*, about the anti-apartheid martyr Steve Biko. On the Lesotho side a sleepy black guard waved us through. At the other end we anticipated a jackbooted Boer with a sneer,

---

[23] It became SADC, the South African Development Community, after apartheid ended.

and some harassment. Instead there was another sleepy black
guard, who also waved us through without comment.

From there it was an easy half-day drive on good highways
to the Johannesburg airport. But when we stopped for lunch
in a small town, racially segregated of course, our black
driver had to go elsewhere to eat, and one could sense—or
imagine—an atmosphere of oppression. I did not notice how
beautiful the countryside was, as rural South Africa would
always seem when we traveled through it frequently fifteen
years later.

Among Family and Friends

In January of 1981 the Iran hostages were freed and as the
TV broadcast their release, we had a memorable celebration
to welcome one of them, our colleague and good friend, Ann
Swift. She later called us from Wiesbaden on the way home
to see whether the Iranians had ever arrested our mutual
friend, Louise Laylin Firouz. Louise was a good friend of many
in Teheran's American community, and Ann had been staying
with her just before the hostages were seized. We were able
to determine from the Laylin family that Louise had indeed
been arrested, but had later been released.

Ann told us that shortly after the Algerian aircraft that
took them from Teheran to Algeria was airborne, the crew
broke out wine and champagne. "That is why we looked so
woozy getting off the plane in Algiers," she told us; "it had
nothing to do with 444 days in captivity." At our own party
we were also generous with the champagne, and one of our
best friends got stopped by the Alexandria police on the way
home and required to take a breathalyzer test, "which for
some reason he passed,"[24] but not before spending two hours
in Alexandria's circa 1820 jail, since demolished, seething and
empathizing with the hostages.

Outwardly Ann seemed as chipper as ever, but it became
clear that she had been damaged by her Teheran experience.
She was distressed less by her own captivity, or so it seemed,
than by the CIA's failure to safeguard the identity of her

[24] Barbara letter to Dear Family, January 25, 1981.

Iranian friends, who she believed had fallen into the hands of the Revolutionary Guards occupying the US Embassy. She decided to do no more political work and never sought an ambassadorship, which she no doubt could have had for the asking. Instead she finished out her Foreign Service career as a consular officer, had a prestigious assignment as Consul General in London, and made a late but extremely happy marriage to Paul Cronin. She died in 2004 in a tragic horseback riding accident.

In the summer of 1982, the Pringle family headed west. We parents wanted to give the children a little more education about their own country before we headed abroad again. We visited Margot, who had settled down in Sheridan, Wyoming, where my mother had vacationed and worked from the 1930s, and where I had gotten summer jobs on ranches and construction projects during high school and college. On the way out we saw something of the Middle West, following a route to the northern plains that I was familiar with from childhood trips, across the Missouri River and through the

Kate and her second husband, Mark Massel, take Barbara, Jamie and Annie for a walk in Shenandoah National Park near their cabin in the mountains.

Badlands of South Dakota.

Margot had found Wyoming State employment as manager of a historic house, reestablished her connections with the Northern Cheyenne Indians in nearby Montana, and produced a PBS television documentary on the range cattle industry, which was under threat from massive strip coal mining.[25] We visited her at the ranch of her dear friend Ellen Cotton, a Boston blue blood (descendant of Ralph Waldo Emerson) turned cowgirl for the love of it. This is where the photo of Annie with Ellen's twin dachshunds, Rough and Ready, was taken.

After visiting Margot, we drove on to Yellowstone National

On the family trip to the western US, Annie is enchanted with a pair of dachshunds, Rough and Ready, on a ranch in Wyoming.

---

[25] Later a book: Margot Liberty and Barry Head, *Working Cowboy, Recollections of Ray Holmes*, Norman, OK, 2002.

Park, where even in mid-June we found the trail to a seldom visited geyser basin which we wanted to see blocked with enough melting snow so that Annie's tennis shoes couldn't make it through, and we had to turn back. Glacier National Park also presented a challenge to Annie's footwear, but we were able reach a lodge at Sperry Glacier, where we had reservations, on horseback. Later, going over the highest mountain pass in the park, we rented small cabins rather than try to camp out in the icy wind; Barbara prepared a one-pot supper on our camping gas stove in the shower stall.

In March-April, 1983, Barbara and I returned to Indonesia, lecturing on board the *Pearl of Scandinavia* cruise ship. The trip began in Singapore and included bits of Sumatra, Bali and Java. Barbara was able to come along thanks to her colleague Bill Brown, who covered her classes at Madeira even after the cruise, originally scheduled at the same time as the Madeira spring break, was delayed for two weeks.

The most interesting stop was the island of Nias, off the west coast of Sumatra. We had never before seen this spectacular remnant of Bronze-Age Indonesia, with its communal houses built around big stone-paved courtyards. Bali was becoming crowded as tourism boomed, but Nias was still wonderful.

Aside from the onboard, slide illustrated lectures we gave for any passengers who cared to come, we enjoyed showing the "real" Indonesia to one-third of them who elected to rough it on several overland trips. On Sumatra, there was a visit to Batak country and Lake Toba, with a night at a very local hotel on the way across the island. We remember particularly translating the group's way through a thriving food market on that trip. Then there was the trans-Java expedition, from Surabaya to Jogja by train. We don't remember anything about the visits to Borobudur and Prambanan, which must have been a high point for our guests, but we do remember that the train had non-functioning air-conditioning, a situation which the hostesses tried to remedy by plying the passengers with ever more food and drink. Returning to the ship, we demonstrated our Old Indonesia Hand prowess by smuggling a durian on board to share with our table, something no Indonesia-savvy crew would ever have allowed to happen, given the notorious smelliness of this fabled Southeast Asian fruit.

On the way back to Singapore, our ship docked at the Jakarta port of Tanjung Priok, intending to refuel and install a spare part for the still underperforming engine. But the ship arrived late, after the end of the work week on Saturday noon, and the *Pearl of Scandinavia* had to make the final leg of our journey across the Straits of Malacca at slow speed. We didn't care; it had been a great, free trip.

Once home, in June we took the kids to Bob's twenty-fifth Harvard reunion, a splendid gathering as always, although it was a shock to be having my own 25th, after years spent as an undergraduate crashing the reunions of ancient graduates. (Our fabled cartoonist, David Royce, had been adept at forging passes to get us in as alumni offspring so that we could enjoy the copious free food and drink.)

By this time we knew that we were bound for Embassy Ouagadougou (WA-ga-DOO-goo) in the landlocked West African country of Upper Volta, now Burkina Faso. Chet Crocker had asked me to extend in AF, but we did not want to delay our move, because it was Jamie's final year at the Potomac School, and we wanted him to have the three years of high school all in one place. For me, Ouaga was a good, if not spectacular assignment; I would be a DCM, or Deputy Chief of Mission, in other words the ambassador's deputy. Never mind that Ouagadougou, thanks mainly to that name, was the assignment that all FSOs hoped to avoid. Any DCMship was a requisite step along the career path. Indeed, Upper Volta turned out to be an enjoyable introduction to Africa and to the very real pleasures and occasional quasi-comic hazards of life in a small, isolated embassy where everyone gets to know everyone else, including, to an unusual degree, the people who live there. Moreover, to the extent that most of Africa consisted of countries with similar problems, Upper Volta was also important.

9

From Upper Volta to Burkina Faso, 1983-1985

Ouagadougou, Haute Volta[1]

Our introduction to Africa began with a thud, as the front wheel of the embassy car we were in collapsed into a hole in the center of an unpaved street in Ouagadougou. Just arrived from Washington, we were in the middle of a thunderstorm, the night was dark, and the street unlighted. Perhaps because of the pouring rain, our driver had not noticed a tree branch placed in the hole as a warning, the customary manner of indicating such hazards. The hole itself was evidence of an old well, inadequately filled in when the dirt street was widened. And we were nervous, because the latest coup d'état, bringing a radical young army officer to power, had taken place less than a week earlier and curfew was drawing nigh.

---

[1] This Christmas card was created in Ouagadougou, but we have lost all but a photograph of it, so to the artist the only credit we can give is to say "Thank-you; we really liked your card."

My predecessor as DCM, Tony Dalsimer, with whom I overlapped by a few days, had given us dinner at his house, the one we were about to move into, and we were going back to our hotel, keenly aware of the risk of appearing to hurry past any of numerous checkpoints manned by nervous young troops. The only casualties of the recent coup had been some foreigners driving home, who had made this mistake and died for it. The curfew (*couvre feu*, or "cover fire" in French) clicked in at 11 p.m. and was not to be taken lightly. This may sound grim, but like many things in revolutionary Upper Volta, before long to be renamed Burkina Faso, it proved to have a bright side: there was no such thing as a long, tedious diplomatic dinner party. All such events had to be over and the guests on their way home by not long after 10 p.m. Nothing encourages punctuality like the risk of being shot.

Barbara's First African Job

We both started off our gainful employment with a bang. While Bob almost immediately became *chargé* because Ambassador Julius Walker left the country, Barbara began teaching the day after our plane touched down, before we were even in the house. Not a major feat, when one is teaching fewer than twenty students, and twelve of them are sixth-graders! By then, I knew the ropes of teaching, and I could wing it with introductory essays in which the students introduced themselves (English class) and stage setting for the world and American history, the other classes I would teach. Besides, the academic school day lasted from 7:15 a.m. to 12:30 p.m. Then students and teachers, as well as all embassy staff and those at every other workplace and school in Ouagadougou, went home for lunch and a siesta. The Marine Guards and the principal offered PE (physical education) some afternoons, but aside from a stray faculty meeting now and then, I had the whole afternoon, if I needed it, for planning and grading.

The International School of Ouagadougou (ISO), while it paid a pittance, was more fun than a challenge. As I described it:

The school makes me pine, intellectually, for Madeira, but it is a nice little establishment and a pleasant place to teach. The

The highly international teaching staff of the International School of Ouagadougou, a mix of local residents, Americans, and Europeans. Barbara is on the extreme left, and the gentleman in the center is the principal, David Chojnacki.

junior high, consisting of sixth, seventh, and ninth grades (There are no eighth graders), is taught by me, an English science and math teacher, and a local teacher for French language.[2]

I went on to describe my game plan for my two years there—to convert teaching in seventh and eighth grades to techniques preparatory to high school, rather than a continuation of grade-school workbooks, construction paper projects, spelling and one-line sentences. In this I succeeded somewhat, to the extent that even the director of the school admitted, when he left at the end of my first year, that his bright, but not genius, son who had skipped a grade to be in the three-student ninth grade, was way underprepared by his previous years at ISO to enter tenth grade in his new school.

---

[2] Barbara letter to whom not clear, n.d.

But my greatest success came with the seventh-grade son of missionaries who had been home schooled, very, very well, for the six years his parents had been in the hinterlands way up near the desert. He wrote beautiful, correct, and interesting sentences, but had no idea how to write a paragraph, never mind anything longer. I taught him what good grammar and spelling was supposed to be used for, and by the end of his only year at ISO he could turn out a well-organized and thoughtful essay. He went on to greater things, finally earning an MA at the Georgetown University School of Foreign Service. He invited me to his graduation there, and I have always regretted that I was out of town and could not attend.

Ouagadougou's ISO was up for reaccreditation by the Middle States Association in 1983-84. That meant that the teachers and other staff had to produce a series of essays in answer to probing questions, correlate them all, and then, after a suitable interval, receive a delegation from Virginia or the Carolinas to see if it was all true and satisfactory. Partly because writing did not scare me and partly because there would be quite a bit of staff turnover, not including me, in June, I was assigned the task of overseeing the exercise.

We passed with flying colors, in rather unusual circumstances during the inspectors' visit, as will become evident, but during our conversations, one of them remarked that he had never seen such a well-organized and stylistically coherent report from a school. It should have been; we were a small operation, with teachers of various nationalities, and I rewrote the whole thing. I was later asked to be on the evaluation committee for the school in Abidjan, but by then we were in Port Moresby, and nobody could afford the air fare from there back to West Africa. It was a good example of how nomadism is not always helpful for one's career.

For Annie, now thirteen years old, her big adventure had started in Paris, on our way out, when we were lucky enough to get tickets for an evening concert at the Sainte Chapelle. (Jamie had started his first year at Milton and was not with us.) Annie wrote:

. . . *What a waste of an evening. Stained glass windows? What a waste.*

Well, I supposed I couldn't disappoint Mom and Dad. Well,

from my first step inside the hall I loved it. The windows, in case you haven't seen them, are gorgeous!! . . . I loved every minute of the gothic music they were playing. I drifted away into an unreal world, barely clapping at all, absorbed by the beauty around me.

The next day we boarded the plane for Africa, and I took with me a very valuable lesson—the lesson of keeping your ears, eyes, and most of all your mind open . . . . [3]

This became the nucleus of her essay for admission to Madeira.

Then on to Africa via the "other" French state airline, UTA (*Union Transport Aérienne*), the one that served the colonies, while Air France flew to more prestigious destinations. In what would become a familiar routine, we flew an hour over France, a little less over the Mediterranean, then fully two hours over the vast Sahara desert, before landing in Ouagadougou, at its southern edge. The flight gave us plenty of time for a good meal, with good wine, but the meat course was "*lapin.*" Oh dear, what to do? We let nature take its course. Only later did Annie inquire what she had eaten. It was rabbit, Barbara explained. "You mean I've eaten a *bunny rabbit?*" was the inevitable, genuinely distressed reaction.

To Be a DCM

As for Bob, he hardly had time to figure out what his new role as Deputy Chief of Mission was supposed to be before he became *chargé d'affaires* (acting ambassador). Ambassador Julius Walker, his experienced and respected boss, had to be medevac'd to Paris because of chronic nosebleeds, a serious problem because he had previously had heart surgery.

I became *chargé* for the first time in strange and unsettling circumstances. Almost immediately I was summoned to the airport along with all other chiefs of mission to see Upper Volta's young and radical new President, Thomas Sankara, off on his first trip abroad, to neighboring Mali. I remember meeting Blaise Compaoré, Sankara's number two, the officer whose support, as commander of the paratroop regiment, had

---

[3] From one of our scrapbooks.

been essential to the success of his coup. Campaoré[4] seemed evasive and unfriendly, and indeed he never displayed any of Sankara's wit and charm. I was *chargé* only for a week or so and Julius returned to post with his nosebleed problem fixed and in fine fettle.

What on earth were we doing in this place, Ouagadougou? I had just become the DCM, in an embassy of about fifty American officers, technical staff, and local employees (not including a varying number of Peace Corps volunteers). It was a much smaller post than either Manila or Jakarta, with fewer agencies represented: only State, USIS, AID, Peace Corps and a Marine security guard detachment. We didn't even have a CIA Station.

US interests in the country were minimal. We provided humanitarian food aid, mostly through Catholic schools, augmented in times of famine. Through AID, we were trying to encourage more efficient and profitable agriculture. Underlying these objectives was the competition with communism and its champions, whose evil machinations were to be resisted wherever possible, for hearts, minds and stomachs. This meant having US embassies just about everywhere, a tremendous change from our *modus operandi* before the Cold War.

Having said that, Upper Volta did seem to be an unlikely battlefield. It is landlocked, slightly larger than Colorado, with only seven million people in 1983 (fifteen million at this writing). Its population subsisted almost entirely by drought-prone subsistence agriculture, without mineral resources worth mentioning (or yet exploited) and no major rivers. Under the French, it was a minor colony within French West Africa, one of two French colonial conglomerates, the other being French Equatorial Africa. Most of their component colonies were never profitable, certainly not Upper Volta. In 1932 the French, themselves hard-hit by global depression, gerrymandered it out of existence in an effort to reduce administrative costs.

But when in the early 1960s De Gaulle, anxious to avoid another Algeria-type conflict, decided to bestow

---

[4] Campaoré and his fellow junta members assassinated Sankara not long after we left the country and ruled until 2014.

independence on France's sub-Saharan possessions, whether they were ready for it or not, this place had something special: a considerable Roman Catholic population. It included Paul Zoungrana, Archbishop of Ouagadougou (more commonly known then as "Bancoville," literally "Adobe Town") and West Africa's first cardinal. It also mattered that Zoungrana was a Mossi, the country's most important and best-organized ethnic group, with a history of independent statehood. Many upper-class Mossi had become Catholics, at least nominally, after the French arrived, probably to compensate for the waning power of their traditional kingdom.[5] Together the Mossi and their French allies succeeded in having Upper Volta reinstated as one of the eight independent countries created in 1961 to replace French West Africa.

For the first decade of its independence the new country was relatively stable. Then a succession of coups d'état ensued, each bringing to power a lower-ranking, more left-leaning army officer. The latest head of state in this sequence, whose coup had taken place just before our arrival, was a mere captain named Thomas Sankara. He had been prime minister for a brief time until the previous president, a major, made the mistake of firing him. He was half Mossi and half Fulani (Peuhl), a mark of low social status, born into a Catholic family, suggesting a classic "marginal man." He was clearly a radical, but although no one knew what that really meant, pro-communist sympathies were assumed by everyone. Sankara would alternately tease, charm, amuse and frighten foreign residents, and many of his citizens, until his assassination in 1987.

Life in Ouagadougou

For American Foreign Service Officers "Ouagadougou" was code for a dreary hardship post, and our two years there did have some tiresome and fear-tinged moments. Upper Volta was hot, flat, dusty, impoverished, malarial, devoid of

---

[5] Virginia Thompson and Richard Adloff, *French West Africa*, Stanford University Press, 1957. This book gives a good account of French rule up to the date it was published, but does not cover the decision to give Upper Volta separate independence.

television worth watching or first-run movies, politically unstable—the list could be extended. But the people were charming and their rich art and culture was largely intact. As is so often the case in such places, opportunities to travel outside the capital were numerous and rewarding despite bad roads and worse lodging, if any. We learned quickly that one should always travel prepared to camp out, or to stay with Peace Corps volunteers in "their" villages, invariably a learning experience. As in Jakarta but even more so, servants, usually at least two or three of them, were a necessity not a luxury, especially when entertaining was part of the job.

In the absence of supermarkets, shopping required time and skill. Drinking water had to be boiled and double filtered. There was a washing machine, but laundry had to be hung out to dry and then ironed to make sure that no biting flies had laid eggs in it. Drivers and gardeners were expected, if not totally necessary, and a night *guardien* was essential. One of our friends employed an elderly man who arrived each evening with a traditional spear. The ubiquitous dust required constant cleaning, especially during the September-May dry season.

As a result, we all had "villages" that had to be recruited, paid, taught minimal hygiene, trained on the varying requirements of foreign employers, given medical advice, and loaned (or not) money for family emergencies. In our house, Barbara was the mayor of this village, instructing all but the driver and the gardener, and being banker and health consultant for even those. The bright side was that, with the worst will in the world, managing servants made it impossible to live in isolation from African society. We learned fast the meaning of "It Takes a Village."[6]

In such places, the American community bonds more closely than in larger, more advanced countries. On the evening of the August 4 coup d'état in which Sankara seized power, many of the American children were at the home of Karen Rugh, the embassy nurse, practicing for a variety show they were planning for the end of school vacation, when the

---

[6] The full quote is "*It Takes a Village, and other Lessons Children Teach Us*," a book published by Hillary Clinton in 1996.

older ones would depart for boarding school or college. They ended up spending the night on her floor after firing broke out. Coups having become almost routine, foreigners knew that Rule Number One was Don't Go Outside, especially after dark, until things calm down. The rule worked because, at least in Africa, foreigners were rarely the target of political unrest. Every house had a two-way radio, which all adults and teen-age children knew how to use, thanks to weekly radio checks.

As to flying back and forth from boarding schools and colleges to darkest Africa, the students, on the whole, managed fairly well. In our case Aunt Kathy helped Jamie obtain both tickets and visas. We became fairly confident about him after his flight out that first spring, when Barbara observed,

I am still skeptical about Jamie's making a connection through Charles DeGaulle in half an hour [as another student had just done because his flight from the US had been delayed]. I have to admit, though, that he is fast becoming a seasoned traveler. He spent the night in Paris with friends who did not know he was coming (thanks to the fact that we thought his ticket had been changed to Friday) and he managed to phone them, get directions, and then take a bus to their house, all with 'Merci' being his sole word of French.[7]

The next morning before his plane left, he explored by himself and managed to see the Eiffel Tower, walk under the Arc de Triomphe and "see a lot of Victorian (sic) houses." (The latter were probably those post-Hausmann mansard-roofed mansions along the Champs Elysée.) Later, despite Annie's determined suggestions that she would travel alone when she went to boarding school, she accompanied her brother until she got the hang of things.

Esprit was high in a situation where the community had to pull together, which it did through entertainment, school activities, expeditions in the country side (*en brousse,* literally "in the bush") and sports and cultural events with other expatriates, if only because there was little else to do. Everyone

---

[7] Barbara letter to family, n.d.

in the American community socialized together, with the
"Marine House," where our Marine Guards lived, providing a
traditional Friday night gathering place. Often they showed
a movie or organized special board game competitions, and
always they sold food and drink to finance the annual Marine
Ball, a high point of the social year. We had seen nothing like
it in our previous, much larger posts.

There were other distractions. The American kids hung
out together, their numbers augmented by boarding school
returnees during the summer, at Christmas, and during spring
vacation. The day after Jamie's arrival for his first spring visit,
after he had almost been snowed in leaving the US, "we piled
seven of the teenage crowd into a large van lent by USIS and
went out to a thank-you feast in a village about four hours west
of here."[8] (We can't remember what the "thank-you" was for.)
The nice thing was that all older children were welcome to
participate in such trips, from shy Sven Trahan and ebullient
Patrick Weinhold in sixth grade right through Scott Weinhold,
a couple of years older than Jamie. Despite Ouagadougou's
periodic bouts of political jitters, the teenagers also liked
to visit the *Pavilion Verte*, a somewhat dubious chicken
restaurant, as well as to ride bicycles and mobylettes (motor
scooters) around town if their parents allowed.

There was one nice restaurant in Ouagadougou, The
Zoo, so-called because a menagerie of small creatures lived
in cages in the garden. Once, just after the restaurant had
stopped taking American Express credit cards without any
notice, we celebrated a wedding anniversary there and had to
come back the next day to pay in cash. No problem; of course
the proprietor knew us.

Not long after we arrived, we saw a hilarious video of a
Ouagadougou-style golf tournament. The course had been
scraped from the thorn-scrub savanna; it had no water, but a
surfeit of sand (traps). Its "greens" (or "blacks") were made from
oiled desert grit. The video parodied big-time golf tournament
coverage, with the narrator solemnly describing the reaction
of the enthralled spectators, as the camera panned to some
ragged urchins herding goats and a parade of market women

---

[8] Barbara to Dear Family, March 18, 1984.

American children (Jamie and Anne Pringle, Scott and Patrick Weinhold) explore the local market. Their smattering of French language, plus a willingness to use gestures and smiles was all they needed to enjoy the local scene.

with baskets on their heads nearby. Especially for those who spoke reasonable French, there were plenty of opportunities for socializing with the French and other expatriates: aid workers, diplomats, researchers, missionaries and volunteers in organizations like the Peace Corps.

Our soft-spoken ambassador, Julius Walker, was thoroughly charming and very effective. He had a rich Texas accent and looked a bit like Colonel Sanders. Together with his wife, Savannah, a fellow Texan and veteran Capitol Hill staffer, he provided perfect leadership in a small post setting. His hallmark locale in Ouagadougou was the embassy rose garden. The roses were planted along paths, which crisscrossed the big embassy compound courtyard.

The embassy consisted of a rectangle of modest buildings set flush with the unpaved street, with no setback at all, around four sides of a city block. The complex had once been the villa of a Mossi notable, and included his stable, servants' and wives' quarters, and so on. It was constructed entirely of mud brick, "banco" in local parlance, the same as adobe. Except for the embassy communications unit, which had been lined with concrete to approach normal security standards, the walls could easily be penetrated with a hand-held steel reinforcing rod. They were in constant danger of dissolving during the summer rainy season when, I discovered soon enough, my office roof leaked copiously.

Ambassador Walker arrived every morning about twenty minutes before opening of business to prune his roses, planted along the central courtyard paths. They were a special orange variety which did well in the African heat, and I have always wished I had them to plant in Alexandria. If you had a problem to chat about with the Chief of Mission, this was when and where you could find him, without fail, ready to listen.

For a while, Ambassador Walker also ran an informal chicken business. Good eggs were in short supply in Ouaga, small and expensive, so he set up a row of coops in back of the Residence and sold the eggs to friends and embassy personnel. They were nice big ones from obviously well-fed, American-style chickens and I told him he should brand them "Eggs Plenipotentiary," but his wife Savannah decided that that it wouldn't be ambassadorial for him to sell them. However, he liked his small chicken farm, so for the rest of his tour, we got them for nothing.

Julius had other seemingly un-Texan habits. One of his hobbies was doing needlework to relax; one year he provided a whole nativity scene for the annual Christmas fair, or *kermesse,* at the International School. And he was an extremely talented actor, performing in several expatriate drama productions while ambassador. But he was a real Texan, no doubt. He came from Plains, a very small town in the West Texas panhandle, and while he was in Ouaga he discovered that, by an incredible coincidence, his secretary was also from Plains. A short time later, she married one of our communicators, who was also the US Embassy golf champion. As you can see we were never short of things to talk about.

A month after our arrival, we got a taste of the ambassador's thespian skill when the Ouagadougou Way Off Broadway Players staged Woody Allen's *Please Don't Drink the Water,* about a confused American tourist who gets ensnared in a devious communist plot "somewhere behind the Iron Curtain." A sizeable proportion of the American community was involved in the production. Julius, wearing a loud Hawaian shirt, played the befuddled tourist; Savannah was a confused Slavic countess who gets caught up in the drama; Carroll Bouchard, our Peace Corps Director, who looked more like a senior diplomat than the ambassador did, was the US envoy to Yuckovakia; USIS Public Affairs Officer Bill Weinhold was a devious communist operative; Russell Perdue, a very talented Marine security guard, was the ambassador's obsequious aide; the director of the International School was the ambassador's son and the Peace Corps nurse the tourist's daughter; a missionary from up country was an Orthodox Priest (he happened to be named George Zagarac) and so on. Everyone of course got a bang out of seeing friends, some of them authority figures in everyday life, in hilarious transformation, and indeed we have rarely seen anything that could beat Woody Allen in Ouagadougou for sheer entertainment value.

Aside from occasional bouts of *chargé*-ship my duties as DCM were not onerous. I did not need to spend much time

The Way-Off-Broadway Players present *Please Don't Drink the Water*.

"managing" the Mission, in theory the primary role of any DCM. Our major agencies, AID and Peace Corps, had competent heads of their own. Our consular and administrative officers rarely needed my assistance. As noted above, morale, often another major DCM preoccupation, was good at this "hardship post." I had time for plenty of reporting on whatever topics I found interesting, backing up Joyce Leader, our political/economic officer. Our workday was divided by a two-hour lunch/siesta break. Since the drive home took less than five minutes, I could return for lunch or a quick nap or swim, or have guests for lunch, or stay at the office for two hours of undisturbed work.

Somewhat surprisingly, we had quite a few official visitors. One of the first and best was the Director of the US Peace Corps, Lorette Ruppe, the great-granddaughter of the man who established the Miller beer company, and not unaccustomed to luxury. But she was also a dedicated, capable Peace Corps Director and a very pleasant visitor. We enjoyed taking her to visit volunteers and showing her a Ouaga *dolo* (beer) "factory": rows of earthenware pots in a dusty courtyard, boiling down the millet-based contents of the local, non-Miller, non-Light brew. But the highlight of her visit was a call on the President, accompanied by the local Peace Corps Director, Carroll Bouchard.[9] It produced one of the more memorable Thomas Sankara stories.

The meeting took place at Sankara's "temporary" office, not far from where we lived, in the *Conseil de l'Entente*, one of many West African regional organizations, which he preferred to the official presidential residence. It was dusty and miserably hot in his office, really hot, making it hard to concentrate on the agenda.

Finally, as the meeting appeared to be ending, Sankara asked his perspiring guests, "I suppose you wonder why it's so hot in here?" There were murmured negatives; no one could say, "Well we suppose your AC isn't working, like so many other things in Africa." So Sankara explained that after he became president, two of the young Peace Corps Volunteers who had been his friends during his political exile in the provinces had

---

[9] The Ruppe visit is partially covered in Barbara letter to Dear Family, November 13, 1983.

come to pay him a visit. They had looked around at his new and luxurious surroundings. "Well," one of them said, "you didn't live like this when we knew you in Dedegou. You didn't have air conditioning then."

So, concluded Sankara, "I always turn off the air conditioning when I have Peace Corps visitors."

By this time we had pretty well settled into our new African home. Our house was roomy with a big yard and swimming pool. Every American had a swimming pool, including our AID employees, despite an AID regulation forbidding them, which had resulted from some idiotic Congressional investigation. Before our arrival the embassy had gotten around the ban by arguing that pools served as auxiliary water supplies, which was true.

During the winter, when hot winds blew from the desert, the pool was covered with a thin film of dust. "This is one of the few places in the world where you can be wet and dusty at the time," someone joked. In the garden there was a big tree that our little dog Pax loved to run around, soon wearing a circular path. He also liked to sit and cool off on the top step of the pool, to the point where his constant fluffy white dampness resulted in a skin infection and a trip to the vet.

I did a lot of gardening and discovered that American sweet corn, the seed acquired via the diplomatic pouch, grew beautifully outside our compound wall—no disease problems at all in the dry climate. Silver Queen was a hit at several dinner parties, the only corn available locally being tough as nails. No one ever stole my corn, although in the end a soldier told me that growing it in our dead-end street was forbidden for security (sic) reasons, so that we had only one season of Silver Queen.

We were in a "high security zone" because of our proximity to Sankara's office. The neighborhood was heavily guarded, and we had a machine gun emplacement on the corner. "Fort Apache," as we called it, became progressively more fortified, its bored crew having little to do other than rearrange the sandbags. Of course they were friendly to the American kids living nearby, and when several of them, including Annie's best friend's little brother, went out with a camera, the soldiers wanted to pose, holding their Kalashnikovs, as his horrified parents discovered when the film came back from processing.

For adults, even carrying a camera could be dangerous, especially around airports. Early in our stay, a group of Peace Corps volunteers went to the airport to welcome a contingent of new volunteers. As the deplaning volunteers walked toward the terminal, their colleagues on the balcony above them gleefully unrolled a big banner reading "Welcome to Peace Corps Chad!" This was supposed to be funny because there was a hot war going on in Chad at the time, but when several of the newcomers pulled out cameras to record it, the rest of us nearly had heart attacks.

Then there was the "Waiting for Godot" episode. Across the street from us lived a French aid technician who was the kingpin of a very active music and drama group with wide-ranging tastes. Although he adored American jazz and had a jazz ensemble, he didn't seem to like Americans and we never got to know him. During the frequent rehearsals at his house there was always a crowd of cars in his compound. On this occasion the play being rehearsed was *Waiting for Godot*, and the performers stayed way too late. When they realized it was curfew time they all left at once, buzzing their motors and stirring up a cloud of dust. I was out walking Pax in front of our gate when the guard at Fort Apache, just down the street, suddenly woke up as the cars passed by, and expressed his unhappiness by firing a burst from his gun, fortunately in the air and not at the cars or me.[10]

Annie in the French Lycée

Annie was thriving during her big adventure in the fourth year (*quatrième*) class, the equivalent of our eighth grade, at the French *Lycée St. Exupéry*. We had naturally worried about her sudden immersion in French education. She had virtually no French beyond a few weeks of tutoring in Washington and Ouaga. We had heard all the stories about how tough French schools could be on foreign students, and Bob remembered his initially unpleasant experience at age twelve in Switzerland. We were also taken aback by the apparent casualness of

---

[10] Bob letter to Dear Family, October 24, 1983.

the *"Lycée St Ex,"* as everyone called it. Although our French friends had a high opinion of it, and it got high ratings in the annual surveys of all *lycées* everywhere, many of its faculty were very late getting back from their long summer vacations.

We need not have worried. It was clear from the beginning that whatever Annie's academic achievements at the *lycée* might be, she was going to be a social success. Both faculty and students found it just fine to have this bright, charming American in their midst. She rapidly discovered that she was learning enough French vocabulary to communicate well with her friends, but she also concluded that learning grammar was less important to her social life, a shortfall that would later cause some trouble in formal French classes back home.

Her friends included the class leader, the *chef de file*, son of the French aid mission director, whose aristocratic name (François Peyredieu du Charlat) caused us to have frivolous visions of her marrying a French nobleman. The English teacher, instead of requiring her to follow British grammar and spelling rules, viewed her as a resource who could introduce everyone to American English. Some of her success was no doubt attributable to the fact that *quatrième* was a down year in the highly standardized French system; it did not precede any of the important, threshold tests, and everyone could afford to be a little relaxed.

By the end of 1983, we were feeling at home. Barbara had acquired some bourbon whiskey on her first trip to the West African Overseas Schools Conference in Lomé, Togo, and some angostura bitters had arrived with our shipment of consumables, so by my birthday we had the makings for Old Fashioneds, my favorite cocktail.

Ouagadougou itself seemed mostly like a big village, and because it was so flat one could get thoroughly lost in it. There was one avenue of modern office buildings and a station for the little used rail line connecting us with Abidjan, on the coast in Côte d'Ivoire. There were one or two old, French-era hotels near the market plus a new one with more modern facilities on the edge of town, the Silmandé, where many foreign visitors stayed. There was a ramshackle central market, the most famous aspect of which was the meat section, which boasted big vultures perched over the stalls. This impressed our Marines so much that one year they used a vulture motif to decorate the T-shirts they designed and sold to support their annual birthday ball (about which more below). In general, Ouagadougou retained its traditional African character, far less Europeanized than the country's commercial capital of Bobo Dioulasso, half a day's drive to the west.

The most interesting sight in Ouaga was its *raison d'être*, the palace of the Moro Naba, the Mossi king. In a weekly ceremony the monarch, fed up with squabbling among his subjects, decides to leave. His horse is saddled and ready to go, when, at the last minute, his courtiers cluster around him and beg him to stay, which he finally does.[11]

Thomas Sankara, Our Tragic Leader

Our biggest preoccupation was, and remained throughout our stay, Sankara's radicalism. Was he fundamentally hostile to the West, or simply waving red flags to mobilize his people? His revolutionary rhetoric and gimmickry intensified over time, but he never did anything truly radical, like breaking Upper Volta's tie to the French franc and establishing his own central bank. Of course he knew that other radical African leaders, like Sékou Touré of Guinea and Modibo Keita of Mali, had taken such steps in the 1960s, without any positive results.

Instead Sankara did things like mobilizing his civil servants to build a railroad by hand to an allegedly rich manganese deposit in the north of the country. He held show trials for corruption, proof of which included transgressions like owning a refrigerator. He invited his friend Jerry Rawlings, president of neighboring Ghana, to visit Ouaga and join him in giving fiery speeches. By this time conditions in Ghana, just to our south, were so bad that Peace Corps volunteers there were being evacuated from small towns in the interior where food was no longer available unless you grew it yourself. Things were never as dire in Upper Volta, thanks largely to its hard, French-backed currency.

---

[11] The current (2012) Wikipedia version, in which the monarch is dissuaded by his subjects from going to war with enemy tribes and makes peace instead, differs markedly from the version we saw in 1983, see http://en.wikipedia.org/wiki/Moro-Naba_Ceremony. Oral history by its nature changes over time.

Indeed, with the help of a European aid project, the country had made real progress in developing exports of fruits and vegetables to Europe during the northern winter. It worked so well that at one point there were too many green beans to fit on the French UTA flights. Sankara portrayed this as an imperialist plot, and it became everyone's revolutionary duty to consume more green beans; the local radio station broadcast recipes for cooking them. At the same time he ignored obvious possible sources of revenue like seriously taxing alcohol, mainly consumed by the imperialists, whoever THEY might be. For much or our stay we could buy single malt scotch whiskey and the like from a mud-brick shop owned by a Lebanese resident, at prices much lower than at any duty-free outlet elsewhere.

Increasingly, Sankara did things that seemed designed simply to pop Uncle Sam's garter. In November of 1984, he ordered us not to hold the annual Marine Ball, among the biggest events on any American embassy social calendar, always a black tie event held on or near November 10, the anniversary of the founding of the Corps. This was serious indeed. In a letter home, Bob had explained, only partly in jest,

The Marines are a great addition. Their main role is to provide entertainment to the teen-agers, including Annie, who now has her room decorated with ferocious Join the Marines posters. Secondarily they provide security for the Embassy.[12]

There were five of them, all under twenty-one, plus the detachment commander, or "gunny," for gunnery sergeant. They had been working for weeks, "selling tickets like mad all over town but primarily in places like the Dutch Embassy which is well supplied with rosy-cheeked secretaries."[13]

The alleged reason for the banning of the Marine Ball was that the recent US invasion of Grenada had aroused bitterness among the Upper Volta people, making it unsafe for us to hold the ball. The real reason might have been that Reagan had stated that our invasion was to safeguard foreign citizens.

---

[12] Bob letter to Dear Family, October 30, 1983.
[13] Ibid.

To Sankara, that could have sounded like a pretext for what we now call regime change, in Upper Volta.[14] In any case, the cancellation attracted the ire of none other than Secretary of State George Schultz, an ex-Marine, who had never before paid the slightest attention to our little country.

Evidence of Sankara's dark side continued to mount. At about this time he created Committees for Defense of the Revolution (CDRs), possibly inspired by Cuban practice, to emphasize the dangers facing Upper Volta. There were frequent flights of Libyan and Soviet aircraft into Ouagadougou and since our house was near the airport we could often see them landing and taking off. What were they up to? It was obvious that there was tension between the young president and other members of his ruling group, in particular a few alleged communists even more radical than he was. In fact, we had little information about the internal workings of the regime and relied considerably on briefings by French military intelligence officers at their embassy. Having had a CIA station might or might not have improved matters.

One of the annoying things about this situation was that our neighboring US Embassy to the north, in Niamey (Niger), kept sending reports to Washington about what a dangerous radical Sankara was. The ambassador there, William Robert Casey, was a Republican political appointee and, in real life, a mining engineer from Colorado. He had been active in Republican state politics, so he wrote the White House asking to be named ambassador to Niger. It just so happened that Niger was a major uranium producer, but no one saw any conflict of interest, so his wish was granted.

The Nigerien president, Seyni Kountché, was a crusty general, somewhat to the right of Attila the Hun and a great friend of the Free World, the antithesis of our own young Thomas, whom he detested. He kept telling Ambassador Casey what a scoundrel Sankara was, and Casey, hanging on his every word, reported all his remarks whole cloth to Washington, copying his cables to us. But if we had appeared to be defending Sankara against what we saw as exaggerations, our views would of course have been dismissed as clientitis, all the more so since Julius was

---

[14] Barbara letter to Dear Family, November 13, 1983.

already suspected of not being tough enough with Sankara. So there was nothing we could do but steam.

Then we learned that in the course of a call on his Nigerien contact, Ambassador Casey's CIA Station Chief had parked his Volkswagen in the wrong place at Kountché's presidential palace. For this mistake, Kountché's nervous guards had riddled his car with bullets, one of which grazed the Station Chief's head, effectively scalping him. He was not seriously injured, but for weeks he had to wear a big bandage on his head. We liked to think that Embassy Niamey minded its own business a little more after that.

Not that we didn't have excitement of our own. One morning in May, 1984, while Julius was away and I was *chargé*, Barbara and I were awakened by a loud BANGBANGBANG noise. To my sleep-clogged ears it first sounded as if someone had grabbed hold of our gate and was shaking it violently back and forth. Annie came hurtling down the corridor from her room and jumped into bed with us. The noise was coming from Fort Apache, whose machine gun had been upgraded to an anti-aircraft piece, probably brought in by one of those Soviet or Libyan flights. It soon developed that the new Committees for Defense of the Revolution were holding an exercise to repel imaginary, imperialist-backed mercenaries parachuting in to seize Ouagadougou. Next day the government newspaper would proclaim triumphantly "Le Peuple à Repondu Prêt." (The People have Answered at the Ready.)[15]

The first phone call came from the principal of the International School, where classes had to be cancelled and our citizens warned to stay home. This was awkward, because the team to accredit the school had recently arrived from the United States, and on this, their final day, was going to visit the school in session. Staying in an empty house near the airport, not only were they scared to death, but they never did see any actual teaching going on at the school. They accredited the school anyway.

As *chargé*, I authorized a diplomatic note to the government pointing out that bullets fired in the air had to come down

---

[15] Bob and Barbara letter to Dear Family, May 2, 1984; the *Sidwaya* editorial quoted is in the relevant scrapbook.

somewhere, maybe in the nearby "Zone de Bois," where many US Embassy families lived. The recipients had probably never read "I Shot an Arrow in the Air," but they were not amused.

Not long afterwards Sankara summarily executed seven officials for alleged coup plotting, apparently due to tension between him and the more radical (left-wing) group. Never before had there been this kind of political killing in Upper Volta. At about the same time, he closed *L'Observateur*, the only remotely independent newspaper in the country. His random potshots at the US became more frequent. In a letter clearly understated for family consumption, Barbara wrote:

Politically the situation continues somewhat iffy, with our hyper-talkative young president continuing to woo the Cubans and other "progressives," lambast us over issues like Nicaragua, which we think are none of his business, and generally talk as if there were an invading mercenary army behind every bush. We are compelled to tell him if he continues this behavior it will have a bad effect on our relations, which given the political realities in Washington is probably accurate. Presumably that means cutting aid, but since the food aid, which is the most valuable aid we give, is sacrosanct, "humanitarian," the message gets somewhat garbled. Also we are well behind the French and Germans as donors here, and just barely ahead of the Dutch and Canadians, none of whom gives a hoot about what they say in the UN ....[16]

Cultural Wealth in a Poor Country

All this sounds a bit scary in retrospect, but we continued to enjoy the country and the many interesting things about the work. Early on we had discovered a fascinating area south of Ouagadougou, near the Ghanaian border. It included the Nazinga game park, featuring some elephants, not many by East African standards, and hard to find because of the roadless, scrub-forest terrain, but elephants nonetheless. Also, although we didn't fully appreciate it at the time, Nazinga had a population of horse-size Roan Antelope,

[16] Barbara letter to Dear Family, Memorial Day, 1985.

among the most sought-after sightings in Africa. There were plenty of huge baobab trees and interesting Gurunsi villages, beautifully painted structures reminiscent of American Indian pueblos, with all residents in one rambling mud-brick structure. Barbara described one of them:

The chief has twelve wives, and they live in twenty-eight rooms, all connected by narrow hallways, that are half sunken in the ground and then roofed over with branches and mud, creating the effect of caves, lit by holes in the roof. There is only one entrance, aside from the entrances by holes in the roof, which is also a living area. On the roof are also little round, straw-roofed huts for young men. The whole is spotlessly clean, swept incessantly to get rid of dust, and the kitchen hearths are adorned with whole walls of stacked up, nicely decorated clay pots.[17]

These villages became favorite destinations for visitors who wanted to see some exotic African culture, but had limited time. We later learned that the term "Gurunsi" was a somewhat derogatory Mossi term for anyone who was not a Mossi; the more correct term for this group, which straddles the border with Ghana, is "Kasena."

The family reunited for Christmas of 1983 in Ouagadougou. With lots of logistical help from Kathy and Barbara's parents, Jamie came out from Milton to join us. Because there was no English-language high school in Ouagadougou, the government was paying for his boarding school costs and up to three round trips per year to join his parents, as it would later do for Annie at Madeira. We decided to visit Mali, where our friend Parker Borg was serving as US Ambassador. Bamako was a 600 mile round trip from Ouaga, and of course we had no idea that we would be living there three years later. This was a "familiarization" trip for me, so we got to use one of the embassy's Ford Broncos, an initial effort to manufacture an American 4x4, unreliable and leaking dust through every joint, but required, until several years later, by our "Buy American" policy.

Parker was engaged to Anna Lehel, whom I had known when she was the Liberia Desk Officer and I was in AF/EPS. They gave

[17] Ibid.

a lunch for us and for archaeologists Susan and Rod McIntosh, already famous for their landmark work at the ancient Malian city of Djenné-Djenno (old Djenné). Their excavations had demonstrated that, contrary to prevailing opinion, urbanization had taken place in sub-Saharan Africa prior to the arrival of Islam (i.e., that black Africans had developed cities without "foreign" assistance). Almost three decades later, and partly because of this connection, Rod McIntosh, by that time a professor at Yale, would enable Barbara to find a new home at Yale's Peabody Museum for the unique Timeline of Beads from the Bead Museum in DC, which had had to close due to lack of funds.

The next stop was modern Djenné, half a day's drive down the Niger River from Bamako. We admired its great mosque, surely one of the most spectacular mud-brick edifices in the world, and we were able to photograph not only its exterior but also the interior, later not allowed. Our visit even included a climb to the roof, interesting and imposing in its own right, but also giving a marvelous view of the main market square below. A very special photo in our Mali album shows Jamie and Anne enjoying Djenné from the roof. We would visit the mosque again many times during my tour in Mali as ambassador; even the children, in Bamako on school vacations, took friends to visit it again.

From Djenné we followed what would become a well-worn trajectory, down the Niger to Mopti. There we admired the great riverine market, with its fleets of *pirogues* and slabs of Saharan salt, "a great place to buy fifty-foot long Tuareg wedding blankets [actually Peuhl wedding tent liners], just what we need to wrap around 216 Wolfe Street."[18] (But we did not buy any, at least not for another four years.) We spent the night in a *relais* (modest French-run hotel) facing on the river that would become familiar to us. After a morning drive into the nearby Dogon Country and a final night in the *campement* at Sangha (an even more modest, and in this case Malian-run, lodging)[19] we drove back to Ouagadougou, a thirteen-hour trip over dirt roads, mostly atrocious. Jamie left the next day to return to Milton.

The next big adventure was an International School outing

---

[18] The Mali trip is covered in Bob to Dear Family, January 1, 1984.

[19] In the standardized French system of naming hostelries in colonies and former colonies, a *relais* is the middle quality lodging and a *campement*, though not necessarily tents, is the most modest.

to Park W, a little-known tri-national game park shared by Niger, Upper Volta and Benin. It was supposed to last for three days. Barbara was one of four chaperones for twenty-two sixth-, seventh- and ninth-graders, plus Annie. Remembering very sensible Girl Scout practice in the US, Barbara informed all parents that, in case of trouble, the DCM would be the emergency contact person.

Getting to Park W by road required an all day trip, mostly over "*pistes*" (unpaved tracks), so the school hired Air Volta's only plane, a Fokker Friendship, augmented by a much smaller aircraft to take the group out and back. Accommodations in the park were at another *campement* near a river, and while the kids didn't see lions or elephants (they both existed at Park W but did not show themselves), there were many types of antelope plus buffalos, warthogs, hippos, and interesting birds. In addition, the roar of lions could be heard each night; the hotel manager told his guests they all lived across the river in Benin. The students had a good time chasing little rodents called agoutis around a hillock, and, while out game viewing, they got a kick out of going to another country by stepping across the international border with Benin on small unguarded bridge.

However, when departure time arrived, only the little plane showed up at the appointed hour; it left right away with two chaperones and several of the older students who had weekend commitments. I, Barbara, can remember wondering what would happen if the big plane did not arrive at the grassy, unlighted landing strip before darkness set in. As dusk loomed, I persuaded the manager of the *campement* to radio the Ouaga airport, and the answer was supplied: the plane could not land, and in fact it had never left the capital. No explanation as to why, but it left stranded almost twenty students and two chaperones, me and a parent volunteer who spoke only English. The big plane didn't appear the next day, a Saturday, either; I spent most of the day on the radio in a fruitless effort to figure out whether, and if so when, it was coming.

One of the advantages of Foreign Service, missionary, and other International School kids is that they are flexible. And so the students made their own amusements by climbing "Agouti Hill," all of about 20 feet high; swimming in the puddle-sized pool; and in general fooling around, in a good way. The *campement* staff laid on a couple of extra game drives, which occupied time, but to the kids' chagrin, they sighted only more antelopes—no big game, though they all swore they heard the lions roar not far away.

Meanwhile at the *campement* food was running low, so the cheerful staff ignored the park's "no fishing" rule and caught big Nile Perch for dinners. *Pintard* (guinea fowl) eggs and then some of the *pintards* themselves provided other meals. There was still lots of bread, or else flour to bake it, and the innkeepers opened the last bottles of wine for the adults. They produced some appropriate-for-tweenagers French dance music (*"Comment ça va? Comme ci, comme ça!"*).

By Saturday evening, parents of the stranded children were getting more nervous by the hour. So the emergency contact person, aka Bob, started to organize a rescue flotilla of all-terrain vehicles, mostly from USAID, for a road trip to Park W on Monday, in case there was no progress with air transport on Sunday. Happily, some Air Volta pilots were French and one of the Dutch parents knew them; he found out that the difficulty was that the insurance for the plane had lapsed, and, correctly, Air Volta would not fly without it. What machinations took place we will never know, but the insurance was somehow paid early Sunday, and the plane finally did appear, late in the afternoon and at a landing strip with some lights farther away from the park.

Pupils, chaperones, and even the *campement* manager and his wife, by then exhausted, got back to Ouagadougou forty-eight hours late, well after dark, only to have the immigration authorities insist on stamping all the kids' passports, which I had fortunately required them to bring.[20] (Of course, we had never officially been out of Upper Volta.)

Princess Anne Visits

At about this time the embassy learned that Her Royal Highness (HRH) Princess Anne of Great Britain was coming to Upper Volta in her capacity as the royal patroness of (British) Save the

---

[20] The Park W expedition is covered in Bob and Barbara letter to Dear Parents, February 6, 1984.

Children. The British Embassy advance team contacted Julius with a dilemma: they had looked at all the hotels in Ouaga and had deemed none of them appropriate for Royal Occupancy, not even the Silmandé, which we thought was pretty good. So they asked, since there was no British Embassy in Ouaga, if the Princess could stay with Ambassador and Mrs. Walker at the US Residence? Julius said she could, with three conditions. Most importantly, the British (not us) would have to get permission from the Upper Volta government and explain to it why Upper Volta's hotels weren't good enough. Second, it would be appreciated if she could attend a small dinner party at the Residence to meet some resident Americans. Finally, he concluded, would she greet the rest of the embassy staff informally? And so it came to pass, exceeding all expectations.

She did stay at the Residence, in a downstairs suite looking out on the pool. The dinner happened the evening of her return from visiting Save the Children projects in the north. It included Julius and Savannah, the British Ambassador and his wife, based in Abidjan, the head of British Save the Children, HRH's Private Secretary, her Lady-in-Waiting, our AID Director, Emerson Melaven, and Barbara and me. Just before Princess Ann came upstairs for dinner, her Equerry (security person) told Barbara, "YOU talk to her; we've been talking to her for three days."

I got to sit next to HRH. She was very pretty, very talkative, and very knowledgeable about humanitarian aid to poor countries. The Lady-in-Waiting, Legge-Bourke, the wife of a wealthy businessman in Wales, was "a real firecracker, replete with flowery wardrobe and rapid-fire commentary on everything." We learned that there was a pool of "LiWs" who took turns accompanying HRH on her travels, in the role of combination senior staff and companion. There was also a dresser who turned out to be a wardrobe mistress and errand runner.

Next came the promised meeting with the embassy and school staff. First there was a photo op with the Marine Guards at Post One, outside the entrance to our offices. The Marines were a bit nervous and had trouble smiling. HRH announced, "They always say 'Cheese' is the best way to get people to smile, but there's a better word . . . BITCH!" which indeed produced grins. Then we went outside for the main event.

*Ambassador Julius Walker escorts Princess Anne into the embassy courtyard
to greet staff members and ISO teachers and pupils, on the occasion of her
visit to Burkina Faso as patroness of British Save the Children.*

HRH had asked us to include everyone. We were to
distribute ourselves as is done at the Queen's Birthday Party at
Buckingham Palace,[21] in small groups around the big embassy
courtyard crisscrossed by the ambassador's rose bushes. We
were not to move; she would move to us, accompanied by one
or two of her staff and Julius, who would make introductions.
She spent forty-five minutes doing this, speaking with the
Americans in English and with our Voltaic staff in fluent
French, not missing anyone. Annie was very annoyed because
although the older students from the International School
were invited, the Lycée kids were not. Barbara, having met
our royal guest the evening before at dinner, stayed at school
to supervise the children in kindergarten and Grade 1, who
were not invited to the embassy garden function.

When HRH departed, there were no more skeptics about
just how good British Royalty could be, and not a few who

---

[21] The Princess Anne visit, including direct quotes, is from Bob letter to Dear
Family, February 25, 1984, typed on the back of a January 31 cable from the
British outlining a preliminary version of the schedule for HRH's visit.

couldn't help wishing that she instead of her brother Charles could have been heir to the throne. But in fairness we had never seen him at work. Julius named the room where Anne stayed the Princess Anne Suite, with an appropriate plaque.

Back to real-world Ouagadougou: The month of HRH's visit brought another wave of coup rumors and new check points sprouted all over town. Some overeager soldiers shot and killed a local driver about two hundred yards from our house. In the same letter describing Princess Anne's visit I wrote:

If you go very slowly and talk to the soldiers you are really quite safe, but most people who don't thread this maze [of checkpoints] every day (and some who do) are put off and frightened by the whole thing. The reason for all the nervosity [sic] seems to be rumors of anti-government plotting by various exile groups in France and the Ivory Coast. Having done it himself, Sankara knows how easy it is.[22]

In addition, an American researcher with an aid project we'd just visited broke her neck in an automobile accident and needed immediate attention not available in Africa. We called an excellent new Swiss-based medevac service and their flying ambulance took off from Europe, but lower-level authorities in Ouaga said it couldn't land after the curfew, which would have diverted the flight and delayed its arrival by a day. So Julius called Sankara, who was most gracious, said of course the plane could come in, told his people to cooperate and offered us a helicopter (which we didn't need). "Even so, taking the ambulance through a series of itchy trigger checkpoints at 3:00 am turned out to be somewhat hair raising."[23]

We also experienced our first really bad dust storm. They got worse as the rainy season approached, perhaps even more so in the dread circumstances when the rains were failing, as they did in 1984-85. This may have been one of the few days when Barbara's sixth-grade class, normally a model of good behavior, refused to settle down. She reported that they were totally distracted by the fact that the sky was red and

[22] Ibid.
[23] Ibid.

the street lights stayed on; they said it should be a holiday—
like a snow day at home. (Of course they had already had one
unexpected holiday on the day of the live-fire exercise to repel
the imaginary mercenary invaders.)

In March we had our first visit from Chris Roy, Professor of
Art History at the University of Iowa. He had been a Peace Corps
Volunteer in Upper Volta and had helped set up a state art and
crafts center, which slid into mediocrity after his departure.
Now, having finished graduate work in art history and become a
professor, he was returning on a series of Fulbright Fellowships,
studying, as he would title his eventual book, the art of the Volta
Rivers.[24] He focused mostly but not exclusively on the masks that
were danced for ceremony and entertainment.

Some of this art had been famous in the world of museum
curators and art dealers for decades, but few people had seen
it in use in the communities where it came from or knew what
kind of art was still being produced, a gap that Chris aimed
to fill. Unlike some scholars, he loved to share his knowledge
with anyone who was interested. We were, and he took us to
where the art was, opening our eyes to wonderful things that
we would never have seen without him. And, of course, we
learned more about rural areas, which was part of my job.

Upper Volta's art was barely beginning to be commercial-
ized. There were very few dances or other cultural displays
put on for tourists, no doubt because there were hardly any
tourists. Dancing with masks was a dry season activity, when
there was no farming to be done. Many masks represented
an animal that was the totem of a certain lineage or clan:
antelopes, fish, serpents (sometimes toweringly tall),
"butterflies" (actually bats) and much more.[25] Styles and

---

[24] Christopher Roy, *Art of the Volta Rivers*, Paris, Alain et Françoise
Chaffin, 1987. He also wrote a book on Mossi art, the subject of his PhD
dissertation: Christopher D. Roy, *Mossi*, Vision of Africa Series, Milan,
Continents Editions, 2015.
[25] See especially pictures taken at a Cotton Harvest festival at Dosi, in March,
1985, to which we were taken by Chris Roy. Some of the pictures he took
there, of the same subjects I photographed, are in *Art of the Upper Volta
Rivers*. Our pictures are captioned in the relevant green scrapbook but not
in the big portfolio, and the original slides are in material I've given to the
Smithsonian Museum of African Art, as part of their Eliot Elisofon collection,
although we do have copies of them.

Plank masks like this one are among Burkina Faso's most famous art, and "dancing" one, as shown here at what was just a rehearsal, obviously requires a great deal of shoulder strength.

customs varied greatly, from one ethnic group to another. The Mossi, many of whom were still animists despite their nominally Roman Catholic elite, took the religious function of mask ceremonial seriously and did not often display it to foreigners.

Others groups were more relaxed, and their art was just as interesting. On the main road to Bobo Dioulasso there was one village of the Bwa people, with a Catholic Mission, which staged relatively well-known public performances of the approximately four-foot tall plank masks for which the country is famous. These are so heavy that the dancer must have linebacker physique; even though all he does is rotate his shoulders rapidly, causing his rough fiber costume to fly around. Unlike the animal masks, it is not clear what the plank masks represent.

Dancing was sometimes, but not always, done on market days. Finding such performances was not easy because some markets happened on specific days of the week (e.g. every Saturday), while others took place at intervals of four or five days (Monday, then Friday, then Tuesday, etc,). One of the newspapers in Ouaga printed a list of upcoming markets, with dates, which helped a little. Many were a long way away, and getting there meant either arriving at the village the night before, or at dawn. Performances took place as the market was winding down, but exactly when that might be was anybody's guess. However, via his contacts, Chris found out how you could see masks that would make a museum drool with envy.

These market dances were always festive affairs. The masks seemed to be in friendly competition. *Griots*, members of the musician/entertainer class, and traditionally very low on the social scale, drummed away furiously to guide and encourage the dancers. Women, who rarely had a role in serious ritual dancing, joined with gusto, as if showing the dancers how it should be done. Everyone kicked up clouds of dust, a necessary part of the artistic ambience; Barbara noted that if a Voltaic dance troupe ever went abroad, it would have to take bags of dust along.[26] "Policemen," wearing monkey masks, chased the children around under the guise of keeping the dance floor clear. There were sometimes huge clay pots filled to the brim with *dolo* (beer) for all

---

[26] Bob and Barbara letter to Dear Family, January 27, 1985.

Masked dancers in the village of Mou; this is during a recreational session at the end of a market day, rather than a full-fledged ceremonial performance. The masks with the big, round horns are buffalo and the tall, thin one is the monkey.

and sundry, as was the case at Mou, one of our all-time favorites. Masks being danced there included a wonderful black buffalo with fiery red eyes, a towering red, black and white mask which Chris told us was a spirit mask, and at least two particularly interesting monkey masks, aged and worn from years of use. One could see very clearly, by the way people dressed, and the solidity and neatness of the mud-brick houses, that Mou was a prosperous place, even though, like almost every other village in the country, it had neither electricity nor running water.

Masks were not for sale at such performances, but anyone who wanted to buy local art had no trouble doing so. We explained the connection between society, art and commerce to the family:

In the areas we have visited most, especially around the town of Ouri, the blacksmiths (forgerons) made masks for at least five surrounding ethnic groups. Forgerons are always a family

*group. I think they are endogamous [meaning that they marry
only within the lineage] and certainly patrilineal (for Margot),
and always very high class, unlike the weavers/musicians who
are ex-slave family groups. We just read in a book that the family
we know best, named Konaté, came to Ouri many years ago from
Mali because their skills were needed to make weapons for wars
then going on against the French. The whole region was ravaged
by punitive expeditions in 1914-16 after people revolted to resist
being conscripted for troops in World War I—it was all a huge
misunderstanding; if they had known they were going to be
paid, [be eligible for French pensions], see the world, etc., they
probably would have welcomed it, but all people knew was that
their children were being stolen by the white man. And of course
they thought in terms of the slave trade.*[27]

*Today the Konaté family makes masks for ritual purposes
and also for sale to tourists. The real ones are better; they have
to be in order to be used in dances. Or you can order a "real" high
quality one. Chris introduced us to the family through one of the
younger members, Poboye, who (as a result) is now becoming
something of a culture broker and businessman; although he
has never been to school he is quite bright and speaks French
and circulates regularly into Ouaga peddling masks and
carvings to a widening circle of western acquaintances . . . .*

*At other levels the market is very sharky indeed. Large
amounts of junk is carved and peddled . . . . If you are a glutton for
punishment you can have "antiquaires" on your doorstep to the
tune of a dozen a day. A vast subterranean industry fakes things
to be "tres anciennes;" treatments include burying carvings in
mud, putting them in the rafters to get all smoky, and even soaking
them in old and exceedingly dirty motor oil. This is popular in
the Dogon Country [of Mali] north of here, perhaps because lots
of cars get wrecked on the execrable roads and there is always
a good supply of dirty oil. [Here in Ouaga] there is a great flea
market in front of the railroad hotel, stacked to the rafters with
this stuff. Some of the dealers operate from their houses, where
they have rooms full of objets d'art (?) all invariably covered with*

---

[27] The anti-conscription unrest was finally halted in large part due to the
efforts of Felix Eboué, a half-Guinean who was the first black to reach the
senior ranks of the French Colonial Service, later to become famous for his
efforts to rally support for De Gaulle and the Free French during World War II.

layers of red dust. Some of these people know very well what they are doing and much of the top quality stuff gets shipped directly to major dealers in Abidjan and Paris without ever being seen by innocent collectors in Ouagadougou.[28]

We failed to mention in the letter that the wives of *forgerons* were potters. We found the Voltaic pottery irresistible; it was beautiful, inexpensive and useful in the garden, and there were infinite regional styles. And of course it was fragile. A trip *en brousse* always seemed to end with one of us balancing a gigantic pot in our lap all the way home.

At about this time Barbara acquired a pair of carved Nigerian panels that had been subjected to the mud-immersion aging process, and she spent hours scrubbing them. Despite the mud, they were obviously brand new, and years later we made them into very classy cupboard doors for our furnished attic at 216 Wolfe Street. Like the story of Poboye, the doors proved a rule of African "antiquing": that "fakes" are often made by the same craftsmen who make the "real thing," and often to equally high standards of craftsmanship.[29]

Before long Barbara was taking her students to visit some of the interesting places we had learned about.

Yesterday we took two classes from the International School, plus straphangers, to see some dancing in our favorite town [Ouri] about two hours drive west of here. The only problem was that our informant, Poboye, told us that the dancing was going to be in his town; instead it turned out to be another hour's drive to the north. This made us too late; the villagers had already danced (supposedly to drive away some bad winds that have been blowing lately). However when the army of foreigners descended they obligingly got their masks out again,

---

[28] Bob and Barbara letter to Dear Family, March 10, 1984.

[29] Probably the best Voltaic art we bought, according to Chris Roy, is the old crocodile mask on the second floor stairwell of 216 Wolfe Street. We also acquired a very nice buffalo mask which Anne now has, and a small but good plank mask destined for Jamie. The miniature masks at PKS were obviously made for tourists, but they are good examples of Voltaic style. In the Indonesian breakfront there is an interesting old ivory anklet, stained brown either by soaking in tea or from old age.

but needless to say when all this was over it was dark and we were faced with a four-hour drive back to Ouaga, about two-thirds over dirt roads. In the end no one had flat tires or ran out of gas and the seventh and eighth grades had a fine time. One of the irrepressible seventh-grade girls asked Barbara, "Mrs. Pringle, wouldn't it have been fun if we had run out of gas on one of those dirt roads and had to camp overnight?" Answer: No. [In the days before cell phones, we were worried mainly about distraught parents in Ouaga.] *There is something about an African nighttime road, ankle-deep in powdery dust and running through mile after mile of featureless, pitch-black countryside, that is unlike any other driving experience, especially if you are at the rear of a procession eating dust.*

This letter, which as usual covered a week or so of varied activities, ended on a culinary note:

We had eighteen people to dinner on Friday night; I was chargé; the Nehers [our new ambassador and his wife] *were in Lomé, picking up their car and we served one roast lamb, along with couscous which Duna, our cook, is very good at, which (the lamb) cost the vast sum of $13. If you are into cheap sheep, Burkina Faso is it. (Tender too.) Unfortunately most people here can't afford to eat sheep, even at $13 a head.*[30]

Our Own Village

As in our previous posts, the burden of managing our obligations to the servants landed on Barbara. She had to be a banker, a doctor and sometimes a social advisor. Our most memorable experience involved our houseboy and laundryman, Prospère. Under Voltaic law, he was entitled to Social Security, including not only a pension, but also an allowance of seven dollars a month for each of his five children, payable immediately. That's right, in one of the poorest countries in the world, with a serious overpopulation problem, the government subsidized fertility. This had nothing to do with Sankara's radicalism; it was just good old fashioned French socialism, with a bit of Catholicism thrown

---

[30] Bob and Barbara letter to Dear Family, January 27, 1985.

in. And of course it was operative primarily in urban areas.

The problem was that Prospère had never completely paid his bride price of two cows and eight sheep. He still owed one cow (*boeuf*). And until he did, the village "magistrate," probably a relative of his father-in-law, would not register the couple as married, no doubt muttering "*Ou est le boeuf?*" (Where's the beef?) the whole time. No certificate of marriage registration, no child payments. Fortunately the *boeuf* could be monetized for the huge sum of US$80, which Barbara lent him, insuring that he would be in debt to us for the rest of our stay. Then she gave him $10 for bus fare back to his village near the Ghanaian border to make the payment and get the certificate. That done, she tried to make certain that the embassy administrative section would guide him through the maze of enrolling for Social Security.[31] Unfortunately, that is where the story ends, and by the time we left in 1985 Prospère was, for some bureaucratic reason or other, still not getting his child support payments.

In June, 1984, Jamie arrived from Milton and got a summer job writing a computer program for AID, no doubt a prophetic bit of employment for someone who now spends much time helping his parents out with their electronic dilemmas. (Don't ever think that spending some of your tax dollars on foreign aid is just throwing money away.) Then Barbara and the kids left on *Le Point*, the budget French Airline, for a long vacation in Europe, first visiting the family of Michele Antoine, her friend from Girl Scout exchange student days, in Lyon and at the family farm at La Chapelle de la Tour du Pin. Then they went to Switzerland to see Liz Eschler-Sutter, a friend from Camp Ross Trails, where she had been an exchange counselor, followed by some hiking in the French Alps. Finally, they met Kathy in Paris for a road trip to Mont St Michel in Normandy. [32]

Annie had had a grand time at the Lycée St. Ex, although we almost concluded that the French succeed intellectually in spite of, not because of, their educational system. In her classes that year, the famous emphasis on rote learning was a reality. The program was chopped into an intellectual mishmash,

---

[31] Barbara letter to Dear Family, February 9, 1984.
[32] Barbara letter to Dear Family, Labor Day, 1984.

The Country Team of American officers at Embassy Ouagadougou.
Ambassador Leonardo Neher is seated in the center and almost seated is DCM
Pringle, who ran back from setting the camera's self-timer to be in the picture.

and what really seemed to matter was keeping a beautiful
cahier—literally "notebook," but more like a scrapbook, the
history class *cahier* complete with little stickers—as evidence
of one's learning experience. We concluded that although one
year of this had been wonderful, two years, especially the one
which would be her freshman year in the US, might not be a
good idea, and she did not resist.

Our first choice, and hers, was Milton, so she could be
with Jamie and at a coed school, but she was placed on the
wait list. This resulted mainly from our inability to provide
meaningful information about her curriculum and grades for
the seventh and eighth grades. The Alexandria school system
could not cough up anything when requested to do so by mail,
and the only available statement of the Lycée curriculum for
quatrième was a thick government document, the French
law that decreed everything to be taught on every day of the
school year in all lycées, down to the last irregular verb. We
copied the relevant pages, but that didn't do the trick.

We ruled out St. Stephens, an American school in Rome,
which did not have a strong reputation. Besides, as her dad

noted, "I think Italianizing Annie might be gilding the lily."[33] So she ended up at Madeira, where they remembered her fondly as a little sprite who showed up now and then, when she had a school holiday that Barbara didn't, or when the infirmary agreed to look after her on days of sickness. Barbara wrote, "She thinks being a boarder will be a lark, a perpetual slumber party."[34] It turned out that there was also lots of studying involved, but she now looks back upon that period as a key in both her intellectual and social development, and still has friends among both teachers and fellow students.

Moving to Burkina Faso

In July of 1984 Ambassador Walker's term ended and he departed post the day after our July 4th celebration. We gave him an African stool, symbolizing chiefly leadership. On August 4, on its independence day, Upper Volta became Burkina Faso, meaning noble or upright (Burkina) country (Faso)—so that calling it Burkina without the Faso was and is quite acceptable. However, this change plus Sankara's increasing hostility led to a tongue-in-cheek column in the US press accusing the Republicans of "losing" Upper Volta. This could not be brushed aside lightly, the columnist intoned, because "There is no Lower Volta."[35] (He was wrong, of course; Lower Volta is Ghana.) In any case, the country will henceforth be referred to here by its new name.

Ambassador Walker's successor, Leonardo Neher, arrived in mid-August, but I remained *chargé* until the third week in September, when Nard, as everyone called him, finally presented his credentials. Sankara had decided that all such presentations should henceforth be done in rural areas in order to introduce new diplomats to "the people," who by his definition were not to be found in capitals. Nard's ceremony took place at a small town called Boromo, several dusty hours from Ouagadougou, and it was no accident that he shared it

---

[33] Bob letter in four postcards about trip to Bobodioulasso, to Dear Char and Clay, March 30, 1984.

[34] Bob and Barbara letter to Dear Family, April 21, 1984.

[35] Arthur Hoppe, "Who Lost Bourkina Faso?" Panorama, *San Francisco Chronicle,* August 31, 1984. Hoppe was a widely syndicated columnist for that paper.

with two thoroughly anti-imperialist diplomatic colleagues, the North Korean and Cuban ambassadors.

The government's campaign of insults and irritations against the US had been accelerating for some time. An article in the official press only days before the credentials ceremony, swallowed whole from a Soviet press release, asked, "Is Reagan another Hitler?"[36] (Desired answer: Yes.) Burkina Faso had decided to boycott the Los Angeles Olympics. Sankara had asked us to let him fly to the UN in New York in a Cuban aircraft, which was also taking him to Cuba, a request we refused. Then he was angry because he couldn't get high-level appointments in Washington on twenty-four hours' notice.[37]

Sankara did succeed in getting our official attention. Nard arrived with instructions to get him to cool it or risk retaliation of some kind. He led off with a tough speech at his credentials ceremony along the lines of: How long do you think the US will be willing to help a country that keeps heaping verbal abuse on it and refusing to send its two athletes to the Los Angeles Olympics? Sankara struck back *ad lib* with something like: Burkina is an important, independent country just like you three, referring to, besides the US, Cuba and North Korea, and should be respected and treated as such. He also managed to work in an uncomplimentary reference to the Bay of Pigs.[38]

Things continued in this unpleasant vein for the remaining year of our tour in Burkina. In October, 1985, the government newspaper ran another toxic column insulting and threatening Nard ("the representative") and Reagan ("the represented").[39]

---

[36] Barbara letter to Dear Family, September 22, 1984. A note at the top says "Bob says to please keep this letter in the family."

[37] Bob letter to Dear Family, October 21, 1984.

[38] Ibid.

[39] "The Representative and the Represented," *Sidwaya* [the official newspaper], October 11, 1984. It referred to Reagan as a "cowboy" and, with regard to Neher, "Usually representatives of this type have acted through goons and mercenaries, but it happens that this representative, as the represented has been in the past, is a lone gunman. He meddles, makes contact, recruits, yes recruits agents to quickly clarify what is expected of him. With whitish hair, tapered mustache, the eyes of a militant, this "diplomatic animal," so recently landed among us, believes he is in conquered territory . . . . Mission for mission, the August revolution should quickly finish with him." Nard told me in July, 2012, that one of Sankara's aides told him the President himself had written it.

In response Nard called on the President, and I went along as note taker. Sankara said he couldn't understand what it took to be on better terms with the US. Nard gave him a long list of what it would take, and later concluded that the meeting marked a turning point in US-Burkina relations, meaning less name-calling and improved access to Sankara, at least until the US air attacks on Libya six months later.

But after we had left the President's office, one of his aides came after me and said Sankara wanted a word with *me*. So back I went, and he asked me politely whether I had been tape recording our meeting. I had not; proper *diplomats don't clandestinely record official calls! Of course not. Where was I?* It was only then that I noticed that Sankara had a revolver on his desk.

This episode gave credence to one of Nard's main points, that if Sankara's insults were taken in context, they were not as dangerous to us as Washington was inclined to think, although we had to respond to them if only to keep Washington from going ballistic. Sankara was a populist, not a communist, and he was facing a serious threat, the only one, from real hard-line communists supported by enemies of the US. He had to be seen as attacking us harder than anyone else. Suppose I had recorded a conversation in which Sankara was trying to *understand* us, and it had been acquired by (or given to) his enemies?[40]

Sankara kept his wife almost entirely out of public view, a curious trait for such a militant progressive. I never met her, but Barbara did, at a diplomatic convocation to wish the President, and by extension all Burkinabé (the form for someone from Burkina), a Happy New Year. The President made brief remarks, witty as usual, suggesting that while diplomats had to do what their governments told them, their wives might be able to persuade them to be more reasonable. As for Mrs. Sankara, "[she] is a strikingly pretty young woman, fairly tall, slim, who lived up to her reputation as a stylish

---

[40] Drawn in part from Interview with Leonardo Neher, Association for Diplomatic Studies and Training, oral history program, p. 36; also Bob letter to Dear Family, October 21, 1984. When I interviewed Nard in July, 2012, he told me that the pivotal meeting with Sankara, described here, was January, 1985, but if indeed it followed the representative-represented insult, which he thinks it did, it was in October, 1984.

dresser, with a sash around her hips and a simple gold chain and earrings . . . ." The President recognized Barbara and chatted her up, calling her "Mrs. Springle," as he always did.[41]

We continued to travel for business and pleasure. We toured Bobo-Dioulasso, Burkina's commercial capital, with its bustling market, impressive mud-brick mosque (similar to many in Mali), and extraordinary gigantic spring, which gushes forth not far from town to produce an instant river. Further south, Banfora had the most spectacular market in the country, featuring wonderful mats, tremendous mangos and yet another kind of pottery.

We went back to the game park at Nazinga on the Ghana border, and Annie got to go up in its ultra-light aircraft on a mission to locate some elephants within viewing distance, which it did. But in the process of piling into vehicles to reach them on land, Barbara was bitten by a monkey belonging to the Canadian managers of the reserve. Fortunately the monkey could be observed, so she had to take only the prophylactic version of the rabies shots.[42] Peace Corps volunteers were assisting Nazinga's Canadian management, and just before our departure in 1985 Jamie had a brief summer job at the reserve helping them.

Bereft of snorkeling and shelling, and with no game parks within easy distance, we became bird watchers, *faute de mieux,* at least at first. On a walkathon organized by the Marines to benefit Save the Children,

. . . we discovered that our local park, [adjacent to] a Ouaga suburb and full of typically scrubby savanna vegetation [the so-called Zone du Bois], is crawling with birds. Fortunately we also got a copy of the only West African bird book[43] after months of trying. On one subsequent outing we've seen cuckoos and coucals, flycatcers with tails like birds of paradise, wonderful things called long-tailed starlings, with long lustrous tails most

[41] Barbara Pringle, "Wishing the President a Happy New Year," memo to files, US Embassy Ouagadougou, January 28, 1985.
[42] Barbara letter to Dear Family, March 26 [no year but it must have been 1985].
[43] W. Serle, G.J. Morel and W. Hartwig, *A Field Guide to the Birds of West Africa*, London, 1977.

unlike any regular starlings, Abyssinian rollers and Senegal fire finches and the common sorts of hornbills. No lyre-tailed honey guides yet.[44]

By the time we left Burkina we had formed a life-long hobby.

The Land of the Lobi

In February 1985 we traveled to Gaoa (not to be confused with Gao in Mali), a small town near the Ivorian border in the heart of Lobi country. The Lobi are a militantly animist people famous for their art, architecture, jewelry and evil tempers. Europeans liked to have Lobi men as *guardiens* (house guards) because everyone else was afraid of their black magic. At home, they still hunted with bows and arrows. We admired the two-storey Lobi houses, pristine in their traditional style, their mud-brick walls often decorated with fetishes smeared with chicken blood. "*Cabarets,*" or *dolo* bars, were often attached to them.

We saw Lobi ladies firing their exceptionally beautiful pots on open fires, slapping them with green leaves as they cooled to achieve the chocolate brown finish. They "calabashed" for artisanal gold (i.e., panning with large gourds, called calabashes), earning 2,000 to 3,000 CFA francs a week. The French, especially the women, liked to come up from Abidjan to buy gold from the Lobi, convinced that it was a great bargain. A Peace Corps volunteer working with a Dutch project exploring more ambitious mining possibilities had already concluded that there was nothing there exploitable on a grander scale, and I concluded that "Artisanal gold working will continue and the bare-breasted Lobi ladies will never be displaced by dredges."[45]

We stayed in a rustic, thirteen-room hotel, clean and air-conditioned, run by a Lebanese couple, M. et Mme. Damien, who had fled Lebanon after a failed Maronite (Christian) coup.

---

[44] Bob and Barbara letter to Dear Family, May 2, 1984.

[45] Quote from Ouagadougou A002, "Gaoa Trip Report," February 22, 1985; see also Bob and Barbara letter to Dear Family, February 22, 1985. However, the women calabashing for gold were not getting wealthy either: 2,000-3,000 CFA francs equaled roughly US $5-6 in the 1980s.

Everyone ate together, boarding-house style, enjoying Mrs. Damien's excellent cooking. At the time of our visit, Gaoa, which is near Sankara's boyhood home, had just hosted National Cultural Week, recognition which the Lobi certainly deserved. The government had lengthened the airport runway from 1,000 to 1,800 meters and had run an electric line into Gaoa. It was a good idea, but the event was marked by confusion and maladministration. The government reserved the Damien's hotel for the diplomatic corps, but neglected to inform the diplomats, so most of the invited excellencies flew in for the opening and then left, leaving the hotel empty for the rest of the week at a time when the town was full of visitors.

The local people, irritated but also flattered by all the uproar, enjoyed the excitement. They built a path to the top of the highest hill so the President could look out over his old home. "It was a good example of how personality cults pursue African leaders, whether they like them or not."[46] On the way home we saw an overgrown stone fortification at Loropéni,[47] supposedly used by slave traders in the bad old days to spend the night when traveling to the coast with their captives.

Wherever we went, we were preoccupied with drought. In the Lobi country, relatively far south, the granaries were full. But we couldn't forget that we were in the Sahel, an Arabic word meaning "edge of the desert." The further north you go, the drier it gets. It rains only during the summer months, roughly June through August. The rub is in the "roughly." Timing and amount of rainfall is determined by something called the Intertropical Convergence Zone, which advances northwards every spring. Early rains are often dust storms, all dirt and fury. Then liquid begins to fall, most often in thunderstorms but occasionally in day or two-long soakers.

It was impossible not to worry about whether the rains would fail after the initial dust storms, because you knew that would be a tragedy in the making. On the other hand, to see everything turn green, whole villages disappearing

---

[46] Ibid.
[47] A current (2012) Wikipedia reference says that the ruins may have been linked to the gold trade, or were possibly the residence of the King of the Kaan people. They were in any case made a UNESCO World Heritage site in 2009. See Wikipedia article on Loropéni.

behind fields of millet and sorghum, was deeply comforting. It was already conventional wisdom that the desert was advancing because of climate change. But three thousand years ago the Sahara itself had been green, and after that it had been even drier than it is today.[48] We saw ancient sand dunes in Mali well south of where the desert is now. Clearly the desertification problem is a combination of changing climate, however cyclical, and human activity, mainly too many animals. People cherish their cattle and tend to sell them only in drought times after prices have plummeted. (In Ouagadougou, beef filet was extremely cheap, and still excellent eating even from malnourished, if not starving, cattle.) In Burkina, AID had an interesting project in the arid north; they simply fenced off a tract so that over-grazing could not occur, and sure enough the desert stopped advancing, but there only.

The two years we were in Burkina, 1984 and 1985, were among the worst drought years on record, and much of our official activity, when Sankara wasn't distracting us, was focused on improving "food security." What could be done? In the short term, bring in grain when local harvests fail. Then try to get emergency care to refugees coming south into better-watered areas. Over the longer term, establish grain stockpiles in drought-prone areas that can be tapped in bad years. Much effort was devoted to amassing such stockpiles and providing proper storage for them, but since then more than two decades of normal and sometimes above normal rains have ensued—the gods are always ahead of you. In addition, push economic development, the only long-run sure cure for overpopulation of humans and their flocks.

All this has been tried, and things would be worse without such efforts, but the population of Burkina today (2018) is over fifteen million, compared to seven million in 1985, and it is still, like most of the other Sahelian countries, among the poorest anywhere. Why not promote birth control you may ask? Unfortunately, in the absence of machinery, having more children is economically rational because they are all too

---

[48] For more on this complex subject see Roderick James McIntosh, *The Peoples of the Middle Niger*, Malden, MA, Blackwell, 1988, esp. pp. 72-73.

often an essential source of farm labor.

One of our immediate concerns was getting the food aid through clogged ports and over bad roads into the interior where people were at risk. The worst time of year is always just before the rainy season, when the previous year's grain has been consumed and the new crop, however good or bad, has not yet been harvested. In January, 1985, I wrote:

Last week I went up north to the Yatenga area. It doesn't look any worse than the area we were in yesterday [Ouri] but we know that it is in fact much harder hit; they produced about 30,000 tons of grain as against a minimum requirement of 120,000 tons. Normally, young men migrate out at this time of year to seek work in the Ivory Coast; this year we know some whole families are leaving but information on how many (or where they have gone) is hard to come by. There are also migrants moving in from the Mali border areas; these people are nomads and "foreigners" and thus relatively easy to keep track of but probably not as serious a problem as the settled local population because they are much less numerous. Much of our food aid will be focused on this area; either distributed through well-established Catholic Relief Service programs or via village cereal banks run by the villagers. There will be the usual cliff-hanger to get all the food delivered before the rains make roads impassable; it's all the more difficult because the neighboring countries to the north are much worse hit than Burkina and all transport facilities will be overtaxed.[49]

There were still plenty of activities around Ouagadougou: the diplomatic community Christmas festival, or Kermesse, the fundraising event where Julius sold his needlework; a fashion show, in which Annie was one of the models; and a visit by John Denver, who was not allowed by his manager to perform commercially in the country, but who, sitting on a folding chair in the middle of the embassy tennis court, gave the embassy and school crowd a special, unamplified, concert.[50]

---

[49] Bob and Barbara letter to Dear Family, January 27,1985.
[50] Bob letter to Dear Family, October 6, 1984.

A big local attraction was the Pan African Film Festival of Ouagadougou, or FESPACO, with many of the films presented outdoors on portable screens. It is now in its twenty-third year and is well known internationally.[51] Finally there was the annual softball tournament, SOFANWET (Softball Fanatics Weekend Tournament), one of three held more or less annually among American Embassy-sponsored teams in the region, an event second in importance only to the embattled Marine Ball. The stars of our team, Sahel's Angels, included an Assembly of God missionary from upcountry who gave up seven runs in the three games he pitched; the commander ("gunny," for gunnery sergeant) of our Marines, who routinely hit home runs deep into the surrounding scrub-thorn savannah, and the director of British Save the Children who amazed the Americans by fielding bare-handed, cricket-style; he and his wife Hillary are among the Ouaga friends with whom we long remained in contact.

Barbara wrote:

So that accounts for this holiday, as you can see a typically American Memorial Day Weekend. Oh, I forgot [that] the final game yesterday was called after five innings because of a dust storm. The other holidays were Anti-Imperialism Day last week and Catholic Ascension Day the week before. One good thing about Burkina, it's syncretic; we don't miss a holiday.[52]

She also mentioned that the softball tournament was held under a shadow, because shortly before it began we had medevac'd one our five Marines, who happened to be black, with a severe case of sexually transmitted hepatitis, which he probably picked up from one of the Ghanaian prostitutes who frequented the local bars. As he had done a year previously, Sankara, in response to a call from the ambassador, personally made sure that the patient could be taken to the airport safely well after curfew to meet the Swiss flying ambulance. However, after eight days in intensive care in a military hospital in Germany, he died.[53] We fully expected a full-blown

---

[51] See http://www.fespaco-bf.net/ .
[52] Barbara letter to Dear Family, Memorial Day,1985.
[53] Ibid.

investigation by the Marine Corps, but, for whatever reason, there was no such reaction.

It was at about this time that we experienced a kind of literary political crisis, proving again that the pen is still mighty, especially when it's dipped in slease. It all started when a French author named Gérard de Villiers arrived in Ouaga with several assistants, seeking background information for his next book.[54] De Villiers wrote an endless stream of very dirty, very violent paperback spy novels on sale in every French airport, with titles like *Amok au Bali*, *Mort à Beyrouth* and *Le Tueur de Miami*, about a Hungarian count in the employ of the CIA. That should have been enough, given the political situation, to scare the French-speaking community stiff, but instead *le tout Ouagadougou* excitedly wined and dined the famous novelist and, like lambs going to slaughter, answered all his questions about the local scene.

Putsch à Ouagadougou[55] came out few months later. Malko, the Hungarian count-cum-CIA agent, parachutes in on a mission to assassinate President Sankara, who like some other characters in the book is identified by name. One of Malko's first encounters is with the nubile daughter of Ouaga's leading Lebanese merchant, one of the ones who had entertained De Villiers and his team. A few pages later, Malko is having sex with the wife of the CIA station chief in her heart-shaped swimming pool. This was one of several digressions from accurate scene-setting since, as mentioned earlier, we had no CIA Station in Ouaga, and there was no heart-shaped swimming pool in town. Another bit of fiction, really, was the portrayal of CIA agents implanted in the Peace Corps.

For the balance of the book Malko duels with some genuine real-life characters, one being the mixed French-Burkinabé head of Sankara's security detail, Bangaré in the book, truly feared and detested by the expatriate community and forever

---

[54] For more on de Villiers see Robert F. Worth, "The Spy Who Knows too Much," *The New York Times Magazine*, February 3, 2013, pp.18ff, which portrays him as greatly admired by intelligence professionals. A copy of the article is with our copy of *Putsch à Ouaga*. De Villiers had written more than 200 of his penny dreadfuls, with the same hero, Malko, by the time he died in 2013.

[55] Librairie Plon/Gerard de Villiers, 1984.

trying to pick fights with our Marine guards when they were off duty. Finally the assassination of Sankara fails and Malko escapes, barely.

The real Sankara, perhaps pleased because he emerges unvanquished in *Putsch à Ouaga*, signed a copy and sent it to Ambassador Neher, who, shame on him, later lost it (according to him).

Epic Drought

Our last big trip, in April 1985, was to the drought-blasted northeastern area of Burkina and across the Niger River into Niger, accompanied by Chris Roy. Once again we saw settlements of displaced nomads who had migrated south in search of food and water, mostly Peuhl (Fulani), Tuareg, or Bella (black ex-slaves of the Tuareg). We talked with local officials, missionaries and aid workers, including a team from the US Centers for Disease Control (CDC), which was testing levels of malnutrition. At one embarrassing stop, the people greeted us as heroes, on the assumption that we were going to distribute some grain that had already been delivered; instead they had to wait for a local government official due to arrive in a day or two. It was often hard to tell who was worse off, the nomad-refugees (many from Mali) or the inhabitants, but we were as usual amazed at the stylish dress and jewelry of some of the refugees. We got a glimpse of the Burkina government's revolutionary zeal on the wall of a local office:

> *On peut tromper tout le people* [sic] *une partie du temps*
> *On peut tromper une partie du people tout le temps*
> *Mais on ne peut pas tromper tout le people tout le temps*
> *La Patrie ou le mort, nous vaincrons!*

There was no attribution to Father Abraham; the last line was the national slogan of Burkina Faso. (Once again, the verse may have been lifted from Cuban practice.)

Not far from Gorom-Gorom, our Ford Bronco broke down and Chris and I had to walk seven kilometers to get a Toyota Land Cruiser from the bare bones hotel to tow our car into town, where the staff discovered a broken coil and got it running with one scavenged from a Land Rover. The hotel, a mud-brick exercise in "appropriate tourism" linked with the *Le Point* budget airline, was booked solid with a French tour, and our reservation had been lost, but they found a spare room for us, with a baby camel in the adjacent courtyard.

Not far from Gorom-Gorom, we stopped at Salmossi,

... a settlement of Songhai (or Zharma or Djerma) people more numerous in neighboring Niger [and especially in Mali]. The village appears decrepit from outside, and the people tell us there is nothing in their cereal bank. Unlike Toulfe, our previous day's stop, there are virtually no men of working age in evidence, all having departed to seek employment elsewhere. In this distressed setting, the house compounds turn out to be gems of traditional African architecture, heavy mud-brick construction, with exterior facades gaily decorated in polychrome low-relief, interiors cool and inviting, kitchens and bedrooms floored with scrupulously clean sand, walls lined with neatly arranged calabashes and other utensils, beds decorated with hand-loomed blankets and set off with curtains. It tells you something about the human spirit and adversity.[56]

The leitmotif photograph of the trip, taken near Gorom-Gorom, was of a cow, too sick to walk, being hauled to market on a donkey cart.

Our next stop, Aribinda, was partly an effort to solve an art history question: was the Aribinda Antelope still being made? This attractive mask, usually referred to as Kurumba style,[57] had been illustrated in a well-known French African art book years previously, and since that time innumerable fakes had been carved and marketed, including one to us. Chris wanted to see if they were still being made in what might (or might not) have been their place of origin. We had some trouble getting an answer but finally an elderly man sent a small boy scrambling into a mud-brick granary, and out he came with a

---

[56] "Trip Report: Northern Burkina Faso to Niger and Return," Ouagadougou A-004, April 12, 1985, travel April 2-8, 1985 [pasted in green scrapbook]. See also Barbara letter to Dear Family, from Ayorou, Niger, April 6, 1985.
[57] For an illustration see William Fagg, *Sculptures Africaines: Les Univers Artistiques des Tribus d'Afrique Noir*, Paris, 1965.

miniature toy mask of unmistakable Aribinda style. That was as the end of our quest; Chris gave up.

Niger (the country) came before the Niger (river). We had to fill out the same entry forms at four different checkpoints to satisfy its notoriously prickly immigration authorities. As a result we crossed the Niger by ferry after dark, still forty kilometers from our destination, the river town of Ayorou. The road was covered with seriously blowing sand, so Zerbo, my driver, had to go fast, exceeding the range of his headlights, and in four-wheel drive, to keep us from getting stuck. (Although we don't have a copy of that letter any more, Father Clarence's reaction to that bit of news was "Don't do that again; it's dangerous.")

What a relief when we finally arrived, to discover that the same French couple who had hosted Barbara and her students at Park W a year previously was now running the *campement* here, which had a fine view of the river in one direction and of the marketplace in the other. So although our reservations had once again gone astray, her old friends found a room for us, which we all shared even though a capacity-size French tour was coming in to see Ayorou's Sunday-only market later that night. The market, which was the main reason for the *campement*, lived up to expectations and we bought a necklace of very large *kopal* amber beads as a true souvenir.

The next day after market, we headed for Niamey, Niger's capital, hoping to unwind at its fancy French hotel, a product of Niger's uranium boom. No *campement* this time; the Hotel Gaweye had, in addition to its big swimming pool, a fancy cold buffet every Sunday evening which we headed for with gusto. That was a bad mistake, because Barbara and I came down with food poisoning, especially me. Chris, who had had traveler's tummy as result of something eaten en route to Ayorou and had eaten little at the Gaweye, escaped—clearly pointing the finger at the buffet. Going home the next day was a nightmare, because although a modern paved road was being built to Ouagadougou, it was not finished. Meanwhile the old road had been shredded by construction machinery, leaving ruts and axle-deep dust for miles, after every few of which I had to get out in the 110 degree plus heat and throw up.

Expecting to leave Africa for good in the summer of 1985,

we planned a real African safari as our family swansong. In June, as soon as Annie and Jamie returned from boarding school, we all left from Abidjan, via the east-west Air Ethiopia flight, for Kenya. But first, we had to manage to board the often overbooked Air Afrique flight from Ouaga to Abidjan. Friends on the incoming plane alerted us that the check-in counter in Abidjan had issued more boarding passes than seats, and some would-be passengers had boarded through the tail, only to walk the length of the plane and be told to get off.

In the course of her periodic visits to Abidjan to get her braces adjusted, Annie had become the family expert on flying in West Africa, characterized by unpredictable routings and chaotic boarding procedures. Therefore, we parents gathered all the hand luggage and it became the kids' responsibility to hustle onto the plane at the head of the crowd (none of this Zone A, B and C stuff) and make sure we all got seats. This they accomplished.

In Kenya, our family of four qualified for a pop-top van, the most popular game-viewing vehicle of that era, with a driver/guide all our own. Although we had seen an occasional elephant at Nazinga and along the road to Bobo-Dioulasso, antelopes at Park W (Barbara and Annie) and Nazinga, and a few giraffes on the trip with Chris into Niger, wildlife in Burkina had been few and far between. So we were thrilled to see our first animals right in Nairobi, which has a small game park in its center.

Then it was the floodlit waterhole at Treetops, the famous lodge where Elizabeth II, when she was in her early twenties, learned that her father had died and that she was Queen of England; it was still an exciting place to see game. Barbara's favorite was the next stop, Samburu National Reserve, up north in the dry plains country; our rooms looked right out on those plains and the antelope bounding over them.

Driving in that area of the country, we saw wonderful grassland birds, the most memorable of which was the Broad-tailed Paradise Whydah (I think, records are unclear) undulating and swishing its long tail as it flew; our driver turned out to know as much about birds as about the larger fauna. The next stop was the chain of lakes in the middle of the country—the alkaline Lake Bogoria with its hundreds of flamingoes, and the fresher, but muddy, Lake Baringo. There we stayed at the Island Camp in fancy tents with facilities attached and little birds (weavers) that raided our sugar bowl at breakfast.

Our stay there ended dramatically when Annie, a strong swimmer, banged into a submerged piling and got a bloody scalp wound. Luckily a nurse who was also a guest at Lake Baringo assured us that the wound, though bleeding furiously, was not deep. She referred us to a nearby Catholic mission clinic on the mainland where Sister Margaret sutured it with adhesive tape—in the shape of a cross! We felt embarrassed being ushered into the treatment room ahead of a long line of patients waiting to be seen. It being near the end of the month, the government clinic was out of medicine. Sister Margaret, who took us to her little house for a cup of tea, badly needed a rest and easy, English conversation, which we supplied. She didn't want to accept payment, but we pressed the equivalent of the grand sum of $25 on her.

Our final stop was Masai Mara, with its extensive lodge complex. It lived up to its reputation as a world class game viewing park, and it would have been even better, especially for Jamie, if high winds hadn't caused cancellation of the early morning balloon ride we were supposed to take. We could not even consider going to Tanzania and its equally famous parks, because at that time Kenya and Tanzania were embroiled in a border dispute, but the trip was nonetheless a spectacular introduction to African wildlife and not, as we feared, our last such opportunity

By this time Bob had decided that although two years in Africa had been fine, he should try to refresh his Southeast Asian (or at least Asian) credentials. We still needed a post where we would be eligible for boarding schools at government expense, which left only one suitable opening for the summer 1985 transfer season, namely DCM Port Moresby, Papua New Guinea (or PNG). It was not strictly speaking Southeast Asia, but it sounded like an adventure. That meant a direct transfer to Port Moresby, with time for consultations in Washington and a vacation at Pine Knoll Shores.

There was an uncertain moment when my future ambassador, Paul Gardner, an old Indonesia hand whom we knew well, cabled me in Ouagadougou to say that his secretary had just asked for a transfer because she was so upset by the crime situation in Port Moresby. Did we really want to come? I replied that we did. So we prepared to leave, never dreaming that in less than three years we would be back in Sahelian West Africa, although not in the same country.

We would not visit Burkina Faso again until the summer of 2007. In October, 1987, Sankara was eliminated by members of his inner circle. The leader of this coup, Blaise Campaoré, became President and ruled until 2014, when yet another coup claimed him. He was an orthodox African dictator, with none of his predecessor's radical panache, but he kept on conspiring with the Libyans and became notorious for his links to Charles Taylor in Liberia, the peddling of blood diamonds, and other noxious habits.

It seems a pity that, after we left, the United States felt forced to retaliate against Sankara's insults by cutting AID programs that benefited the people of Burkina. Sankara got back at us by suspending Peace Corps, which did not return until 1995. I agree with Nard Neher that Sankara didn't leave us much choice. Had Julius Walker remained, Washington would have ordered him to do something similar, although he would not have done it with quite the gusto that Nard did. Nard believed that without some retaliation, our relationship with Burkina would have descended to an even lower level.

It is true, as Nard believed, that he got along better with Sankara than Julius did. He was more like Sankara's stereotype of an American Ambassador. The young dictator preferred his "cowboys" tough and had trouble wrapping his mind around a contemplative, soft-spoken Texan who grew roses and did needlework. This is not to suggest that Neher was a "better" ambassador. Though differing in style, both represented the United States well.

After his death, Sankara was revered by African youth, achieving almost Che Guevara status. There are now at least three biographies of him, and a *Sankariste* opposition was among the political parties that competed (unsuccessfully) to succeed Campaoré as president of Burkina Faso in 2014. Sankara is often credited with enhancing his peoples' reputation for hard work and keeping promises. Perhaps, but

I think the real credit goes to certain cultural habits, especially among the Mossi, which long predate Sankara's brief rule.

It was always hard to take his anti-imperialism seriously, despite his passionate rhetoric. As mentioned earlier, he did not expel the French, or the Lebanese business community, or end Burkina's membership in the franc zone, or even nationalize foreign holdings. It was as if he yearned to be truly revolutionary, but could never figure out how to do so without causing more harm than good. He would have been remembered as charming and admirable, had he not killed quite a few people in pursuit if his hopeless ambition. I believe that by marginalizing his fellow junta members, he was consciously or unconsciously setting himself up for martyrdom, and he achieved it.

End of Volume 1

It turned out that, despite an interesting and enjoyable tour in Papua New Guinea, Burkina Faso was the beginning of a whole new area specialty for Bob. The rest of our time overseas, as well as Bob's Washington assignments, would be concentrated in Africa. Volume II will cover these years and a bit of what we did afterwards.

www.ingramcontent.com/pod-product-compliance
Lightning Source LLC
Chambersburg PA
CBHW020512100426

42813CB00030B/3205/J